"BELOVED HOMELAND"

Also books written by Patricia McClaflin Booher

Reflections of a Wyoming Shepherd on the
23rd Psalm

Soon to be released

Timmy the Tender, Timmy the Timid,
Tools for Coping with Grief

Lessons of Life I Learned in my Garden Patch

"BELOVED HOMELAND"

"GROWING UP ON A WYOMING HOMESTEAD"

Patricia McClaflin Booher

ROCK PAVILION PRESS
www.patriciamac.com

Copyright 2020 © Patricia McClalfin Booher

Cover Design: PEL – PHOTOGRAPHY

All Scripture quotations are taken from the Holy Bible, New King James Version, NKJV. Copyright 1982

Printed in the United States of America

$15.00
ISBN 978-0-9601025-0-1
51500>

9 780960 102501

DEDICATION

To my parents

Wallace and Edna Mae McClaflin

To all the fathers and mothers in the Heart Mountain Homestead
Community that have passed the baton of courage, grit and honor to their
children and grandchildren that has given us a true meaning of a

"Sense of Time and Place."

To all the first generations of homesteaders who were so willing to sit
around their kitchen table with me.

They let me record their stories.

To all the rich memories of those no longer with us and their dedication to
the children of Heart Mountain community

They have given us wings to fly.

TABLE OF CONTENTS

INTRODUCTION

years ago, I returned home to my childhood community of Wyoming for my 50th high school reunion. I think all of us could say in unison, "Oh, my goodness! Where did the years go? It was a wonderful celebration. I think we were all relieved that the Committee had the foresight to remember to have name tags. It meant that, as a group, we were coming together with the consensus that the community we called home as children was a unique place to live.

At the turn of the last century, this fertile valley in the Big Horn Basin of northern Wyoming was only a picture of sagebrush as far as the eye could see. With the introduction of irrigation, this arid, high desert became a lush and thriving place where homestead families came to settle. I was the fortunate daughter of parents who had the grit it would take to be a part of the 1949 group of homesteaders who would take part in one of the last homestead communities in this country.

As young children growing up in the Heart Mountain homestead community, we all felt a strong sense of belonging. It was not an easy life, to be sure, but a life which seemed to take on a depth of meaning and caring I would later come to cherish and honor.

When I came back to Wyoming to assume a position with UW Extension Service and met my friends again after thirty years, it was if I had never been away. My three children had grown and were establishing their own families. As a child, the University of Wyoming Extension Ag programs played a major role in our community and county. And now, I was coming back to assume a position as an Extension Family Consumer Education agent.

Because the 4-H youth program had been such a vital part of my own childhood years, I once again took part in the many facets of leadership in educational programs dealing with youth and families. I worked cooperatively with 4-H Extension agents throughout the state.

13

I often found myself at conferences with 4-H agents with which I had grown up in Park County. The friendships that were formed in those childhood years came back into focus as if thirty years were only yesterday. I remember one particular afternoon at a conference in Casper, Wyoming, sitting next to several of my very close friends from childhood. The presenters were from Search Institute. The institute has developed a research-based program that focuses on forty positive, developmental assets that enable young people to grow up to be healthy and productive citizens.

It was the last session of the conference, and the speaker was tying everything together. As I sat there, I was moved to tears along with my close friends sitting on each side of me. We looked at each other and in unison said, "We grew up with these assets."

It is often said that there is a moment in time that can be looked back upon as a pivotal point in one's journey. That afternoon, while sitting there with my very dear childhood friends, a seed was planted in my heart that would change the pattern of my own destiny. I knew I had to tell the story of my childhood community.

A few weeks later, I was at the university working with UW Extension Family Life Specialist, Ben Silliman. I had been telling him of my desire concerning my childhood community. He connected me with Professor Sue Williams. She graciously met me in her office that morning. I believe she was intently listening to the story I was telling her of my childhood. In many ways, I believe she planted my dream into a real place where those seeds could take root. She informed me about the method of Qualitative Research and how it could be used successfully in the adventure into which I was about to walk.

I often refer back to that morning in Professor Williams' office at the University of Wyoming. I had seen her collection of the Foxfire Series on her bookshelf. Later, I would find several copies of my own. Hopefully, one day I will have the complete set of twelve volumes.

Eliot Wigginton, an English teacher in Rabun County High School in the Appalachian Mountains of north Georgia, began the Foxfire Series with

his int ٱnd tenth grade English classes in 1966. The project was part of
a lٜ gu ə arts curriculum. The students taped interviews with the local
res en ɔf the community--recording history, folk life practices, and other
cus ɩm ᵉlated to farming and rural life. That was the beginning of the
Fo⟩ ɩre ₐagazine which would reach out to a national audience. Articles
we cᴄ ɒiled into the first Foxfire book in 1972. Wigginton later would
be va ᵉd "Georgia Teacher of the Year" in 1986. In 1989, he received
the ⁄a ᵣthur Fellowship. A connection with the extensive work Eliot
ach vᴄ with his students gave me courage, as I launched out into new
ter᷈ orᵧ ₙto which I had never before ventured.

m ᵉ an appointment to see UW Extension Director, Edna McBreen.
To ᵧ ᵣeat delight, I discovered she had an extensive background in
res ᵣcᴵ She gave me the green light to go ahead with my project. I have
fonɩ m ᴵories as I look back on that meeting with Edna. As she looked
acr ˢ ᵗ desk, she saw a person so full of excitement and drive, I would
say ᵤy ᵢrector just had to say "Yes"-and she did. She took the time to
giv diᴵ ᵗion in what I needed to get started. I took her advice on what
boᴄ ˢ ᴵ ould need to purchase in order to understand how to conduct the
res ᵣcᴵ In the next few weeks, I read the books backwards and forwards.

ΓHE PROCESS OF QUALITATIVE RESEARCH

ɩ those formative months of the homestead project, I found myself
rea ᵰg ₙto the night, learning all I could about this process called
"Q ᴵit ᵥe Research." I took interest in the controversy over this type of
res ᵣcᴵ ᴄompared to others. At first, I felt overwhelmed, to say the least.
I w ᵢlᴄ ₐve to say, it seemed after a while, the research did take on a life
of ᵢ oᵥ ᴜ

ᴴhe ⎞ualitative Research method deals with gathering information
thrᴄ ₉ᴵ ᵢe documentation of oral interviews, compilation of various kinds
of stᴄ from old pictures, newspapers, official documents, and so on.
Hiᶳ ɔriᴄ data found in libraries, government documents and community
ageᴄ ᴄiᴄ ᴵlso add to the research project.

In some ways, I think it would have been easier for me to conduct the Qualitative Research project in a community with which I was not familiar. One could also add, "Wouldn't the outcome of this research be from a biased point of view?" And I would respond with, "Well, of course." But on the other hand, the passion and commitment I felt to this group of courageous homesteaders would propel me on when obstacles stood in my path.

When I began to conduct those first interviews, I was anxious and even fearful. But after a while, there were specific questions I always asked, and then I just sat back and let those old friends tell their stories.

This would be a very expensive project, so I began to write for research grants. Before it was over, I think the number topped around twenty grant proposals. Looking back on that time of work, I ask myself now, "How did I ever do it.?" What did come out of the process of refining the project over and over, as I wrote for one grant after another, was that I was able to focus on the portion of history of the Heart Mountain Homestead Project in those first, early years. I would soon learn that I had taken on a gigantic task, and the careful outlining of goals and outcomes kept me on target.

I made a brochure that was concise and to the point. It took a great deal of refining, because this project had by now expanded to more than I first would have imagined. This small brochure proved to be a very important tool to keep me focused when I was sitting in front of a Board of Directors or CEO of a company.

I have enclosed within this portion the contents of the brochure that found its way to many destinations.

PROJECT TITLE

"THE IMPACT ON THREE GENERATIONS FROM LIFE ON A WYOMING HOMESTEAD"

RESEARCH DIRECTOR

Patricia Booher
Family Consumer Science
Extension Educator
University of Wyoming
Cooperative Extension

HISTORICAL BACKGROUND

ince the turn of the century, the Big Horn Basin was the location
of : ve   homestead projects..

he Heart Mountain homesteads were developed after WWII with
vet an)f that war as the participants.

he Ralston Bench Project consisted of 120 farms. This was the
las)f : eries of homestead projects in Wyoming.

)n f the significant factors of this project was that the homes which
we   p ided for the families came from the Japanese Relocation Camp
nea)y. t was no longer in use.

he Bureau of Reclamation was the agency in charge of
de\ o] g the irrigation systems which were used in this project.

his community was a close-knit group of people who developed
a u qu set of strong, family values and a work ethic that has seen three
ger rat s of families coming from this heritage. The triumphs, tragedies,
suc ess , and failures have been woven into a part of American history.

RESEARCH PROCEDURES

Qualitative research will be carried out through interviews with three generations of homestead families to gain an oral history.

Documents, photographs, diaries, newspaper articles, and materials from archives relating to the Bureau of Land Management will be used to gain insight into the organization of this project.

Background history of the Japanese Relocation Camp will be investigated to evaluate the impact it had on this community of families.

Local citizens will be interviewed to examine the impact of the homestead project within the community.

OUTCOMES OF RESEARCH

The Impact of family values, work ethic, and courage of these homesteaders will be preserved in a historical setting.

Manuscripts, oral histories, photographs, documents and diary excerpts will be preserved at McCracken Research Center, Buffalo Bill Museum, and Cody, Wyoming and at the American Heritage Center, University of Wyoming in Laramie.

Qualitative research findings will be published in Educational Journals to enhance Healthy Community development.

Multi-generational communication will be encouraged and developed in this project

RESEARCH DIRECTOR

This research project carries a special significance for Patricia, as her parents received the first drawing for a homestead allotment on Heart

Mc nt 's Ralston Bench in 1949. Patricia's parents brought their family
to ' yo ng in 1950 to begin life in a new frontier.

he work she does in building Healthy Communities and Family
We ne has strong roots in the opportunities she was given as a child.

ie always felt her upbringing had a special significance. Her
bac gr id in Family Life and Counseling has given her many
op rtu ties to research the impact of life on a homestead.

ie has a unique interest in working with multi-generational
gro os.

itricia received her B.S. and M.S. degrees in Human Resources,
Fai ly fe and Counseling from Eastern Michigan University. She has
tau it ondary and adult education.

****

came to realize very early in the first stages of the historical
res rc project I was conducting, that it was not just about me or my
fan ly, it this expansive endeavor was part of an entire community. And
no a am in the last stages of completing the historical narrative that
wil e e of the outcomes of this Qualitative Research Project, this is just
the e ning of something far bigger than myself. I trust future
ger at is of writers who come from the Heart Mountain homestead
cor nu ty will add many more stories of the richness of American history.

those early stages of the research project, it seemed as if I just
cou ln' et enough information under my belt. I found myself searching
out th writers, especially the seasoned sages of the research process. I
dou t would ever place themselves in this category. Maybe if I had
sta d s writing process when I was a child, the feeling of needing to
"ca h " wouldn't be a central theme now. While attending a writer's
cor ere e in Jackson, Wyoming, I perused through the workshops and
cho " chniques for the Research Writer." As I sat there, I looked around
anc vo ered if everyone else in that room was as excited with their own
res rc s I was at the great opportunity that lay before me.

19

I thought if I sat quietly, everyone else would not realize what a novice I felt I was. But finally, my exuberance overpowered me, and I raised my hand. "When do you know you have enough research to write your book?" I don't remember the answer from the speaker, but I do recall that, as I left the room, a gentleman approached me. "Ma'am, I just want to make a comment. Just start writing-- then you will discover where your research needs to be more extensive." I thought that was advice from a seasoned writer. For those of us who have headed down this road to research, we would probably all be in agreement. We never feel we have enough research data.

When the research project began, I thought it would deal mostly with the homesteaders from the 1949 drawing. I believe I felt from the onset of the research project that a book would unfold out of the process, and now the last words are being penned to the page.

It wasn't long into my own research that I realized I needed to have knowledge of the entire four phases of the Shoshone Irrigation Project. I remember, as a young child, how scary it was driving up the old, narrow road in the canyon next to Buffalo Bill Dam. I found the history of building the dam fascinating, as well as the Shoshone Irrigation Project in its four phases. The books I acquired, written by Beryl Churchill, were a valuable resource. I had no idea what a monumental undertaking the irrigation project had been.

As I became more involved in the Heart Mountain homestead story, I found I needed to go back and research the story of the Japanese Relocation Center, as it had made an indelible impact on our community.

When I was a young girl, I remember one morning session of Vacation Bible School at our Mountain View Clubhouse. I was alone, standing very quietly in a back room, looking at the yellow oil cloth on the wall. This had once been the small home of a Japanese family during the war. As a young child, I didn't understand or know much about the situation with Japanese families during the war. But for some reason, as I stood there, I began to cry. As I became more involved in the research project, I found myself delving more into the story relating to that time

20

dui g WII and the story of the Heart Mountain Relocation Center. I
rel 11 vily on the excellent research conducted by Mike Mackey, also
fro th Jniversity of Wyoming.
hroughout my adult life, I have been very aware, whether as a
par it in my teaching career, or just living in a neighborhood, that my
life va greatly influenced in those childhood years in a very rich and
wo ler way.
have spoken briefly in the closing chapter about my "Russian
Co iec n" when I taught in Saratov, Russia. There have been many
tim I ave thanked God for my childhood upbringing, but especially
dui g stint of teaching in that Russian university, I knew the stamina I
pos ss came from the strength and courage imbedded in my DNA from
my hi lood community. Hopefully, one day that experience I had will
ev(e to another narrative. During that period of teaching at Saratov
Un er y, I relied heavily on my experiences as a child which helped me
to i at those dear college professors and students. I saw the glint in the
eye of lose young people who have survived a Communist regime and
nov wa to "head into the wind." I could identify with those young people
fro s ar away, as I had seen that same tenacity and courage in my
par its d neighbors of our homestead community.
s I think back on the 50th high school reunion and the many
coi er ions around the tables with old friends, I am intrigued at the multi-
fac ed e experiences we have had from this Wyoming community. At
thi po in the journey, I believe those of us who grew up in that
ger rat have come to the realization that this was a very special time
anc la in history of which we had the privilege to be a part.
nd now that I have introduced a portion of research that draws
on(ac n time to a story involving young families who were courageous
anc es nt, let us begin our journey together.

ACKNOWLEDGMENTS

A description often used in portraying how a person views life is if they see a cup half empty or half full. I would say that afternoon as I sat with my friends listening to a speaker from Search Institute describing the effects of forty positive assets in youth development was a "half-full" cup experience. The seeds planted that day in my mind and soul would launch me into a quest that would lead me far beyond what I could have dreamed.

It would be impossible to put down on these pages every person that came along my path in this great adventure of writing, but I will highlight just a few.

I was coming into the home stretch of writing and knew I needed an editor. Not just one who would read through the passages and look for mistakes. This story has been written with such passion and dedication, that I needed someone who was able to grasp onto the power and courage in this story of modern-day pioneers, and that special person is Nancy Gullet. What has come natural to Nancy throughout her career of editing has been a challenge for me. I have found myself learning volumes from her, and for that and her dedication to this story; words cannot come close to how grateful I am to her.

The story evolved out of a Qualitative Research Project I conducted while on staff with the University of Wyoming Cooperative Extension Service. Professor Karen Williams of the UW Child Development Department introduced me to the process of Qualitative Research. Ben Silliman, UW Extension Family Life Specialist gave "wind to my sails," giving me the courage to believe in the possibility of writing down the story of my "growing-up" community. Edna McBreen, State Director for Extension, gave me the first green light to begin research. The next Director of Extension, Glenn Whipple, would make it possible for me to apply for a sabbatical to be used for research. A

spe al   anks goes to Virla Harrell for transcribing all of the homesteaders'
int vie s which will be stored for future use at UW American Heritage
Ce er   Laramie, Wyoming, and McCracken Research Center in Cody,
W) mi   .

    ira writing became an integral part of research and compiling
his ric data. Rick Ewig, Associate Director of the UW American
He ag   Center, Phil Roberts, UW Associate Professor of History, and
An L(ard, UW Director of College Relations were instrumental in
giv g   e valuable components in the procedures and process of
Qu ita e Research. I fondly called the Extension Staff in Big Horn
Co ty   y comrades. They were such an encouragement to me during
tho m   y months of writing for grants and writing chapters in the story.
A   ec   thanks to my secretary, Dori Noyes, and fellow staff members,
Gr hu   Gasvoda-Kelso, Carolyn Karhu, and Eric Morrison.
    he   hn Anson Foundation presented me with a grant which was used
for e   earch process.

    Jo   nly would a book be published from the research information
col ct(but a second vital component would be making the research
ava ab   to future writers and researchers. The McCracken Research
Lit ry   oused at the Buffalo Bill Historical Center in Cody, Wyoming,
anc U\   American Heritage Center in Laramie, Wyoming, will be the
loc io   or the research that has been compiled.
    w(distinguished authors who were invaluable resources for the
Sh ho   Irrigation Project and the Japanese Relocation Center were Beryl
Ch ch   and Mike Mackey. Several members of the Heart Mountain
W) mi   Foundation (HMWF) contributed greatly to the research relating
to e l tory of the Japanese Relocation Center. They were the former
Pre de   of the HMWF, Dave Reetz, Curator LaDonna Zall, and Mary
Bl kb   . Many of the documents used in compiling the history of the
He t N untain Homestead Project were found at the Powell Tribune, Park
Co ty   ibrary, and Shoshone Irrigation District Office

23

I want to give special thanks to Lori Startin at Shoshone Irrigation District, Jeannie Cook, Park County Historical Society, and Rowene Weems, Director/Curator at the Pioneer Homestead Museum in Powell. The impact on my life as a young child in the 4-H youth program would be a great source of endurance in this process of writing. Several heroes in my life while growing up were Cooperative Extension Agents Jimmy Nichols, Edith Anderson, Harold Hurick, Lyle Bang, and many others. I was grateful when my childhood dream of a college education became a reality. I was greatly influenced by many of my professors. I will name just a few: Dr. Williston, Dr. Found, Dr. Young, Dr. Barber, Dr. Del Campo and Dr. Laws.

My children, Craig and Sandy, Shana and Paul, and Rachel and Mitch came alongside and believed in Mom. And, of course, the eleven grandchildren were frosting on the cake.

My brothers Mike and his wife Linda, Wayne and his wife Pam stood in the wings cheering me on.

From the beginning, I had what I like to call "Forever Friends," who faithfully prayed for me and never gave up their belief in my desire to complete this project. I will mention just a few: Teddy and Ronnie Jones, Phyllis and Ray Sammons, Virla and Gordy Harrell, Mary Martin, Joyce Johnston, Ruth and Joe Shadler, Linda Bearup, Margo Satterfield, Mary Ellen Fraser, Pat Vess, Carol Leyme, Esther Collins, and Georgia King.

I believe it would be appropriate to give a standing ovation to my parents, Wallace and Edna Mae McClaflin and all of the other homesteaders in the 1949 Heart Mountain Homestead Project, as they truly are champions of courage and endurance! The times spent around the kitchen table drinking coffee and renewing childhood memories with dear neighbors will forever be imprinted on my mind and spirit

I am most grateful to God in Heaven who has looked down on that homestead land and given me time and courage just to keep marching.

CHAPTER 1: BELOVED HOMELAND

looked out over a shimmering sea of glistening stars, so bright it
wo   d   m the darkness of night had been splashed with the brightness of
day   H   vever, these were not stars but sparkling diamonds of snow upon
a n   un   n side I had never seen before. Pushing the sleep from our eyes,
my   ro   r Mike and I looked out from the window of a Greyhound bus.
We   ve   a small sister and brother, only six and seven, who came from
sou   er   California, seeing, for the first time, snow upon the great Rocky
Mc   nt   s.

e had talked about this faraway place called Wyoming, knowing
we   ou   see snow but never able to imagine how beautiful it would be.
An   no   in the middle of the night, our mother had awakened us, knowing
we   ou   not want to miss this moment of wonder and enchantment.
         o   ny years have passed now. My own children are grown, and I
hav   be   blessed with grandchildren. I try to push away the years to allow
my   lf   remember the excitement of that time in my life. I experienced
all   e   otions and wonder of a new land of sagebrush, rugged mountains,
anc   nc   which had never been a part of my life before.
         t w   the spring of 1950. The Second World War had ended. Families
we   re   ited and trying to begin life over. Some fathers did not come
hoi   .   en as a young child, I can remember feeling a sense of loss but
did   ot   iderstand. I was a few days old when my father went to Europe
anc   ln   t two when he returned home. Time lost during those infant years
wit   ou   father could never be given back.
         ou   g the war years, my mother had moved to southern California to
live   vi   relatives while our father was overseas. My brother Mike was a
yea   ol   than I. I was born in October of 1943.
         y father, Wallace McClaflin, came home from the war in
De   m   of 1945. He began to work at the Edison Electric Company in
On   ric   alifornia. We lived in several homes in those first few years. I
ren   ml   we lived briefly in an orange grove. I have talked with my

27

mother of this, and she finds it hard to believe that I remember, but it was the fragrance of the oranges that heightened my memory at such an early age. Our parents also bought a small, ten-acre farm and began to raise corn.

As one gets older, we become aware of how very quickly the years seem to slip away. For some intangible reason, we have the idea our parents will always be with us, but, of course, this is not true. And so, for this reason, I am writing down many of the stories that have been related to me by homesteaders and their families in the community where I grew up. Hopefully, I will be able to retrieve some of those heart-warming stories that were woven into the quilt of the homestead community that so lovingly raised her children.

As you read on in this journey back into childhood with me, you will find many similarities in these homestead families. All of the interviews have become close to my heart. I recall sitting across the table from homestead widows. It was always good to have both the husband and the wife sharing, but most of the homesteaders were in their late eighties, so of course, I interviewed widows and widowers as well. Upon many occasions, when I asked the question of the wife's role in homesteading, it would be the husband who quickly commented on the vital role his wife played.

Many young families had come to northern Wyoming from other states. I think for all of the families who stayed, they felt a deep sense of commitment to their life on the homestead. Leaving family behind, we all suffered a degree of homesickness. I suppose that is why we rallied around each other and developed such close friendships early in the process of homesteading.

Everyone endured living in tarpaper barracks in the brutally cold, stormy Wyoming winters, living, at first, without electricity or running water, constantly irrigating the land, taking care of livestock, and trekking out into the cold to use those wonderful outhouses. It is still amazing to me how my mother had managed to have a clean house without the luxury of electricity for Mike and me to come home to, and I don't ever recall missing a meal. Wonderful smells of a supper cooking would meet us before we ever set foot in the house. And there was also the joy of getting together with neighbors in a community club where there were square

dar es,   -H meetings, Boy and Girl Scout meetings, and so many other
thi s l   pening. Everyone was in the same boat, so everyone helped each
oth .   ave taken all these memories and values of home with me into
my du   years, and it has enriched my life in ways that are hard even to
exp ss

          a stranger were to ask me to describe my early childhood, the
def iti   that would come to mind would be in this fashion. "Well now,
let e   if I can paint my memories on a canvas of words." It was like
tak g   ip through an enchanted forest, but instead of a collection of trees,
we ad   gebrush. The spring brought on the lemon-yellow tint of cactus
flo ers   Little hands learned quickly the danger of prickly thorns when
pic ng   ese delicate blossoms. The trails I followed through the virgin
soi we   not made by man, but rather deer, rabbits, and wild coyotes.
Lo in   ack, I think all of us in that farming community claimed Heart
M ta   as our beloved silhouette in the sky. The magnificent splendor
of ns   that would settle down over the rugged cliffs and ravines to the
we al   ys gave me a sense that God was smiling down on our families
on at   ountain plain in the northern parts of Wyoming."

          ome days, when trying to put words on the page and feeling such
lim ati   s in myself, a picture would come to mind of my father. He would
be an   g at the window in the living room on a hot, summer afternoon,
loo ng   ut at thick, charcoal-gray clouds releasing ice-cold hail on crops
jus re   y to harvest. I can still feel and see his face masked in
dis po   tment, knowing his many months of arduous work were all in
vai

          eeling I dare not break into the silence that would settle over the
hou e,   ould ask him in a voice barely above a whisper, "Daddy, why do
you ke   farming when there is so much risk after you have worked so
har "   Well, Puddin', we'll just plant again next year; what could we do
tha vo   l be a better life than this?" How many times, as my own life has
tak u   xpected and unwanted detours, have those words come back to
me T   re is really only one word that could describe what I saw, as I
loo d   ast the sadness, the lines of weariness, and the great
dis po   tment in the eyes of a father I loved so dearly--I saw a glint of
rav oi   ge.

29

My father was taken much too early from our family at sixty-seven. But I am sure he is smiling on me today as I put into words the wonderful journey our family had as we began a new life in a new community of young war veterans' families, on homesteads just under the shadow of Heart Mountain, on the northern plains of Wyoming.

How does one pay tribute to courageous parents? Those of us so young then, just after the war, were loved and cherished by our farming community on the Ralston Bench. My story is only one, but maybe with the telling, it will cause those in my generation to take a look back and recollect their own rich stories of childhood.

CHAPTER 2: THE HEART MOUNTAIN PROJECT: PHASE FOUR

the turn of the twentieth century, the Big Horn Basin could be
des ib as an arid, high desert covered with sagebrush. Very few ranches
and io s could be seen on the northern plains. The Shoshone Irrigation
Pro ct ould change the fabric of this Wyoming area. Those first few
bui in seen in early pictures, would one day become the beginnings of
the ri ig community of Powell, with a successful community college.
Th ir hree homestead projects had been completed, but there would be
a la e p in time before the last and final project would begin.
v almost thirty years after the first project, the Garland Division
tha or ess on the last, the Heart Mountain Project, would begin.

n January 31, 1939 invitations for bids on the construction of the
ear w k, a tunnel and the canal lining for the Heart Mountain
Div io vere issued. 1
Th w in Europe was making an impact on progress in the early '40s.

The Garland, Frannie, and Willwood projects were slowed
own and the Heart Mountain Division came almost to a halt.
hen the country went to war many young men were enlisting and
her young people were drawn to the high paying war related jobs.

The comparatively low wage scale set up by local
rigation districts made it practically impossible to compete with
e other employers in securing labor for work on the irrigation
stems. When the U.S. Corps of Engineers started construction
the Heart Mountain Relocation Center (for the Japanese
acuees) a large number of Bureau and irrigation district
nployees resigned to accept employment with the Corps of
ngineers. Working on the relocation center, it was possible for a
mmon laborer to receive a bigger paycheck for two weeks then
Bureau foreman received in a full month.

uring the war, guards were stationed at the Shoshone, Corbett,
id Willwood Dam, as well as the power plant. 2

Before the war had ended, much interest was coming from veterans. Approximately 10,000 applications were filed for the drawings for the 1947 and 1949 homestead units. The homestead drawings were big events which were held in Powell and Cody. The 1947 homestead units were located near the highway between the two towns. The portion of homestead history and interviews I conducted were related to the families from the 1949 drawings, as that was the community where I grew up.

Two hundred eighteen veterans of World War II received Heart Mountain farms in 1947 and 1949. Each of them had to pass scrutiny of a settlement committee as had their predecessors at Willwood. 3

The fourth phase of the irrigation project was a huge undertaking for the government. Much had been learned from the first three projects. A benefit to the Heart Mountain homesteaders came from the dismantled Japanese Relocation Center, which was located near the highway. Each homesteader was allowed to buy a barracks for one dollar, and the barracks could be made over and used as a home. In telling the stories of those early days on the homesteads, neighbors related some very interesting stories of moving cumbersome, tar- papered buildings across sagebrush, since there were no roads.

The Powell Valley had been developed out of the endeavors of the Shoshone Irrigation Project. Big Horn Basin was a high desert. Without the capability of getting irrigation water, farming would not have been possible. The community opened its arms wide to this group of veterans and their families. The G.I. Bill of Rights would become a great asset to these young farmers. From past experience, it was recognized that ongoing education about farming, land management, and irrigation techniques would play a vital role in the success of farming.

FIRST APPLICATION DRAWN FOR THE 1949 HOMESTEAD PROJECT

As a young girl growing up on the homestead, I often heard my mother tell the story of the drawing for the 1949 homesteads.

an and Ruth Otto had already received their homestead unit in drawing in 1948. The morning I spent interviewing Ruth, she f that night at the local theater in Powell. "The auditorium was ith excited people from the community. I remember they called)arents' names as the first applicants to appear in the near future terview to determine if they would qualify for receiving a d unit."

:ollected files to begin writing this morning, I went over to the l high with research and picked up the manila folder for "Wallace l." Several years earlier, as I was gathering documents for the)roject, I had visited the Shoshone Irrigation District Office in spent most of the afternoon going back through the files and old)hs of the Shoshone Irrigation Project. Lori Startin agreed to)ies of information I had requested. A few days later when I she not only had made copies of my requested pages but had ut the McClaflin file and presented me with a yellow envelope. .o, once again this morning, I found myself going from page to ng to learn more about this young man from so long ago. As I ough the folder, I came upon my father's "Honorable Discharge." d the document countless times. It is only a copy of the original, now, I am sure is yellow with age. The document was hard to I still read line by line. When I came to the two columns, * and *Efficiency Rating,* there was a one-word description of this dier: "Excellent." What can I say? That's my dad!

g the Depression, my father had grown up in the dust bowl days in the Panhandle near Forgan, Oklahoma. He had "set his sails" ng a college degree. This dream would never come to pass in his le impact it made on his children was a lasting one.

r had grown up in Gage, Oklahoma. She had completed her s a cosmetologist in Woodward, Oklahoma, and was working in Vlamie Irion's Beauty Shop. It was located in the second story of ; with a drugstore and soda fountain on the first floor. She went : in the morning and worked for her aunt in the afternoon and Back in those days, the person who waited on customers at the vas called a "soda jerk," and that was my dad. I remember well

35

the times Mother told of meeting her future husband. During her long days of work, she would say with amusement, "You know, it was amazing how thirsty I would get and just need to go get a drink at the soda fountain."

Dad enlisted in the service on September 13, 1940, when he was twenty-one years old. When our country went to war, life would never be the same. My parents were married on December 14, 1941. By the time the war was over and my father was able to return home for good, he had a wife and two small children.

It was a difficult time for veterans coming home from the war. Those early adult years had been set aside, and now many of them had small families that needed a father and a job waiting for them back home on American soil. My father had been fortunate to find a position with Edison Electric near Ontario, California. My parents both wanted to make a life for themselves and their two small children. My father worked the midnight shift. It seems somewhat strange, the memories we have from those very early years. I would cuddle up close to my mother in the late evening, falling asleep as she read nursery rhymes. I would pretend to be asleep when my father came home, feeling the great comfort of his strong arms as he would carry me to my room and put me to bed for the night.

They purchased a ten-acre garden farm and began the task of growing garden produce, such as sweet corn.

Wallace McClaflin was a young man, just like so many filling out an application, never thinking his name would be drawn. He had found an advertisement in the California Farmer which stated there were 18,000 acres of irrigable land near the vicinities of Cody and Riverton, Wyoming. His was a very brief letter, written on June 8, 1949, requesting information about the land.

His letter was probably written very late one night. The copy of the letter is hard to read, and the page has smudges on it, so I am typing his brief communication.

Jun 8,)49

Bureau of Reclamation
Cody, Wyoming

Dear Sirs:

I have noticed a clipping in the California Farmer
hi states that 18,000 acres of irrigable land is to be
vi l into Homesteads in the vicinity of Cody   and
ive on, Wyoming.

Would you please send me any additional
nformation available and the necessary blank forms that I may
bmit my application.

Is it necessary to be present for the drawing?

Sincerely,

allace L. McClaflin
ox 2420, South Archibald Ave.
ntario, California

e eived this reply from the government:

N ED STATES
EF RTMENT OF THE INTERIOR
U AU OF RECLAMATION
10 ne Project
O ox 900
od Wyoming

July 11, 1949

re y refer to
pp No. 58-1234

Wallace L. McClaflin

Dear Sir:

Your application for a farm unit in Part III of the Heart Mountain Division of this project was received July 7, 1949.

Serial No. 58-1234 has been assigned to your application and any inquiries concerning it should refer to this number.

As stated in Section 16 (a) and (b) of Public Notice No. 58, opening the lands to homestead entry, all applications received prior to 2:00 P.M., July 12, 1949, shall be held and treated as simultaneously filed. Applications of persons not entitled to veterans' preference as set forth in Section 16 (b) of the Public Notice, will not be considered until it is evident that sufficient qualified applicants, who have veteran's preference rights, are not available to enter all the farm units listed in the notice. You may not expect to hear further from this office in regard to your application until sometime after July 12, 1949.

Very truly yours,
A. S. Ingraham, Superintendent
Operation and Development

IMPORTANT
to
APPLICANTS FOR HOMESTEADS
on
HEART MOUNTAIN DIVISION, SHOSHONE PROJECT, WYOMING

Applicants' rating will be based upon the information given on the application blanks, hence you are urged to take every precaution in the preparation of your application, including all substantiating data. Before mailing your application, check the following list of reminders:

you claim veteran preference, attach a photostatic, certified, or
aut nt ited copy of your discharge or certificate of service.

physically handicapped or afflicted, attach a detailed statement
sig d an examining physician which defines the limitations of the
dis ili

ave you shown month and year, indicating beginning and close
of ch riod of farm experience? (Question 7)

you have listed farm or other equipment as an asset, have you
att he in itemized list of equipment, giving make, model, size, year
ma ifa ired and present market value?

ave you shown the present cash value of life insurance and
sec iti ?

you have listed credit as partial fulfillment of the capital
req re nt, be sure to attach to our application a statement from a
res ns le representative of the credit source which describes the terms
anc im nt of the loan which is available to you.

ave you fully answered all questions? The blanks in the first
par ra of the application for listing your priority of choice of farm units
nec nc ie filled in at the time of making application.

as your application been signed and attested by an authorized
off ial

is not necessary to visit the project prior to filing your
app ca n. You will be called in for a personal interview if you qualify
anc re iccessful in the drawing. Maps and directions for inspecting the
far ur ; may be obtained from the Settlement Office at the former WRA
Ca p r lway between the towns of Powell and Cody.

10. Mail your application to the Superintendent, Bureau of Reclamation, Powell, Wyo.

11. Applications received prior to 2:00 p.m., October 22, 1947, will be considered as simultaneously filed. Mail your complete application at the earliest possible moment. You will be notified of all actions taken with respect to your application.

ADDITIONAL INFORMATION

The Shoshone Project is situated in northwestern Wyoming, in What known as the "Big Horn Basin." The Project is composed of the Garland, Frannie, Willwood, Heart Mountain.

The average elevation of the Heart Mountain Division is about 4,800 feet. Precipitation averages 6 inches per year and the growing season averages 148 days in length. Water for the division is diverted from the Buffalo Bill Reservoir on the Shoshone River. An adequate supply of water is available for all the lands to be included in the project. The irrigable lands of the project are in their raw state, covered with sages and grasses, and must be cleared, leveled and the farm irrigation system installed prior to crop production. The soils are low in organic matter and a period of 3 to 5 years of soil building practices will be necessary before maximum yields can be obtained. 3

HOMESTEAD AND RECLAMATION REQUIREMENTS

An entryman must be 21 years of age or head of a family. However, any person under 21 years who established military preference in World War II is entitled to the same rights as those over 21 years. The entryman also must be a citizen of the United

ates or have filed intent of citizenship; must not own more than
50 acres of land in the United States, and must not have previously
hausted his homestead right. No person who owns land on a
ederal Reclamation Project upon which his share of the total
onstruction charges are unpaid, may make homestead entry on a
rm unit. The entryman must establish residence within six
onths of the date of entry, must live on the unit for three years
id have a habitable dwelling at the time of making final proof.
redit for military service may be substituted for the second and
ird year of residence. The settler must clear, level, irrigate and
oduce satisfactory crops on at least 50 percent of the irrigable
reage in the unit for at least two years before patent may be
sued. 4

would discover more and more information in the folder given to
at hot August day at the Shoshone Irrigation District Office in
ach applicant for the Heart Mountain homestead units followed
process as my father. From the beginning to the end, a great deal
nplished in, surprisingly, a short amount of time.

r tired of hearing Mother tell of the afternoon when the men from
newspaper came to the front door. Daddy had already gone to
ey came with the news that the McClaflin application had been
This meant that my parents' names would be placed in the
hat would take place at Powell's Teton Theater on September 23,
e went with the men to Edison Electric that afternoon with the

[y parents' names were placed in the drawing, and on September
23, 94 my father's name was the first one drawn! What an exciting day
it v s! hat meant that he would have first choice in selecting one of the
ne\ ho steads.

[y parents came to Wyoming in early October of 1949 for an
int vie by a special committee chosen to find those families who would
be le meet the challenges of beginning a new community on virgin soil
in ɛ ɪ thern plains of Wyoming. They were okayed by the committee
aft th interview.

41

In telling of that first trip to Wyoming, our mother told of going to a local beauty shop to have her hair done for the interview. That is where she met the owner of the shop, Bessie Hoff, who would become a close friend from the beginning. Bessie introduced her mother, Emma Bosley, who in turn rented a room to our parents. I noted that on some of the papers filed, Emma's signature was used as a witness.

I don't think my parents ever gave up their dream of the homestead. They felt they had been blessed with a sense of time and place. It was a heavy responsibly for this young soldier who had been raised on a dry land farm (with no irrigation) in the Panhandle of Oklahoma. After a great deal of examination, the McClaflins made their final decision and chose Unit No. 200.

After all these years, as I write the stories of this courageous group of people, it brings me a great sense of honor and humility in knowing my parents chose their homestead on October 11, 1949, my sixth birthday.

<u>Final Homestead Proof Accepted</u>
On October 31, 1949, Wallace L. McClaflin made reclamation homestead entry, Cheyenne 081776, for Farm Unit "A" of Sec. 18 or Lot 19 of Sec. 18, Tract 2 of Lot 72, T. 55 N., R. 100W., 6th P.M. within Heart Mountain Division, Shoshone Project, Wyoming, and allowed subject to the Act of June 17, 1902. 5

I found these two articles in the archives of the Powell Public Library, from the local newspaper, the week the McClaflins were picking out their homestead unit in October of 1949.

HE GETS FIRST CHOICE

The No. 1 homesteader, Wallace Leroy McClaflin, with his wife, comes from Ontario, California, and makes a homestead filing. We welcomed him yesterday at the Tribune; a fine appearing young couple originally from Oklahoma but later from California. We gave them the hand of welcome and gave them to

nderstand as best we could that always will they be welcome
sitors at the office of the home newspaper.

Mr. McClaflin, possessing as he does the first priority right
select the farm he chooses of the 104 units just opened between
alston and Heart Mountain, does not find the task too easy of
cking out the best unit in the opening. Put yourself in his place,
range that it is, with all the other successful applicants awaiting
xiously his decision. He has been at the reclamation offices
udying their soil tests, but that is placing much responsibility
on the shoulders of a stranger from a strange land, even though
e may have had much experience in farming.

But welcome to this young homesteader and his charming
yo   g wife from southern California, feeling as we do that any choice
he   akes will not permit of his going far wrong. They tell us they are
go   g to like it here as the Tribune photographer caught their smiles
in   icture snapped too late for Tuesday's edition. Wanting to like it
an   naking a serious effort to like this fertile valley is half the battle,
be   ise any of the homesteaders who are not in the proper mood to
ad   t themselves to this country had better never make the start. 6

LUCKY McCLAFLIN

veryone here is so friendly," commented Mr. and Mrs. Wallace
Mc   laf   from Ontario, California, when they visited the Powell Tribune
off e h   e Tuesday morning.
     [c(flin, you may remember, was the veteran who drew the No. 1
pri ity   the land drawing for 104 units on the Heart Mountain division
of   e S shone irrigation project, which took place here in September.
          he dark, slender handsome young man smiled when asked if he
hac ee   hrilled to learn that he had received first chance at the farm lands
anc ai
     5u   but you know how those things are – you put in your application
anc he   ou figure you might as well forget about it, because you just don't
thir y(could be that lucky." The McClaflins were first notified by their

43

local newspaper which had received a post-dispatch concerning the result of the land drawing.

Mr. and Mrs. McClaflin are recalling the harrowing trip through the park snow storm. They rented an apartment at the home of Emma Bosley and immediately went to look over the project to be their future home and after much appropriate and due deliberation and consultation selected unit No. 200.

McClaflin is an Irishman who was born and reared on a farm in the Oklahoma panhandle. He says he doesn't fear the cold winters here because it got cold and windy down there for the past six years he had been living in California and raising vegetables on a truck farm.

During the war this 30 year-old veteran served for two years in the artillery and for three years with the air force. He was a first lieutenant as a pilot with the famous 92nd bomber group stationed in England, and flew 35 missions over Germany as a member of the Lucky Tiger Squadron.

When the war was over he came home to his charming wife and two children, Pat and Mike. The youngsters are 6 and 7 years of age and are in school presently in California so they did not make the trip to Wyoming with their parents. The mother thinks they will like it up here and that she herself will be happy wherever her husband is.

The unit McClaflin has chosen is about ten miles from Powell. He said the decision was a difficult one because many of the farms look good especially No. 196. He thinks the land is a heavier variety than any he has been used to, but is optimistic on the basis of results obtained from first year efforts in the surrounding area. His present equipment will have to be supplemented and in some instances, replaced, McClaflin stated, as in the case of his tractor which he believes much too small and light for the type of farming done here. Irrigation farming is not new to this army veteran, but as a truck farmer he has been operating on a smaller scale than required here, and also he does not doubt but what the methods will vary.

McClaflin's plans now are to return to California and complete preparations for the final move to Wyoming with their children. Mr. and Mrs. McClaflin will return here about January 1st and set about the task of becoming real homesteaders.

he newest homesteader has the unbounded energy of youth, the
ess ıtiı experience of a farmer, and what is more the ambitious desire to
suc ec   7

PI ICANTS FOR HOMESTEAD INTERVIEWED
UI DAY

Eight more applicants for homesteads on the Heart Mountain
we interviewed in Powell Tuesday by members of the Homestead
Ex ıining Board, according to George Gibson, member.   Ten
ıp cants were scheduled to appear, but one failed to show and
an ıer withdrew.
The applicants, their family members, and units chosen are
lis ı below:
Applicant No. 40 – Albert G. Kamm, Fort Collins,
Cc rado; married with five children, unit 192. Applicant No. 41 –
Kc ıeth J. Cunningham, Powell, married with two children, unit 132.
Aı icant No. 42 – Elmer I. Collar, Arnett, Okla., married with one
ch , unit 153. Applicant No. 43 – Gordon W. Hutchison of Dumont,
[o\ , married with two children, unit 140. Applicant No. 44 – failed
to pear. Applicant No. 45 – Marion Aimone, Kemmerer, Wyoming,
mı ied no children, unit 115.   Applicant No. 46 – Withdrew.
Aı icant No. 47, O. Fielding, Roberts, Idaho, married with one child,
un !10. Applicant No. 48 – Francis B. Meins, Ryegate, Mont. Single,
un 143. Applicant No. 49, Bernard Leroy Fulton, Powell, married
wi five children, Unit 116.   Applicant No. 59, John H. Krauter,
Aı ı, California, married with one child, Unit 192. The board will
int view more applicants on Tuesday and Thursday of next week. 8
/la of the families selected for the homestead units came from other
sta ;.   reviewing the correspondence back and forth, it was clear that it
wa ı d icult decision to decide where to locate the barracks on the farm
uni ›eı e they moved. Upon being awarded a farm unit, applications and
ma / d ıils regarding water service would come into play.
ltl ıgh we were very young at the time, memories of those husbands
and /i\ working so hard are vivid. There were many requirements

those first few years in order to finalize the ownership of land. In the formal government documents, the veterans were referred to as entrymen.

In early spring of 1950, the final closing on McClaflin's ten acre garden farm near Ontario, California, was finalized. The 1947 ¾, quarter-ton Dodge pickup was filled with as many household items as possible, and Wallace drove the truck to Wyoming.

I remember taking the trip to Wyoming with our mother on a Greyhound bus. That was a long trek for two small, rambunctious children. Seeing snow as we crossed over the mountain ranges in the middle of the night was a new experience for my brother and me.

The bus pulled up next to the Home Hotel in a small, white stucco building on Bent Street in Powell. We saw our dad, face cloaked with weariness but eyes that sparkled, standing there on the sidewalk waiting for us. Children seem to have built-in radar at times when they need to be quiet. The embrace of our parents there on that chilly afternoon in early spring gave an indication of how much they had missed each other.

The beginnings of this community can be described as a windswept prairie land with a covering of sagebrush, dirt roads, and irrigation canals. The black, tarpaper barracks held nothing of beauty, but it was home. The men worked hard with what they had. For the most part, families were grateful to have a place to live right on the home site.

Those first two years were crucial for the homesteaders, as they would be expected to prove up the land and furnish a livable home from the barracks. Two seasons of cultivation were required. This was virgin territory never before farmed. The farmers would have to clear the sagebrush, dig ditches, plow, and level the ground for irrigation. These were young families, husbands just a few years home from war. Neighbors grouped together, planning what machinery would be needed, and then it was shared among the farmers.

The homestead farmers received $90 per month for taking agriculture education classes. This was a great asset to the young families venturing out into farming. For their ongoing education, the State Department of Education played a key role in facilitating instructors as well as in-class and on-site visits to farms.

he   was a cooperative effort between the Bureau of Reclamation,
US A   gencies, the Veterans Administration, and the University
Co)er ve Extension Service in furnishing the educational needs of the
far ers
hi is an application I found in my father's file that each of the
hoi st ders would use at the end of the two-year, proving-up period.

NI :D STATES
EI RTMENT OF THE INTERIOR
UI AU OF LAND MANAGEMENT
an nd Survey Office
he nne, Wyoming
at(

Name of Entryman
Reclamation Homestead Entry

Final Affidavit Acceptation or Rejection

Description of Reclamation Homestead

Copy of Certificate of Honorable Discharge on file

ar 43, Sec. 230.60, Code of Federal Regulations reads: "To
)m y with the provisions of the reclamation law as to reclamation
art 3 CFR 181.38 of the general homestead regulations states that
)ef e satisfactory final proof may be submitted on a homestead entry,
ve an (with 19 months or more military service) will be required to
)m y with the homestead laws for a period of at least one year,
:*: *A veteran will not be required to cultivate the land after he has
et e requirements as set forth above: provided he promptly files
)ti(of intention to submit proof."

This regulation, however, does not apply to Reclamation homestead Entries since in those cases cultivation of at least one-half of the irrigable area must be shown and two satisfactory crops raised during the two years immediately preceding the submission of the final reclamation proof.

Perry T. Williams, Manager 9

In those early years of irrigation, unlined ditches across the farmstead were used to water the crops. Canvas dams held the water build-up for watering the crops. In "row" crops such as beans, siphon tubes were used for each furrow of rows across the field. My brother, Mike, with his long, lanky legs had mastered this process of siphoning the water up the funnel and onto the field. Not me! I tried, but I don't know that I ever got the technique down like he did.

When I interviewed Jewel Carter, we both laughed a great deal at our similar experiences. I think both of us had gifts of cooking that outweighed our lack of being able to set a head of water in record time.

It was a heavy-duty project carrying the canvas dams, shovel, and siphon tubes across the fields every day, sometimes several times, but that is how the irrigation was done in those days. Later, I remember how pleased my father was in showing me the cement ditch all along the north side of the homestead.

The technology of irrigation and water conservation has advanced from those early years. Now, as one drives through the farmlands of Heart Mountain, large, white plastic gated pipe can be seen stretched out across the fields. What the eye cannot see is the many miles of buried pipe.

"The work already completed, by reducing the losses to evaporation and seepage, has improved the efficiency of parts of the system by nearly 50 percent, and it is expected that similar results will follow from the work presently underway." 10

In those years of growing up on the homestead, one could see canals along the roadside which dropped every few hundred feet. Some of the canals were much deeper than the one in front of our homestead, so parents

we   a ays careful with their children. In those early years, on hot,
sur   ne ays after work was done, Mike and I enjoyed cooling off in the
car   . later years, there was a greater degree of concern as to the
env on ental safety of using the canal as a swimming hole. Insecticides
use or ie crops could possibly be found in the water.

Al ii drain ran across the back of the original homestead farm. This
wa   un f water from the farmlands above my parents' homestead. As the
yea ; w it by, large trout could be found in the deep holes in alkali drain,
dug iw by years of water moving down the plains.

Vit all this and their own hard work, farmers on Heart Mountain
pro icc crops in 1951 that earned a higher per-acre income than those on
any)f t older divisions of the Project. 11

remember that early summer morning, June 25, 1950, when
Lai a (viness, our neighbor to the east, drove her Willys jeep into the
fro y. l. She was obviously upset. She had on her small, battery
opc ite adio. It had just been announced on the news that war with Korea
wa   dec red. This was a grave concern for our homestead community.
The vet ans were not sure how this would impact their lives.

took some time before wells were in place on the farm units.
Wa   r l to be hauled from town. On our back porch, there was a wooden
ice he. where food was kept cold. Propane gas was used for the cooking
sto s.

h(leart Mountain community did not have electricity for several
yea ;, s families became very inventive in coping. They really looked
for irc) having electricity. It was a big undertaking, burying the electric
pol ; f(miles over new territory. It was a cold winter day when the men
car ; t hook up electricity in our home. Every Christmas, we had
dec rat a tree with electric lights with the anticipation of seeing the
col s \ y soon. Our parents had packed the pickup with all the Christmas
ite ; tl day the men climbed up the electric pole near the well house in
our ac yard. Our family was going to spend Christmas up at Paint Creek
Ra   h \ th Bessie and Felix Hoff and their daughter, Phyllis. Mike and I
loo ;d t the window as the folks coaxed us to go. There was no way we
we   al it to leave until the men crawled down the pole. It was getting
lat n ; afternoon when they finally were able to come down off the

windy perch. Mike and I ran over and plugged in the Christmas lights. I don't believe it would be possible for two young children to have been any more excited! What a beautiful sight those Christmas lights were!

Along with spring plowing and all the other tasks of farming, the young men worked hard on the barracks, making them livable for their young families.

In our barracks, the bedroom had been partitioned off. Our mom had brought with her the lovely, mauve-colored, quilted bedspread from California. We were greeted one night that first spring with a late snow. The next morning, there was a layer of snow lying on top of the quilt!

In the living room sat a large morning stove that had come from the camp. Mike and I had been warned of the danger of getting too close. Many neighbors spoke of that first source of heat. That old stove became a gathering place for the neighbors, as the men would gather around with cups of coffee and discuss farming. The only original stove I could ever locate was at the Homesteader's Museum in Powell.

I remember the presidential election of 1952. It was a cold, blustery November afternoon when the men gathered around the McClaflin morning stove, drinking coffee. Jim Caviness had brought his battery-operated radio for the neighbors to listen to the election returns. Dwight Eisenhower was running against Adlai Stevenson. When it was announced that the former war general had won the election, there was a great cheer that went up in our homestead barracks home.

Our dad had taken a hand in building. His first project was called the well house. It is still being used to hold the pump. The cooler temperature made it a good place, down through the years, where the big freezer and row upon row of canned goods were stored.

MA BELL COMES TO HEART MOUNTAIN

As I look about and try, as best I can, to come to some semblance of understanding of the new ways of communication, I feel at a loss. My small cell phone meets my needs. It doesn't take pictures, and many of the accessories lay dormant in usage. My grandchildren and all their friends cannot understand why I do not use the wonderful technique of texting.

Mo i   ividuals have some source of communication by phone and
int ne   While on a mission trip a few years ago, we could see cell phones
bei ʒ u d in the remotest parts of Africa.
     Av   le back, I was drawn to research taken of young people in today's
soc ty   The data taken from this broad-based information indicated that
the un   er one description of teen-agers today is that they are lonely. That
wa su   ising at first, as the ability to communicate today far surpasses
tho ea   y years on the homestead. Although volumes of words are shared
thr igh exting and e-mails, what is lacking?
     lt   ugh I was only six years old that first year, I can remember the
fee ig   of homesickness. Our relatives were far away in southern
Ca or   and Oklahoma. In that remote place near the mountains, our
fan y   is not alone in this feeling of isolation. I do believe that was a
cat ys   those early years for neighbors coming together and creating
bo   s c   friendship and family that would last for a lifetime.
     he   cal community assisted the Heart Mountain families in those
yea b   re phones were installed. I remember the night when our little
ho   h   settled down to sleep. I was awakened to voices speaking very
lov an   could hear my mother crying. I had a sense it was very late, as
eve in   e darkness, it was hard to get my eyes open in the small bedroom.
Be ie   d Felix Hoff had graciously accepted the task of conveying
inf ma   on that came from a long distance. I knew I should not intrude on
thi im   rtant discussion in the next room. I could hear Bessie telling
Mc er   at her father, Pop Brown, had died in the night. A cloak of
sad ss   ettled over our home that night.
     he   irst phone lines on Heart Mountain were not installed until
No m   r of 1955. Those first few years, neighbors shared party lines.
Co er   tions were kept at a minimum in respect for other families. When
I i er   wed Margaret Olson, she graciously shared information and
cor s   pictures about the process of getting phone lines.

    The committee worked closely with the Rural Telephone
As cia   on. The initial plan was for the telephone lines to be on the Rural
Ele ric ssociation poles. The homesteaders on Heart Mountain waited
lon er   phone service, but it proved to be to their advantage. With the
sal of   e telephone company, more funding was available. In 1955,

underground cable was laid, and the Heart Mountain community telephones were serviced by Mountain State Telephone and Telegraph.

That first year of farming in 1950 was difficult for the farmers, but they still took the time to get together in the community club building. They were an energetic group of families that took on the expansion of their homeland. Lloyd Snider, President of the Mountain View Club, designated a group of men to become the telephone committee. Vechel (fondly called Swede) Olson was designated as chairman. Committee members were Floyd Gay, Robert Jirsa, Jack Hirst, and Herbert Wojahn. They took on this challenge with gusto. It would later be noted that the entire Powell community would be rewarded for their diligence, as the telephone company was privately owned in 1950.

"The 2,000th Telephone in Powell was installed November 1, 1955, in the home of Mr. and Mrs. Vechel W. Olson. Signed by Kenneth K. Kearns, Manager, and by Bertha I. Crinklaw, Chief Operator." A copy of a picture of the ceremony was given to me by Margaret.

Before moving to Wyoming, television was coming on the scene. The large, narrow screens filling up a wall space are a great contrast to those first black-and-white pictures. Early in the spring of 1950, our father had gone to begin working land, while our mother, Mike, and I spent time with Aunt Eileen in Ontario, California. She had a television which was a great fascination to us. When I look back at those first programs, it is hard to grasp. It would take years before TV would make it over the great mountains.

I don't know that any of the homestead families ever went on vacations in the summer in those first years of farming. Work began before sunup and continued long into the night hours, setting the irrigation for the day. When I was in the third grade, our family went to Oklahoma to visit relatives for Christmas. The first night of our journey we stayed in a small "Mom and Pop" type of motel. I don't know why that trip seemed to press on my memory in later years, except I remember hoping, at the time, that I would never lose the capacity to feel such complete joy and excitement. When we walked into the small motel room with meager furnishings that evening, Mike and I broke out with exuberant energy as we saw a small TV hanging down from the corner of the ceiling! There was a metal chain

o the back-- I suppose for fear someone might steal the set. Of
e picture was black and white on the small screen. There was a
quarters to be placed in a slot. I don't remember how long we
ved to watch the little TV, but it was wonderful experience.

se early years of homesteading, there were challenges for sure,
maraderie the families shared together, along with the unified
nd determination to make a thriving community out of the
was evidenced in the communication shared. In the winter
t was a common occurrence to meet in a neighbor's home and
s and visit. As I interviewed the homesteaders, they often
d that after TV came into the home, we didn't visit as much, and
ssed disappointment in that.

the last few years, I don't recall that the winters have been so
hose first years in Wyoming, the snowdrifts would be almost as
e roofs of the houses. When storms were coming, the Heart
school bus was always the first to leave the school, as roads could
d by drifts so quickly. We thought it was fun to be able to go
y from school. After we began to have livestock, the fun was
ssolved, as we would spend hours out in the bitter cold making
vestock had water and feed.

remember storms that lasted for days. At times there would be a
t" which made it impossible to see right in front of you. The snow
ld pile up over the fences. The flocks of sheep would wander
our father would have to go looking for them. It was not
n in those years for ranchers and farmers to become disoriented
to death.

was high desert, so the growing season was short. Field work
done quickly, and when it came time for harvest, all energy went
getting in the crops. Weather could change quickly.
orms would gather over the mountains and bring hail, which, in
f a few moments, could wipe out a whole crop. Wyoming winds
utal. I have to say, I don't miss the howling that could last for
wipe out crops.

determined that the original homestead unit acreage could not
family, so each farm unit was given added acreage, or allotments

53

of land, in 1951. There was not enough land for all of the homesteaders, so eleven of the men would wait a long time. There was acreage at the base of Heart Mountain that was considered, but the expense of another canal delayed the process. Dick Hansen was a key player in bringing this to the forefront again in 1970. By 1974, it was finally determined that sprinklers would be installed on each new unit. Those eleven homesteaders who were finally awarded an added acreage were as follows:

Herb Beslanowitch, Gene Dunleavy, Lyle French, Dick Hansen, Wallace McClaflin, Dale Metzer, Glenn Montgomery, Harold McHose, Tak Ogawa, and Lloyd Snider. In later years, sprinklers could be seen on the lower farms. I always thought it was a beautiful sight, seeing the water circling high into the air with Heart Mountain in the background.

When I was researching for news articles at the Powell Public Library, I came across the article from the Powell Tribune with information about the tunnel disaster in 1986, so I have included it here.

WATER TUNNEL DISASTER

The Corbett project has served the Powell valley farmers well. From 1917 until 1985 there were minimal repairs to the tunnel. In 1983 the tunnel began to show serious signs of old age when several small chunks of concrete fell from the ceiling and leaks in the tunnel became more severe. Voids began to form behind the concrete walls.

In 1984, the Wyoming legislature appropriated a $750,000 grant and approved a $750,000 loan for repairs to the tunnel. Those repairs began just after the water was turned out of the system in late October 1985." 12

When one understands the arid climate of the northern plains of Wyoming, it helps to understand the necessity of irrigation. Driving through the farmlands in the summer months, it is hard to visualize what this country looked like before the canals were developed to hold the waters from the North Fork of the Shoshone River.

Thirty thousand acres of farmlands between Powell and Cody were severally threatened in the spring of 1986. On Tuesday, May 6th, the Bureau of Reclamation Control Center in Casper, Wyoming was put on alert. The controls at the station, which monitor the water levels in the

tun els ndicated, at 5:30 A.M. a drastic drop in water elevation in the
He t N untain conduit. The concrete tunnel is located 2.6 miles west of
Co i hoshone canyon.

wa sh y 11:00 A.M. the water supply to the Cody and Powell valleys
cor ict down. Engineers from the Cody area were immediately
hac us An investigation of the empty tunnel indicated a 40-foot section
we b illen away. United States Bureau of Reclamation tunnel experts
in t e n ight in from four states to help determine the damage and assist
als pl st rapid method of repair. The Heart Mountain Irrigation District
ins ct ed a major role in informing local farmers and helped with
of e d the tunnel. Inspection had to be delayed until 2:00 P.M. because
he ger of sulfur gases present in the tunnel.

yea , t nnel had been constructed between 1936 and 1940. During those
tun el re had been virtually no major problems with the tunnel. The
Th ai is imbedded twelve feet below the surface of Cedar Mountain.
of ite ity of the twelve feet wide conduit was 915 cubic feet per second
to ll Use for irrigation from the tunnel began in 1941. It was not used
hoi est pacity until 1946 when the first drawing for Heart Mountain
ls was completed.

tur d he tunnel had been inspected each year before the water had been
cra s for irrigation. In 1975, it was discovered that there were some
cra s. the cement. At that time $15,000 had been spent repairing the
cra s. irout was pumped into twenty four-inch holes to fill damaged

tun el. ut now in May of 1986, there was a major problem with the
foo se fter the inspection was completed, it was estimated that two 40-
tun el ins would have to be removed and replaced. Another 300 feet of
be ou uld need to be grouted. The repair to the tunnel was estimated to
cor nu $400,000. Irrigation District Manager, Ed Norlin, informed the
Wy mi y of the cooperation that was given to the community from the
Re am Congressional delegation, the United States Bureau of
on, and the Irrigation district.

Vo ers were committed to repairing the tunnel damage as soon as
pos bl as spring crops needed water. Crews worked around the clock.
Th e e as many as fourteen men per shift. By Wednesday, May 28th,

all cracks up and down the patch area were sealed water tight, and monitoring equipment was placed across the cracks of the tunnel. The two sections had been completely removed and replaced.

After three intense weeks for the community, repairs were completed and water was returned to the crops. Some of the alfalfa and grain crops were affected, but there was no crop failure. This was a memorable experience for many of the homesteaders that had been farming in the spring of 1986. 13

In Appendix B, I have listed for you, the reader, the entire list of homestead units for the Heart Mountain Homestead Project. The project was in three drawings, in 1947, 1948, and 1949.

HAPTER 3: HEART MOUNTAIN JAPANESE RELOCATION CAMP OF WWII

he Heart Mountain homesteaders originally lived in barrack
ho⟩ ⟩s, ade from those left by the Japanese American citizens who lived
in ⟩ en⟩ t the relocation internment camp during World War II. These
tar⟩ pe⟩ arracks were moved to the homesteads to provide shelter as the
ho⟩ ⟩st⟩ ders were moving onto the land.

⟩s it in my upstairs office this afternoon, I have a book before me.
It i ⟩nt ed, *I Am an American*. 1 This is only one book in my stash that
has ⟩ee collected during the process of the Qualitative Research Project
tha ⟩ee ed, after a while, to take on a life of its own. On the front cover
of ⟩is ⟩ok is a group of young boys holding an American flag. I
co⟩ ne the author, Jerry Stanley, for the significant contribution of
his ric research that has gone into the making of his book. What seems
a b di ⟩artening to me, as I open the first page of this library book, is a
wo ir ⟩ld, red print stamped "Discard." For many years, it was as if this
wa ⟩oɪ tten history, but now awareness is growing in our country of that
tin⟩ du ⟩g WWII when so many thousands of Japanese American citizens
we ta n from the west coast and forced to live in relocation internment
caɪ ⟩s.

fe ⟩t an honor and privilege that I have grown up in this great nation.
Th⟩ U⟩ ⟩d States of America is truly the melting pot of the world.
Ne le⟩ to say, as we look back over history, there would be portions I
wo d⟩ ⟩rite. But then, I am only one person.

⟩ my childhood years, the lonely chimney sitting out on a wind-
sw⟩ t⟩ ⟩ under the shadow of Heart Mountain was a reminder to me of a
wa ha ⟩ok my father to a far-off land when I was an infant. Along the
wa ⟩ ir ⟩y office is a collection of the history of those years during WWII
rel⟩ ⟩ng ⟩ the many thousands of Japanese families moved to relocation
ceɪ ⟩rs the western states.

⟩ ⟩ ⟩ting this brief history of another time, I am not passing judgment.
Wl ⟩I ll share with you, the reader, are some titles of those books I have

found that have enlightened me and brought back a part of history I hope is never repeated in this nation I love so well. The Heart Mountain homestead community sat right next to the internment camp. I lived in a barrack home from the relocation center, so this history of another time that I am sharing with you has, without a doubt, had an impact on my life.

Life seems to find us in an ebb and flow of seasons. If we are perceptive to those circumstances around us, we can be assured there are lessons to be learned. Webster's Dictionary defines the word "ebb" as, "The flow of water back toward the sea, as the tide falls."

As we get older, our sleep patterns seem to change. I find this to be a great frustration at times. I can be right in the middle of writing with great passion, the words coming rapidly, when all of a sudden, right in the middle of the day, sleep seems to overcome me. If I am not careful, I fall into a deep sleep which robs me of precious time and writing goals for the day. Then in the middle of the night, I am wide awake, mind in full swing. But I am not brave about getting up in the chilly bedroom. I have learned a hard lesson in not allowing myself to write too late into the night, as my mind keeps moving on down the path.

A while back, at about 4:00 a.m., I was having one of those wide-awake experiences. Hoping the sound of the TV would lull me back into a stupor, and needing sleep, I turned on the news.

I sat up in bed and watched pictures of a tsunami sweeping across farmlands and cities in northern Japan. At first, the death toll was a few hundred, but I knew with the rapid rise of water, many thousands would probably lose their lives. The ebb and flow of the tide took everything with it back into the sea. What a terrible sight it was!

In the next few days, as I watched and listened to the news forecast of the surreal unfolding of one disaster after another, I would weep and pray for the Japanese people.

The tsunami on March 11, 2011, off the Pacific coast of Tohoku, was called the Great East Japan Earthquake Disaster and was also known as the 2011 Tohoku earthquake. It has been referred to as the most powerful known earthquake ever to have hit Japan. Since the recorded history of earthquakes in 1900, it has been classified as one of the five most powerful earthquakes in the world. It was a mega-thrust earthquake that lasted six t a magnitude of 9.0 (Mw) [2] [3] with a depth of 32 km (20 is estimated that there were 1,235 aftershocks. At this time, the on I have found lists the deaths at approximately 15,839, with red, and 3,642 missing.

ys turned into weeks, and then months went by, it seemed the t more serious, and the danger to so many Japanese families was here was something about this nation of people I was sure would ered. Once again, as I would follow the news each evening, I was or the opportunity I had been given in learning of those many families that had lived so close to what I now refer to as my Homeland." The Japanese people are resilient in the worst of . In the face of the disaster of the terrible tsunami, they would get and work to rebuild.

Writing this chapter on the Japanese Relocation Camp has been cess, and even now as I put into words a brief history of a part of I feel inadequate.

grateful to those persons who have gone back into archives and o the forefront so much that otherwise would have been lost to the enerations of Americans concerning the Japanese Relocation WWII. In this writing, I will recall only one camp which was st north of Highway 14 between Powell and Cody, Wyoming.

the homesteaders of the 1949 drawing began to arrive, the camp existed for Japanese families. As noted in some of the interviews, homesteaders lived in the camp a few months before moving o the farm units. Some of the offices for agencies involved with Mountain Homestead Project were located at the campsite and moved to Powell. The barracks on the site of the relocation center quickly erected prior to bringing Japanese families to Heart . There were 450 barracks for living quarters. Each barrack was)' with six living quarters in it. The barracks' exteriors were ith black tarpaper.

I visited the location of the Japanese internment camp on Day weekend in 1999 with my daughter Shana, her husband their first child, Kameron, who was almost one year old. Paul's eidi, is Japanese. She was a war bride but has lived in the United

59

States from the time her two sons, Paul and Ritchie, were very small. Paul was born in Japan. He now has dual citizenship

As we drove from my home in Shell, Wyoming, I was apprehensive at Paul's reaction to the site. I wanted to get some pictures of the camp, but to say I didn't have a foreboding heaviness in my heart would be an understatement.

The morning was cold. The drizzling rain gave a bite to the early spring wind that customarily swept across the foothills under Heart Mountain. The sun was trying to push its way through the billowing, gray clouds. As we stepped out of the car, the pungent smell of wet sage- brush filled our senses. From a distance, I watched Paul as he quietly read the memorial for young Japanese men from the camp who had given their lives in service in WWII. What was going through his mind? How did he feel about this place? If we had been born in another generation, would my daughter's family have been required to live in this camp? A hypothetical question, of course, but nonetheless, from the time I was a small child, there were questions in my mind concerning this silent town made of black, tarpaper barracks that no longer existed. Now it was only a ghost town with no houses--just a chimney stack standing alone over on a hill as a reminder of the place in which so many families had been confined during the war.

I stood there, clutching little Kameron in my arms, knowing in just a few moments this precious little grandchild would have to leave me. The rain-streaked sky of gray only increased the tightening in my chest. As I stood there, it was as if I shared a sorrow borrowed from long ago with people I have never met. Why did I allow myself to feel this? So many years have passed, a chapter closed, history forgotten. Let it go. I looked down at my grandchild--his face so beautiful, with dark olive skin and eyes the shape of his mother's, and I knew there was a part of long-ago history I would play out.

The portion I have committed to has required a long and arduous journey into history and research. In just a few days, I will sit down with all of my children and grandchildren for Thanksgiving dinner. Around that table, I will see the family resemblances to great grandparents from Germany, a son-in-law born in Japan, and my own Irish heritage I like to hold onto as well.

o, once again as we go back to that "ebb and flow of seasons," if
were living in a different time, would my daughter Shana find
ing in a barracks during WWII? Or, would my son Craig be
to be a soldier fighting under the evil hand of Hitler, if his
had not immigrated to the United States?

ther day, my daughter Shana was frustrated. Her oldest son,
had come home from school confused and upset. That afternoon,
udent had called him a "Jap" and said, "We hate Japs." Well,
sure that twelve-year-old boy does not really hate Japanese
e was probably just trying to get a rise out of my grandson. But
me, those kinds of comments are hurtful.

always been drawn to children. I am sure that impacted me
choosing to be a teacher. Down through the years, I have often
comment, "Children can be so cruel," and I come back with, "And
they learn prejudice?" And I quickly add, "From their parents!"

ny years have passed, and for young people, WWII is not even
dar. I was a war baby during the time of the Japanese relocation.
ot taken on this Qualitative Research Project about the Heart
Homestead Project, I would have vaguely remembered those few
nd the lonely, old, brick chimney left up on the windy hill near
ay where almost eleven thousand Japanese Americans had been
uring WWII.

all the business of completing this research and writing, one day
grandson, Kameron, and I will spend an afternoon making bread
As we sit drinking hot chocolate and eating our hot rolls, right
oven, I will tell him my stories of a group of Americans who
e and made the very best of a hard situation. And with the telling,
e the opportunity to inspire, not only Kameron, but many others,
nmon quality of humanity where we can respect and care for one
egardless of the station in life we find ourselves.

six years old when our young family moved from southern
and began homesteading in 1949. I remember hearing the adults
t the camp. Unfortunately, very little remains of the original
few buildings and the large chimney, which was attached to the

61

hospital, can be seen from the highway. A memorial has been erected on the location and can be viewed by the public.

Early in the spring of 2011, I had been given the news that the visitor center was almost complete. It would be dedicated in August with many dignitaries present, along with many others who had worked so long and hard to bring this portion of history into view. I had been very ill for several months, so it was impossible for me to travel, but I look forward to the time I can visit the center. My close neighbor and friend from Shell, Linda Kincaid, graciously sent me a clipping from the Billings Gazette featuring this very special event.

I read the newspaper article carefully. As I looked at the pictures, I studied the faces of those dear people that had been at Heart Mountain and wondered if I would ever have the privilege of meeting any of them. As I read through the newspaper article, I once again felt a reverence for these families that had gathered for such a special, long awaited ceremony.

In the many years since the camp's occupants were allowed to go home, Heart Mountain's message has become one of the lessons learned. It is a symbolic reminder of what one speaker called "an imperfect response" to public hysteria and manufactured outrage.

"This is not about the past, but rather, this is about the future," said Norman Mineta, a former internee who went on to become a U.S. congressman and Cabinet member. "History always has the ability of repeating itself. But what you are doing here is drawing that line in the sand, saying that this will never happen again."

Tom Brokaw, former NBC News TV anchor, author of *The Greatest Generation*, was the guest speaker at the Friday night pilgrimage dinner in Powell. He said, "They did not give up on their country that had so mistreated them. In so many ways, this symbol of failure now becomes a symbol of triumph and a light to show us the way forward." 2

For clarification, I will make reference to the generations of Japanese from the west coast at the beginning of WWII. The term Issei is in reference to the first-generation immigrants. Nisei were the second-generation students and young adults. Sansei were third generation infants and young children. I recommend two resource books that I found vital in helping me understand, as best I could, the circumstances and laws that had been passed that would have grave consequences for the Americans with the bombing of Pearl Harbor on December 7, 194 . Mike Mackey's book, *Heart Mountain, Life in a Wyoming ... tion Camp,* 3 and *Only What We Could Carry,* 4 edited by usao Inada, have been valuable resources.

he political climate and prejudice against Japanese living on the t prior to World War II, combined with the mass terror that struck rt of Americans already engaged in a war in Europe, were the hat brought the evacuation of more than 100,000 Japanese and Americans living in California, Oregon, and Washington in April of 1942. There were 107 evacuation districts, and in 2, Exclusion Orders gave Japanese residents one week to ten days or sell personal possessions prior to reporting to a designated point. From the central gathering point the evacuees were tagged, , and sent to one of the fifteen temporary camps known as centers." Failure to report by the designated time was a of federal law. Public Law 503, passed by both houses of without a single dissenting vote, made it a federal offense to a military area once an individual had been ordered to leave. 5

ssembly camps were basically makeshift places for the Japanese vhile waiting to be sent to the relocation centers. There were ssembly camps in Washington, Oregon, and California. Many of quarters were horse stalls on fairgrounds that had been ned over manure.

here was some opposition to the Japanese Relocation Center from Wyoming, but that did not stop the plan established in 1942. Department ordered the center to be built on May 23rd. The Army Engineers was moved into the area, and construction began on the

ome 2,500 workers hurriedly erected 456 barracks and built other facilities to handle the nearly 11,000 Japanese evacuees for relocation at Heart Mountain. Within three months the first evacuees came by special train with military guard from the west

For many of the Japanese, their stay in Wyoming was tragic. Two thirds of them were United States citizens who had done nothing to suggest that they were disloyal to the United States, yet they were herded eastward and imprisoned on a bleak desert. For the most part, Wyoming people displayed little of their famous western hospitality in dealing with the Japanese. "A Jap is a Jap," agreed many Wyomingites as they failed to distinguish between loyal United States citizens and war like enemies across the Pacific. Although there were many fair minded citizens in the state, they tended to remain silent while alarmists and racists were noisily vocal.

Some people in the vicinity of the relocation center were afraid that the Japanese might break out and attack them. Gradually, such fears dissolved. Governor Nels Smith and many other persons however were afraid that the Japanese would settle in the state after the war.
One of the best friends the Japanese had in Wyoming was Editor L.L.
Newton of the *Wyoming State Journal* (Lander). When he learned that the evacuees were coming, he wrote: "Let us demonstrate to them what real Democracy is, that it is the application of the same Christian principles of living and dealing with others which have made America what it is today." A more typical reaction was that of the *Wyoming Eagle* (Cheyenne), which asked: "Has Mr. Newton Gone Berserk?"7

During the many times I would be interviewing homesteaders from the 1949 drawing, my neighbors would refer to Chester and Mary Blackburn. "Patty, you must go visit them." By the time I was able to meet with Mary, Chester had already passed away, so I was greatly disappointed. She no longer lived on their homestead. When I met her, she was living in an apartment in Ralston. I observed she was not in good health so felt I shouldn't stay long. This couple had dedicated themselves to many years of bringing back the history of the camp. One day, while researching through back issues of the Powell Tribune, I came across this article, "Bond of camp life endured." I will share portions of comments made by this dear couple.

Chester and Mary Blackburn were homesteaders with the 1947 Heart Mountain project. In their retirement years they committed tireless

yea ; d icated to preserving the history of the Japanese Relocation camp
of l ear Mountain. They were recognized as national heroes by Newsweek
for lei fforts.

Why were the Blackburns so interested in the lives of people they
nev r e n knew? What was it about the camp itself that made them realize
its sto cal significance?

he answers to those questions are inextricably woven into the
He t M untain homestead experience. It's difficult to separate the stories
so e F ckburns saw themselves as homesteaders and combined that with
bec mi historical preservationists in their retirement years. They
the se s admit the story is a confusing mix of the same elements.

What it basically comes down to is this; in some small ways, the
hor est ders on the Heart Mountain Project shared some things with the
10, 00 panese Americans who lived there only a few years before and
dur g e war. They shared a sense of place and they shared common
liv g c ditions. They were both at the mercy of natural elements over
wh h t y had no control. The homesteaders were free and the Japanese
we n and that is the important difference between them. But in many
wa tl two groups of people had more in common than either group
wo d r realize.

uring the war, while Chester was in Saipan and Mary was home
in l an with their three children, they were not aware that the United
Sta s l l built relocation camps throughout the West and were interning
Jap ie Americans there. "I don't ever remember reading about the
rel ati centers in the newspapers," Mary recalls.

Most of the overt racism against the Japanese was occurring in
Ca or ," Chester commented.

he Blackburns themselves were accustomed to such hardships
rel d cold winters because of their early married years in rural Kansas.
Th ba cks retained very little heat. That first winter in the Relocation
car rc rted record breaking cold spells. For the Japanese who were sent
fro s hern California without adequate warm clothing, the situation
wa gri especially for the older people.

uring their years of homesteading and raising their family, the
Bla kb s were busy and really didn't have much time to become

65

preoccupied with the camp. It was probably always in the back of their minds, but there was work that had to be done first.

For many years, Chester said he assumed the people in the camps were simply warehoused there during World War II. But that wasn't the case at all. The relocation center was a living, breathing community and its residents did all the things that people were doing in other communities.

For the older people interned in the camp, the experience was one of bitterness. But it was not the Japanese way to complain about their misfortune, and so the children were largely insulated from the meaning of what was happening to them.

Over the years, almost every remnant of what was once Wyoming's third largest city was removed. Where once stood concrete foundations and wooden barracks, fields of barley cover the landscape. Only a single building and chimney remains of the original camp.

It was the Heart Mountain Ladies Extension Club that first noticed Japanese Americans coming back to the site of the camp to look for where they had once lived. "It was part of their roots," Mary explained. A bond developed between the homesteaders and the Japanese-American visitors.

In 1978, the Blackburns, along with friends and supporters, dedicated a memorial to the internees at the site of the camp. Other memorials followed. In 1985, a plaque was mounted to honor the Heart Mountain internees who fought for the United States in World War II. Of more than 600 who served, 22 died for the country that could not recognize them as Americans. 8

Although some information has already been stated in Hagel's newspaper interview in the Powell Tribune, I want to share a portion of the interview I had that summer afternoon with Mary, without deleting portions, as it will give you, the reader, a sense of the dedication this couple had for the Japanese families.

"Up until now, many American people knew nothing of the Japanese relocation camps during WWII. It has become a very controversial issue. For those of us who live in this community, it is certainly a part of our history.

The prejudice that surrounded the Japanese Americans goes back over a long period of time. The Japanese families that were detained in the

rel ati . camps left possessions behind that were to be stored. The homes
anc el gings were ransacked and sold. I think the thing that is felt the
mo b he Japanese people was the fact that their loyalty to the United
Sta s s questioned, and their citizenship was disregarded.

some of the books that I have studied, it is not indicated that they
we b g protected, but one cannot help but feel, because of the mass
hys ria nd fear at this time during WWII, that this was an issue.
I h e think that there could have been race riots and the killing of
inn cei Japanese on the west coast during that period of time. But the
rel ati camp did bring with it some protection for these people.
W 1 my husband and I have given slide show presentations in
sch ls e has asked the students some serious questions. Charley would
ask nei "What would you do, or what would you think if you went home
this ve ng and your parents told you that you had to go someplace? You
did t l w where or exactly why you had to go. You couldn't take your
bic le You couldn't take your pets. You couldn't take your radio or TV,
but f urse, then they didn't have TV. Your family could only take 100
po ds clothing and household items.

ometimes we have been criticized for speaking so frankly to
chi rei or fear they might be startled or frightened. But I think we far
unc res nate children and their capacity to have empathy for others. And,
of ur that is where prejudice starts, when children are young.

uring WWI, there was prejudice against German families. A
per n th a German heritage can look like your neighbor next door, but
wit Ja nese, their features set them apart, so it certainly was a problem
for os families on the west coast. As we talk about this situation today,
it i ea hard to comprehend the fear all over the world that came with
W I.)

uring the years I worked with the University of Wyoming
Co er ve Extension, my offices were in Basin and Lovell. I worked
coc er vely with the Extension agents in Park County. My brother, his
wii a my mother still lived on the homestead, so I often made a trek
acr s miles to Powell, which gave me an opportunity to visit the
Po ll ffice Supply. The store was a good resource for books on local
his ry One day, I came across a journal written by Velma Berryman

67

Kessel, R.N., entitled, *Behind Barbed Wire*. She had served as a nurse at the camp. The journal began November 11, 1941, and was completed on November 22, 1945. I was pleased to see that she had included a picture of Chester and Mary Blackburn standing next to the war memorial on the campsite.

I have included a portion from Velma's acknowledgements.

"This is a diary of my thirty-one months working as a Registered Nurse at the Heart Mountain Relocation Hospital in Wyoming. Dedicated to the displaced

Japanese who were forced to suffer in the severe cold, howling winter winds, scorching heat and dust storms in the treeless camp during World War II; and also to acknowledge the dedication of the five Japanese doctors, who worked for nineteen dollars a month to care for their people. Actual names of individuals were used for they were there and were a part of history." 10

As I read through the daily journal of this young nurse, I was impressed by her gift of writing, by which she portrayed everyday life in the hospital. It was evident that the doctors and nurses took great pride in their dedication to serving the sick patients. I will include several quotes taken from the pages of this very historical book of everyday life and the way it was.

December 18, 1942:

When I made my rounds to the Wards, I always checked on each patient. Especially close to my heart was Emiko on Ward 9 who was in isolation. It was particularly hard for her since her visitors had to stand in the hall to visit. I would put on an isolation gown and go in and sit by her bed. She loved to crochet and read but the days were long and she felt left out of everything. Most of the time she was a very cheerful sweet child. 11

December 18, 1942

An elderly man on Ward 6 that reminded me of my grandfather, had fallen and broken his arm between the elbow and shoulder, and it wasn't healing properly and I would stop and visit

little longer. After he found out that I was engaged and that my
ᵕyfriend was in the army, he always asked about
John. During our conversations, we talked about camp life,
ar, his home in California, and his concern for his teen-age
ᵕandchildren. 12

re   ᵕmber it was a very stifling, hot day in August when I finally
wa ᵕbl ᵕo meet with LaDonna Zall outside Powell's 1ˢᵗ National Bank.
Wᵕ n s   stepped onto the pavement, I saw a very petite woman with the
enᵕ ᵕvi s of Wyoming wind and character in her face.   We entered a
bui in ᵕcross the street from the bank and took an elevator downstairs
intᵕ a ᵕ ᵕe, cool room with an adjacent vault.   The bank had dedicated
thiᵕ ᵕto ᵕe vault for artifacts from the Japanese Relocation Center.   As
we ntᵕ d the room, I remember I felt a quiet reverence for this silent
hisᵕ ᵕry   the past.   We put on cotton gloves and began a tour around the
rooᵕ ᵕ.   was evident that LaDonna was well versed in describing the
ma ᵕ, ᵕ ᵕks, and articles I observed.   It was also apparent that this little
lad he a great deal of respect and honor for these families. I read names
ofᵕ ᵕldi ᵕ who had given their lives in fighting for our country. I couldn't
takᵕ ph ᵕgraphs but tried to put pictures in my mind of many wonderful
iteᵕ ᵕ.   m hoping that many of those things I had the privilege of seeing
in ᵕ ᵕt ᵕ ᵕderground vault will be on display at the visitor center.
    ᵕs   ᵕook back on that special afternoon with LaDonna one of the
sto ᵕs ᵕ shared, that I hold I most dear, was of the pictures drawn by a
grᵕ ᵕ ᵕ ᵕrownies or maybe Girl Scouts, many years before while these
yoᵕ g ᵕ ᵕldren lived in the camp.
    ha   always been interested in the art work of children, as it can tell
us ᵕlu ᵕs.   Many times, I have brought out this delightful collection of
pic reᵕ ᵕrawn of happy children, flowers, kimonos, Mickey Mouse, and
oth ᵕsᵕ ᵕ items one would typically see from that era and time.
    ᵕf   ᵕrse, this was a difficult time, and there were many hardships to
ovᵕ ᵕoᵕ . But every time I look over these little pictures, it reinforces in
me ᵕvᵕ ᵕe parents living there in the Heart Mountain camp during WWII

69

tried as best they could to go about life day by day, creating a time and place for their young children.

As we made our way around the room, I was drawn to a picture I assumed had been done in charcoal or pencil. LaDonna told me the story of the Caucasian bride who chose to go with her husband to the Heart Mountain Relocation Center. She told me about Estelle Ishigo, and how she had written a book. Of course, I wanted to find her writings, but LaDonna said she and her husband had both passed away, and the book was no longer in print.

The pictures I saw that afternoon seemed to haunt my memory. Once again, as I started to bring this chapter to a close, I thought about that afternoon. I got online and typed, *Lone Heart Mountain*, by Estelle Ishigo, 1972. Sure enough, a used copy came on the screen. I stopped everything I was doing, ordered the book as fast as I could, and said a prayer that the order would be filled. In just a few days, I went to my mailbox, and there was the book.

Everything else was put on hold that afternoon, as I reverently and slowly read page after page and closely examined the sketches of this woman's story of a place and land where I had grown up.

Daughter of a concert singer and portrait and landscape artist, Estelle was born in Oakland, California into an environment of music and art. From the age of four, she tried to show everyone how she could paint and sing. At the age of twelve, she learned to play the violin.

While a student at Otis Art School in Los Angeles, she met Arthur Shigeharu Ishigo, a San Francisco-born young Japanese (Nisei) aspiring actor. They were married in 1928. Their happiest years were spent on trips to the mountains where Estelle could paint and Arthur could hike and fish. At the outbreak of World War II, they were placed in the Pomona Assembly Center and later sent to Heart Mountain, Wyoming.

During the three-and-a-half years they spent in the camps, Estelle helped with the camp newspapers and played violin in the camp's Mandolin Band. She did hundreds of sketches and water color paintings of life behind barbed wire and text to go with the drawings. 13

\ni   ier book in my collection I have read over and over was found at
Po\ :ll   ffice Supply. It is entitled *The Heart Mountain Story*, by Mamoru
Inc ye   d Grace Schaub, 1997.

         ι January of 1943, Life Magazine sent Hansel Mieth and her
hus an(Otto Hagel on assignment to the Heart Mountain Relocation
Ce1 er   northwest Wyoming. The couple was known for their sensitive
poi ay   of the poor and migrant farm workers of the 1930s. None of their
ph(>g1 ihs of the internment camp were published during the war.

         he photographs of the Heart Mountain Relocation Center
ren in(largely hidden until an exhibition in 1995 of the works of Hansel
Mi   h a l Otto Hagel at the Vision Gallery in San Francisco. 14
         n :   interview with Hansel, after she had become a widow, she
des ib   her sensitivity in the work she was assigned to do.
Ha   el   lt an immediate kinship with the internees.

         he morale of the internees was excellent in spite of their isolation
an(fo   ible separation from their homes and belongings.   The
cir(m: nces were impossible, but everyone helped to make the camp feel
as 1 uc   ike a normal life as possible. I never saw anything like it. It is
not n   tary morale that I am talking about, but rather a complete self-
rul g (self-discipline. 15
     Vh   I gleaned from the photographs and writings of this book was the
det m1   tion and fortitude of this group of people to form a resilient life
for 1ei amilies in spite of the hardships.
     As   study the photograph of the man drawing Heart Mountain on a
col w1   er day, it is as if a bond has been created between the two of us
by   lo1 mountain setting out in the wind-swept plains.
     'o1 1unity spirit was birthed in this town which was built almost
ov(1ig on the wind-swept prairie of northern Wyoming. It is evident
tha ma   r bonds of friendship were created in those war years. I have
app :ci :d the photographs with written text from Hansel and
Ott w1   were able to capture a sense of day-to-day life among this group
of i du   ious people. In just a few years, my family would move to this
tre(:ss nd of sagebrush. Our homestead community would be met with
mi1 ; a   miles of cement irrigation ditches that would be the makings of
a c(nn   1ity that still exists today. The camp evacuees played a big role

71

in bringing to completion the final irrigation project on Heart Mountain. The Japanese farmers brought with them knowledge and experience that became a great asset to local farmers.

Both Mary and LaDonna told me about the camp newspaper. While spending the afternoon with Mary, I was able to glance over several copies, and then while with LaDonna in the vault of historical archives, I once again saw copies of the newspaper. One person I had hoped to meet someday was Bill Hosokawa, but he has passed away. Through many times of research, I have come across his name. He was the editor of the camp newspaper, *The Sentinel*. He wrote a very enlightening portion, used in Mike Mackey's book, concerning the newspaper.

After a great deal of discussion, it was decided to name the camp newspaper, The Sentinel. We settled on Sentinel because the mountain stood like a sentinel over the camp, and we wanted a guardian role for the newspaper. Neil Fujita, who after military service became a prominent New York art designer, designed the masthead which featured the mountain and the word "Sentinel." 16

The Heart Mountain Sentinel was an important part of the camp community which contributed to building the morale of the families. "Two of its promising young reporters, Fred Yamamoto and Ted Fujioka, volunteered for military service and died in action. Another Sentinel associate, Lt. Moe Yonemura, also was killed in battle." 17

The Heart Mountain Fire Department was organized on September 1, 1942 and was made up of evacuees who had worked in fire protection at the assembly centers. 18

That first winter posed great risk to the families. It was a brutal winter, and to make things even more difficult, the pipelines continually froze. The frigid temperatures did not infringe on the determination of the firefighters in protecting the families. The barracks were drafty, and the morning stoves could be a hazard in the night hours. Patrols of men were set up to keep guard for possible fires. The families had already lost most of their possessions, and it was as if this served as a catalyst for those brave firemen who did everything they could to help save the meager belongings of the families.

he Japanese subjugated eighteen hundred acres of virgin bench lan... erproofed a section of irrigation canal; produced pork, poultry, anc... raised more than six million pounds of crops; and supplied much sea... abor in agriculture outside the camp. 19

he children and youth had activities like any other community, suc... as... outs and athletics. The high school teams competed with schools in... a. One particular picture that moves me to tears is the student boc... ting the flag.

n a cold winter day, faculty and students of Heart Mountain High Scl... ol... d by Principal John K. Corbett and Student Body President Ted Fuj... ka... ledge allegiance to the flag. Principal Corbett was concerned; "M... yb... tudents wouldn't want to salute the flag after all they've been thr... gl... He was reassured by Fujioka that there was nothing to worry abc... t. rivate First Class Fujioka was killed in Action in France on No... m... r 6, 1944, after volunteering for service following his graduation in J... ne... 1943. 20

Iol... ays were celebrated. A recreation hall was the meeting place on we... en... Velma Kessel documented many of the activities in camp in her dai... jo... nals. Keeping a semblance of family was difficult, as meals were eat... ir... ess halls, but the resiliency of this group of people held strong in spi... of... is. The Japanese community became organized and used a great dez... of... elf-discipline in managing within the confines of camp life reg... dl... of the circumstances. They set up Block Managers who worked clo... ly... ith the camp directors. I have only briefly shared with you the rea... r, ... emblance of life in the camp so many years ago. Referring back to... e t... nami that was so devastating, I somehow knew that from the pri... leg... I had been given in researching those war years, the Japanese fan... lie... ould again face the challenge given them. In dedication to them I w... te... poem that expresses the heart.

SENTINEL ON THE HORIZON

Life comes to each of us as surely as the ebb and flow of
mighty ocean waters.
The billowing waves of adversity often bring sorrow and pain.
And with it the possibility for courage and perseverance.
And then the sea takes on a calm that brings a peace of soul
that gives one a time of reflection. As seasons of life flow
one into another,
there is that personal choice in every man for good or evil.

In designing this universe with its oceans so wide
and mountains so vast, did God have a plan in speaking
to that quiet place in the soul? As I reflect on that place
in my memory, fondly called, "My Beloved Mountain,"
I must say, "Surely there was a plan."
Sitting there alone on that wind-swept Wyoming prairie in
silent majesty as a sentinel in the sky is a mountain. To
gaze up and see the setting sun over this silhouette in the
heavens brings with it a sense of time and place.

For those so long ago now, who huddled together
there under its shadow
with a longing to go home, there was hope of a better tomorrow. In
just a few years, a young group of families would come from
faraway places.
They would come to call this mountain their own as
they came to find a sense of time and place.
And so now, just as the oceans' ebb and flow of water
Goes through the seasons of personal journey,

74

*ach of us has a choice to look beyond the frame of another
and see As if in a mirror, the reflection of ourselves.*

Patricia McClaflin Booher

ACKNOWLEDGMENTS

any resource people so readily helped me all along the way in thi ro t. I want to acknowledge several individuals who added valuable inp ir the writing of this chapter. I refer to excerpts from the work of Mi M ckey and Velma Berryman Kessel, R.N., as well as interviews wit La onna Zall and Mary Blackburn. David Retz, past president of the He t M untain, Wyoming, Foundation Board of Directors informed me of the ng ng plans for the visitor center which would be built on the location wh e camp had been built in 1942. David was always a source of enc ur ment to me throughout this project, so I came to appreciate him a g at al.

the Photo Album you will find a picture of Heart Mountain taken fro th iew of the Relocation Center. While visiting the camp before the cer r s completed, my son-in-law Paul Lewis took the picture. In my res rc rom the books I had found written by those who lived in the camp the of referred to this mountain scene.

I: THE SHOSHONE IRRIGATION PROJECT

far ing
Th ch
irri ati
hoi est

ior to the 1949 homesteaders coming to Heart Mountain to begin heir land, the Shoshone Irrigation Project had been completed. ter contains a brief history of that project, as well as previous projects, to illustrate what had to be accomplished before ders could move onto their new lands in northern Wyoming.

doc me
Ch ch
ma r
Pr ci
Irri ati
arc ve
pro ct

this chapter, I have relied heavily upon the significant ation, research, and writing accomplished by Beryl Gail in her books written about the Shoshone Irrigation Project. I have rences and quoted from *Land, Water, and People, the Shoshone* ory. The booklet was designed as a guidebook for the Shoshone Project. The information, gained with permission from the oused at Shoshone Irrigation District, has been invaluable in this

Fa
in t 1
I li en
spr kl
aro d
Mc nta

ing has gone through some major changes since those early years 0s. Probably the most drastic improvement has been in irrigation. my brother, Wayne, as he explains the principles of the water to me, and it is all quite amazing how water can be tunneled mountain and be seen spraying up over the hillsides on Heart .

s
pip ly
top f
wh h l
irri te

lrive up and down the roads on Ralston Bench, I see white PVC across fields. (PVC gated pipe is a poly/vinyl pipe laid at the ield or buried in the ground.) Many advances have taken place e impacted the conservation of water, and crops today are being nore efficiently.

hoi est
imj rt
irri ati
thr gl
eac fa

hen I was growing up on Heart Mountain, irrigating our d was an everyday occurrence. The ditch riders played an role in getting water. They administered the allocation of water. Farmers applied for the amount of water needed it the season and the ditch riders turned on the water supply for and were responsible for turning off the supply. It was apparent to me that my father had a great deal of respect and appreciation for these fellows who worked long hours and had a lot of ground to cover in a day.

I am sure some the readers of this chapter will understand all the terminology that goes along with irrigating. You have a grasp of how a dam can be built that holds back tons of water. But for all the rest of us, I am including maps, glossaries, and diagrams to attempt to paint a picture of what a really heroic and adventurous achievement this Shoshone Project has been. I am also including a "Glossary of Dam Building Terms for Laymen" in Appendix A.

When I made an appointment with Lori Startin, secretary/treasurer for the Shoshone Irrigation District, I would later be so surprised at what I found. When I went to the headquarters in Powell, she met me at the front desk, and I was escorted back to a table piled with books from the turn of the century on the work the Bureau of Reclamation had done in the Big Horn Basin. There were books full of fascinating pictures that described all the stages of this gigantic undertaking.

There were some key players in the inception of what is now a thriving farming community contained within the Big Horn Basin of northwest Wyoming.

The town of Powell, Wyoming, is named after John Wesley Powell. Because of the significant work he had done in 1879 with the publication of "*A Survey of the Arid Lands of the United States*," he was named the "The Father of Irrigation." 1

The impact of Powell's endeavors created awareness on a national level of the potential for the development of federal lands in the west.

John Powell declared that the West be developed with an understanding of its arid character, pointing out the potential for irrigation but also the limits that aridity must impose upon growth. He was also concerned that management of water be kept in the hands of those who worked the land. He sponsored, as Director of United States Geological Service, a survey of all the water resources and potential dam sites in the West, and trained a corps of men who later became the staff of the Reclamation Service. After a series of disastrous droughts in the Midwest at the close of the century, and in response to growing fears that the essential character of America was threatened by the tide of immigration

tha wa forcing the growth of cities in the East, the political climate in
Wa iir on by 1902 came to favor a federal effort to expand America's
agr ult al resources by putting money into irrigation in the West." 2

n Act of Congress was passed in 1894 in which the state and
fed al vernments put into motion the promotion of the development of
a m lic acres of federal lands not only in Wyoming, but in other western
stal s. le bill was sponsored by Senator Joseph Carey of Wyoming. 3

he Carey Act entitled each western state to set aside up to a
mil on cres of federal land to be developed for farming, with the
stip lat i that private contractors construct the irrigation works and attract
set rs

"Buffalo Bill" Cody, a world-renowned entertainer from the
tur of century, found a fascination for this area. George T. Beck, along
wit Bi Cody and his partner, Nate Salsbury, were visionaries who could
see 10 this arid, desert land, now with little vegetation other than
sag ort , could one day be a fertile farming community. On May 22,
189 , t two of them applied for a permit from the state to divert water
fro th Shoshone River to irrigate 60,000 acres of land south of Cody.
The e eavor would later be named the Shoshone Reclamation Project.

he own of Cody, named after Buffalo Bill Cody, is situated at the
ent nc o the Shoshone Canyon. The town of Cody was a frontier town.
It v s i orporated in 1901 with a small population of 550. Cody believed
tha his rea one day would develop into a thriving community. The Irma
Ho l, l ilt by Cody, is still thriving. At one time, it was considered the
fin t h el in Wyoming.

ank Mondell, who would later become a Wyoming senator, filed
for pe iit to divert water from the Shoshone River for irrigation purposes
in 95 He had plans to build a canal east of Cody that would irrigate
155 00(cres of land. By 1897, he had not been able to begin the project,
so is rmit was canceled. Bill Cody and Nate Salsbury acquired
Mo del s lapsed water rights.

he iitial plan was to build three canals that would be supplied from
wa rtl had been diverted from the north and south forks of the Shoshone
Riv r. small diversion dam would be constructed to supply water to the
car ls. Although there was great potential for the development of

farmlands in the basin, Cody was unable to raise enough revenue for such a large undertaking. It was estimated, at the onset, that it would take $1 million for the project, but, of course, this figure fell far short of what the project would finally cost.

The Shoshone Project was one of the first national reclamation projects. There was a great interest in the expansion of irrigation in the western states by the turn of the century. The eastern states were rapidly growing, with the influx of European immigrants. Wyoming became a target of interest. Irrigation projects were started throughout Wyoming.

Another major impact on western development came about with the signing of the Reclamation Act by President Theodore Roosevelt in 1902. Senator Francis Newlands wrote this piece of legislation with backing from the railroads.

The Essence of the Reclamation Act was that all money received from the sale and disposal of public lands in 16 western states, including Wyoming, was to be set aside for construction of dams and distribution systems larger and more complex than private developers could afford to build. Congress advanced $50 million to establish the Reclamation Fund, which was to be repaid by those who used the water provided by the new systems. 5

Cody, unable to raise the funds needed, released his water rights to the Reclamation Service in 1902. Now, with the backing of the federal government, the irrigation project turned a corner, and plans for a dam within the canyon were established. The Secretary of Interior, Ethan Hitchcock, designated $2,250,000 for the building of the Shoshone Dam and the irrigation works to go along with it.

The Shoshone Irrigation Project would include the construction of a dam which would later be named Buffalo Bill Dam.

Original plans for the Shoshone Irrigation Project included a hydroelectric power plant. It was put into operation in 1922. Initially, the plant was to supply power for the construction project and to furnish the town site of Powell with power. The Bureau of Reclamation expanded its vision of market power with the expansion of communities in the Big Horn Basin. This would later prove to be a source of revenue that grew in proportion to the farm crop and livestock income.

1922, the power sales generated $16,000 in gross income; in

19_ , a   t was preparing to double its generating capacity by bringing the
He_ t N untain Power Plant on line, the Bureau sold $246,539 worth of
po\ r.   It was netting considerably more from power than from
co_ ru   on repayments from farmers by the beginning of World War II.
6

\ v derful account of the building of the Shoshone Dam can be found
in] ry Churchill's newest book, *Challenging the Canyon*. In 1991, she
ha(he eat fortune of meeting Jean Cole Anderson, the fourth daughter
of] ini Webster Cole, who was the construction engineer for the building
of io ne Dam. Although Jean died before Beryl was able to begin
wri ng e account of building the dam, the Cole family graciously allowed
her o   e the many personal documents and pictures that had been
pre rv by the family.

\s vas conducting research with the Shoshone Irrigation District, I
he_ l a ut the *Canyon* book. I was so anxious to have this book in my
ha_ s t I called the Powell Office Supply and had them mail one to me.
Tw da   later, when the package arrived, I sat down to look through the
pa_ s. vas so fascinated with the accounting of people involved with the
bu_ in f the dam, that by late in the evening, I had read the entire book.

c_ remember the road through the canyon in those early years of
far in_ hen we would be going up to North Fork to fish. The road was
nar w d actually quite terrifying for "flatlanders" from other states. We
use to t amused at the terrified looks on tourists' faces. But now, in my
old y s, I would look at those people with much more compassion. The
ne\ ro and mile-long tunnel through the granite canyon walls is much
mo c venient and safe, but I miss the beauty of the river that now lies
far lc the highway.

he d stories as a child of the lives that were lost in the building of the
dar] upposed there were farms that lay deep under the waters of the
res vo As I looked at the pictures of the bottomland homesteads and
rea ab t the town of Marquette that no longer exists, it became a reality
to ie. With the signature of President Theodore Roosevelt for the
co_ ru on of Shoshone Dam, farmlands within a 10½-square-mile area
of t e v t opening of the canyon had to be sold. Some of these farms had

been homesteaded from as early as 1880. A post office, school, general store, and saloon were all sold to the government.

Purchases of the lands that were overflowed by the Shoshone Reservoir were based on the following compensation schedule:

Land with water right seeded to alfalfa - $45 per acre

Land with water right planted to grain - $35

Unbroken land with water right - $20 per acre

Bottom grazing land along the river with no water right - $7.50 per acre

Rough grazing land with no water right - $3.50 per acre.

Buffalo Bill was paid $3,900 for his holdings in the river valley. Thomas Trimmer received a government check for $12,000 for his 600-acre ranch, and Harrison Arnold sacrificed his 15-acre ranch for $525. Records show that the biggest payments of the reservoir land settlement went to Benjamin F. Martin and Edward F. Grinder. Martin received $18,000 and Grinder, $17,000.

Before the final litigation was over, the government paid this heavy-hearted group about $400,000 for their homes. When the lands were purchased, the agreement, in most instances, provided that the original owners might retain possession until dispossessed by high water. That time came just about six months after the dam was completed. 7

Before construction of the dam could begin, it was necessary to build a road up through the canyon from the small town of Cody. This was a harrowing experience for the work crew.

Before the completion of the dam, three construction crews had been hired to complete the project. The first company, Prondergast and Clarkson, commenced their work on October 19, 1905. The government suspended the construction contract with Prondergast and Clarkson Co. on August 11, 1906.

Another company, U.S. Fidelity and Guaranty Company, was hired on October 1, 1906. A crew of 275 worked under difficult circumstances throughout an extremely cold winter, with equipment needing repair. In the spring, work was progressing at a much better rate. But on July 4, the dam site was disabled, as a record-breaking flood came through the canyon. To make matters worse, a saw-log boom above the canyon broke with the rs. The logs did devastating damage to the diversion dam now nstructed. There were many ongoing difficulties in the on of the dam. Contractors had some difficulty continuing in the ction for further building. By August, the government was once ntemplating suspending the construction contract with U.S. nd Guaranty Co. After negotiations, the company was given chance to reorganize the work crew and make significant ients. Work improved for several months.

probably for the first time in the history of Wyoming work labor strike occurred at the dam. Early in November, the encountered difficulties with the foreign-born laborers who were). Workers demanded a raise in pay to $3.00 a day for common ie construction company officials, realizing they had themselves hard place and a rock, acceded to the labor demands. The history tract is marked by a scale of wages which was perhaps 20 percent n any other in this section of the country. 8

nter came, the raise in pay did not deter the low morale of the 299 The insurmountable expenses that were incurred and the on difficulties caused the company to fail to meet payroll for r and December. There was a lack of necessary materials and ng equipment. The second construction company resigned the March of 1908. They were immediately replaced by Grant Smith r Company who were able to bring the project to completion.

seemed to progress at a much better rate through the winters of 1909. But another strike was called by the workers. This time, ctors replaced the work force with a completely new crew. It ng before the new crew became discontent with the working s.

October through the completion of the dam, labor problems ie contractors. The labor market was tight and it was difficult to) work on the dam. It was even tougher to hold them once they ed a day or two at the grueling task of hand building a 325 foot Agents for the construction company rounded up men all over y - from eastern Nebraska to the Pacific coast, paid their rail fare nd personally escorted them to Cody in groups of 10 to 80 men.

It was hard to hold the workers at the dam site. The contractor employed from two to four "man catchers" who watched the road from the dam site to Cody and brought back the defectors who left the work force at the dam. 9

The cold weather added to the many difficulties in finishing the dam construction. The winter of 1909 was the coldest on record. The final buckets of cement were poured on January 10, 1910.

All three contract companies withstood astronomical financial losses in completing the dam.

The accident report on the actual dam construction shows seven deaths, three workers who lost limbs, three more lost their eye sight and 28 others were crippled or mutilated while employed on the construction. 10

FIRST THREE IRRIGATION PROJECTS

There were four homestead communities contained within the overall Shoshone Irrigation Project. The Garland Division was the first, Frannie/Deaver second, Willwood third, and last, the Heart Mountain Division that would be delayed until after WWII.

When I began researching the Shoshone Irrigation Project, I had no idea it was such a significant undertaking, and that it required so many years to finish the entire system. I read everything I could find, including the books written by Beryl Churchill. I finally just took out the map and studied the layout of each division, beginning with the Buffalo Bill Dam, and finishing up with the canals and laterals in the Frannie community. I will give only a brief overview in describing the entire project, as the accounting has already been so well done in the references I have noted throughout this chapter.

The Corbett Dam was actually finished before the Buffalo Bill Dam. It is located on the Shoshone River sixteen miles east of Buffalo Bill Dam.

Over half of the total acres of the irrigation project rely on waters diverted by Corbett Dam. Nine hundred cubic feet per second (cfs) of river water are diverted into a large, concrete-lined tunnel, which carries the water three and a half miles underground to the head of the Garland Canal. 11

Fa⟩ s west of Ralston, along with the Ralston Reservoir, are supplied
by e (rland Canal, which runs throughout the Powell Valley. Laterals
run ⟩ff ⟩m the canal supplying irrigation water to
35, ⟩3 ⟩res of farmland in the north and south areas of Powell. The
Ga⟩ ⟩n⟩ ⟩anal supplies the large lateral, the Frannie Canal that furnishes
wa⟩ r t⟩ ⟩he Frannie Division of nearly 15,000 acres of land.
A ⟩ ⟩al⟩ ⟩ reservoir near Deaver is also supplied by the canal.
⟩h⟩ ⟩illwood Dam furnished water for the southern far acreages in the
Wi⟩ ⟩vo⟩ ⟩ Division. The Heart Mountain Division would be the final part
of ⟩ ⟩ (⟩rall Shoshone Irrigation Project. This phase was not completed
unt⟩ ⟩af⟩ WWII. It would prove to be more difficult, because the irrigated
acr⟩ ⟩o⟩ ⟩armland were on higher ground. A tunnel was drilled along the
sou ⟩ s⟩ ⟩ of the canyon for three miles. Water is supplied from
res⟩ vo⟩ ⟩using the Shoshone Canyon conduit. A large siphon carries the
wa⟩ r a⟩ ⟩ss the river and along rough terrain for 28 miles.
Vh⟩ the pipe was built it was the longest unsupported span of its size
in ⟩ ⟩ v⟩ ⟩ld. The siphon empties 914 cfs into the Heart Mountain Canal.
Re⟩ ⟩rn⟩ ⟩w ditches collect excess flow, which is returned to supply ditches
fur⟩ ⟩er⟩ ⟩ong the system: a significant amount of water unused or once-
use⟩ ⟩or⟩ ⟩eart Mountain becomes part of the supply for Garland.
⟩ ⟩ a⟩ the irrigation system conceived in 1904 includes a storage dam,
two⟩ ⟩iv⟩ ⟩sion dams, two small off-stream reservoirs, approximately 140
mil⟩ ⟩ (⟩tunnels and canals, and 564 miles of laterals and distribution
dit⟩ ⟩es⟩ ⟩t 93,000 acres, the Shoshone Project today is the largest federal
irri⟩ ⟩ti⟩ project in Wyoming, as well as the oldest. 12
⟩h⟩ ⟩ were two diversion dams that were constructed below the
Sh⟩ ⟩ho⟩ Dam-- the Corbett Dam and the Willwood Dam. The Corbett
Da⟩ ⟩w⟩ built sixteen miles below the Shoshone Dam. A three-and-one-
hal⟩ ⟩mi⟩ tunnel was built to carry water from the Corbett Dam to the
Ga⟩ ⟩n⟩ ⟩anal which would irrigate homesteads in the Garland and Frannie
are⟩ . ⟩ ⟩ e Corbett Dam was actually completed before the Shoshone Dam.
Engineers began with surveys for the Corbett Dam in
Se⟩ ⟩m⟩ r of 1904. Contractors from Billings, Montana, built both the
Co⟩ ⟩et⟩ ⟩am and tunnel. Charles Spear, contractor for the Corbett tunnel
wa⟩ ⟩n⟩ ⟩ e to complete the work at the price he had quoted. He was forced

to go bankrupt, so government workers were called in to complete the work. The final cost of the Corbett Project was estimated at $1,161,663.

"At completion, in late 1907, the remarkable tunnel was 17,355 feet long, 11½ feet wide, 10 3/4 feet high and could carry up to 1,000 cubic feet of water per second."13

Out of the ten irrigation projects that had been scheduled by the government, the Corbett tunnel was the first to be completed. Workers encountered many hardships and difficulties while working on the dam. After the Reclamation Service took over the work, there were between 350 and 400 men employed to bring the project to completion. An added year was required to finish the Corbett project.

Common laborers were hard to find, although wages were from $2.50-$3.00 per day, which was considered a good salary. Workers lived at Camp Corbett which was situated near the project. In September of 1907 many of the workers in the camp came down with
typhoid fever which was contracted from the water taken from the
big cistern. 14

Work on the Corbett Dam began in September of 1906. The contractor for this project was The Billings Construction Company with a bid of $44,750. Excavation began in the fall and continued throughout the winter, until spring runoff in June continued with high waters until October. Both the tunnel and dam were completed by April 27, 1908, thus allowing water to be turned into the Garland Canal, which would irrigate the first homesteads in the Powell Valley. The only problem encountered with the irrigation that first year related to a break in the Garland Canal and a leak in the Ralston Reservoir.

During the first season, 1,500 acres of land on the Garland Division of the project were irrigated. But, by the second year the entire system "was serving admirably the purpose for which it was designed." In 1909, 9,547 acres of land were irrigated using the new diversion system. Bureau records reported 96 farmers watered 80-acre farms and 106 new homesteaders irrigated 40-acre fields. 15

The conception of the Shoshone Project was, from the first, one of the most ambitious of the early Reclamation works. The high dam in the canyon, never a part of Buffalo Bill's plans, was one of the first concrete

arc da ; built, and at 328 feet was the highest in the world. The storage
res vo behind the dam held 456,000 acre-feet of water, refilled each year
by ie ows that melt in the high Absaroka Mountains on the eastern
bor er Yellowstone Park. The dam provides a regulated flow of water
thr gh it the irrigation season. 16

he Corbett diversion dam was constructed sixteen miles below
Bu alo ill Dam. A large, concrete-lined tunnel carried water three-and-
a-h f i les to the head of the Garland Canal. The Frannie Canal, the
lar st eral on the Garland Canal supplies water which would be used to
irri ite e Frannie Division. A smaller reservoir was built to supply the
De er ea. The Garland Canal supplied water for irrigation in the Powell
are 1 e Willwood diversion dam was six miles downstream from the
Co eti Dam. Willwood Dam would supply water to the Willwood
Div io containing about 14,000 acres.

he arland Division was the first irrigation project to be opened in the
fal f i)7. By the next April when the first water became available, there
we s nty-six homesteads opened. The Corbett tunnel and Garland
Ca l e used for the irrigation. The dam would be completed two years
late eadquarters for the Reclamation Service were housed in the
Ga in)ivision in 1906. In 1909, this became a town named in honor of
Joh W ley Powell. As I walk down the streets of Powell today, which I
for y member as my hometown in those childhood years, it is hard to
ima in I look at pictures of those first few years, and there are only a few
bui in and a scarcity of trees.

he Frannie Division was the second project to be opened in 1917.
By 91 the homestead units in Frannie had been taken. This irrigation
pro ct ould meet many difficulties. WWI caused a shortage of workers.
Th ma ets had plummeted. There was much to learn about irrigation of
arid so Later projects would benefit from the mistakes made on the
Fra nie division.

ll ver the Project the topsoil is relatively alkaline and the
gro nd ter table is relatively high. When water was applied in amounts
suf cie to grow crops, the ground water rose and concentrated alkali salts
in t e r t zone, killing or damaging the crops. 17

The term used for this water issue was called seepage. Farmers in the Garland Division had already dealt with this problem. The Reclamation Service began a process of installing a system that would lower the water table. This process was carried out on all the projects from that point. The Garland Division project benefited, but the soil in the Frannie Division was much more difficult, so that almost half of the project was shut down.

The construction of drains was a costly affair. In addition, market prices for crops fell after the war, and the seepage problem had affected productivity.

There was great tension between the water uses and the Reclamation Service over the terms of repayment of construction costs and operation and maintenance costs. In 1926, at the urging of the Bureau of Reclamation, the farmers on the Garland Division formed the Shoshone Irrigation District and took over the operation and maintenance of their part of the system in 1927. The Frannie Division took over its own operation in 1931, and it was entitled the Deaver Division. 18

Although negotiations for new contracts for water took place, many of the farmers could no longer sustain farming.

The third project to be completed was the Willwood Division. The Willwood Dam was completed in 1923. The lessons learned from difficulties impacted the third project. Homesteaders were allowed to rent water and delay construction costs until after the land had been settled. They formed their own district to negotiate the government contracts. For the first time, before the land was settled, the soil and subsoil were surveyed to ensure that farms had enough good soil to sustain families.

A settlement committee was set up to establish that the delegates were financially able to make farming a success. From the beginning, candidates were offered assistance from county agents, the Reclamation Bureau, and the Department of Agriculture. The Willwood Project was far better equipped after learning from the mistakes made in Garland and Frannie.

Although the Willwood Division had advanced by 1930, only 48 units had been taken. By 1940, the farm district was settled. The onset of the Great Depression would affect the irrigation projects, and 1932 would

pro ɔ t   ɔring great difficulties for the homesteaders. But by late 1933,
thi s l   ame better, and by 1935, situations were looking up for families.
     he   Shoshone Project's quality crops were known throughout the
nat n.   1 1935 the project's seed pea crop was marketed in eight states
ran ng   rom Pennsylvania to California and beans were shipped to 22
sta ;, ı st of which were east of the Continental Divide. Turkeys raised
by   ca   armers were marketed in New York State. This crop, which was
big ɔus   ess for area farmers for about 10 years, was sold through the
ag   ɔss   ɔ dealings of the Big Horn Cooperative Marketing Association.
19

     uc   ssful oil refineries in the area would add to the benefit of the
cor nu   y. The oil was of such high quality in the area that it could be
use w   ı farm equipment without a refining process. The Texas Oil
Co   pa   and Husky Oil were located in Cody by 1939.
           /ork on the fourth phase of the Shoshone Project had been set in

mo   ɔn.
     ;y   ɔ end of 1938 the layout of farm units and the lateral systems
un   r tl upper part of the 28-mile-long Heart Mountain Canal had begun.
An   fɔ   the next two years work on the Heart Mountain Division went
alo ; s   ɔothly. In the fall of 1941 the first water was turned through the
Sh   ho   Canyon Conduit controlling works and into the Heart Mountain
Ca   l.   iming of the canal started in early October of that year, and was
cor ɔle   ɪ a month later without any serious problems. 20
           /ith the onset of WWII, the fourth phase of the Shoshone Project
wo   d l   greatly curtailed. Work continued on the project during the war,
but ıe   vernment work force was limited. Much of the work done on the
lat ıls   ıd canals was carried out by the Japanese evacuees. The first
wa   r d   very to the fourth division began May 29, 1943. It was used by
sev al   ivate landowners and the relocation center.
           he last of the evacuees were removed from the camp by
No   ɪm   r 10, 1945. Construction work moved slowly because of the cost
of ı ıte   ıls and a limited work force.
           he Heart Mountain Division would not be ready to settle until
aft W   II. There were three drawings for the settlements in 1947, 1948

and 1949. With the opening of the fourth division, the Shoshone Reclamation Project would be complete.

On October 3, 1946, Public Notice No. 53 advertised the opening of the first unit of the division. Four thousand applications were sent out to interested persons wanting to know more about the new Wyoming project. After an intense examination period, 212 veterans were declared eligible for the homestead drawing which was held in Powell on February 4, 1947. Eighty-two of these applicants became owners of new Heart Mountain farms totaling 7,720 acres. 21

HAPTER 5 LIFE IN THE HEART MOUNTAIN COMMUNITY

'o   ve you, the reader, insight into the day-to-day activities of the
gro) (homesteaders from the 1949 drawing for the Heart Mountain
ph; :,   1ave made a collection of some of those heartwarming stories
sha :d   )und their kitchen tables.

'h(aining the veterans received, funded by the GI Bill, proved to be
an ; de   :omponent in the success they achieved in farming. This monthly
all(ne   received by the families helped to furnish groceries and items
nee ed   making improvements to the barrack homes. I don't think any
of ` e 1   iilies in our community considered themselves poor. There just
wa `t   uch money, so we all managed to live frugally. The Heart
Mc nt;   homestead community was on the Ralston Bench. There was a
sm. l t(n, Ralston, between Powell and Cody with a grocery store and
sm l p   (office in the store front. In the very beginning, the homesteaders
hac)o:)ffice boxes at Steck's Grocery. Bud Steck was a gracious man
wh su   orted our community a great deal. Many of the homesteaders
sp(: (1ow they had appreciated him in those early years.

MOUNTAIN VIEW COMMUNITY CLUB

/hen interviewing the homestead families, it was evident that the
cor nu   :y club was looked upon as a hub for activities that brought the
fan lie   )gether. Several barracks were given to the community in order
for ier   o form a clubhouse. The community chose "Mountain View" for
the an   of our clubhouse, as I believe we all felt Heart Mountain was
"ot ` 1   untain. In the beginning months, when the families gathered
tog he   for organizational meetings, they brought their children. I
ren m   · much needed to be done to make this a safe and satisfactory
clu 101   :. While the adults were busy planning and developing a

clubhouse and community, the young children were busy in the back barracks rooms running from room to room playing hide and seek.

The families gathered together for community meetings, wedding and baby showers, Scouts, and 4-H youth meetings. The UW Cooperative Extension Agents did a great deal of educational training in the community clubhouse. Many of the couples shared with me about the fun they had during the time they had formed a square dance club. When I was given pictures of the dances, I studied them carefully. The couples looked so happy and healthy and full of life-just as I had remembered them so well as a child.

The Mountain View Clubhouse would not be considered a very fancy building but rather seemed to melt into the landscape. But for our families who had a special bond of friendship, I would say, the building spoke of giving us "A Sense of Time and Place."

The following article describes how the community club Started and the dedication of the community.

COMMUNITY CLUB FORMED BY HEART MT. HOMESTEADERSAT ORGANIZATION MEETING

The homesteaders on the Heart Mountain project who live west of Ralston and north of Eagle Nest Creek held an organizational meeting at the Ralston Community clubhouse on July 7, 1950.

The purpose of the meeting was to form a community club for the settlers in the north and west area of the project. The following officers were elected: president, Lloyd Snider; vice president, Mrs. Charles Nunley; secretary, Mrs. Vechel Olson; treasurer, William White. The board of directors includes Harvey Adams, Vechel Olson, Edward Schaefer, Robert Van Dyke and Albert Kamm.

Five acres of land located near the Adams' "Mountain View" store and a building have been allocated to the organization by the Bureau of Reclamation. When farming operations are less strenuous the settlers plan to start work on the construction and repair of their new community club building. 1

VACATION BIBLE SCHOOL

here is a an old photograph of that first year the Mountain View
... organized a Vacation Bible School for all of us young children.
... studied the faces of those children, trying to remember all of their
... The mothers, all lean and suntanned from summer work, have
... accomplishment. Our parents all worked so hard in those early
... required a great sacrifice of time and energy for the mothers to
... weeks bringing the children to the Bible School each morning
... take part. It was a special time for our community, as it was a
... nding the varied faiths together in gratitude to God for the new
... ture with which we had been blessed.

RATTLESNAKES

ne of the hazards, especially in those first years of homesteading
... the many rattlesnakes encountered in the fields, as well as
... barns and houses. The irrigation water would draw them out.
... field workers had to be on the alert. It was not good enough just
... or the sound of the rattles, because a snake, if coiled, could fling
... great distance. I never wanted to come upon a deadly rattler
... ng my horse, as horses have a sense of the danger about such an
... and can quickly shy away, leaving a person on the ground if they
... prepared.

... the death of our father in 1986, I was living in Michigan, but the
... calls my mother out in the fields with certified seed that needed to
... d. It had been an exceptionally dry year, so the snakes had come
... n the hills and would lay in the grass for shade. She had hired a
... w, but when they discovered there were rattlesnakes in the field,
... ft. She went to town, bought some irrigation boots and went up
... those rows pulling weeds. We worried about her out there in that
... ut knowing the mindset of these pioneer women, many times in
... coped with their loss through hard work. I am not so sure the
... ld have given her that much protection, but that summer passed,
... here were other seasons that came and went.

The following story, shared by Margaret Olson, is very typical of how these farm husbands and wives managed when confronted with the rattlesnakes.

One of the crops that we grew on the homestead was peas for seed. They were combined when dry enough, sacked, and the sacks left open to dry thoroughly before being tied for delivery to the elevator.

Relatives had visited us for several days, and shortly after they left one morning in the 1950s, the truck came to pick up our peas. I said, "They are not tied and tagged." The men said, "We'll load and haul a neighbor's sacks this morning and come for yours this afternoon."

The boys and I grabbed the tags, jumped in the car, and went to the field where the untied sacks of peas stood in a row several sacks deep. I tied the first sack and started for the second one, when I heard a buzzing noise. I thought "There's a bug in that sack, and he really wants out." Then I realized that it probably was a rattlesnake. I stepped back to see a coiled rattlesnake on the ground between the sacks. Had my foot, in toeless sandal shoes, been moved forward only a few inches, I would surely have been the victim of a snake bite.

Up to that time, when I went to the field, I always wore heavy shoes, took a shovel and snake-bite kit. That day, I had none of these, so I sent Vechel, Jr., and Ronald to the neighbor's to get a shovel. Barbara Long was ill in bed and told the boys to go to the shed and find a shovel. Finding no shovel, they hurriedly returned, with Vechel, Jr., dragging a big sledge hammer with a long handle.

I had stayed by the sacks to keep my eye on the snake. Well, I could not be quick enough with that "weapon" to pin the snake, so I did not try, but had Vechel, Jr., wiggle that sledge hammer slowly in the dirt to keep the snake's attention. I got up on top of the sacks (standing up) and hurried with the tying. After a while, the snake disappeared in the sacks; but with watchful eyes in all directions, I managed to complete the tying and tagging.

I watched for the truckers and gave them the word about the snake. They assured me that they would push the sacks over before loading them.

HUNTING, FISHING, AND GARDENING

ot only were the husbands learning the many skills of farming,
but he ives planted wonderful gardens. Now, I wish I would have paid
mo at ntion to my mother out in the garden. One of the summer jobs
wa to le cabinets with canned goods, and later, when electricity was
ava ab products could be frozen to be used in the winter months.
Pre rv ç the produce required a great deal of work, but there was
sor th ç very gratifying at the end of the day, looking at the rows of jars
on e inet and hearing the popping of seals, knowing the day's labors
had ec successful.

)n f the pleasures of living in northern Wyoming is the mountains
nea y. enison and elk were a main part of one's diet in those early years.
Th ne vorked hard getting the plowing completed before the snow came
in l v ber. Almost all of the men became hunters.

n t se first few years, if our dad could get the final irrigation set early
in e ening, he would come into the house and say, "Edna, lets go
fisl ng. She kept a wooden box handy that she could quickly fill with
foc it s, and off our family would go in the pickup to North Fork. In
late ye , I fished with my parents, but as a young child, as the folks fished
for ou I would dreamily create little communities, building roads and
hou es ing sand and rocks near the stream bed.

)n fternoon, Dad came into the house with a box he had gotten in
tow . hen our mom opened the lid, she saw a small pair of leather
mo ita boots. She was so proud of those boots; I remember her wearing
the fo ears when we went fishing and when she went hunting with Dad.

FISHING TRIP WITH BILLY WOODRUFF

illy Woodruff, an old gentleman thought highly of by our
cor nu y, had a sheep ranch north of Powell. In the spring, Billy would
tak ba s of sheep to summer pasture on Heart Mountain. One of the
hig ig for our family was when we went with Billy Woodruff on a
fisl ng p, so I wanted Mom to tell the story.

95

Billy invited us many times to go with him up into the Beartooth Mountain Range, up high where his sheep were taken for summer pasture. Finally, one year Wallace said, "Okay, we're going to take three days and go." I remember the kids were so excited.

Before we left, I asked Billy if he wanted me to take some lemonade. He looked at me like I was nuts. It was primitive up in the mountains, and we just drank water, as there was nothing fancy about that trip.

So, off we went, way up into the Beartooth Mountain Range next to lakes where there were no roads. We slept in his sheep wagons and would ride on horseback before dawn to the most wonderful fishing spots. Patty can still remember eating those trout with the red fins and how delicious they were. In the evening, we would come into camp, and the men would get a big fire going and fry up the fish with fried potatoes. In the morning, Billy fixed sourdough pancakes with bacon and eggs. In the evening, after supper, we would sit around the campfire, and Billy would tell us some of the most outlandish stories about the early years in Wyoming.

When Billy caught his first fish, he cut off the red fin, and that is what we used for bait. Everyone caught fish. We would ride horses way back to deep blue, mountain lakes along deer paths. It was high in the mountains, so the sun rays were intense. We would begin at four in the morning to load up and ride for a long distance. We would be tired at night, but we all enjoyed being with Billy so much.

Afterward, we were so glad that we just decided to go, because that winter he found out he had cancer and passed away. I believe he was eighty-one. Such a nice fellow; we missed him so much, as we always had enjoyed the times he would stop by the house for a cup of coffee or a meal.

2
I am grateful I have my mother's voice on tape and the words she spoke in transcript form. The trip to the Beartooth Mountains with Billy Woodruff is a highlight in our family's collection of memories. I can still remember the fun of catching the "brookies" in those icy cold, mountain streams. Years later, after I was an adult and would come back to the homestead, Dad would be up at sunrise, down at Alkali Creek, catching fresh trout. By

the m ny family was getting up for the day, he was frying the fish. He
wo d back and enjoy watching me, as with great delight, I would enjoy
my av te kind of breakfast. But I think, even to this day, the most
del io trout I ever ate was when we were sitting around the campfire
wit Bi , listening to his scary stories.

HUNTER'S PEAK RANCH

unter's Peak Ranch was another special place on Crandall Creek.
Wl n ave the pleasure of driving north on the Chief Joseph Scenic
Hig w #296, thoughts go back to many childhood times of spending time
wit A n and Garnet Cary. They owned an old, rustic lodge situated in
the un ht area. In those years growing up, the road through Clark's Fork
wa a v y precarious, and at times, scary adventure. It would take hours
to t t he Cary's. The quaint, log cabins and huge, rock fireplace in the
lod w e a fascination to me. Our dad enjoyed being the camp cook for
Alv 1 v en he would take groups of out-of-state men elk hunting.
Vh relatives came to visit in the summer, we would often take them
to llc stone National Park. But when it was just our family, we tended
to to iose more remote areas. I would say that most of our neighbors
enj /ec ie mountains as well as our family.
re mber once when we had relatives visiting from the Los Angeles
are \ had taken them to Hunter's Peak. Late in the afternoon, after
fisl ng /e were lounging on the grass in front of the lodge. Our guest
ma tl comment, "It's hard to imagine enjoying being in such a remote
pla a y from the city." I remember thinking, "You must be nuts, this
is j t ut as beautiful a place as anywhere on earth," but then, just like
my ar s, I had a great love for the mountains.

ELK HUNTING TRIP

ate in the fall, Dad and Mom would go hunting with Felix Hoff
up 1 l d Ridge, in the Sunlight area above Paint Creek. There was a
dec ra ie called the Natural Corral. There were several deer paths down
int hi eep ravine, but if it began to snow, one did not want to be caught

97

in this area, as it was impossible to get out of the enclosure made by the massive, rocky cliffs.

When interviewing Mom, this is one of the stories I wanted her to share.

The most memorable hunting trip for Wallace and I was with Felix Hoff. We went up to Pat O'Hara, set up camp with tents, and brought horses with us. That first night of camping, the men had put the tents right on the edge of an old, abandoned sawmill. The wind came up in the night, and the sawdust blew right into our faces. The next morning, we got up early and rode the horses up on the top of Pat O'Hara. I remember how cold it was, and I wasn't about to complain, as I was so glad to get to go on this hunt with the men. My face got wind-burned that first morning out.

The temperature began to drop during the day, and Felix became concerned about his house on Paint Creek, as he was afraid the pipes would freeze. It was the last of October, and it seems that back in those years, it got colder a lot faster in the fall. We rode over Bald Ridge and down through the Natural Corral to get to his ranch. We spent the night, and the next morning we were going to ride back up to the camp. During the night, it began to snow. The men asked me, "Do you want to stay here at the ranch?" I wasn't about to stay there and miss out on the hunt. "No, I'm not staying here, I'm going with you." We began the trip back up to our campsite. We took the horses up through the Natural Corral. There were only two ways to get in. There was a trail below the corral, and up on top, a horse could come down a narrow passageway. It was a rock formation that encircled about a hundred acres deep within the ravine. It was a good place to hunt for deer and elk. Fortunately for Wallace and me, Felix had hunted this territory for years and knew all the trails.

We decided on our way up to the camp we would hunt down in the Natural Corral. Wallace and I took the horses, and Felix went on ahead to spook the elk down into the ravine. Felix left us about 11:00 a.m., and after a long while, Wallace began to get nervous, as the snow was coming down so heavy. A heavy fog was rolling into the canyon, and we had no way of knowing how to get out. We kept trying different paths but would come right up against the rock ledges. The snow was up to the bellies of the horses, so Wallace thought he would leave me with the horses and try to

get ut   foot. But he came back in just a few minutes. "Edna, it is getting
so   ıld   ınd I don't know if I could ever find you; we had better stay
tog he
          A   ɔut 4:00 p.m., we heard a gunshot. It sounded like it was right
abɔ ɘ ı   We answered with a shot back. Felix shot back, and then he
sta ːd   lling us. He was up on top of the ledge, so he guided us up out of
the on   . When we finally joined Felix, he told us the only way we would
get ff   ː mountain was to follow the fence line.
          F   ıx was a good guide. He found the fence and we followed it. We
car : u   ın a big herd of elk, but we knew our situation was a serious one.
Th   ɘ ʌ   ; no way we were going to try to shoot one. At about 9:00 p.m.,
we   ɔt   o camp. Felix said, "If we don't try and get out, we will be stuck
up   ɘrɵ   ɔr the winter, because all the roads will be closed." We didn't
haʌ a   ır-wheel drive, just the old Dodge pickup loaded with rocks for
we   ht.   Ve were all just starved, so we quickly ate something and loaded
evɵ /th   ʒ in the back of the pickup. Felix instructed us to turn the horses
loo :, ɐ   ıe said they could find their way back to the ranch. Sure enough,
a fɵ / d   s later, they returned home.
          ℸ   ː camp was about a mile from the road. Felix got on one side, and
I gɵ oı   ıe other side of the pickup, and Wallace drove. We shoveled a
pat foı   ıe wheels, because the snow was so deep. It was the old dirt road,
not ıe   ıe that we drive today going to Sunlight. We needed to go to the
top f]   ıd Indian, which was about five miles away.
          ːlix and I would sit on the back end, and Wallace would drive a
littl wɐ   , and the chains would break. There was some bailing wire in
the   ıcl   /e used to tie the chains together. They kept breaking, and we
woı d j   ɾ be inching along.
          \   got into Paint Creek Ranch about 2:00 in the morning. I can still
ren ml   · how relieved we felt when we drove down the hill and saw the
old an   house. Wallace and I never forgot that trip. I think we both
gai :d   . awareness of the mountain storms and how they needed to be
res :ctɵ   . Without a good guide, we would have been lost and probably
woı d]   ʌe frozen to death up there in the canyon. We had many good
huɪ ; ʌ   ı Felix in the years to come but never had another experience that
waː ıs   ghtening as our first hunt in the Natural Corral.

Felix and my parents spoke of that special elk hunt many times through the years. As I think about the circumstances of that trip down through the Natural Corral in such a heavy snowstorm, I can't help but feel there was a heavenly presence guiding Felix and my parents to safety. 3

HOMESTEAD HUSTLERS

I have asked my mother, Edna Mae McClaflin, to help me remember how the 4-H youth program was introduced into our community. I was still very young at the time, and it is such a part of the history of so many of us in the community, that I needed some help.

At that particular time, Jimmy Nicholls was the UW County Extension Agent. He came out and interviewed Wallace and I and asked if we would be 4-H leaders. I remember I said, "Well, yes, I will be a leader if Wallace will be a leader." We both agreed. He took over the livestock part of the program, and I took the sewing projects.

I had most of the project meetings in my home, with only one sewing machine. Lots of times, the little girls would be sewing on the machine, so Patty would be left on her own or would be busy helping the little girls. Patty always liked to sew when I wasn't there, so we did a lot of ripping.

Okay, Patty, that first year Mike was in 4-H, he took a livestock project. The next year you began 4-H and took sewing with Hannah Bodle.

Probably, the 4-H years were one of the highlights of our homestead days, because we did it as a family. I remember the judging tours that we had for the different projects. Most of the fathers were working in the fields in the summer months, so many of the mothers would take turns driving all over the county with the 4-Hers going to the contests.

One year, Mike had sheep, but then he decided on hogs. Patty loved her sheep. She started out with Suffolk. They were so beautiful with their black faces and black feet. But after just a couple of years, it was discovered that the ram that had sired many of the herds of sheep in our county was infected with a disease called Scrapes. Patty was not the only 4-Her this affected; there were many broken-hearted 4-H children that had to give up their sheep at that time. Then her father helped her to find some

100

nic Co mbia sheep, and that is what she had for the rest of the years she
wa n H.

/e formed a community club, and it was called the
"H ne ad Hustlers." At one time, it was the largest 4-H community club
in \ yo ng. Ann Nelson was the community club leader for several years.
We ac eetings once a month, and then the different project clubs would
hav ii vidual meetings. Some of the project meetings were at the
clu ot ;, but most of them would be held in the individual homes. There
we m y of the parents that were leaders, and all of the families helped
in (e \ y or another.

Many of the 4-H members in our community club won trips.
Mi a Patty both won trips to National Club Congress in Chicago. Mike
wo a t) to the Denver Livestock Roundup. Many of the trips were won
thr gh eeping good record books. That was not the fun part of 4-H, but
it t gh ne kids a lot about keeping records and paying attention to details.

Back in those years, a 4-Her could be in 4-H until they were 21
yea -o I know Mike went on to the University of Wyoming and
cor nu citizenship and leadership projects until the cut-off age.

will always remember those 4-H years with Jimmy Nicholas and
Ma e l kam. Then Edith Anderson, who followed Marie as our UW
Ex si l Home Economist, was such a dedicated person to the 4H
prc ar Edith was one of those rare persons who took such an interest in
all tl kids. I treasure the years we had with her. Jimmy Nicholls was a
wo ler l Extension agent. He soon went on to be the state 4-H Director
anc la d a vital role of leadership throughout the state for many years.

arold Hurick, Bob Bledsoe, and Lyle Bang came to us after
Jim y t. They were with our county for many years. The 4-H program
wa les ned for the whole family, so these people not only helped each of
us d r children, but they became very dear friends down through the
yea . l nink that those young people who went through 4-H together still
hav la ng ties to each other. 4-H made a positive and lifelong impact on
all os /oung people.

l aybe one of the reasons 4-H played such a significant role in our
cor nu y is that we didn't have many other programs at the time. None
of h TV. So 4-H was a major part of our lives. They had 4-H camp

101

up in the mountains, Junior Leader Camp, State Fair, and many national trips. The 4-Hers have some good memories of all the things they did together. They stuck together and encouraged each other.

If a young person went all the way through their youth years in 4-H, they learned many healthy life values, such as a strong work ethic, honesty, integrity, leadership, good citizenship, caring for others, as well as all the skill development in the many different 4-H projects.

Back in those years, there wasn't such an emphasis on the separation between church and government, and so every year we were able to have Rural Life Sunday. It was an interdenominational service, held in a different church each year. The 4-H members were the ones that put together this service, and it was something very special for the whole community.

I remember one summer going up on the North Fork for a livestock judging day. It was raining that morning when we left, but we had no idea there would be such a cloudburst. Torrential rains are not that common in the Big Horn Basin. The livestock judging would take most of a day, so as we came home early in the evening, we were met with a lake of water down in Eagle's Nest. I had a car full of 4-H kids. Canals were all full and running over. I managed to get everyone home safely, but that was not a fun experience. The potato crop was washed out, and we almost lost the bridge over the canal.

HEART MOUNTAIN ADVENTURES

Those of us who were the oldest group of homestead kids have great memories of our teen-age years. Our group consisted mostly of 4-Hers who could make our own entertainment from the most basic elements. In our teen-age years, most of us classified Heart Mountain as the Mount Everest of the Great Northern Plains as she lured us and beckoned us to climb the rocky peaks on hot summer days.

Summer did not seem complete without at least one hike up her steep and rocky crags.

I recall the first time our little group of about a dozen 4-H teenagers decided to make a day of it. We decided to have a picnic.

102

limber was assigned to carry part of the feast up the   mountain. I c 't nember anything else we took, except someone had brought an an f I cake with orange frosting.

T northern plains can be dreadfully hot on a July afternoon. The ten er re must have been hovering around 100° F that day. The hike up the oc trail is an endeavor in itself, but we were never satisfied just to cli u the trail. We would surround the huge boulders at the top and hoi o elves up to the precipice to see spectacular views of the basin flo

W had decided to wait to have our picnic until we had climbed to the p. s we ascended the rocky cliffs, it was hazardous, to say the least. I w ld ot put the blame on any individual, but somehow, as we climbed up ve he ledges, the water jug was broken. As there is no water an he on the top of the mountain, this was not a good situation for any of . decided to have our picnic anyway. We managed to choke down the na course, but as we delved into the angel food cake with orange fro ng ve all realized how desperately thirsty we were.

O nother summer's hike, we had some visiting 4-H teenagers from the ar s City area. On that trip, my brother Mike was driving the old far pi up. By the time we counted how many of us there were, we had eig ee passengers, three riding in front and the rest of us in back-- scr m , yelling, and singing our favorite choruses at the top of our lun .

M e could always be counted on to be the Master of Ce mo es. I really don't think he set out to be such a comedian, but wa a ural. I have never met another person who could make magic tric c of thin air like he did. His nickname in those teen years was "R ." lthough he had a ferocious appetite, he was long and lean.

O this particular trek up the mountain, Mike detoured just a bit, fee g was his duty to give these city kids a joy ride they would be sure to m ber. He wound his way up the mountain, trying to pick the ste es ills the old clunker could manage.

T hike up the hill doesn't have any special memories, except that the ie or those "flatland" kids had to be quite fantastic and scary. We sta d the mountain much too long, so we decided we had better load up and make our way back home. As we began our descent on the first huge mountain-top plunge, Mike realized, to his horror and excitement for thrills, that the brakes had gone out.

Looking back on that trip down the mountain, I now have different feelings, as I am much older and have grandchildren. On that day, we did have some realization of danger, but as we would hit the bottom of each hill with a crashing thud, we would encourage Mike more and more. How we managed not to lose at least half of us out of the back is amazing to me.

Finally, the last hill was conquered, and we could begin to wind down the dirt road to the homesteads. We passed a lone sheep wagon in the distance. This, of course, was of interest to the city kids, as they had never seen a sheepherder or the inside of a home on wheels.

We all piled out of the pickup and ran up to the open door of the sheep wagon. The sheepherder looked at eighteen teen-agers, their faces pressed into the open door and mouths open in amazement. Of course, Mike led the group in quite a ridiculous, spur-of-the-moment question. Most of the time, he was better on his feet--but not that afternoon. It was apparent the old fellow was disgusted with the lot of us. Mike made his classic blunder, of which we still remind him with great delight. "Could you tell us how to get out of here? We have been up on the mountain and seem to be lost." The sun-baked face of a man, in no mood for nonsense, and with an old shotgun lying at arm's length, replied in a voice that let us know we were trespassing. "There's only one road in here, the same way you drove in." With that, we all turned on our heels and retreated back into the pickup as fast as we could. I am sure the old couple took no delight as we drove away, singing and shouting as if we were the only people left on those vast Wyoming plains.

By now, the sun was setting, and we were at least an hour late getting home. A couple of the girls had dates with two of the guys who had not been able to go that day. Looking back on this situation, we all agreed that it was not one our finest moments in politeness. We should not have stayed so long up on the mountain. As we came down the dusty, dirt road, making just a terrible commotion, we saw Keith and his Kansas City guest, all dressed up, standing by Keith's parents' blue Mercury. Mike picked up speed, and the guys jumped into their car to make the chase.

us s we flew by, we got a glimpse of Ted Ley's front porch. Mike
and k v we were dead. From the road, we could see our dad sitting on
the ey front porch, and we could tell he was mad. Our dad always wore
a s w at to keep the sun off his head. The brim of the old faded hat
did t   guise his anger as he sat there smoking a cigarette. Suddenly, his
sm de g face vanished from view as we were rapidly flying down the
sw hb ks of Eagle's Nest. It took all of Mike's wiry strength to keep
the ld kup from careening off the edge. We could see Keith in our rear-
vie m or. He had no way of knowing what was ahead of him on the
flat F a day that had been filled with so much fun, it could have ended
in   sas r. We managed to get to the bottom, collect ourselves, and then
we ne we were going to have to face the music at the top of the hill.
     ac of the 4-H families had taken guests from the Kansas City
del gat i. Mike and I each had a guest with us. It was a somber four that
dro e t mile-and-a-half home that night after dark. Upon arriving home,
Da wa sitting there in his chair, but for the life of me, I can't remember
wh he iid. I do recall the deathly silence that seemed to settle down over
tha itt farmhouse that night. No yelling, nor choruses, just stillness.
     Jo ll the stories told of those 4-H years were happy. We all worked
har S netimes we won contests, other times someone else received the
Gr: d ampion ribbon. But we cheered each other on and became the
bes of ends.

4-H SHEEP TRAGEDY

     he old lambing shed, full of dust and shadow, would seem to give
esc e m the August blast of heat, but not on this late afternoon. The
me l r f, turned to a burnt umber shade from years of Wyoming's brutal
Jar ry old and wind, was on this late afternoon a sun-baked oven for me
as   vo d steadily, combing and carding the Columbia ewe I would take
to t c nty fair.
     Su mers on the McClaflin farm were filled with long hours of work
and l-I ctivities. My elder brother, Mike, thirteen months older, had a
sta ol urple ribbons on his bedroom wall from several years of having
the rea thrill of winning Grand Champion for his prize Hampshire pigs.

105

It wasn't my intent to compete with my brother, but the lonely red ribbon from last year's Columbia ewe didn't have the same place of royalty in my thirteen-year-old way of thinking.

The suffocating heat pressed down upon me on that afternoon, but the words from my father kept me pressing on, steadily combing, carding, and combing again.

Several weeks prior, my father came in for dinner with that look on his face that clued me in to something exciting that was about to happen. "Well, Puddin', I was out in the pasture and I saw your Columbia ewe and checked her out. I think you have a Grand Champion there." That set the wheels rolling. This was my year. I had worked so hard on my 4-H sheep, and now my time had come. There would be a purple ribbon on my bedroom wall, just on the east side, where the afternoon sun's rays would show it off in all its splendor.

Living on a homestead near the east gate of Yellowstone Park was a draw for friends and relatives from afar. We were blessed with many guests in our home, probably because both Mom and Dad were such gracious hosts, in spite of the heavy workload they carried. "Fair time" was the busiest week of summer for our family, as we all participated in the 4-H judging activities. My father's Uncle Elmer and his wife, Aunt Lizzie, had come the day before. I had spent some time with them last night after supper, and then back out to the barn I went and worked late into the night. Mike would come out and check on me and help me some, but most of the time I quietly worked away on my Grand Champion, always with my dad's words propelling me on.

My Columbia ewe patiently stood on the fitting stand, her head in a leather harness, as I worked with diligence hour after hour. The late afternoon sun was accompanied by 100 degree temperatures that left me dry and parched. The family was all in the house drinking iced tea and visiting with my elder relatives. I was tired. I was lonely and missing out on all the fun. My thirst reached an unbearable level of Dust Bowl proportions.

I quickly ran to the house, leaving my ewe harnessed to the stand. As I entered the kitchen, I could hear Uncle Elmer telling one of his many stories. I filled a large glass with ice cubes, let the cold water run to the top

of e l m, and then stood for a minute by the living room door. One
mi te rned into five, and then I knew I must run quickly back to my
cha ipi sheep.

It s been over fifty years since that late afternoon in August, but
eve n as I pen the words, I feel that same quickening of breath with
wh I ind in the sheep shed that day.

T silence--where was that beautiful head of white wool? As I
car in the wooden framed doorway, the first impact of tragedy was the
hai ss illed tight around her neck, taking the breath out of her body. She
hac ou t against the tethered leather just enough to lose her footing and
hac all off the fitting stand.

I t ied, screaming with a cry of anguish. A cry from the very depths
of r ning as fast as my body could fly, "Daddy, Daddy!" The screen
doc fl open as my father ran through it, my brother close on his heels.
Of ui , they both tried to resuscitate the beautiful prize-winning sheep,
but he as gone. There was no way to console that young girl with sun-
bak d s n for many days to come.

T ook on my father's face coming through the screen door has lived
on ith e, and the recollection is burned upon my memory. The look of
cor en n his face has come to me at times when I have needed that same
me y l loving kindness from a Heavenly Father, who is touched with
cor as n, too, for persons who cry out for a father when they least
des ve . 4

T 4-H youth program had been an intricate part of the fiber of Park
Co ity The Homestead Hustlers on Heart Mountain was a thriving
cor nu y club. As we grew into our teen years, we became close-knit
wit fri ds across the county. The Extension agents, Harold Hurick, Lyle
Ba ,   l Edith Anderson played huge roles in the youth. After I had
gro n , I wished over and over that I had told each of them what heroes
the we in my life. As young people, we all worked hard on our projects.
It v sn until I became involved in 4-H as an Extension Educator myself
tha r ized how much work and dedication was required of those who
wo ed faithfully with us.

T it first year at the state fair, after I had returned to Wyoming, I
fou lr self working side by side with friends with which I had grown up.

It was late Thursday evening, and most of the big contests were behind us; we were exhausted. The Park County adult group had gathered together on the midway, at a concession stand that sold homemade pies. With great delight, we all began to share those many stories of growing up as friends in 4-H, and the last thirty years that had come and gone seemed like only yesterday. Each of us still had that keen sense of a bond of friendship that had taken us through the teen years and propelled us into the adult years.

MEMORIES OF THE SNIDERS

It was going to be one of those hot summer days. Although it was only midmorning, the air seemed to be close. Bertie Snider came driving into the yard, which was such a common occurrence in our neighborhood. All of our community felt close to one another, but we tended to form the closest attachments to those neighbors right around the perimeters of our land.

As a child, I took great delight in sitting off to the side in the living room, listening to the farmers discussing their work. Each of them, in their own right, became a wonderful storyteller, but most of all, I appreciated the common feeling of friendship the most. The wives would usually sit around the kitchen table, or if there was work to be done, they would join in and lend a helping hand.

Looking back on that time, I can't help but feel what extraordinary treasures those times were. Everyone had so much work to do, but friendship with neighbors always seemed to be a part of life.

So this was just another day in the summer activities, Bertie Snider driving into the yard at midmorning. She came in as she always had, a smile on her face, but there was something different about her countenance on this day. I was a young girl, so I could quietly slip into a kitchen chair unnoticed.

She had been to the doctor, and the report had come back. She started to tell us, and then the tears came. Just a few words from her lips, but they carried steel hammer power. Just above a whisper, "I have breast cancer!"

With a huge gulp of air, I was suddenly propelled into adulthood in a matter of seconds.

I ... 1 not know what this meant. I knew the word "cancer" was life ... g, but I had no context with which to place this exclamation of ... with this special person in my life.

... mother stood there in the middle of the kitchen floor, a large ... n in her hand. She had already poured Bertie a cup of coffee. I ... w why she did this, because she had a cream pitcher she kept on ... er, but she opened the refrigerator and scooped a spoonful of ... the top of the milk, freshly brought in from the morning chores. ... he plunked the cream down into the coffee, she realized what she ... They started laughing, both of them there hugging each other ... g together. But I was not fooled. I knew this was a serious ... and I just did not know how to handle the emotion I was feeling, ... outside.

... oked out at the barn and began to stroll out there with the sun ... wn. I found the kittens snuggled up asleep next to the mama cat. ... p the black and white one with the long furry hair. I cradled her ... ill hands and began slowly to make my way out into the field. I ... ong way from the house, looking back every few strides to see if ... ar was still there. I slipped down underneath the potato plants. I ... small, little kitten. And I cried. I sat there a long time, and I ... I thought I could hardly breathe.

... rs later, after I was grown and had a family of my own, we would ... k to Wyoming on vacation. It never seemed that we got to come ... t often, so when we were home, I tried to just relax and enjoy ... lf. But I always knew that when we drove away from that homestead ... n, the agony of missing my parents and old friends would return. ... ardless of how short the stay, we always tried to squeeze in a visit ... d and Bertie Snider. We would sit around their kitchen table and ... se stories of whatever. Regardless of what we said, we always ... ne reaction of enjoyment from those two, dear old friends. I think ... v the second generation of us felt about that windswept farmland ... ing. We felt loved. A great deal of sacrifice and hard work had ... raising this bunch of war babies, and we certainly did not want ... int those people who invested so much in each of us.

Sandy, Lloyd and Bertie's daughter, was a few years younger than Mike and I, but we always included her in things. She was only an infant when we came to live in the barracks. I remember how cute she was as a baby. She possessed a bubbling laugh that never ceased to bring me pleasure. In a matter of minutes, Mike, the natural-born comedian who still is, could have Sandy laughing so hard she would be crying. Later, in my high school years, I was the lucky candidate that helped her with her sewing project in 4-H. I have her to thank for somehow acquiring the patience of Job. Actually, one of the greatest pleasures in my adult life is in teaching young children to sew. It is interesting to look back over one's life and see how those early, youthful experiences many times grow into the most satisfying careers.

Once, when our children were small, Bertie and Lloyd came to visit us in Detroit. We made the mistake of going shopping in a big mall right after Thanksgiving. The crowds were horrific, but they wanted to buy the kids some games, so we waded through the throngs of people. When we came home, I watched the two of them as they played and played all evening with the children.

A few years later, when I was going through one of those valleys of life, I came home. By now, my father had passed away, and I was painfully feeling his loss. I also knew that Bertie was gravely ill at this time. They called and wanted to see me, so my mother and I went over to their house. When we walked in, they were both sitting at the kitchen table. Bertie had tubes in her nose for oxygen, her face was puffy, and she was having such a hard time breathing. All I can remember about that meeting, with the two of those old friends, was how concerned Bertie was for my welfare. I don't think she ever knew what that meant to me, as I have pondered it so many times down through the years. She passed away a few weeks later, and even after all this time, I miss her keenly.

A year later, I was in the midst of selling my home. I was feeling quite overwhelmed as to how I would ever be able to manage all the details. One morning, I got up before dawn and was praying for wisdom and strength. Later in the morning, the phone rang, and the voice on the other end of the line was Lloyd Snider's. "Patty, how are you doing?" I managed

to ı ın e something. "Well, I am down in California on a visit; I think I
wil ea ınge my schedule and come to Oregon and help you."
     S : enough, he came. He stayed for a couple of days, helped me
pac , n /ed furniture, went with me to the house closing, and helped me
put ıe ıney in the bank. That last afternoon of moving the furniture, we
we   b(: so tired, and I am sure his nerves were as frazzled as mine. He
wa   dri ıg his pickup through the evergreens on a mountain road. We
beŗ ı t talk about my dad and Bertie, and there was just such a heavy
sac ess t missing both of them.

          ıt only did his visit mean the world to me, but it is a much
tre(ır(memory for my daughters, as they could finally realize why this
Sni ır nily had always meant so much to me.

     I   n't say that I have ever seen an angel in human form, but I
sor :h(have a sense that Wallace McClaflin was looking down from
He   er) a daughter in need, and a commission was sent out to an old
fri(d t)e an angel of mercy to me on those days when I so desperately
nee ed e advice of a wise and kind father.

LLOYD SNIDER TALKING ABOUT MY DAD

          ıad the privilege of receiving an M.S. degree in Family Life that
bas al went through all the stages of life from infancy to death. One of
the ɔu s I have returned to time and again was entitled, "Middle to Later
Ye   s.' Dr. Laws was the instructor. Throughout my studies at Eastern
Mi   ıg University, I had come to acquire a great deal of respect for this
edı atɔ One day, I asked him why this course was required in my
prɔ :aı of study. He replied that, if it wasn't required, many students
wo   d ı take it. I realize I was one of the older students, but through the
yea , l ıve returned many times and remembered many of those topics
tha ve covered. In one particular lecture, Dr. Laws explained that, for
the ıoʂ ıart, men are so busy with careers that they don't take time to have
clo fı ıdships until after they retire. After that day, I often would see
old g(lemen sitting together in the park or having coffee in a restaurant,
jus ho ıghly enjoying each other's company.

111

From the very onset of sitting with the original homesteaders of 1950, drinking coffee with them and hearing their stories, an awareness came of those young veterans, who from the very onset of farming, developed very deep and lasting friendships with each other.

In some ways, this interview with Lloyd Snider is very personal to me, but I felt I needed to share it with you, the reader, because I think all across the homestead community, this same kind of friendship took place with the men. Lloyd speaks of my father, but I think many of the things said about him would also describe, in very like manner, the other very special farming men who made up the fiber of the Heart Mountain community.

When I came back to Wyoming to take a position with UW Cooperative Extension, it was not unusual to meet 4-H and agricultural colleagues who had worked with and been friends with my father. I missed him so keenly, so when this happened, I wanted to hear everything I could about my father, as if somehow that would bring him back or at least soothe that sad place in my heart.

This is how it was the afternoon I went to see Lloyd. I had to stop the tape several times, as we both would be moved to tears. He and my dad had been the greatest of friends and also worked together from the beginning of the homestead project. I am sure there are other friendships in this community that are just as endearing and unique. And with the telling of my father and Lloyd, hopefully it will give a spark to other families to tell their stories of those first years in their corner of that homestead community. I will write the conversation as closely as I can, to give you, the reader, an awareness of what made this particular friendship of two homesteaders a glimpse into "A Sense of Time and Place."

"Talking about Wallace McClaflin, what a nice guy. He was one of the candidates we met. We met him and Edna Mae at the first opening interview. He was number one. He had first pick, and we had the second pick. Wallace said, "I don't know what do for sure. I have picked two or three units."

Wallace was a nice guy. He was interested, very concerned and somewhat nervous, coming to Wyoming taking on this new venture. You don't usually homestead except once in your lifetime. We became neighbors, fast friends, shared machinery, philosophies, and enjoyed it.

W ac had a truck farm background, and I had my own farming
exp rie es. We all brought our knowledge and experience with us. We,
of ur had a good Extension Service. People tried the best they could
to g ve a good start. Nobody was giving us anything, just an opportunity.
We ad lenty of sunshine and water.

V llace already had a family, and we just barely had one. We
enj ec /atching the kids grow up and saw the school buses begin to grow
in ı ml in our community.

I joyed fishing with Wallace. We fished a lot down through the
yea , t I could never catch the amount of fish he caught.

e was well organized. In fact, he worried when this wasn't the
cas V learned to raise different kinds of crops. We had to learn what
we er loing. We worked together a lot. Wallace was a good friend and
nei bo

had a good philosophy in managing his farm. He understood
tha o times you don't know what you did wrong--and then he thought
ma e metimes the Good Lord doesn't intend for us to know exactly
wh is ıing to happen to crops and nature.

Ie ıd a good philosophy, both social and personal. I began to
gra al understand that he was a peculiar guy, in that you just could never
get im) say something bad about someone. Wallace used to say, "If I
car sa ;omething good about someone, I'm just going to keep still." We
wo d t together with the other guys, and sometimes we would say
sor th ; negative about someone, and then we would recognize that
Wa ac vould be still, and I began to understand where he was coming
fro .

those first years, economically it was difficult; we didn't live very
we l /as hard at first, but I don't think Wallace ever thought that we
suf rec We were here, because we wanted to be here. From knowing
Wa ac don't think he ever wanted to live anywhere else. He had started
the ro s of retiring. It is just too bad his life was cut short.

allace and I both enjoyed our sheep business. He enjoyed his
live too his dogs, and his pets. He enjoyed his family and took good care
of em I think the enjoyment we shared in this farming enterprise is the

113

way we looked at things. We both enjoyed the community and were on the Lamb Board together.

He was on the State Fair Advisory Board for a number of years. He went for the full eight days to the state fair. I would only stay a few days showing my sheep, but he felt this was a contribution to the young people. He enjoyed the children and the 4-H program. We both felt our future outcome depended on informing the kids and trying to help them get going; he did this very well. We still managed to get back and get the harvest in and take off for four or five days to go hunting.

I was with him at state fair when he had his heart attack, and that was a hard experience. I think he felt very humbled that he didn't die and felt like he needed to take better care of himself. I had faced that myself in early years, and the doctor had told me I had to pace myself. Wallace had always worked so hard, and so he learned from that experience.

After this comment, I had to turn off the tape for a few minutes so we both could regroup, as sadness had come over us at we sat there together.

I remember Wallace never got in a hurry. He enjoyed the wildlife and enjoyed being with Sandy when she took pictures. Sometimes, we would be out and get stuck in ditches, but we always managed to get back in time to set the water.

We got started a few years later going wild turkey hunting with Harold Hurick. We went east over by the Black Hills. I think we took nineteen trips hunting. There were six or seven Extension agents and some ranchers who also came every year. Wallace was a pretty good cook, so he was the one that prepared the meals. It was a great country to be in, but we had to have a guide so we wouldn't get lost.

In November, we used to go elk hunting up in the Clark's Fork. Sometimes, the kids got to go along, so that was a lot of fun we shared.

He was the head chaperone at state fair for a number of years. He liked to judge the livestock showmanship. He would take the kids aside and give them help on how they could improve. He was successful in this, and the kids always received well from him. He wanted to educate them. We both felt the importance of the kids gaining general knowledge from

par its   d leaders and schools, and it needed to be in balance. He felt it
wa   m   rtant to understand what goes on in the community.

W   lace was fundamentally an optimist in life. Your dad liked to
sch lul   things, but something would often interrupt his plans, so he had
to l rn   pace himself and roll with it. Your dad was fussy about how to
do   in   wanted to do them well, but he had to learn to live a little along
wit w   k. Most of the time, farmers work by themselves. Wallace
enj ec   arming. He was a thinker and had a lot of ideas. He was a very
int st   constitutionalist and believed in freedom. He felt you needed to
run o   ife and take care of problems. He was philosophical about life.
He   lt   ur actions are your own doing. The government doesn't owe you.
If y u   ke a mistake, you can profit from it, if you learn and don't do it
aga .

I   ink most of the men out here would talk about the service time
tog he   ut didn't share much with their families. We had things we
ren m   ed, and there were things we wished we didn't have to remember.
Wa   ac   lew the heavy bombers over Germany. On one flight, they didn't
get ac   They had radioed ahead, and that is what saved them. But it was
so   ld   nd it was hard to stay together in the channel. Most of the men
we   d   vned. He used to say the patrol boat was a welcome sight. He
use to   l me he wasn't afraid to fly. We all knew we might have to ditch
anc ni   t not get down, but that was the risk. He enjoyed the Air Corps
anc nj   ed his crew. He always regretted losing his crew. "Why was I
sav l a   not someone else?"

W   llace was sad that you didn't get a college degree. He used to talk
a l ab   t when you went back to college. He and Edna enjoyed so much
goi b   k to your graduation when you got your B.S. degree. One day,
he   m   y and told me you had gone on and completed your M.S. degree.
"Y k   w, I think Edna and I are just going to go back to Detroit and see
Pat g   her diploma." He was so happy about that.

W   ace and I were good friends. We enjoyed thinking together. I
ren m   he used to say, "If we always agree on everything, we probably
are ot   oking at all the sides of a situation." I am just sorry we didn't
hav m   e time together. With that comment we stopped the tape.

115

CHAPTER 6: PAINT CREEK RANCH

w many more stories will be written about our families on Heart
M nta ? I have no way of knowing. I can only hope that many others
of y ieration and future generations will be compelled to write. Of
cou e, e chapters contained in this book give only a brief overview of
the ral iterviews which have been conducted with the homesteaders.

A of the families interviewed have spoken of neighbors and friends
on e l nesteads, but I think that most of us found longlasting friendships
in t s ounding communities as well. Since the Big Horn Basin has been
ma ly ttled by homesteaders and ranchers born around the turn of the
cer iry he people in this valley possess a quality of rugged kindness, an
abi y reach out to others.

here were several families who adopted the McClaflins that first
yea of imesteading. Many families would make their way to
Po ll the fall of 1949 to apply for homesteads. On that first trip to
Wy mi in October of 1949, my parents rented a room from Mrs. Bosley.
Th is iw they became acquainted with Felix and Bessie Hoff. They
ow d int Creek Ranch. The Hoffs had a daughter, Phyllis, six years
old tl i I, who became the big sister to Mike and me. From the very
beg ini , it was as if our family had been grafted into the Hoff's family,
anc ha iendship has lasted down through the years.

3es owned a beauty shop in Powell. There was a small house in
fro o the shop where we would get together from time to time.
So ti s, in the winter months, Mother would work for Bessie, but
sur ne as much too busy on the farm.

ime of the greatest memories of childhood were spent up at the
Ho r h on Paint Creek. I will share just a few of those treasured
me or as they were woven into the tapestry of my childhood.

3es passed away in the spring of 1991. It is such a shame that she
is i t l to tell us stories of her childhood growing up on Paint Creek.
Ra h. don't know when Bessie and Felix bought the ranch from her
par its ut that first spring our family was in Wyoming, they were living
on in Creek.

I well remember that first trip to the ranch. When I scrambled out of the truck, the first thing I saw was the corral and the horses. I felt joy and delight so stupendous, a little six year old could hardly contain it!

When I was in the fourth grade, Bessie had a baby girl named Melanie. We were at a program in the old auditorium at Powell High School. I was sitting next to Bessie. I remember that my mom and two other ladies were dressed up in cowboy outfits. They had just sung a song, "Cool, Clear Water." It wasn't time for Bessie to have her baby, but I could tell she was very uncomfortable sitting in that folding chair. Bessie had spent several hours backstage before the program styling hair, so I thought maybe she was really tired. After the program, I can remember my mother running down the hall with a scared look on her face. Bessie had gone into labor. It was cold that night, so I stayed in the hallway. I watched through the window as Felix, a very uncomfortable Bessie, my dad and mom stood there on the sidewalk, frantically deciding what to do. I don't know what they were saying, but I could tell they were all upset. So off they all sped to the hospital in Cody, leaving Phyllis to manage two scared kids. Phyllis, Mike, and I stayed in the little house in Powell that night. The three of us went there to spend the night, but none of us could sleep. Mike and I had endless questions for poor Phyllis, who was only a freshman in high school. She did the best she could, but I am sure the questions we were asking were not easy to answer in grade-school terms. I was in the fourth grade at the time. The next morning, as I told my fourth grade teacher of the prior night's events, I was surprised that she wasn't taken with the drama of it all, as I felt exhausted from the entire happenings. Although Melanie was a bit small, she was fine, so now we had another member of this happy family of Hoffs and McClaflins. Two years later, the Hoffs had another baby girl, Colleen. She was a happy, curly headed blond. I adopted them both as my little sisters.

THE OLD RANCH HOUSE

The old ranch house wasn't fancy. It was typical of the kind of house one could find in the foothills of the Wyoming mountain ranges back in the fifties. I don't know how old it was when our family met the Hoffs

118

in 49 The old logs were seasoned with years of hard winters and high
wii s. lthough it was nestled down in a ravine, shaded with old willow
tre tl old house had seen her share of hardships.
      he itchen had running water but very few modern conveniences. We
wa ed shes in an old basin. The walls seemed to permeate the smells of
ma r ch-cooked meals, the sweat of horses, and leather. There were
two sm bedrooms and a living room with a wood-burning stove sitting
aw fi n the wall. I can remember standing close to that old stove on
col w er mornings. The old, outdoor John could be found out behind
the un ouse.
      he vell-worn stairs to the attic were dark and scary, with just one
sm l, (watt light bulb that cast eerie shadows. The stairs were located
at t b k of the house behind the main bedroom. The attic seemed large
to , it ran the whole length of the small house. It was full of old relics
anc or lden treasures that would fascinate any young child. There was a
do or ne back of the house in the attic. There was a long rope with a
kn at e end of it attached to the old willow tree. We could grab hold of
it a l s ng ourselves up to the old door. There were no outside stairs, so
I o n ondered why a door had been placed there in the attic.
      Ve ould come up the back stairway and make our way to the front
par of e attic on a narrow path through the boxes and antique relics.
Th e only one small window in the attic located way at the front of
the ou . There was an old cast-iron bed near the window piled with old
qui a pillows. There wasn't any heat in the attic, so one wanted to be
sur to ve shoes on in the winter months when one had to get up out of
bec Tl is where the three of us youngsters slept on those wonderful trips
to int reek Ranch. Even though Phyllis was the oldest, she still hadn't
ma ere her fear of the dark. Mike would pick up on her superstitions and
sug est hat those antique relics could be, as the moon would cast its
gh tly ght over images looming in the dark up there in that old attic. We
lik o times up there away in our own secret world of childhood.
      n f the great delights for me at the old ranch was when Bessie would
ma S edish pancakes. I did just as Phyllis did. I would cover my
par ak with butter and then sprinkle sugar over the top. I can still see
the mi on Bessie's face as she anticipated me on those mornings at the

119

ranch, bounding down the stairs and asking, "Are we going to have Swedish pancakes this morning?"

Now Felix, being the faithful Swede that he was, had a New Year's Eve custom of eating lutefisk. Of all my memories of the ranch, the smell of that slimy fish is the only negative recollection I have to this day.

One New Year's Eve, I remember that I had the flu. I was feeling miserable, knowing I would not be able to eat any Swedish pudding. I honestly don't know if I really had the flu, or the smell of the lutefisk cooking in the kitchen and the dreaded anticipation of it sliding down my throat that brought on this sudden sickness. Anyway, I lay in the bedroom feeling sorry for myself but also relieved as I heard the adults in the next room at their merry dinner party eating fish that had been soaked in lye. A few years ago, over the holidays, I was visiting Felix, Melanie, and her family in Idaho. They were excited about taking me to a Scandinavian celebration. On the drive to the party, I was talking to myself. "Oh you were just a child. What did you know? I am an adult; now I am sure I'm just going to love lutefisk." We took our plates and started through the buffet line. Oh, there it was! It had that same smell! I went and sat down with my dear friends, and with a weak smile on my face, I desperately tried to be a good sport about this whole situation. I took a bite, and suddenly the same flu from so many years ago suddenly gripped me with violent speed. I began to sweat as I rolled the fish around in my mouth. When Felix turned his head away to speak to a passerby, I lifted my napkin to my mouth, and that is the end of the story.

PAINT CREEK HORSES

It has always been a mystery to me just where one gets the love and fascination for animals. For as long as I can remember, I was intrigued by horses. As we drove down into the yard there on Paint Creek for the very first time in the spring of 1950, I remember seeing the corral over on the hill. As the adults were greeting each other, I was making my way across the creek and up the path. I crawled under the old wooden poles of the

cor l a walked into the herd of huge horses. I had no sense of fear and
did t n realize the danger of walking directly behind the mares. My
fath r f nd me and tried to explain the importance of staying out of the
cor l, t from that point on, a keen eye had to be kept on this young girl,
as a unt of scolding could convince me to stay out of the corral.

le ed to ride on Lady; she was a wonderful sorrel-colored mare.
Sh ac colt we named Nosy. I rode Nosy in the Fourth of July parade
in w when she was still a small colt. She wasn't "broke," so I don't
kn h I managed to lead her down the main street with people yelling
an ll other commotion.

y d built a fence around some pasture. When Nosy was weaned
fro h nother, we brought her home to the homestead. I never heard the
bus es ransaction that transpired between Felix and my dad, but I finally
ha h se of my own. She was swaybacked, not much of a beauty, but
she va horse, and I spent many summer afternoons after all my work
wa lo mind you, riding on that little horse.

n early summers of the fifties, the three of us kids spent many
ha y es together, galloping our horses over cliffs and down through
the ill es of Paint Creek.

h cond spring in Wyoming, I was up at Paint Creek Ranch with the
Ho . ad been there a few days, and I was excited, because my folks
we c ing up later in the morning to help Felix brand the calves. Felix,
Ph is d I had ridden out early that morning to start collecting the cows
up t bench. We came to a big ditch, and I was hesitating, because I
kn r horse would have to jump to get over. Phyllis came up from
bel d d swatted my horse on the rear with her reins. I didn't see her, so
wh n horse jumped, I flew out of the saddle and up on the horse's neck.
I g ob her ears, as she began to run down the ravine. I was just a little
tyk at time, so I was plenty scared. Felix, seeing what had happened,
im di ely took out after us, bringing his horse up next to me. He reached
out nd ok hold of me, but I didn't even know he was there. I held on
wit a p like steel. My horse was jumping over sagebrush, and I lost
hol of r neck and fell off. I lay there on the ground, knocked out. When
I re air consciousness, I was crying at the top of my lungs and wanting
my na real bad. I had a big knot on my head, so I had to go back and

121

stay in the house, which made me very unhappy. When I saw that old, blue Dodge truck coming down the hill, I ran out and crawled up in my mom's arms. I don't know if my folks realized how serious this situation was, but in my little girl's mind, this was really a big deal. Anyway, in a few hours I was back up on a horse.

In my childhood, I was bucked off many times, but I would always just crawl back up in the saddle. Nosy was my first horse, and there were several others that followed. But Lady was the best. She was a wonderful horse for all of us kids, and when she finally died at the age of 30, it was a sad day.

THE TURKEY CHASE

One summer, Bessie and Felix had the idea of buying 1,000 turkeys. Now, if it had been a band of sheep, or a herd of cows, or anything but turkeys! I was only eight years old, and even I knew better than that. Well, anyway, I am not sure why I was chosen, but I was invited to the ranch to help Phyllis herd the turkeys up through the hills. Now, I don't know if she was lonely for someone to talk to; if she was, she must have been desperate, or if she was just bored and needed to be the general of this army of two humans with 1,000 turkeys, I really don't know to this day.

But anyway, it doesn't matter, I would use any excuse to go to Paint Creek Ranch and spend time with Phyllis. It's really been so long ago, and remember, I was only eight, so I wasn't trying at that time to remember small details.

I have vivid memories of Phyllis, and even after all these years, we are the best of friends. Phyllis was a tall, statuesque Swedish blond. I thought she was the most beautiful young woman in the world. She was all wise and kind. She could do no wrong, so I followed her instructions explicitly.

We commenced herding those stupid turkeys. Nothing was going right. They went right through fences. They were just scared of everything and would go flapping and squawking noisily in every direction. Well, naturally, this would spook the horses. Oh, of course, we weren't on foot--we rode horses. I don't think the horses liked the turkeys.

Phyllis got a very clever idea somehow to attach a white sheet to
d run through the turkeys, waving it in the air. That didn't work.
imes she would command this little private first class to take a
;h the flock. Naturally, the horses' hooves would usually step on
ead or two. That meant we would have to take the dead bird back
se and dress it.

ould sleep out on the hill, so we could be close by to protect the
They would be on the move long before the sun came up, so those
n the hillside seemed endless. By the time the sun was at midday,
ribly hot, riding on those horses. I decided to wear my bathing
my clothes, so I could peel off clothes when needed. I would tie
the saddle horn. One day, my feet got so hot, I even took off my
tied them to the saddle.

now, we got so we were getting quite a chuckle out of running
iis flock of turkeys. I was usually sent out first. One by one, my
lothing were falling off of the saddle and would seem to get lost
ds.

t remember how many turkeys had been killed, but it was several.
d I vowed that we probably should stop our merry chase; besides,
in the ranch house were getting quite upset with the two of us.
ing, Bessie announced that she and Felix were going out for the
That was nice; we could come back to the house and have it all
es. We were happy at those prospects. So out to the field we
more time, watching those silly turkeys. Maybe we could have
nore chase. By now, I had lost all my clothes and was wearing
)athing suit. So off we went, being careful not to hit any of the
the head, but one duffer wasn't paying attention, and my horse
)ver him.

'hat were we going to do? We didn't dare take any more dead
< to the house. We took the turkey and put it up in the spring, so
nountain water would keep it cool. In the evening when we rode
e house, we waited as long as we could. Phyllis slung the dead
wn over the other side of the saddle as we rode into the yard. The
ill there. Why hadn't they left yet? We rode around the barn, she
e the turkey, and she went into the house. She came back in just

123

a few minutes, her face all red. "They decided not to go!" I didn't need to ask her if they knew about the turkey now weighing heavily in my small arms. It was very late that night when we finally had plucked all the feathers and were escorted off to bed.

Our days of herding turkeys came to an end that summer, and I was taken back to Powell. Bessie dropped me off at Mrs. Bosley's, as she had some errands to run. Phyllis always looked out for me, so she had kindly loaned me shoes, jeans, and a shirt. I was happy to wear anything that belonged to Phyllis-- never mind that her clothes hung on me like an old feed sack. I remember my mother driving up. Oh! I was so happy to see her, as I had spent quite some time at the ranch.

She didn't have a happy face. She pulled up to the curb. "Get in the car. Where's your clothes? You look like an orphan!"

REMEMBERING ANOTHER TIME

Much to my sorrow, the Hoffs sold Paint Creek Ranch in 1957 and bought land over on Clark's Fork River. Soon after that, they moved to Idaho. We remained good friends, but unfortunately, our visits were few and far between. I was always very sorry that I didn't have the privilege of watching Melanie and Colleen grow up. But now, after so many years, we still seem to have that bond that was created back then, even though they were so young when they left Wyoming.

Phyllis, Mike, and I have not been together for many years, so when we finally do get together, we reminisce about the many childhood experiences on Paint Creek. These sessions can go way into the night. I have always appreciated Ray, Phyllis' understanding husband, for tolerating all the stories we delight in telling and retelling.

A few years ago, I was visiting Phyllis and her father, Felix, at their ranch on the Clark's Fork River. Phyllis had come up to the ranch on the river to spend some time with her father. On a Sunday afternoon in late August, I had gone over for a visit. Melanie's daughter, Amy, about eleven at the time, was with Phyllis. As we sat there watching the lazy river

... rough an arid, dry land, telling the childhood stories, we decided ... e old ranch on Paint Creek.

... hildhood memories of the old ranch were rich with the brilliant ... childhood forty years past. They had already warned me that all ... ngs had been burned down by the new owner. I was excited to ... t a dread down inside of my adult mind, knowing the old ranch ... be as I remembered.

... /e all piled into the van and drove around the hills on a dusty dirt ... int Creek. The ranch was situated on a wide plateau just under ... ls of the Beartooth Mountain Range. The ranch house and ... gs had all been built down in a ravine where Paint Creek ... d for miles. As we stopped and unhitched the gate, I could feel ... pounding of my heart. We drove to the top of the ravine and ... own under the hill to what used to be one of my favorite places ... th.

... astures were still lush and green. Across the meadow were the ... rock formations that could evoke wild and terrifying scenes for a ... orseback, pursuing imaginary conquests. Up along the crevice ... was the old cave, which held secrets and stories told long ago by ... hievous children.

... reverence, we silently climbed out of the van and stood on a ... of overgrown weeds and grass that was once where the old ranch ... od. The old house was not a mansion, mind you, but it was our ... ur place in time, our keeper of holidays filled with laugher, music, ... friends.

... t help but feel a crime was committed. How could a house, so ... be wiped away by such a thoughtless act--as if we could bring ... ld logs stained with the seasons of life?

... stood there, we each desperately tried to remember just exactly ... h room was located. We walked past the back part of the old ... n of the house where the old willow tree once stood. When the ... burned, the tree caught on fire. All that was left was a portion ... k.

... ny times on those warm summer days, I would climb into the ... at willow tree for comfort and solace. Felix had anchored an old bed springs into the tall branches long before we arrived on the scene in that first summer of 1950. Those afternoons Mike and I spent with Phyllis in the old willow tree, as she shared her wisdom of life, are close to my heart. There were times the three of us found ourselves in a good deal of trouble with the older generation. Somehow, they did not comprehend our zest for life, or maybe they did? It was at these times the mighty old willow tree called us. As we would ascend its mighty branches and sway back and forth, it would seem our troubles were not so bad. It was a safe place for us to contemplate our next adventure. So now the three generations of us, Felix, Phyllis, Amy, and I stood over the poor old charred stump of a once beautiful tree.

We made our way across the creek and up a small bluff to the corral Felix had built. Most of the posts were still standing. The strong fences had held me many times, as I would gaze upon the horses. We examined the moss that had crept into the wood as the years came and went. We decided we would have to talk to the owner of the land and see if we could have a few of the logs to build a small fence in memory of the ranch.

As we moved away from the corral, we walked over to the old barn. We peered into the dark and dank building. There was a ray of sunlight that pierced through the small remains of dust and smells of animals long dead now.

An object caught our attention as our eyes pierced through the darkness. It was an owl glaring at us from his perch. His face carried a defiant look of ownership, as if to say, "Go away, this is my home now, you are trespassing, the ranch you had is now in memories."

As we quietly walked down the hill, we each fought back tears, but we also had a feeling of love, life, and goodness in all the smells, sights, and the sounds of childhood coming back in waves of happiness.

So the stories could go on and on about the wonderful old ranch house, the barns, the creek, corrals, horses, and the smell of sagebrush on a rainy day. I can still feel the anticipation of fun and hear the laughter that was shared within the walls and out on the hillsides. I am personally grateful for the memories that are still with me today after so many years.

'ART II: HEART MOUNTAIN HOMESTEADER INTERVIEWS, SECTION 1

LOIS AND DICK ASHER

suc ess
as i y p
as i e ii

sof all
par its
tha he
cor t
did or

I jo ec
wa: ov
to ( )lo
guy o (
anc ha

a P i N
50(32
anc at
tim tl
cor)ar
wo d (
We , it
jus o
Ye ve

remember Dick and Lois Asher well. They were a big part of the
our community 4-H Club, and I spent many summers with Lois
ject leader in foods. We sat together that morning, drinking coffee
rview began.

Lois and I both grew up in Page, Nebraska. I was playing on a
am when she came and met me at a game one night. Both of our
ere dry land farmers. It wasn't long after we came to Wyoming
egan to irrigate in our hometown area. Maybe we wouldn't have
ive on the homestead if it had come sooner, but we are glad we
to Wyoming.

vas in the infantry during the war and was stationed in the Pacific.
e service in 1941 through 1944. When my time with the service
I remember we flew into Seattle and took a train ride from there
lo, and that is where I was discharged. Four or five of us hired a
ve us into Columbus, Nebraska. I took the bus home from there,
vas it. I was very glad to get home. Yes, very glad!

e had a sergeant who had a friend in the Air Force, and he flew
istang. Every morning before the war was over, there would be
that would fly over, and then fighter planes would fly over later
up with them. A lot of planes would come back all shot up. One
e was a crew that bailed out right near us and landed right in our
area. The plane went on out to sea and just blew up. The men
ne back so sunburned from sitting in the cockpit for eight hours.
as just a very hard time. The war was terrible, you know. I was
d when it was over.
glad!

Lois's family had come to Wyoming on a family trip in 1948 or 1949 and heard about the Japanese Relocation Camp, but I didn't know anything about it until then.

It was just a bad situation along the coast for the Japanese families. I know there are bad feelings both ways. We weren't original homesteaders, so when we came four years later and the saw the barracks, I thought it had to be very hard for the families interned at the camp. The barracks that was on our place had really deteriorated pretty fast, so we just tore it down and used some of the lumber." Lois spoke up.

"I first heard about the Heart Mountain camp when I was not very old in Nebraska. I heard about it at our MYF youth group at church. Our minister's daughter had been the recreation leader at the camp. When she came back, she talked to us about it. That was the first time I had heard about it. I guess I didn't pay too much attention to the fact it was like a concentration camp. It was just a place they had brought the families to keep them safe. Of course, after we came, we learned so much more about it.

The living conditions at the camp were very primitive, and they had no privacy for their families. I have read some of the books written by those that lived in the camp, and they tell of how they formed some very deep friendships.

And many of them did survive, and I am happy for that. When they did go back, so many of their homes and possessions were gone. For them, it wasn't just a period of their time; it probably affected the entire rest of their lives.

I think it is important that we know about the internment camps as a part of history and learn from it. But we need to move on, as we didn't plan this or our children, but we shouldn't forget it. We cannot go back and change the situation, but certainly we need to learn from that part of history.

Dick had come out to Wyoming to hunt with his uncle, Harry Cullen, and that is what drew our attention to the Heart Mountain homestead community. We came to Wyoming in 1952 and bought the Thawley homestead. It is between the Beslanowitch and Roland homesteads. We later bought the Nunley unit."

Lois laughed as she said,

Nhen we first came, I cried a lot. There was so much to do, and

we ll j ɾ worked so hard just to get started. We didn't want to fail in our
far ing All of our neighbors felt the same way, so we all worked hard
tog he The church and friends in our community helped us to just keep
goi ʒ. ck and I feel it was a once-in-a-lifetime opportunity for us.

ncle Harry helped us when we built our house. It was 24 feet by
30 et. Vith the four small children, we needed the space. Fred was born
in)5(ɪnd Pam was born in 1951. They came with us from Nebraska.
Ric w: born in 1954, and John was the last, and he was born in 1956.

red lives in Laramie and has been a coach. Pam lives in Omaha
anc ik her occupation as a grandma. Rick never wanted to leave the
hoɪ ɛst l. He now farms with his sons, Andrew and Brian. John lives in
Co ɪr (Alene, Idaho, and is an elementary school principal.

he community club was a very important part of our community.
Mc o ɪe work, like the foundation for the building, had been done by
the m ɪe arrived on our homestead. But we all worked together through
the ea to improve the building.

think the square dances were really important for all of us. We
wo d the water and then have a few hours to dance before we would
haɪ to ɪt the water that would take us through the night." Lois spoke of
the -H ɾganization.

Of course, 4-H was very important, not only to our family, but to
the ʌh ɛ community. We thought Edith and Niles Anderson were
wo ler l. Niles received the "Outstanding" award one year. I practiced
my pe h while driving the truck, but when it came time to introduce
Nil ɪ, I ɪst cried, as he was such a help to Edith and all of the Extension
age ts. Ve remember Harold Hurick and Lyle Bang as well. They were
wo leɪ l role models for our children. They each took such an interest in
the hil ɛn in Park County.

was privileged to be the State Chairman of the 4-H Leaders'
Co ɪci ɔr several years. I remember the great trips we took to Laramie
wit yc folks and other leaders. I was the project leader for foods for
ovɪ tw ty-five years, so I received the special pin, which meant a lot to
me

Our kids were involved in many 4-H projects like crops, gardening, sewing, rabbits, beef, hogs, and many others. They enjoyed their years of 4-H.

We didn't realize at the time we came to Wyoming what we were getting into and how hard we would have to work, but I think we would do it all over again if we had the opportunity. I think the most important things that our family learned were the importance of hard work, but then to learn to have a good time as well. Faith and understanding became very important to all of us in this community.

When it is our time at the church circle to do the dinner, everyone knows it is the group of ladies from the original Heart Mountain church circle, because we are so noisy in the kitchen. We giggle and laugh, you know, and the men use our Heart Mountain menus; you just can't get away from it. We would make fresh cookies and homemade ice cream. We used to be a lot more ambitious than we are now. But it was just that we had so much fun doing things together, and we still want to. We have given wonderful showers for our kids, and everybody wants to come. Not everybody is able to now, but they still want to come, because they know it is going to be a special occasion. It just can't be replaced.

Dick and I have moved to town now, but we love the Heart Mountain community, and it was good to us. When I see a storm coming up, I still go out to where I can see and say, "Oh, is it hailing on the farm?" I think about the families farming and wonder if their crops will survive the hail storm.

But even now, there is nothing like coming to the top of the hill and looking at Heart Mountain."

Dick chuckled.

"When I look at Heart Mountain, I feel a little closer to Heaven. It is peaceful."

Lois said they had their picture of Heart Mountain in the TV room. I had noticed in most of the homes I visited that on a wall somewhere, there usually was a picture of the mountain. I think we all felt like that mountain belonged to our community.

RUTH AND McKAY AVERY

uth and McKay have retired from homesteading and are now
Cody, Wyoming. The day I interviewed them, McKay said he
eling very well, but they were both so gracious. When I got ready
McKay went back into his collection of rock jewelry and came
lovely necklace, and he gave it to me. That afternoon, as I drove
n their home, I was gripped with how the project is so important
up of people who made up such a special community.
s I started the interview that afternoon, I began by asking McKay
had grown up.

grew up in southern Utah, about halfway between Provo and
nyon. I wanted to farm after my time in the Army. I was
d in March, 1946, after the war was over. I saw an ad in the paper
rt Mountain. I applied, and I believe the number I drew was 39.
Then I came and saw the land, my first impression was that it was
re place, and it made me wonder what kind of ground we were
We were excited, but of course, we wondered if we were doing
hing. We had three children when we came to Wyoming. That
we were busy getting our home. There wasn't electricity or
it was quite an experience for a family.
e attended church in Powell regularly, so that provided some
ngs for our family. We attended the community club meetings
th. We liked to square dance with the group here.
square danced until about four years ago, when I had to quit
f health problems. We danced at the community clubs at Heart
, in Powell, Cody, and even in other states. I think we had
neighbors. Our children adjusted to homesteading." Ruth added
ments at this point.

didn't come to Heart Mountain until I married McKay in 1971.
was an adventure to be here on the farm. It was so peaceful and
I I thoroughly enjoyed it. I loved the neighbors on Heart
. I was involved in the community club, so that allowed me time
any friends.

133

I was raised in Sunlight Basin, Wyoming, so I knew some of country life. My father had a ranch there in Sunlight, and he raised all kinds of livestock--cattle, horses, sheep, and pigs. He died when I was only two years old. My mother took over the ranch, and she stayed on the ranch until she remarried. I grew up there and helped on the farm. I learned to do all kinds of things, between the animals and chopping wood and carrying water.

My grandfather built the schoolhouse that still stands up there above Sunlight Creek going towards Crandall. It was a one-room schoolhouse with several grades. They don't use it for school anymore. They used to use it for square dances, but now it is owned by a private individual. I went to school there until the eighth grade and then attended high school in Cody.

I think the main thing I especially liked was when we used to get so much snow, we couldn't get out. So in some ways, living on the homestead was easier than how I lived as a child.

When McKay and I married, I had one ten-year-old son, Mike Riley, still at home.

He went through high school there in Powell, and then he also went to college. He loved the farm. He especially liked working on the tractor.

I attended the Extension Club meetings. It helped me get acquainted with other ladies in the community, so it made me feel more a part of the community. There were different education programs that were given at the club meetings, so that was a great help to me." McKay talked about the life on the homestead.

"I think our barracks must have been one of the colder ones. It wasn't fixed up very well, but we accepted it, and I think we enjoyed it. I put in a coal furnace to heat the home. Of course, it was so nice when we got electricity. In the early years, we sometimes wished we had a little more money, but we never considered ourselves to be poor.

Our first daughter is Carol. She now lives in Cowley. Our second child is named Linda, and she now lives in Lovell. Lorna lives in California. Our son Ivan was born here, and he died about ten years ago.

those early years, we raised a big garden and had a milk cow.
Th cr   I raised were peas, and then I went into raising beans, alfalfa,
an ar . I never did raise sugar beets, though.

off e j m glad we raised the children on the homestead. When I had an
sto ec , I always had headaches, but when I came here, the headaches
o I think I was a lot healthier." Ruth spoke.

When I married McKay, I learned to drive a tractor and a combine.
I th k   role of the wife was very important. When McKay needed help
wit in ation, I learned to do that too. I think a wife's duty is very
im rta on the farm. It really helps the husband a lot, and I certainly
enj ec ll of it. I think the wives that came here were really courageous
an ra to endure what they did. I know it was very hard at first. I never
he t wives complain when I was around, although they sure could tell
so i resting stories.

e had three horses for a number of years the children used to ride.
W ls lid rock hunting. We looked for dinosaur bones over near Shell.
An th when I retired, I joined a rock club. I have polished rocks for
so y s now. The main rock I liked to polish was a dried agate I found
aro d vell."

cKay said he retired from farming in 1981 because of problems
wit hi yes.

The doctors said if I kept farming, I could lose my eyesight, so it
wa g d time to retire.

e have enjoyed fishing. We like to fish in Clark's Fork and up
on or Fork. I used to go up to Clark's Fork fishing when they had the
old oa nto the canyon. The new road up to Sunlight makes the drive
mu e ier, but it takes away from some of the scenery we enjoyed on
the ld ad."

oth Ruth and McKay agreed that they had enjoyed their
ho st ling days. But they also appreciated the retirement years which
all ec hem more time for rock hunting and fishing. They were two
ver gr ous individuals, and I enjoyed my time with them.

DOROTHY BAKER

Several homestead families met together on that late summer afternoon at a favorite fishing spot--Horseshoe Bend, on the North Fork River above Buffalo Bill Dam. The day was still warm, as some of our parents were busily preparing a picnic lunch over a wonderful campfire. My dad had waded out to his favorite fishing hole with a bamboo fly-rod in his hand. He was deftly casting into the curve of the river, just under a massive rock which had been eroded by centuries of icy, cold rapids.

I was sitting at the dark, wooden picnic table, coaxing just one more story out of Dorothy Baker. I knew that she was an elementary teacher, so of course, she must love all children and be very patient. What could be more important to her than sitting for a long span of time with a pigtailed, six-year-old child, telling her one story after another of mystical fairy lands, so much like this present place of mountain beauty?

I don't think Dorothy Baker was five feet tall. She had raven black, curly hair, infectious laughter, and a beautiful face. I was enraptured with her. Getting together with friends for fishing trips on the North Fork was a treat, so I am sure on that afternoon, she would have much preferred to visit with her neighbors. But there she was, patiently telling me one story after another.

So many years have passed now, as I sit across the sofa looking at Dorothy. She is in her eighties, a widow, and her raven black hair has mellowed into beautiful salt and pepper gray. But I still see the twinkle in her eyes. I hear that same infectious laughter that speaks of a woman who is still enraptured with life and still has a spark for adventure.

Dorothy, what did you think of coming to the northern plains of Wyoming to begin life on virgin soil covered with sagebrush? After I asked the question, I somehow knew what she would say. "Oh, it was an adventure! Lyle and I were going to begin our lives together. We were so excited!"

I wondered what such a petite, southern California lady could find so appealing about living in a black, tarpaper barracks in the brutal, winter storms of Wyoming.

D   othy Baker grew up in Kingston, New York, an upstate town
abc t s y miles from New York City. She received a degree in primary
edu ati . Winters could be severe there, so she was familiar with snow
anc vii r's cold.
     Tl war was on. The young men in the community were off to war.
Do   th ound herself allured by the warm climate and sense of adventure
she :o l find in southern California. Her mother's sister lived in
Sou ng :, California.
     U| n her arrival in southern California, Dorothy found a job working
for xe on Manufacturing Company, a defense plant. After the war, men
we   cc ing back and resuming their jobs they had left behind. Dorothy
dec lec t was time to get back to teaching, so she found a position in
Ora ge ounty as a first grade teacher. Kindergarten, at that time, was not
sup ort by the government, so there were no positions open.
     Tl school was located in Irvine, which was surrounded by a farming
cor nu y where beans were a major crop being produced. Other fruits
anc ve; ables were abundant on the small farms, so Dorothy thought it
wo   d   a good experience for her students to visit a farm. She made
arr ge ents with a farmer nearby who grew strawberries. Upon arrival
of 1 : f t graders and their teacher, Miss Smith, they were greeted by Mr.
Ba   r,   vell-respected farmer in the community, and by his son, Lyle, just
hor : f n the war.
     L\ took one look at Dorothy. He knew he had to find a way to meet
this /ot ; beauty. He lived next door to one of the first grader's parents.
He   sk(his neighbor if she would call this young teacher. In a few days,
a n e \ s on the teacher's desk from one student's mother. "Miss Smith,
do   )u ite boys? I don't live in a great house, and I could walk over to
Lyl an let him get in touch with you. I would love to entertain you, but
I ar ju going to turn your name and telephone over to him."
     G   ig to Hawaii had been one of Dorothy's goals while she lived in
Ca   or l, so after must cajoling, she talked Lyle into letting her take the
trij)f \ ich she had always dreamed. About three months later, after she
retu ne(rom this adventurous holiday, Lyle and Dorothy were married.
     Tl newly-married couple settled on Lyle's father's farm in El Toro,
Ca   or l. One evening, Lyle and Dorothy went to a dance with two

137

friends from the El Toro Marine Base. One of the Marines began to tell Lyle about some literature he had read at the base about homesteads being opened for war veterans in Wyoming. Lyle had all the qualifications needed, so his friend encouraged him to send in an application.

Lyle asked Dorothy if she would go. "Well, of course," was her reply. She was always ready for an adventure, and the thoughts of moving to the "Wild West" summoned dreams of excitement and intrigue.

In the next few days, Lyle filled out the proper application, fulfilled requirements outlined by the Reclamation Project, mailed the packet, and then forgot about it.

One Sunday, Mr. and Mrs. Baker, Sr., were attending Sunday services at the local Presbyterian Church. Several friends approached them, excited with the news that the application for Lyle and Dorothy had been drawn for a homestead in Wyoming. This was a surprise, as the family had not been notified. But sure enough, the Baker name had been drawn as the fourth candidate for a homestead in Wyoming.

In October of 1949, Lyle and Dorothy loaded a small camping trailer and began the trek across the western states to northern Wyoming.

Those first few days in Wyoming are forever imprinted on the veterans and their wives. A vision of a strange, new land lay before these young families. It had possibilities for a future home on virgin soil, the Rocky Mountains silhouetting the sky, and a valley that would one day be a fertile homeland for many families.

There were four couples in that first group of candidates coming from many parts of the country to pick out units. Lyle's former experiences as an irrigation farmer helped him, as he studied the lay of the land. He decided on unit 139, which was about in the center of the Ralston Bench homestead project.

Lyle and Dorothy became close friends with my parents from their very first meeting. Lyle needed to stay in Wyoming and get some plowing done before winter, so Dorothy went back to her teaching position. My parents had to go back to southern California to sell their small garden farm, so the three of them made the trip together.

Dorothy resigned her position as a first grade teacher and was able to come back to Wyoming with Lyle on the fifth of March. The barracks had ed onto the homestead unit, but it had not been insulated, so the er became home. There had been a severe snowstorm, and it was rch in Wyoming.

ailer was heated by propane. During the day, it was comfortable but because of safety hazards, the propane was shut off before r the night. During the night, the young couple was cold, and in ng, they were greeted with icicles hanging from the ceiling that ed from moisture condensed by the cold. That first spring in , Dorothy cooked meals on the two-burner stove in the trailer. . Smith, Dorothy's father, came early that year and began to e barracks to make it warm enough in which to live.

nd Dorothy had both moved from their families on the east and sts, but both families supported their decision to move to . Many relatives came to help in those first years and to enjoy d beauty of Wyoming. The barracks was transformed into a le home in those early years of homesteading. The visitors all come in the summer, wanting to tour Yellowstone. Family was welcome sight to the homesteaders, but the summer months were days beginning before dawn and ending way into the night. a farm was a grueling task.

rviewing the homesteaders, I think most of them felt they were r those barracks. The black tarpaper was not a thing of beauty, give some protection from the northern winds.

were frequent visitors, and every family probably had stories to se quiet little creatures. After moving into the barracks in the e evening Dorothy began to laugh and tell Lyle, "A mouse is y feet." Lyle was exhausted, as he had put in a long day plowing. go to sleep, there isn't a mouse in the bed." With more peals of "Yes there is, he is tickling my feet." The mouse then moved over Lyle a jolt. In the next few minutes, there was a wild chase on len floors, chasing a poor little mouse who only wanted to share h of the covers in the cold spring of 1950.

e Baker was born in 1953, and Ginger, the fiery, little redhead in 1957. They were both born in the Powell

I cherished every minute of the interview with Dorothy. After each interview with a widow or widower, I would sense a pang of regret that I was not able to speak with that missing partner, but their memories are now in our hearts and minds. Hopefully, as we read the accounts from those first few years, we can fill in the stories between the lines. Lyle passed away in 1987 of congestive heart failure, and he is still greatly missed by his family and many friends.

I asked Dorothy a question. "After living in southern California, didn't you miss the many conveniences you were used to?" Looking across the room into the face of a lady, who as a child I much adored, I can't help but hope that she has influenced me today. If I have the privilege of living into my eighties, I just hope I have some of the humor and spontaneity for life as dear Dorothy has. "Oh, no, Patty, we really had all we needed--there was Bud Steck's grocery store, the lumberyard, and the homesteaders were all in the same situation, so we stuck together. We did seem to manage without electricity and running water. Yes, it was an adventure, it was a great adventure."

GINGER BAKER

So many of the second-generation families from the Heart Mountain homesteads live in other states now, so I was extremely happy when I heard that Ginger, daughter of Lyle and Dorothy Baker, was spending a few days with Tak and Emmy Ogawa.

Ginger came to my mother's home that day. Of course, I had not seen her since she was a tiny, little girl. She has the same petite frame of her mother. Instead of dark brown hair, Ginger has fiery, red hair, but as our interview progressed, I could see that zest and energy for life had been passed on to a daughter from a homesteader's wife I could still remember well. We sat at the dining room table drinking coffee as Ginger began her story.

"Yeah, I think I was six years old, and I had started the first grade when we moved back to Tuscan, California. My brother, Joe, was four years older than I, so I am sure he can remember a lot more about those early days on the farm. He now lives in Laguna Beach, California.

Sor eti :s we go through old pictures, and that brings back memories. My
son s r v sixteen. He was only a year old when my dad passed away.
Ou mo is still healthy and living an exciting life.

M nom has told me that she and Dad were happy with the homestead
the we able to pick out. They were excited to come out here and farm."
hinking about her mom, Ginger chuckled
She was a little girl from New York, but she married this man
fro sc hern California who was a farmer. When they came, they lived
in ; ea rop trailer that was heavy-laden inside and out with icicles in the
wii :r. hat was their home for about the first year, and then her dad, who
wa ; c penter, came out and built them a home.
V at I remember about that first year in school was that the teacher
ma : n drink milk--and I hate milk. That was the year John F. Kennedy
wa sh I was out on the playground with my classmates. It was
No :m r, and there was ice on the playground, so we were all ice skating
in (r s es. The older kids were very upset, but I didn't really understand
the /h(situation. At the time, the leaves were still changing color in the
tre(n(the playground. I just thought it was all so beautiful.
I solutely loved living on the homestead. It was the most fantastic
pla : t(ve. I remember looking up in the sky and seeing the Canadian
ge(: a other birds flying south for the winter. The fields were beautiful,
an(ve d lots of animals. We had cows, and pigs, and all the kittens in
the ay cks. It was just a fun place for a kid to grow up.
I as an independent six year old. I would go out to the pigpen and
per 1 u high on the fence and watch the animals. That seemed to be my
spe al ot.
I) remember leaving home one time when my dad was supposed
to t w hing me on his tractor. He apparently lost sight of me. I decided,
Go ;, t is kind of boring. I didn't want to stand in the field, so I walked
ov(ab t a quarter of a mile to Tak and Emmy's. My dad thought I had
got n i) a drainage ditch or something. So I guess I started hiking early.
Th(fol always warned me about the drainage ditches.
I 1ought my parents were crazy for leaving Wyoming. I loved
W) mi ; I wanted to stay. I remember the auction at our house.
Ev(yth g was sold, even my cat, dog, and my horse. I remember driving

141

to California at night through all the traffic, with all the little lights, and Mother in her positive way was saying, 'Oh, look how beautiful the lights look,' but I was unhappy. Now that I'm an adult, I understand why they sold the farm. Dad was having back problems, and Mom was away from her family.

I think I have passed my love of Wyoming on to my son. That is why we are here this summer. He wanted to come and enjoy the beauty. When we were here on the homestead, we spent a lot of time with the Ogawas and the Sniders. Kathy and Jenny Ogawa were my friends. Sandy Snider was my brother Joe's age. I remember how I used to sit with Emmy and shuck peas.

We liked to go to the community club for a lot of things. One time, there was a cake walk, and I won a cake Sandy Snider had made. That was something really special to me. The frosting was pink, and it had little marshmallows on it.

Since we lived a ways from our neighbors, we didn't see them all the time. I would entertain myself out with the animals. I would walk in the cattle trough and pet the cows. I liked to have them breathe on me. And, of course, I loved my horse. My dad had a sled behind the horse, and he would pull Joe and me around on it.

We had little bum lambs we fed. Joe and I entertained

My mother made pickles and put them in the window. The women did so much canning. Coming back now, I realize how important it was when everyone got together, the farming, food, and family all bonded us together.

The other day, Emmy and I were walking outside, and as we talked, it helped me have real vivid memories of childhood here. The smell of fresh air, and the fields, and the sagebrush brought back my childhood. When I would come here during my junior high school years, I would take some sagebrush back home with me, just so I could smell it.

In the summer, so many of our relatives came to Wyoming. Our grandparents came up every summer. All the city cousins would come up to the farm and enjoy it. One time, my grandfather was here, and he took all of the boys fishing, but I didn't get to go because I was a girl. That was not so good for me.

[y mom was always spunky, and she is still full of energy. I hope

I c b ike her when I get to be her age. I do remember a very vivid
me or vhen I thought my mom was super-woman when we were on the
far . l dad must have been gone somewhere. We were out in the barn,
anc he iw was having babies. In my mind, I still have the total vision of
my 10i helping the sow have her babies.

    I can still remember being out in the garage plucking chickens.
On of y favorite meals is still chicken and dumplings.

ven though I was only six when we left Wyoming, a work ethic
hac lro ly been instilled in Joe and me. We were taught, "You get the job
do1 , c your work before you go out and play. That was the kind of
atti de at our parents had.

'e had quite a few dogs, but the most special one was Lady. We
hac i j crabbit we found as a bunny. It would go over to Lady, and she
wo d it nurse. The dog and the cats just treated the jackrabbit like it
bel igc

think every kid remembers their first day of school. The school
bus lro up, and I got on. Of course, my older brother, Joe, got on, and
he 1e\ vhat he was doing. I thought I knew what I was doing, so I went
anc iat ith Sandy Snider, because she was a friend of ours. After the
sch ol y was over and we were home, my brother asked me, 'What were
you loi ?' I replied, 'What do you mean?' He looked down at me, 'You
we ai sat by Sandy--you don't go sit with older kids, you sit with the
litt ki ' I don't think Sandy cared; she never said anything.

fter we left Wyoming, I tried to hold onto all of my memories.
Wl n would get together with the cousins and aunts and uncles, I
ren ml sitting at the table, and even though I was still very young, I
wo d , 'I want to move back to Wyoming and live on the farm.' They
wo d tease me a great deal. 'Oh yeah, Ginger, you want to go back.
Yo wa to be a farmer and go back and live on the farm.'

fter all these years, I still love to come back to Wyoming. This
tim I me back with my son, Kelly, who will be seventeen in August.
I'n jus hrilled he wanted to come here for our vacation and enjoy the
bea ty. still tell people I am from Wyoming and always try and describe
the un s. My foster daughter now has a three-year-old daughter. When

143

she came to live with us, she rode my horse, and she loves to garden, so I guess my love for farming rubbed off on her. I still love to garden.

When we moved back to Tuscan, we lived on a city block. I somehow managed to keep a sheep for 4-H on our place. I always wanted a steer, but there was no way for that in the city. The first year I had the sheep project, the neighbors complained about the noise. So I had to send my sheep up to my 4-H leader's house. The next year, I got two sheep so they could keep each other company and not make so much noise. They would start bleating real early in the morning about five. My bedroom was upstairs, and I didn't want to come down that early, so I would take a big bucket of grain to my room the night before.

When they would wake me, I would just open the window and dump out the grain. My dad used to think that was real funny, because I had figured out how to be a farmer in the city and not get out of bed real early.

Being in 4-H was fantastic for me when I was growing up. I would go to 4-H camp and the fair every year. Our club had wonderful leaders, and we had lots of friends that my dad had known growing up.

My projects included rabbits and sheep. I tried the sewing and cooking projects and also participated in judging. I do remember doing a demonstration on television. I thought that was something really special. I think the Junior Leader project prepared me to enjoy working with children. I enjoy being around people and love kids, so I know that 4-H had a big part in helping me to become who I am today.

I have so many good memories, and in some ways it is sad to come back to Wyoming, but it is also just a wonderful experience to be here again."

ALICE AND HARLEY BRIGHT

From the onset of this research project, Harley and Alice had encouraged me. I remember early on they had sent the most gracious letter. Whenever I would see them, it was the same--always a smile, and "How is it coming?" I looked forward to this interview, and I was not disappointed, as they are both wonderful historians.

I began with Harley. Tell me about your service time.

was in the 25th Infantry Division, which was called "Tropic
Division," that is based in Hawaii. I joined them over in New
and from there, we went to New Caledonia and up to the
s where we were in battle for five-and-a-half months. After that,
came the atomic bomb, and things were settled to where we were
an for occupation. My job basically dealt with communications
United States.

/here did you meet Alice?

Well, after I got out of the service in 1946, I went in partnership
cle, with my dad's backing, in western Colorado between Aspen
t, Colorado. It was an interesting little place called Snow Pass.
ranch on Snow Pass Creek, and it is beautiful country. While
there, I would go to the Saturday night dances at Basalt,
le, and so on. I finally had the good fortune to meet Alice, and
on she was the number one girl, I'll tell you!

/e have been married since October 4, 1950. By that time, I had
tten word of the good drawing on the homestead project up here
, Wyoming. So then, after our wedding and honeymoon, we
in this old 1947 Studebaker pickup and brought most of our
s, shall we say, and came up here. We got here in December.

must have been quite a shock for Alice when she saw this
ome, a tar-papered barracks from the internment camp. Some of
er was flapping in the wind. But she was a brave girl and stuck
e didn't catch the next bus back to Colorado." Alice related her

guess it was what I had expected to a certain extent. It was much
en and dry than I thought it would be. But these were just two
at we had to overcome.

/e rented an apartment in town while we fixed a kitchen in our
and then we lived in the kitchen and the so-called "utility room"
s large enough for just the bed. We had to take the door off in
et the bed to fit. But that is where we spent the first winter. In
n was born while we were still in the kitchen area before we got
remodeling done.

145

We started building partitions and putting in sheet rock. One thing I remember about that was the boards in the rafters. The wood was real hard, so I would have to get up in the attic with the sledge hammer to hold the boards down while Harley was pounding up underneath. He would say, "Go north, go south." Well, I didn't know my directions. We had a lot of fun doing that, trying to get those boards to hold still long enough to get the sheet rock on.

I grew up on a farm and ranch in Colorado where we did irrigation and had cattle, so I was glad to come with Harley here. My parents never really said much about us coming to Wyoming. I am sure they would have rather had me closer to home, but they just accepted it as life."

Harley added a comment.

"I thought the Ralston Bench community was great. We were all in the same boat, you know. It was really neat, a bit of education and experience, and even adventure. To think, here were 104 families, all about in the same boat. They all seemed to be readily willing to help each other when the time came. It was a rare experience that a very small percentage of the people have had the opportunity to go through. How do you feel about it, Alice?

Well, I guess I never felt it as a hardship as such. To me, it was more of a challenge. We did what needed to be done from day to day. And always looking forward to better crops next year, developing a bigger garden, doing this, doing that, it was just life. I think the wife had a big part in making the homestead successful and in raising a family, of course.

We did a lot of canning. We would go to the pea viners and get green peas, but because we didn't have running water, by the time we washed off the dirt, it would have been less work to pick them ourselves. We always had a big garden.

We used to take our clothes to town to wash at Humphrey's Trailer Court.

After we got the barracks moved to our unit, the very next improvement was building an outhouse." Alice continued.

"That first year we were here, we did get homesick. I guess it was because all of our families were back home, wherever home was, and being newly married, I guess I was quite homesick. The first holiday that we

146

we   h   , we were invited to a family's house that we didn't really know
too   el   out Harley had gotten acquainted with their son, and she just took
us   .   e was a lot like my mother, and we just had a great time, so that
is c et   ig that we did. We were married the first part of November and
car   u   here the first part of December. Why we didn't stay and enjoy
Ch   tn   with the family, I don't know. In the wintertime, we didn't have
to l d   g any plowing or anything, but we thought we had to be up here
for   iis omestead. I guess we were excited. We must have really thought
we   ar   d to get started!

            remember one thing that we did, when you talk about making do
wit wl   you have. When I was pregnant with Duane, which was the first
chi , t   husbands were taking agricultural classes in town. Harley, Leon,
anc qu   a few of the guys were going to town in the evenings together.
Th   w   ild take turns driving, because all the families only had one car.
Ha   y   ould put a five-gallon bucket out with sand and light in it. This
wa   to   e used in case I went into labor. Laura was supposed to be
wa   hii   Of course, we didn't have trees at that time. If I needed help, I
wa   su   osed to light the oil bucket, so she could tell I needed help. It
nev l   opened that way, because most farm children are born in the
mic le   the night.

            /e had waited for electricity for a long time, so when the REA was
put ng   our lines, we just wanted them to hurry. That was an important
tim

            think the most important thing for us was the closeness of our
coi nu   y. Everyone was willing to help, and it created such a
coi oar   nship and support for each other. I mean, we didn't think
any iin   about correcting our kids and the other children as well, if they
we   ir   anger or getting hurt or something. I think the time element had
a l to   with the way we lived. We just had so much
wo   t   o, we didn't have time for disrespect." Harley
     ol

            Getting back to the importance of the wife--in Alice's case, she
hac rai   ng in growing up on a ranch and running a tractor. So we could
lite lly   ike turns at times, where if I had to be gone, she could keep the
sch lul   going, you might say, by running the tractor or combine. She did

147

all the hauling when we were raising beets. I can remember our son at that time. Gary was hardly a year old, riding down on the floor of the truck as she would go back and forth to load the beets. But that was really an added help to me, because she had previous experience on a ranch and farm and knew irrigation, and those

were important pluses for me, that was for sure." Alice

added a comment.

"One thing that Donna, who is our daughter, tells us that she remembers, and Duane, too, is when we used to walk across the field to go down to the Banks' for an evening of visiting or whatever. She says, "I can still remember the stars and how it looked at night to be walking out across the field." This is something that I can remember from parents--that we walked to the neighbors." It is things like this I think that our kids remember more so than other things--the quietness, and the brilliance of the stars, and the family unity.

We visited with all of our neighbors, but those that lived closer we spent more time with. We were real close to Leon and Laura Banks, the Montgomerys, and the Cobbs. We played a lot of canasta.

We had a milk cow. We made our butter and had our cream and all that. I sometimes wonder if my thumbs bother me now from milking so much. Harley milked in the wintertime, but when he was irrigating, I did it.

We had pigs and chickens, too. I can remember building little old wire chicken pens to keep the chickens in, and the eggs and the whole bit.

In the early years, we raised seed barley, oats, and peas, both seed and the canning peas. Gradually, we graduated to pinto beans, and we fed cattle. We had corn for silage and alfalfa as our hay crop and cash crop. Then we got into sugar beets when we could get an allotment. I think the sugar beets took the most work and expense in raising, but they were a good all-around crop. Tak Ogawa helped us with the spring and fall work while I was finishing my degree. So when we retired from farming, he rented our place.

The two older kids were in 4-H. We never felt we had the time or the money to bring them into town for football or whatever was going on. The kids' 4-H projects were gardening, and Duane was in leather craft.

Ed M e taught Donna sewing. She still makes her own clothes and so
for ."

arley commented.

One of the activities Duane enjoyed was hunting. I really didn't
hu   ur   our oldest son got a license, and we went out in Sand Cooley
no   t o Ralston Bench. He got his first buck deer. We would hunt
sor tir s on the South Fork. It was mostly because of his interest in
hu   ng   Of course, I had lived down in Colorado, and we had deer on our
pla y   r around. Now, fishing--Alice and I enjoyed the trout fishing up
in   is   untry and got to go occasionally, but the farming was such a
pri ity hat you didn't let other activities interfere too much. Sunlight and
No   1 l k were our favorites for fishing. It was always nice to get up in
the 10   tains, but we have certainly always enjoyed the Ralston Bench.
Lo   a   ne whole perimeter and see the Rocky Mountain ranges. It was
nic to   t into them occasionally and see them, to actually camp under
tho tr   up there near the fishing creeks. When we moved to Powell and
lef ne   rm
aft 4:   ears, we felt we had been fulfilled." Alice
          lded this.
          had mixed feelings. You hate to leave a place where everything
is s me   ing you have had a hand in. When we first moved
out o t   unit, there was not a stick or can or anything."
          huckling, Harley recalled what they encountered.
          There wasn't even a worm. We brought worms from my folks'
pla ir   olorado to get worms started in the soil. But as we got older, we
ren ml   ed the years that we were snowed in and so forth, so maybe living
in   wr   the sensible thing to do. And I have enjoyed it, as there are
adv nta s to be in town also. The oldest son, Gary, now owns the
hoi st   d, and the land is leased. So, in fact, it is still in the family.
          think all the children feel an attachment to the homestead. Our
old t s   and daughter do not live here now, but they always enjoy coming
bac h   ie, renewing their ties, you might say. Gary worked for the
aer pa   in Salt Lake and then moved to Dearborn, Michigan, and worked
for or   s a mechanical engineer. He gravitated to the east, but after he

149

was married and had their third child, he decided perhaps out west was best, and they moved back to Wyoming."

Alice described the windbreak of trees.

"It was a good stand, but in farming, we were so busy we didn't always care for it as we should have. Harley planted 400 trees with a shovel, and I think they all lived. Now, some of the elm trees are dying."

Harley spoke up.

"For the most part, we do have a windbreak on the homestead. I planted the trees before Alice and I were married. That was the first smart thing I did. A windbreak is important, because we do get wind on the Bench.

We didn't buy more land, because we thought we would have to get larger machinery and hire someone to help and didn't think it would be worth having the extra amount of work. Our first major change in our lives came when we decided to add another job that paid a definite salary. That job could be depended on, and we thought that would be good for us. There were times the hail, early frost, late or early snows all hurt us. So we took a three-year gamble. We took three years for me to go back and get a degree so I could teach. Of course, during this time, Alice did the farming. In order for our family to do this, the children had to go to a different school for two years, while I went to school. I went to Northwest College for one year and finished my degree at Arizona State University in Tempe. We decided on Arizona, so we could enjoy a warm winter.

Well, we found out that it was a hot place, and you shouldn't go there 'til November. When we came back to the homestead, I completed my teaching credentials by commuting to Billings. I got to be a student teacher here in Powell. The experience helped me to become a part of this school district. I taught for fifteen years. That made a long time for Alice to do most of the farm work in the fall and spring. I taught fourth and fifth grade.

When we went to Tempe, we put a tarp over our farm truck with the cattle guards on it. I fixed a couple of swinging beds for the children, a bed for us, and put the deep freeze under the tarp. When we found a place to rent, we had a hard time getting the truck parked for the winter. I guess we were looked at as hillbillies to be moving in with a farm truck,

but t w ked great. We just slept in the truck until we could find a place
to 1 nt, it it was so hot, we couldn't stand it.

he great thing about our community was the fact that we never
loc :d r doors when we were living there. In the early years, we could
lea fc 1 month's vacation to go see Alice's folks before the kids went to
sch ol. Ve could be gone that long and never worry about locking our
do(s.

he basic thing about our community is that we all started on a
coi no ground. The family all came together, and we all worked together
to 1 ilc ur community. A man's word was gold. The community club
wa 1 c esive unit and a gathering place for the 4-H kids and for different
bir da parties and celebrations. We had square dances there. Alice
enj /e(at more than I did. She grew up dancing so was better at it than
I w . e all worked for the same goal; we were working to survive. We
wo ed make our homes, raise our
far ie and develop the homestead into a farm." Alice
lked of the early years.

Dur children were all small, we didn't have hired help, so the
nei lbc just had to help each other, and we did. There were no
bat sit s. We helped each other, if there was a need to help with the
chi rei If I were talking to young people today, I would tell them to have
pat nc for one thing, and another thing would be to approach life with a
pos iv(ttitude. Sure, you are going to have ups and downs, and you are
goi g t(ave spats within the family. You are going to have kids that don't
mii at mes, but that is just something to overcome. You never throw up
you ha ls and say, "Well, I'm done, I'm through, I'm quitting," because
you :ai quit, and keep going, just hang in there.

/hen we first irrigated, we didn't have siphon tubes. The ditch
bar s v uld wash out. We would grab some straw bales or whatever we
hac 1ai / to hold the ditch bank. Walking in all that mud up and down
wa 10 l fun either.

he children were with us all the time, even when they were babies.
We vo l set them at the end of the field in a cardboard box and strap them
on tra or. They were always in the field with us.

After the children were in high school, they became involved in wrestling, gymnastics, and swimming. Our daughter was the state diving champion for two out of three years. So then they would be gone from home, but we expected them home at a reasonable hour. There is no doubt that the impact of both parents and the togetherness that we all felt for each other helped make them great kids and adults.

It was hard to imagine how quickly a snowstorm could take on dangerous aspects out on Ralston Bench. It was just a few miles into town. Powell could not even be having snow, and within an hour, our community could be having a white-out with snow drifts too deep for a school bus to get through. It was always a worry to parents, because it became a dangerous situation for the children to be put into. There were times when the Heart Mountain community had no other alternative but have their children stay in town with other families. This was a sizeable number of children to find homes for in short notice.

I think all of the families have memories of being snowbound. It created more work with the livestock, but if our families were safe at home, it was kind of fun. That meant you didn't have to clean the house. You didn't have to do anything. You could just sit and watch it snow and hear the wind blow. But, of course, the worst thing is that the chores were terrible. You just didn't want to be out in the snowstorm.

I think four or five days was about the longest stretch before the graders could finally come and get us out. The worst year was in 1978-79. We had drifts 12-15 feet deep on each side of the road. We had drifts by the house where our oldest son could crawl up on the drift and step over onto the roof of the house. We really had some snow that year, but that happened to be an unusual situation. As far as the roads being drifted up for car travel, that happened many times over the years.

I didn't like being snowed in sometimes when we thought we should be in town for something, but hey, we always had canned goods and stuff on hand. It wasn't that bad. It was just kind of fun to play in the snow and walk on the drifts and dig tunnels with the kids. That was great.

Growing up in the mountains of Colorado, we were used to snow. We can remember in those early years when we would ride from our ve would pass through Vail Valley, and there was only one ranch. are hundreds of people in condominiums and ski resorts.

he winters in Aspen were easier, in a sense, because we didn't wind. When we had snow, we had snow. It was graded, or or whatever needed to be done, and then it stayed there until

Alice reminisced.

When I was in high school, I went to school in Aspen, and we had town during the week, and the folks would come to get us on the My roommate and I would go peek in the windows of all those s that were closed. That was just the time they were starting to first towers of the ski building. Of course, all the farmers thought he silliest thing they had ever heard of. This will never work and We herded sheep right in through Aspen when I was a kid. But, , that has been a long time ago." Harley sat listening with a ook on his face.

Well, I don't know what is really going on. I do know that, in this te nineties, and now into the new century, the farmers are having me, because prices are not keeping up with the growing cost of There have got to be some major changes in our government's ith other countries, if we are going to save our own agricultural very year, we hope that these renters that are taking over our those sons and daughters that are keeping the homestead going r break on prices so they can stay in business. This is a life that ple love and enjoy, but things have got to be better balanced on mic situation so the farmer can stay in business."

lice talked of those early years before there were phones on ench.

The thing I missed most was probably the telephone in order to ontact with relatives back home, because that was the only thing d, and I can remember going to Ralston to call the folks.

he friends in Ralston brought out the message that my mother was pital and that type of thing. We have been talking about being hbors. She was in the hospital with a stroke at the time, and they ect her to live. Jack Donnelly brought his car over and said, 'You are not going to Colorado in a pickup,' because that is all we had, and I was pregnant. He said, 'Take my car!' So we took his car to Colorado to be with my mother."

Harley commented that they drove the car 1,000 miles. So that is how neighbors helped each other.

"Sometimes, we don't appreciate the beauty of nature until we get older. But the green of the barley fields when they are first in the spring and then when they start to turn in the fall and almost make a golden wave. Ah–these are things that just make you feel unexplainable, I guess. They are things that you appreciate and you enjoy."

Alice thought her favorite seasons were spring, because of the newness and the trees of year. "It is a time when you have too much of everything."

Harley added to the conversation.

"I know. I certainly feel sorry when I think of all those kids in the big cities that don't even know Mother Earth, you might say, just asphalt and concrete. They can't even get out and see the stars, or the moon, or the sun at the different stages. I think country kids really have a bonus, an asset so many of our world's population doesn't have, so I am very happy and thankful God gave them to us to grow up on a farm. As Alice said, I think seasons are tremendous. I would not live so far south that all you had was summer, or as far north that all you had was winter. Even though we had cattle and would have to get out and suffer a little cold, or even get frostbite, it always felt so good to come in where it was warm.

The canals were a concern when the children were small. We had cement tubes that came down over our property. It was dangerous, and yes, we did worry about it. In fact, for years we covered it in the spring with pig wire, and in the fall we would take it off, because the snow would build up on it."

Harley gave a capsule of his thoughts of the homestead.

"I think one of the great things this homesteading experience probably taught everyone, including the kids as they grew up, that to be successful in life, you had to be willing to work, to apply yourself, and certainly to be willing to obey the laws, because these all help to make the well-rounded person. What is yours is yours. What belongs to someone

els(is (:irs, not yours to steal or take away from. I think the feeling of
sha ng 1d being unselfish in our actions, in our relationships with other
pe(le : : things that we all learned well, being on this homestead project."

N .RGIE AVERY BRUSAU AND DAUGHTER, LINDA CHILDS

met with Marjorie Avery Brusau and her daughter, Linda Childs,
in 1 y o ce in Lovell. The conversation began with Marjorie telling us of
her irs npressions of Wyoming.

Th first thing I remember about Heart Mountain was the sagebrush.
My 1us nd and I came to Wyoming May 7, 1949. We were living in
Ri(fie , Utah, when we saw an advertisement in the paper announcing
ap[ca ns to veterans for homesteads in the northwest part of Wyoming.
here were no trees, only the barracks, canals, and dirt roads. I
did t a ually arrive on the homestead until March of 1950. I came with
the nil en to a barracks with no modern conveniences. Margie Carol was
bo1 ir 946, Linda was born in January of 1949, Lorna was born in
Fel 1a1 of 1950, and Ivan was born in April of 1955. When we came to
the on stead that March, Lorna was three weeks old, and the oldest was
thr . 1 oking back on that time, I wonder how we managed. It was just
sor th ; we did. We were young and knew we had to get that farm in
sha :. lidn't resent working so hard. We had a sense of pride in having
the arr

'e raised a big garden and did lots of canning. We lived in the
bar ck vith the small children. It was so badly built that the wind just
wh tle n through the cracks. The baby didn't even catch a cold that first
wi1 :r. he was a healthy little baby.

didn't know about the Japanese Relocation Camp until I came to
W) mi . I had sympathy for the people who lived there. I know it had
to 1 h: l. What we did with the barracks we received was to use part of
it f a achinery shed, and we built the house out of the other half. The
ho1 e i till there and being used."

larjorie's daughter, Linda, began to talk about the homestead.

155

"I guess I didn't know anything else. It was just life, but I really enjoyed growing up out there. It just seemed like everybody was really close, all the kids were close, and we played with the neighbors. I never thought I would have wanted any other childhood.

Since I was only a year old when the folks moved to the homestead, I don't have any first impressions. I do remember we had a potbelly stove and a couple of wood stoves in the barracks. When the folks were remodeling the kitchen, the stoves kept being moved to different places in the house.

Of course, riding on the school bus is a great memory. We had to get on awfully early, and we kind of got home late. Half the time, you didn't get your homework done, so you finished on the bus. You got help from somebody else in the class, and we just had fun, but it was cold on the bus. Everyone tried to get in that one seat that was right in front of the heater. On the lane where we lived, the snow would drift over the roads, and there were a lot of times we would be snowed in.

One year, there had been so much snow, and we had missed a lot of school. Dad decided to put us all on the tractor and drive across the field to meet the bus on a road that had been plowed out. We were home a lot in those early years during the winter.

There was always something to do when we were growing up on the homestead. We were out riding our horses or playing. Lorna and I liked to go down to the drainage ditch where there was a dugout. We found fox holes and old, petrified wood. We learned to entertain ourselves with the simple things, but I just don't ever remember being bored. We never watched much TV.

We kids were in charge of separating the cream from the milk. That never seemed like much of a chore, because when the bucket of cream was full, we got to go to town, and we got the money for the cream.

I never did learn to milk the cow. My sister, Carol, thought it was because I always had such long fingernails. I don't know, but that was something I never did.

One thing that was kind of sad was when Dad would be out mowing the hay, mother rabbits would get caught, so he would bring the

bal ra its home for us kids to raise. Sometimes, we would raise the baby
pig)ns r pheasants, or other small animals.
'e had cows, and horses, and sheep. We never liked the sheep
ver m 1, because they would always get out of the fences.
'e had a lot of 4-H projects, and we took a lot of animals to the
fai W ad horses, rabbits, calves, and that sort of stuff. The 4-H program
hel d mendously as far as introducing us to different things. We were
rea y i ated out there on the homestead. In those early years, we didn't
do lo 1 town. Our 4-H program was really strong, and it just seemed
tha oi g 4-H was what everybody did. We really had so much to do in
our ow community that we didn't need to go other places. Our
nei ib ood was close. If I needed anything, I knew I could have gone
to y my neighbors, and they would have helped us.
remember one winter when a storm came, and we lost electricity
for re r four days. We had a coal stove, but it had an electric thermostat,
so di 't work. I guess we had what you would call a "block party" in
on ft homes until the electricity came on. I don't know how the adults
ma ge but we kids had a great time. Our neighbor's house was just
pac ed t with people, but everybody was warm, and everyone had a good
tim I ou lived on Heart Mountain, you were just part of the group."

Margie added a comment.

t's hard to explain, but we were all just so close that the children
all ne to respect their neighbors and elders. We watched out for each
oth 's ildren, and they were just taught to behave." Linda talked about
goi t he neighbors'.

When we went over to each other's houses, we knew we had a
tim lin . If we got to be there for half an hour we thought that was a treat.
here was a lot of snow out there and a lot of wind. We had a shed
out ac hat was probably about eight feet tall. The snow would drift up
to t t of the building, and the neighbor kids would come over, and we
pla d the snow. Lorna and I would go treasure hunting in the snow,
anc ve ed to watch it sparkle when the sun came up.

one of those big snowstorms, our front yard was covered about
fou fe leep. Dad went out with his big shovel and started digging us out.
A s ow ow came up the road, and the fellow saw my dad out there, so he

157

just pulled into our yard and cleaned it all up and went on his way. All the neighbors gave him a bad time over that with a lot of teasing, because our yard was the only one cleared out, so I guess he was just lucky that day.

Living out like we did, with the mountains surrounding us, we grew to have a real love for the beauty in nature. All three of my children are good artists. One of the teachers at Northwest College commented that it was unusual. "It doesn't just happen that three children in one family can draw so well." I told him it didn't come from me, but I do have a love for beauty, and I think I have instilled into my children an appreciation for life. And I suppose that has come from growing up out there on the homestead. I still love a snowstorm." Margie talked about raising the babies.

"In order to have warm milk for formula for the babies in the middle of the night, I would boil the water before I went to bed and put it in a thermos and then mix milk with it. It was hot water, and it would be just about the right temperature in the middle of the night. We didn't think this was a hardship; it was just our way of life. I don't remember the wives sitting around and complaining. We were all in the same boat. We had left our families, and our neighbors became our family. I really don't think we resented working so hard. I worked outside a lot. I drove the tractor."

Linda wanted to tell me how her mother took care of the children when she worked in the field.

"Our mom would help out on the tractor all the time except for the plowing. She did just about everything else. She would put us in the car at the end of the field with a bunch of toys, and then she would make one round on the tractor. She would stop and check on us and see how we were doing and then make another round on the tractor and stop and check on us. That is how she managed to work out there with little babies. You know, you couldn't put them on the tractor.

Before we had electricity, we used kerosene lanterns. We would have to pump them up, and they had mantels on them. We went to town to do the laundry and then would haul water back to the farm for drinking. We didn't have a well until we got electricity. I guess it was about three years we hauled water.

When we get together with the family, we like to tell the stories about the horses. Carol was the one that was so good with the horses. She

wa ... a "horse person." She traveled all over on her black horse. We
ne... to ride with a saddle. I think we had a saddle, but Mom wouldn't
let ... with it. I think she was afraid we would get caught in it. You
kn... off and get caught in it or something. I had a horse that tripped
all ... e. She would go down on her front feet, and I would always slide
off ... ck, and then she would be looking down at me like, "What are
you ... down there?" Our farm was near the badlands. We rode horses
out ... a lot, but most of the time we stayed close to home when we
pla ...

... om was afraid of the canals, so I didn't play in them, but Carol
wa ... more adventurous; she lived in the canals. Carol and Ivan would
go ... the drops. But I mainly caught water skippers and frogs. I
ren ... going out toward the badlands and finding a great big puddle of
tad ... nd would bring home bucketfuls of them. We would bring them
hoi ... watch them grow into frogs, and then we would put them out in
the an...

... doesn't seem to matter how many years down the road it is that
we av ... een away from Heart Mountain. All of us that grew up there in
tho ... y years still feel so attached. We still feel closeness.
It v ... ecial way to grow up."

... argie and Linda both agreed that the homestead was a special
pla ... many wonderful memories.

JEWEL CARTER

... those years, how delightful it was to be near Jewel Carter. Her
cor ... s exuberance for life would spill over onto everyone around her.
I lo ... orward greatly to our interview. She is just as I remembered her.
He ... nd, JB, had passed away in the last few years. He would have
ad... or to this afternoon, but we can only fondly remember his stories.
As ha ... read over the transcript, I realize I can never paint a picture in
sto ... Jewel has done with her erupting laughter, so many of the
dis ... will be in her own words.

159

I began the interview by asking Jewel how they had heard about the homesteads in Wyoming.

"Okay, well my aunt and uncle, Charles and Merle Nunley, homesteaded in 1950, I believe it was. And, of course, they regaled us with all the stories of this wonderful country in Wyoming.

At the time, we had just built a new home between Lawton and Apache, Oklahoma. We had been raising white-faced cattle. We got an idea to raise sheep which was a great big disaster. We went to Oklahoma City to see some friends and go to the Barnum and Bailey Circus. We made a fast decision to buy the sheep, and when they were delivered to us, we couldn't even recognize them. One of the sheep had a broken back. Telling the details of that would be quite a story, I will tell you. When we started lambing, the dead animal truck made its regular rounds by our house.

After the sheep experience, we began to settle into the community. JB became clerk on the school board, and we stayed busy taking the boys to basketball games. All during this time, the stories kept coming from Wyoming about what an exciting place it was to live. The twins had gotten with their friends and got to smoking some grapevine on the creek. They both broke out so bad, they couldn't go to school, so we decided to just pack them up in February of 1953, and we made a quick trip to Wyoming.

When we came through the Wind River Canyon, it was snowing, and the roads were so slick. I think it scared all of us. There was a blizzard on Heart Mountain when we arrived. We didn't have any idea how to get to Charley and Merle's, but some neighbors helped us, and we were so glad to be in a safe and warm place. They weren't home, but we knew they lived in a log home. After a while, we became nervous thinking we might be in the wrong house, but we saw some mail with the name Nunley, so we relaxed. After a while, Charley and Merle finally made it home with the help of their neighbor, Elmer Collar. We weren't used to the high altitude, so with the combination of that and the bitter cold outside, we had a hard time staying awake in the evenings. We had such a wonderful time visiting. Charley kept persuading us, so we decided to look for a homestead. We talked with Loran Otto and made a decision to buy his original homestead.

We moved to Wyoming. We discovered that first spring we knew nothing about irrigation or wild oats or Canadian thistle. We had never

160

hea l c them. The neighbors kept reminding JB always to remember,
wa   r r s downhill. But when he set his dam and the water would hit it,
he   vo that water ran uphill. At the time, we just had earth ditches. He
wo   d   notches in the ditch to let the water run down, not pulling the
dar T   water would just go everywhere. In those early days of learning
the iys ries of water, JB could hardly make it back to the house, he would
be   ) ti d. One day, he got so thirsty, he lay down on his stomach and
beg n t drink out of the ditch. A neighbor happened to come by. "JB, I
dor t tl k you had better be drinking that water; there is a dead deer up
the at ie head of the ditch.

When JB got the irrigation tubes set, he wanted to take us camping

in   ell stone. We all came back refreshed, but when we saw what had
hap en to the water while we were away, it became apparent we wouldn't
be   nn g off during the irrigation season any more.

e was always worried about his irrigating, so I thought I could

hel ou vith a ten-acre patch. I just couldn't set those tubes. I couldn't get
the vat to come out. I lay down on my stomach and sucked it out, but
the w just a little trickle. When JB came in he began to laugh, as I had
a r nd ne of mud around my mouth. He had to set all the tubes over, as
I ju d i't seem to have the knack.

would try and start the John Deere, but every time I would get on

the ld iosaur, I would forget about the gears, and JB would have to show
me   ga But we would finally get it started. Everybody did what they
had o and we didn't question it, because there was so much to do, and
it h i t e done.

When we told the twins about the outhouse, they said they

wo   dn go, and I said, 'Well, I guess you will.' During the big snow, we
wo   a ep path out there, and they decided the outhouse must be a way
of l e i his new land.

e didn't have running water, so every morning when JB would

lea , I ve him a bucket for water, and he would carry it into the house
for ie. i the evening, I would have him get me another bucket of water.
On   da I went irrigating with him, and after that, I never asked him to
car ai more buckets of water. I just decided I'd better do it myself.

161

Margaret Olson was visiting one day when we got our first hail. I didn't think it was doing too much damage, because in Oklahoma, the hailstones are so large, but these were fine pebbles, but it riddled our crops. We didn't have much to harvest that year because of the hail. The next year, the hail got our garden, but the neighbors were all so good to help out. Leonard and Edna Schaefer lived across the corner from us. She and I would can the garden produce. We would pick windfalls, cut out the bruises, and can the apples. The men all went hunting, and they helped to supply us with meat.

That first fall, JB's folks came. His mother was appalled that we would live there with weeds around the house. JB's Dad said, 'Well, I don't suppose there is anything here the cows won't get.' She always spent half a day cleaning the oven when she would come. I spent so much time cooking, the stove couldn't get cooled off before I was cooking again.

Everything was exciting to us, like when we got our first pig. When the sow had her first pigs, the boys hung over the fence, and it was a very special time.

The county fair was a very important time for the farmers. Every community had a booth just laden with produce. All of us took such pride in the exhibits. The kids were all involved in 4-H. Our social life revolved around the community and Mountain View Club. We had Brownies for the girls, and the boys had Scouts. The summer Bible School at the clubhouse was so important to us.

The summer Bible School at the clubhouse was so important to us. For several years, we had about 100 children attend from our community. The mothers taught the classes, and we just all worked together to help our children."

CARTER FAMILY

I knew this interview would be an enjoyable occasion, as the Carter family has always possessed a zest for life the whole community has enjoyed down through the years. Ronald and his wife, Helen, were unable to be with us. It is apparent that the family keenly misses their father, JB. He has left his children his sense of humor. JB was referred to as the great

sto tel :, and after listening to them, I couldn't imagine how Ronald
cou l h e topped what I heard. Tolbert and Ronald were twins and the
old t. hn was a few years younger. Roger and Julie were born after the
fan y d been in Wyoming for a few years.

w n't always easy to determine who was talking from the recorded
tap sc me of the stories will be told just as I heard them with very little
edi ig. n writing this chapter, I found myself laughing so hard, at times I
wo d l crying. I hope you, as the reader, are also able to paint pictures
in ur ind of life on the Carter homestead. "Well, this is Roger Carter.
We ot come with the folks to Wyoming to check it out that first winter,
bec isc ve three boys had been smoking grapevines, and all had poison
ivy nd uldn't go to school. We visited Merle and Charley Nunley in a
big no torm. Right off, we saw Jake Fulton on a horse named Smoky,
so w the first cowboy we saw in Wyoming.

he folks bought Loran Otto's place. There was a barracks with a
lot li rooms, as I remember. By the time we came to Heart Mountain,
the w electricity, so we were real modern. We had an outdoor toilet
abc t l hundred yards from the house, and none of us boys were going
to e i We had a potbellied stove in the kitchen and some propane heat.
e had a little hand pump about fifty feet from the house. It was
rea ;oc water. Sometimes the neighbors would come over and get some
wa r. e water seemed to taste better if you hauled it by bucket into the
hot e. lbert would carry the buckets of water in, and Mom would heat
it a l p it in a big galvanized tub. We would fill up the tub with water,
but t v too much trouble and too time-consuming to do it more than
onc , s ve would always see who was going to be the last one to take a
bat l rybody wanted to be first. Since I was a little smaller than the
twi ;, l elieve I caught the last bath, and I sometimes wondered if I was
dir r c cleaner when I got out than when I went in. And, of course, there
wa no ay of rinsing or anything. Needless to say, we didn't take a bath
mo th once a week. Real cowboys didn't take baths.

here was another part of a barracks on the homestead that had
blo n wn before we came. Dad wanted to save the barracks to build
anc ier ilding. He sent us boys out there with sledge hammers and was
goi ;t ay us for our job. He had to go to town for something. We got

those sledge hammers, and we just busted it all up so he couldn't use one plank. We didn't save nothing, we just thought he wanted it tore down, and we did. We tore it down. We was awful good at tearing up stuff. When Dad got home, he was upset with us for some reason. Dad said he would pay us to tear it down, but he didn't pay up."

"I'm Julie Carter Kipp, and I am the youngest of the five. I was born in 1959. I think my life was a little easier, because we had plumbing by the time I was born. I remember we stayed at home and enjoyed life. Mom was always there, and when we were old enough to start 4-H, we went down to the clubhouse. There were probably 30 or 40 kids, it seemed like, that would meet there, everybody in the community. We would all have our projects like gardening, sheep, and sewing. That was pretty much our life outside of school. We never watched TV very much. We were busy with our animals or our
projects and going to meetings. It was a lot of fun." John
talked about his mother's cooking.

"The best thing about living on the farm was the great food. Mom always cooked really good meals. We had three big meals a day if not more, and then we had desserts in between. Meat was at every meal, and my favorite meal was the fried chicken and mashed potatoes with a lot of gravy and corn, and then, of course, homemade pie afterwards. You know, you have to have pie too, so that was just one of the meals. And then for breakfast, we would have the bacon and eggs and all that. I guess one thing I remember growing up was that we never had junk food. On Fridays, we would have hamburgers or tacos besides the seven-course meal, and that was what we considered junk food."

Tolbert told about the time he was supposed to be baby-sitting his little brother, John.

" I remember our dad did not allow us to cuss. Well, I was taking care of John one afternoon while the folks had gone someplace. Ronald and I got into a big fist fight and somehow managed to knock some holes in the wall. We moved some of the pictures around to cover the holes. In the meantime, John had gotten down one of Mom's jars of homemade plum jelly. It was half full, so he filled the rest of the jar with water.

) the next morning, we were all sitting there at the kitchen table

eat g] ıcakes. Dad saw the water floating on top of the jam jar. Since I

wa he ıe that was supposed to be in charge, Dad looked at me. 'What's

the ıat with you, why did you let John put water in the jelly jar?' I said,

'H(, 1 dn't see nothing wrong with it!' I couldn't believe how fast Dad

jun ıed) and jammed my head in that jar. I didn't know a head could fit

in ₂ vi(mouth mason jar, but my head

did I ₅ v immediately what was wrong with the plum jelly.' John

turned to Mom's cooking.

t's a wonder I lived, when I hear what my big brothers used to

ma ₂ n eat. Well, anyway, if there was anyone in the yard when a meal

wa rea ⁄, they were invited in to eat with us. Well, once we had a crew

of ₁ ₂n the farm shearing our 600-head of sheep. They came in from the

she , a it had been real hot out there working. Well, I remember I sat

ne∖ to ıe of the fellows, and he smelled like one of those greasy sheep

out ıeı ın the barn. Well, that day Mom had done her usual best; she had

co(₂d ⊃ast beef and everything, and my most favorite dish, boiled

cat ag(I sat there and ate my cabbage, and all of a sudden it tasted just

lik(⊃n(⊃f those old greasy sheep. So that was the end of my cabbage-

eat g ys for years. Just recently my wife, Gail, who has an Irish

bac gr(ıd, got me to eating boiled cabbage again. I am sure those sheep

she er vere good old boys, but that day eating cabbage will always stick

in ı ⁄ n ıd.

'hen I was only four or five, I liked to go out with my big brother,

Ro r, ıen he fed the sheep. But I was afraid of those big sheep, because

the w(d all come close to me, so I would have to stay outside of the pen.

On da Roger went up on the canal and shot a muskrat. He brought it

hoı ₂ t(ne. Well, that evening I went out to the sheep pens with him,

car ın₂ ıy dead muskrat. Well, those sheep all stayed away from me that

nig . for as long as he let me have it, I carried that old dead muskrat

aro ıd ₂ sheep pen feeling very brave for being such a little boy.

oger and I were great buddies. I remember before he went away

to ı ₂ ⁄ ıy, I was only six at the time. I was in the first grade, so I had to

go ₂ b at 8:00 o'clock. Well, Roger would stay up late, and I liked to

sne ⊀ (after our folks had gone to bed and watch TV with him. We

165

would watch "Inner-sanctum" and "Twilight Zone." I was already pretty scared watching those spooky programs, and then Roger would have to go to the bathroom during the commercials. He would tell me to be sure and watch out for the mama mountain lion sitting over there behind the big chair." Roger joined in.

"Yeah, I remember John was a little guy then. We would sit up real late, but the folks didn't know about it, because we were real quiet. John would have to go to the bathroom, but he would hold off just as long as he could. I would warn him, "Be careful, I'm not sure, but I think I just saw a big, curly tail over there. I think it's that mountain lion again." I could hear him running down the hall as fast as he could. Well, when it was time to go to bed, John didn't want to sleep in his own bed. He wanted to sleep with me every night, but he kept snuggling up so close to me, and I didn't want to crush him or roll over on him. He was pretty little, and I don't know how many times during the night he'd have me forced off on the floor. I'd just get up and come around on the other side and get back in bed, and then he'd work me off the bed. I complained all the time that I couldn't sleep, because he was underneath me, but we were such good buddies that I would let him crawl in with me every night."

Tolbert told about the time he and Ronald wanted to become veterinarians. They were quite young at the time. They had watched their dad out in the barn with the animals when he would have to vaccinate them. The folks had gone to town, so the boys decided they would get into the medicine chest and pull out iodine and whatever else they could find. They went out to the chicken pen and injected the hens with some of the concoction.

A few days later, Mom needed the boys to catch a chicken, so she could dress it out for chicken and dumplings. Well, Jewel began plucking the feathers off the chicken and discovered the skin was green, and blue, and red. She went and got JB, and they were real worried that the brood of chickens had a terrible disease. Now, Tolbert and Ronald figured the safest thing for them to do was to keep silent about the whole incident of wanting to become veterinarians. The folks got so worried, that they were going to call the vet to come out and tell them what terrible disease their chickens had, so the boys had to break down and tell them what they had done. For

the est f the summer, if the chicken they were plucking for supper had
mu cc red skin, it had to be thrown away. "Thank goodness, the folks'
trip o vn was a short one, or the whole brood of chickens would have
bec in ulated." Jewel talked about the cooking.

t was just the normal thing to do. I would just keep cooking. You
wo d breakfast over and start right into cooking for the noon meal. I
alw ys ent to town to buy groceries in the afternoon and would hurry
bac fo uppertime. There was always someone there. A few years before
my not r died, she commented, 'It sure would be nice to know how many
to s th able for.' I said, 'Why don't you just go out in the yard and count
hea s?' But that was when busy people didn't have time to visit, you know.
Wł n t y are eating, it is an opportunity to visit with people. We have
hac l of good times and exchanges around the table." Roger began to
tall

The 4-H program was a big thing for us. I took gardening projects
fro D othy French. Wallace McClaflin and Lloyd Snider helped me
dec le Hampshire sheep. Lloyd helped me pick out three older ewes
fro hi flock. That was how I got into sheep. I kept them for eleven
yea ;. d then Julie got into 4-H sheep. Dad was our flytie leader. When
we ad e fly-tying project, the Spierings and several other neighbor kids
car o r to the house."

onald started talking about his neighbor friend, Chris Fulton, who
hac '? Ford Roadster he was using for an irrigating car. The twins were
abc t fc teen at the time and thought it would be nice to have an irrigating
car)o. heir dad heard about a '36 Oldsmobile over in Cody.

he car was owned by a retired nurse who didn't know how to
dri , v ose husband had died. The sun had faded the top of the car, but
it h l r hair seats with a trunk on the back, and 20,000 original miles on
it. he r had sat there jacked up so long, that when we fired it up, the
wa r p np went out. We were able to drive it home, but it was a rough
rid wi those old tires. You couldn't get tires for the old car. Dad paid
her we y silver dollars for the car. But we kids were poor. We needed
tire fc our car, so we saved up and bought $2.00 tires at Merlyn's
Jur ya at Ralston. We put sixteen-inch tires on the car. Anyway, the car

167

gave us freedom. Dad had a spray outfit, so that winter we painted the car metallic blue and had red wheels with big whitewalls."

'When we were fifteen, we went and picked up all our friends. I mean, lordy, you couldn't believe all the kids we could get in that car. We'd go down to the community building and square dance. Oh, we loved that! That was when the Bebop came out. Oh, we were awful good Beboppers. We entertained the neighborhood from then on." Jewel talked about the twins' sixteenth birthday.

"On their sixteenth birthday, we had a party down at the clubhouse with that little 45 phonograph. We put streamers of paper across the ceiling and bought I don't know how many gallons of root beer, put ice cream in them, and they had root beer floats. JB would have the broom dance, and he kept them all dancing. A lot of them didn't want to get out on the dance floor, but JB saw that everybody was out dancing. They really had a good time. They danced to the 'One-eyed, one-horned, flying purple people eater.' That was one of
the biggest hits at that particular time, I recall."

Tolbert told of his fascination for farm equipment.

"We had modern equipment back in them there days. Dad had a B-John Deere for cultivating and for harrowing, and then he bought this huge G-John Deere. He just couldn't keep me off of it. It was a tumble bug plow. And I was almost 12 years old. I would go from sunup to dark on that tractor. I would put that G in low, and even under, and plow that sod. When I got done at the end of the day, it would be just a little strip. Hell, I thought I did so much.

That was the same year I was plowing up on the bend up there by Sand Cooley. I had gone to a movie the night before and got up about four o'clock to plow, and I got sleepy about nine or ten o'clock. I started shutting my eyes after I dropped the wheel in the furrow. I could catch me a little catnap, but I must have miscounted. I would close my eyes, count to ten, and that would give me enough time to hook my feet into the light bar and turn backwards, and get the pull on the tumble bug rope to make the flip. But my timing got off, and I went over a cliff, and the tractor turned over on top of me. I was pinned there for several hours before anyone found me.

didn't show up for dinner, so they came looking for me. The
almost drowned me. I had to hold my face out of the stream of
had rained the night before, so there was a heavy dew in the air.
r was still running while it was on top of me. The tractor got so
afraid it would set the diesel fuel on fire. When Dad came down
n me, he saw the wheels sticking up in the air, and boy, he was
un to Acott's place to get a tractor that had a farmhand. But then
d his mind and came down and got the old crescent wrench and
d that three-point hookup that I was pinned under. The bar was
ee which had gone dead hours before. So Dad took all the skin
ds, because the crescent wrench wouldn't stay adjusted. He was
ag me out from underneath the tractor. Dad took off running
ie house. Roger and Ronald were in the kitchen, where they had
e mousing all day. When Dad busted through the door, yelling
d to get me to the hospital, he found the both of them robbing the
d pecans we had picked." Ronald chimed in.

Ve thought we were in terrible trouble for stealing the pecans, but
ealized there was a bigger crisis on hand. Roger and I went out
look at Tolbert laying there. He was alive but looked real bad.
he seat down in the Nash and laid Tolbert
ere and took him to the hospital."

wel began to recall the events of the day.

was over at the Nunley's doing some ironing. Merle had gone
linois to her mother's funeral, so I was helping Charley with the
k. JB came and got me, and we went back and got Tolbert and
hospital. Tolbert had gotten some new irrigating boots, and he
ud of them. He was still wearing them, so they had to be cut off.
were just soaked with the diesel fuel. He had a dent in his leg
knee that stayed, and it had lost all feeling. If it had been much
would have lost his leg." Roger wanted to add his story of tractor

Vell now, we were at the point of no tractor, so Leonard Schaefer
d his international tractor. We were getting low on plowboys, so
ittle, bitty old me take that big tractor and plow. I would have to
lmost off the seat to depress the clutch. We were used to the John

Deere that had a hand clutch. A little boy wouldn't have too much trouble as long as the clutch was adjusted. So here I am coming in to refuel. I had never seen a tractor that could go so fast. I was pulling a tumble bug plow. The other tumble bug had been totaled out, so Dad was able to scrape up enough money to get a John Deere plow, but it wasn't a tumble bug. On one side, you would flip the rope, it dropped down, and then you'd get to the end of the field, turn around, or you would trip the rope. That side would come up and turn around, and then I would pull the other rope, and that side would go down. It was working alright, but I guess I was a little bored on the way back to refuel. I was happy at how fast it was going, but that wasn't exciting enough, so I started weaving the tractor and watched the John Deere plow. One wheel would come off the ground, come back down, and then the other wheel would come off the ground. I was having so much fun, but when I got to the corner, I was going just a little bit too fast. The plow just turned over and twisted itself off of the hitch. It went bouncing into the field. Needless to say, it was scrap metal when it came to rest. I eased the tractor into the yard, turned off the ignition, and came into the house to see if Mama had dinner ready. When I came into the kitchen, Mama kept on cooking and didn't even turn around. 'Why don't you go get the tractor fueled up, because it's going to be a few minutes before I have the food on the table.'

"Well, I said, I don't think there is no need of refilling the tractor. Dad looked out the window at the tractor. Well, man, all Dad could say was, "Well, that's my boy." I can't remember off-hand what we did from there on out, but we were shut down pretty bad right there at that time.

John didn't want to be left out of the tractor stories.

'Well, that reminds me of years later. We had a Ford Tractor, and I was raking hay or beans. I was coming home to get fuel. I was probably eight or nine at the time. I was coming around the corner where the telephone pole is. Well, it was a short pole those telephone wires were hanging on. I had the rack on the back, and I forgot I was going wide open. I was doing the Mario Andretti, cutting the corner, when all of a sudden I heard a "Wham!" I was making that corner in road gear when the rack hit the pole. The tractor spun around sideways and just bent the frame on the

Joh D re rake. I didn't tear up much machinery except that particular
tim

highlight of the summer was going up to Crandall fishing with
the -H nior Leaders. My dad was one of the chaperones, so I
got g We would go fishing with the flies we had tied."
he family talked about raising beets. Tolbert began.
When we started growing beets, we hated them. We literally
spe th ntire summer in that beet field. We tried to convince Dad to hire
pro ss als to thin the beets; we would water them, and then he could
ma a ofit. When we started out thinning the beets, we didn't have any
hoe got down on our hands and knees. And with our hands, we
thi ed eets. We were supposed to leave one beet every twelve inches.
On ev ing, Dad came home with some little, short handled hoes for us
boy er all we had been through, we saw those hoes, and we were so
pro 1 hem. I told Dad I was so proud of my hoe, I was going to save it
for y n, not knowing what I was saying.
I w ild ever have made a beet worker out of him.
we just got after it, and after a little while, our backs started
hu ng vful bad. Then Dad went back to town, and he came home with
lon h lled beet hoes. We stayed out in the beet field, until it was all
we ed We did a lot of talking. Brother Ronald was the storyteller. He
wo d p us entertained out in the field telling long, tall tales where we
we c ourse, always the heroes. And so we did, literally, spend the
ent s mer in the beet field, until just about the time we saw the beet
har st coming in. Then we knew it was time to be done for the year.
hen we were working, we could bitch and moan and complain,
but h Dad turned us loose, we would immediately take off running. We
wo d plum to Heart Mountain and the Woodruff horses up there.
We 1 se those horses until we caught the slowest one of them. Then
we re y to the next faster horse, until we all had horses. We had a chunk
of y e in our pockets, and after we ran the horses down, we'd tie the
rop ar d their chins, and then we would ride those horses to death. We
like to all over Sand Coulee exploring caves and catching rattlesnakes
anc tu If we had worked as hard as we played, we would have got a lot
mo d .

171

The big trip for the family every summer was July 1st when we would go to Yellowstone Park. Lyle and Dorothy French and their kids would go with us, and sometimes other neighbors would come too. Dad would get up early and set the water, and we would leave by first light. We would stop and have breakfast on North Fork on an open fire. No one had camp trailers in our group. We would tie a rope between two trees and hang a tarp over it and fill the ends with blankets. We three boys would have our blankets and pillows there under the tarp and tell bear stories all night. And Mom and Dad had this Nash with seats that folded down, and that's where they slept. They had plenty of security, and they slept rather comfortable, but we weren't that scared, you know, because we had each other for protection.

And then we would go fishing up on the bridge. Back then, people were allowed to fish on the bridge. Now you can't. Then we would rent a little boat, and in thirty minutes, we would have our limit. Dad, unfortunately, had to spend all his time baiting hooks and untangling lines, but he kept us all really excited. I mean, we really enjoyed it."

John spoke.

"When Roger went to the Army and the twins left for the Navy, I was the oldest at seven. Dad taught me how to drive the Ford pickup to go help set water. I would drive, following him, and bring him back and stuff. Later that summer, I graduated up to be able to set water while he was farming.

I caught a toad, and he became my pet. I would get up into the pickup and put this pet toad in the seat beside me when I went to set water. One day, as I was driving out to set the water, the toad jumped off the seat onto the floorboard. I reached down to pick him up and pulled the steering wheel along with me. I hit the borrow pit, went up through the fence, and hit a couple of fence posts. I got the pickup shut down. I remember thinking; 'Oh my, this is just terrible. I wrecked the pickup.' I went right back to the house and asked my mom if I was going to have to go to jail. Luckily for me, Charley Nunley came along and helped me pull the pickup out before Dad got home.

ad continued to train me to farm after my big brothers went off
to   rv   , but it was costing him money. That training doesn't come
che ɔ."

ɪlie talked of her days on the farm.
/Vell, I remember when I was little. In the summertime, it was so
mu ɪ f , because we would get to wallow in the waste-water ditches that
hac ɪll ɜ chemicals. The water was solid brown. You would just push
the ɪa ɜ aside and swim. We caught frogs down at Acott's where there
wa ɪ p ɪd that had black, stagnated stuff, and really good tadpoles grew
the .   ɜ'd go down there and catch buckets of tadpoles and frogs. That
wa ɔuɪ ɪg adventure for the summer.
         ɪ 1964, Vada Tirrell started a kindergarten class, because back
the th didn't have public kindergarten. So in her basement, she started
up cl ɜ. All the neighborhood kids that were five went there. Yeah,
the w Wayne McClaflin, Joanne Jirsa, Jenny Ogawa, and myself, and
the ɪsh / girl, and I can't think of all of them. But anyway, we learned
ouɪ ɪB ɜ and how to socialize. That was a real big thing, because I was
rea y s and had a difficult time socializing, because I was stuck on the
farɪ al he time. We had a cap and gown ceremony, and it was real
eve tfu

         adine Ashby taught tap dancing, and Mrs. Johnson down the road
gav pi o lessons, so we got a year of that, until we wouldn't practice
anɪ ɪoɪ "

         hey all talked about the clubhouse, and how it was the central
foc ɜ o he community. So many fun times, so many good memories, so
mu ɪ h ɪ work, such a great place of which to be a part. They all agreed
the wɜ glad they had come to Wyoming in those early years of the fifties.

EDNA COBB

         his afternoon, I am sitting in a comfortable living room with Edna
Co). ɜ and Charley had moved to town in 1987 because of his health.
Co pli tions relating to Parkinson's disease were the cause of Charley's
deɜ ɪ iɪ 991. Edna remarried after his death, and I did not realize until
thiɜ ɪftɪ ɪoon that Edna was twice widowed.

173

I remember Edna to have a quiet but gentle temperament. At first, she was a bit shy talking about her past, but I felt her interview was an excellent recording of the many details of those first years on Heart Mountain.

Both Charley and Edna Cobb were born in Arkansas, just fifty miles from each other. Both parents moved to Glendale, Oregon. Edna was a year old when the move was made to Oregon.

Charley and Edna met at a dance when she was only seventeen. They were married several months later. Charley was in the Army. He was sent to Europe; he landed in France and ended up in Austria. Edna mentioned that the crew with which Charley was stationed lived in a castle. I would have enjoyed hearing more of the details of that story.
He returned to the states in October of 1945.

One of Charley's friends, Samuel, kept telling him about homesteads being opened up for veterans in the western states. Samuel applied for all the homestead projects, and as far as Edna could recollect, his application was never chosen.

Ralston Bench Homestead Project is the only one Charley applied for, and he was successful in being chosen 24th on the list for receiving a homestead.

Charley came to Wyoming in December to move the barracks onto the homestead. Edna and the girls—Helen, five, and Barbara, three, came back with him in February 1950.

"That day in February when we arrived, it was twenty below, but the sun was shining with not a cloud in the sky. I was glad I could look over and see the town of Powell. It helped to give me a feeling that this place was not so desolate. When Charley came back to Oregon in December, he had brought with him some Celotex which was used to build a storage box for the canned goods I had laid up that summer. We were so grateful the jars withstood the cold in that little box, as that is what we lived on that first spring.

Our barracks wasn't ready to move into, so our family stayed in a small barracks apartment at the relocation camp. I remember meeting Ann and Earl Nelson, Bob and Vaudine Jirsa, and Loran and Ruth Otto. Ann made us some sandwiches that first afternoon. A friendship developed in those first few days that has lasted all these long years now."

E(ı did you feel homesick? Did it seem a bit overwhelming arriving
in /er -below weather with two small children?" "No, I never got
hoı ᵉsi(. I just made up my mind; this was going to be home, so that's
the /a) was."

looked over at Edna. So many years have gone by. The girls
are ro\ , both with grandchildren. Charley has passed away, but here
sits dr with a quiet dignity and resolve for life, faltering a bit in her
spe ·h. hat brief interview with this gentle soul spoke volumes in
relɛ on courage and tenacity.

ɪ t se first years, the family garden was a vital part of the summer
prc ct Edna described her first pressure cooker.

t would hold twenty-three pints. I would spend all day shucking
anc ut g the corn kernels off the cob to fill one load for canning. At that
tim w ɪad a wood stove that could hold the big canner. We carried water
fro th water pump across the driveway. We had a small ice chest that
wo ed ɪuite well for refrigeration. After we got an electric stove, I got
anc ıeɪ ressure cooker. After the girls got married, I would help them
wit th(canning. I don't can anymore, since I have quit raising a garden,
but ı t ᵴe early years, the canned food was very important.

don't think the girls minded the barracks too much. When the
wiı b v, the Celotex walls would wave in and out, but it never cracked
the /al ɪper, which was surprising. Each family was given a warming
sto ᵹ, t we also had a coal stove until we got electricity.
We)ui he new house in 1955.

ɪat first year on the homestead, the girls got on the school bus at
7:0 a.ɪ and got home about 4:30 in the afternoon. I remember that
Sw e (ᵴon was the bus driver in those first years.

was nice when we got phones. There were four families on each
linɛ so was important that the phone wasn't tied up for a long time. We
see ed ɪ all work together to make it manageable.

/e belonged to the Mountain View Community Club and the 4-H
Cl .] ɪught sewing for a while. I only had a treadle sewing machine, so
tha s \ at both girls learned to sew on. I didn't feel I was very good, but
wit a ᵈle pushing here and there, we managed to get the 4-H projects
doı . ᵉlen and Barbara don't sew much now because of their jobs.

175

Helen's daughter, Rhonda, sews an awfully lot. She took top honors with her 4-H goats and received honors for her sewing projects.

For a few years, we raised green garden peas for seed. I have tied several thousand sacks of peas. We raised dry beans, barley, and hay seed that first year. We were lucky when we were able to buy some more land. The prices of barley and beets and beans were high, so we got better money and were able to pay off our house finally. We only owed for a John Deere tractor, a small disc, and spike-tooth harrow. Our neighbor made a wooden float that used to level the ground off. We had hardly any sagebrush and some cactus. Charley used a two-way plow that he had to trip at each end of the field.

I did enjoy the farm, but after Charley got Parkinson's disease, he could no longer drive, so we had to move to town in 1987."

ELMER AND TINY COLLAR

The interview with Elmer and Tiny was interesting. It was hard for Elmer to hear some of the conversation, but they helped me with some of the details of homesteading I hadn't known before.

Tiny recalled the years the children were born.

"Well, Judy lives up on the South Fork now. Her last name is Baggs. Bill lives in Athena, Oregon. He works for the Forest Service. His office is in Walla Walla, Washington. Randy lives in Texas. He has his own business as a contractor. Marsha lives in Longmont with her husband, Mike. They have a 30-acre farm with cows, horses, chickens, and ducks. She swore she would never marry a farmer, but they farm there.

Judy was the oldest; she was born in 1947. Bill was only six weeks old when we came; he was born in 1949. Randy was born in 1952, and Marsha was born in 1954. We were pretty busy those first years with young babies and starting the farm.

We came up to the homestead in February of 1949. We could have stayed at the relocation camp, but the conditions were about the same, so we came on out to the homestead.

Boy, it was cold the day we got here. Man, that wind was a blowing and tumbleweeds a-coming at us, and I asked Elmer, 'Well, where's our

pla ?' [e said, 'I don't know?' The landmark we looked for was an old
plo tl sat down here on the corner of the road. Elmer found the plow
but till asn't for sure where our land was.

/e stayed with the Montgomerys for a week while Elmer got the
bar ck noved to the homestead. We swept it out and lived in one room."

iny told of her first feelings.

just thought it was cold and windy, and, oh, with the little
nev)or Elmer added, 'You wanted to go home.' Tiny replied, 'Yes, I
did I b ged Elmer that night to go back home. I was really homesick for
a w ile Oh, I just thought, How am I going to live here with this baby?
He iac it better than I did. He just slept. So we did okay, but boy, it was
qui a ange."

had to stay home and have a baby when he came up to pick out
the nii

lmer was excited about the place. He wrote me a letter and told
me ov retty it was with the snow on the mountains. He just loved it.

f course, you know, we had to haul water and had to take the
lau lry town, and it was quite a thing. We had an outdoor toilet, but we
we us l to that, because we had the same in Oklahoma.

ll of us that came in those first years were in the same boat. No
mo ;y t lots of kids. I mean, we used to get together and play cards and
do in together, but when TV came, that ruined it right there."

Elmer talked about the irrigation.

Yeah, the irrigation was quite a thing to learn. All we irrigated
wa ora e dogs out of their holes. I couldn't imagine how I was going to
get ie iter all over this land. One day, I was sitting up there on the ditch
bar w ching my irrigation job, and along came Leon Banks. He says,
"Tl t v er will run just fine without you sitting here watching it."

ow, when the kids get together, they tell a lot of things that we
did t l)w they did. Marsha was the smallest, and she had a hard time
kee ing p with the rest of them. Sometimes, when she would be lagging
beh id. e older ones would tell her a bear was going to get her to get her
to 1 a.

arold McHose lived just down from us. I remember whenever
we ot be snowbound, here he would come with a bunch of groceries in

177

a bucket. He wanted to make sure our kids were being fed. He lived alone all those years up here on the homestead. He was sure good to our family. He was out working on his tractor when he had a heart attack. For some reason, he had taken the tractor out of gear. Rick Asher drove by and saw him out there, didn't think he looked right, so he turned around and came back, and sure enough, he

had passed away. Rick said he lost a little sleep over that."

Elmer talked of how the kids worked.

"Well, one thing, the kids had to work for what they got. We didn't just go along and buy them a car and give it to them and let them take off.

We liked to fish. We would go up to Buffalo Bill Reservoir and Yellowtail and even would fish in Alkali Creek. I haven't wet a pole for four years. Some of the best fishing is right down there behind Wallace's on Alkali.'

Tiny talked about Gage, Oklahoma where she grew up.

"Well now, I knew Edna Mae. We all went to Skunk Hollow School. I knew her sister, Pauline, too. It's a small world. I knew their dad, Pop Brown. He was our mail carrier.

The house we are living in was the original barracks. We turned a portion of it around to make an L-shape. We stuccoed it on the outside.

We used to have so much company. It seemed in the summer that we had company all the time. Elmer's folks came that first April and helped move a portion of the barracks around." Tiny talked of her folks.

"My dad hated it here. He wouldn't live in this 'so and so country,' but my mom, she thought it was pretty. JB and Jewel Carter used to tease us about having so much company. One time, we were up at Beslanowitch's picking some green beans. The Carters drove by, and the next time they saw us, they just teased us and laughed and laughed, said we were up there getting beans to feed all our company. But then, I think all the homesteaders had lots of company. Everyone was so curious about this group of homesteaders out in Wyoming near Yellowstone Park. But it was good to have family come from back home."

Elmer talked about the ditch riders.

"They were our friends. The ones that come to my mind were Luke Moore and Jim Brown. And then there was Bob Fagerberg. He loved it

His wife, Barbara, used to say, 'This homestead project on Heart
was Bob's baby.' He was so much help to us. And then there
House who lived down in Ralston. He was a carpenter, and he
helping some of us make our barracks more livable."

I asked Elmer how he felt about the Japanese Relocation Camp.
Well, I went to school with the Japanese in Downing, California.
were over there fighting, and people were so scared. I lost a
the war. They were good people, but I'm afraid if they hadn't
em, many of them would have been killed. I never had any
it against the Japanese. They were doing their job; we were doing
men from the relocation camp here did a lot of work on the canal
They worked for the farmers all over and taught them a lot of
Well, it was a terrible war for everyone, just a sad time for

mer chuckled as he talked about one of the neighboring farmers.
Lyle French saw this guy out in his field with one of those old
ng to break up the new ground. Those old plows were awful. It
st of spring, and he was out there destroying his plow. The guy
g car, and Lyle thought he was from Texas. He had on a big hat,
ots, and was wearing a suit. The man said this was a
ken place and left; don't know if he ever came back."

Elmer and Tiny talked about those first years and how difficult it
y thought they had made the right choice and felt it was a good
ise their children. I knew the interview was difficult for Elmer
f his hearing, but once again, like so many times before, they both
nd and gracious.

179

LYLE AND DOROTHY FRENCH

'e had the opportunity to develop many homespun talents in those
yea o omesteading, and storytelling was enhanced on those long, winter
nig s. s I sat with Lyle and Dorothy, so many fond memories came back
of ilc od. I certainly hope they enjoyed visiting with me as much as I
enj /e em on the several interviews we had.

yle and Dorothy talked back and forth during the whole session,
cle in ames and dates. I had never realized before how funny Lyle
cou l b and he had honed his gift of story- telling into a fine art, to be
sur

e began with how they were able to get the homestead.
he fellow that drew this farm didn't want it. He decided
W mi was not the place he wanted to spend his life, so he let it go. My
sist , N rgaret Olson, and her husband, Swede, had the unit adjoining this
far . 7 y were in Colorado for the winter, because their barracks was not
rea / t ve in.

came up and had to be on the land on January 3rd. I needed two
sig tu , so Palmer Win and George Long went with us to Powell where
the ffi l papers were notarized. The papers had to be in Cheyenne, and
sin v were right down to the last hour, I was going to take them by
pla . new the plane was to leave by nine or ten o'clock, and when we
got t airport, they were closing the doors. I waved, and shouted, and
ran T / let me into the plane at the last moment.

ob Fagerberg, who had been so dedicated to this project, wanted
the ni was applying for also. Another fellow by the name of

Jack Black wanted this unit, but he wasn't a veteran, so he had his nephew apply for it. His official papers were on the plane I was flying on.

It was a bad day for flying. The plane was held up in Riverton because of the weather conditions. When we finally got to Laramie, they wouldn't land the plane, because there was a 95-mile-an-hour crosswind. We were flying in an old DC3 plane. We flew on to Cheyenne, and as soon as I could get off the plane, I grabbed a taxi. It was ten minutes of four, and I knew the land office closed at five. I told the taxi driver to hurry, and if he got a fine, I would pay it. So off we drove back to Laramie.

When I got to the land office, the man was just putting the key in the door. The secretary was standing there, and it was still three minutes 'til five. I told him I wanted to file on a farm. "Oh." He was so cranky and grouchy. "What are you doing? Stealing the farm from somebody?" No, I am not stealing it from somebody, it is legal, and I intend to make my home up there. He looked over the papers. "You didn't notarize this paper." I looked at the papers and realized in the last-minute rush, one had been missed. Can't you notarize it? "Well, yeah, we can." So he notarized it. I came just that close to not getting the farm, because the next morning, the other fellow's papers came in the mail.

So anyhow, we were twenty-three years old and didn't own anything and didn't have much money, but we did have enough to meet the requirements when we met the Board in May in 1949.

I looked across the dining room table at a couple in their twilight years, noticing the twinkle in both sets of eyes. "How did you feel about getting the homestead?"

"Oh, I was just tickled to death," spoke Lyle with gusto. "The opportunity to own a farm," Dorothy said with a tone of amazement. "Yeah," and it was perfectly flat and didn't have to be leveled or anything. And I was just tickled to death to get it."

"How did you feel, Dorothy?"

Well, at first, of course, why go to Wyoming on a homestead? But then, well even after the first year, I wouldn't have wanted to live anywhere else. This is truly home for us. When you first see something, and there is

182

not ng ut sagebrush, and we'll put a house here, or we'll do this, or we'll do at. ind there is nothing there, you know.

Well, the barracks? Well, now that is something else. Oh, they we co .

here was no insulation at all in those barracks. To live in the Los An le rea and come out here and live?"

t had to have been terrible for the Japanese at the relocation cer r.'

t this point, the conversation changed. "Where did you both me ?"

'e met in high school. We went to school in Gill, Colorado, ten mil e of Greeley. Lyle had gone to Gill as a freshman, and then his fan y ved to Hereford for a year. Then I moved to San Diego and att de iigh school there. Lyle joined the Navy and did his training in Sai Di . We got married, and in June, we will have been married for fif fo years.

"So how long were you in the service, Lyle?"

went in the service on Thanksgiving Day of 1944. I was sev ite years old. When the war started, I was only fourteen. I was in the er e from the first of December of 1944 until April or May of 1946.

ly parents were homesteaders. Yes, Mom and Dad got married, anc he ook a homestead east of Denver and south of Vono, Colorado. Th to n was Vono, Colorado. It was all dry land, of course. They were sou c Vono about twenty miles. Someone relinquished a homestead clo to 'ono, six miles in, and they took that homestead. A lot of times, pe le ould relinquish their homestead back in those days; someone wo d them a little money for it, and they'd leave it. Our family lived the fi n 1913 until 1926. My parents built a sod house. My sister, Ma ar was born in the sod house. They left the homestead in 1926 and mo d Colorado Springs, where I was born in 1927.

f course, the dry land farming was a lot different than the irri tic we have here. And the equipment they had! My dad bought a

183

new Titan tractor with steel wheels on it. It was the forerunner of the John Deere, the two cylinders. It burned kerosene and water.

They had tremendous hailstorms down through the country, and grasshoppers ate them up one time. The grasshoppers were four inches long, and they just darkened the sky. Some of the hailstones were as big as gallon buckets. It just beat them to pieces, so finally they just gave up and left the farm. But then in 1936, he farmed again, this time with irrigation, so I had some experience with him in that.

I hadn't used up my GI training, so when we came, I used it for welding classes. And then I had a GI teacher on the AG end that taught me all about fertilizer and bugs and everything, plus my dad had taught me about irrigating, so that all helped me when I began with the homestead.

Lyle settled back in his chair, "Okay, Patty, now I'll tell you some stories."

I was plowing here south of the house about halfway or a fourth of the way down here from the house. Oh, my Lord! The wind was blowing 100 miles-an-hour, and I was freezing to death. I was so bundled up, and I came to the shop and got some asbestos off the old barracks. I wired it up to the tractor, and then I draped it with canvas and got a tiny bit of heat in there. I had to keep plowing, because I had to go back home to Greeley. I was plowing away, and a big Oldsmobile, a brand new car, drove up there. A guy got out, crawled over the fence, and came over there to me. He was dressed in an overcoat and everything, business hat on. Boy, that wind! We talked a few minutes. He was from Chicago, Illinois. He had drawn one of the farms down below here, and boy, that wind took his hat, and it was making fifty-foot leaps at a time down across the prairies. With a disgusted expression, he watched his hat hit the piles of plowed dirt. "I'm not going to stay in this darn country. I'm going back home!" And away he went. So there were a lot of them that couldn't take those winters or the wind.

We lived in the barracks, and then we built this home in 1953. We lived here for I don't know how many months with no curtains. We couldn't afford curtains and anything else.

184

he Bureau of Reclamation told us all, "Don't farm more than half
of Y   can't possibly farm over half." I farmed the entire thing. It was
not ng) me, and people would come along and tell me, "Oh, you are
ma ng big mistake. You can't irrigate the whole thing." After my dad's
hel I   t like it was duck soup.

ve got to tell you a funny story. My dad was not used to fertilizer,
anc ll   e sugar company pushed was phosphate. I had learned from a
col ge   rofessor the importance of fertilizer. So when I still lived in
Co rac I took over the little farm Dad had. My brother had a fertilizer
spr de   so I ordered fertilizer. I put potash, phosphate, and nitrogen on
the irr nd just like the professor had taught me to do. My dad came over
the , a   the ground was white with fertilizer. He said, "My Lord! What
are ou   tting on there? Your sugar beets won't even come up. You've
jus oi   ned the ground for probably twenty years." Well, anyway, I had
21 ns   beets with high sugar average – 18.3 sugar average which was
rea / u here.

) when I came here, I made some mistakes, of course. I didn't
put no   h barley seed on the first year. My friend in Greeley, a topnotch
far er, id, "You have got to put 125 pounds of seed to the acre if you are
goi g t get a high yield." I had planted 80 pounds to the acre like all the
res of   e farmers around here. So then the next year, I put nitrogen,
phc ph   , and potash, and 130 pounds of seed to the acre, and boy, did I
hav a   p!

learned a lot from picking out the best farmer in the community
anc co   ng him. We all learned a lot from each other. We shared with
eac ot   r. Learned sometimes from our mistakes.
Th ma   thing that helped was the financial credit in town. We could
cha ge   oceries, gasoline. Without that, I don't know what we would have
doi . . d then we traded machinery.

e had some accidents with our machinery. Wallace got hurt with
the on   ne, got his arm broke really bad. Then Leroy Holmes got his
hai in   e cylinder of a combine, and it chewed the palm of his hand all
up.

185

I think the worst machinery accident was Ralph Compton. He went in under the front auger. What he was doing, there was alfalfa seed in the curls in the wheat. Dick Asher was running his combine. Ralph was pouring the wheat seed out of the sack, and he slipped on the wheat seed, and like that, the combine just grabbed him up. Dick saw it and shut the combine down, but it had already chewed clear through his hip socket. They got Ken Cunningham's new acetylene torch and came driving in and got me, and I cut him out of the combine. What kept him from bleeding to death was because Dick got right in there and put a rope around the cut to try to stop the bleeding. We got him in a car and met Dr. Beaver. They left with him, and I was standing there by the side of the road, but then someone picked me up and took me home. I think that accident happened around 1955. It took the doctors eight hours to sew him up. I think that was very upsetting to the whole community. It wasn't long after that, the Comptons sold their farm.

Both Dorothy and Lyle talked about the barracks they had torn down. Lyle commented.

We got a hold of several barracks and tore them down. Some of the wood was rotten, but I stored a lot of it in the barn. Oh my, this house is, I'd say, 90 percent barracks, good barracks lumber. I cleaned it and took all the nails out. The subfloors are all barracks. The roof is all barracks. I done a lot of the work on this house myself. I laid the linoleum. I laid the countertops.

"And you did the tile in the bathroom, remember."

The tile in the bathroom? Oh, yeah! They both laughed. I didn't know how to lay tile. I never laid a tile in my life. So I went down to Jim Lanik. He was a professional tile setter from California and asked him how to do it. And he explained to me how to do it. My brother-in-law laughed at me. He says, "You'll never hold that tile on there. I've never lost a tile yet."

In his bathroom, he had a professional lay his, and in three years, he had at least a dozen fall off. But I made sure, you know, I had time to do it perfect, you know. I had time to put enough glue on, and where a professional, he is in a hurry making a living, that's the difference.

186

...ed some of the wood to build barns for the livestock. We raised hogs, and we always had chickens. We would buy baby calves, ...feed them out.

...ne time, we had 200 baby chickens in our barracks. I had torn ...buildings and had this sheet rock stacked up, and the wind come ...pped over and killed about half of those baby chickens.

...hen, one time, we went to Billings. It was raining here when we got to Billings, got our shopping pretty well all done. We were ...the street, and it began to hail--hailstones about, oh, golf-ball size. ...nately, it didn't hail very many, because it didn't dent the car. ...rotected from the building, and I said we'd better get home. Boy, ...around by Frannie, and there was no snow at all, but the wind was ...erribly, you know. When we came out of Ralston, we started ...avy snow. I chained up down there by Bob Emery's. I had a car ...d go in the snow; it was a '54 Ford.

...But Lyle, we still didn't make it home, did we?" Lyle ...ntinued.

...plowed through heavy snow that went clear up over the ...s, clear up. And when we turned and got to Harold McHose's ...got just a little ways up from the corner, and it overwhelmed us, ...uldn't go any further. We had 300 baby chickens here at home ...ts, and we didn't know where the kids were or the school buses. ...rick came along on a tractor to pull us back out and took us home ...He says, "You can't go any further." There were several families ...at Don Roderick's.

...orothy began. "There was no electricity, we didn't know where ...en were, and we just knew we had lost all those chickens." ...yle chimed in.

...was two days before we got home, and those chickens were ...hey survived. I got on the phone and finally found where the kids ...town, you know. We have had some awful blizzards here; ...the 1950 was a bad year.

187

And the roads weren't built up high like they are today. A storm could move in so quickly, and in no time, we would be snowed in, or that time we were snowed out.

Lyle began to speak of the children.

Let me tell you about the kids, Patty. Well, Judy helped on the farm as much as she could. She helped her mother a lot. She was the oldest and the only girl, so she did double duty. I taught her to drive tractor just briefly, because she wasn't really needed, and that wasn't what she really wanted to do. But boy, she helped irrigate and everything.

Dorothy added her comments. "Helping, like with the irrigation and stuff.

She was real good. She liked the outdoors. Had a lot of friends here on Heart Mountain."

They both laughed. "Yeah, there were girls here all the time. Judy and her husband, Gene, moved away and then later came back to the farm, and Gene says he loves to farm," added Lyle.

Larry, from the time he was three years old would say, "I'm going to be a farmer like my dad," and that is all you ever heard out of him. We were in the yard working here, and, of course, the trees weren't grown up then, but we missed him. And we started frantically looking for him, because he was only four years old, or maybe going on five, and here he is out across the road talking to Billy Woodruff. Billy Woodruff had stopped out there, and Larry is out there carrying on an adult conversation. And so Billy would always stop there, so Larry would come over there and talk to him. And anyhow, it is ironic he is the one that isn't farming. But then the rest of them would say, "We heard a lot from Jerry, we can't wait to get off the farm and on and on."

Well, I just wanted to tell the funniest thing that I remember that happened was when Larry was about 12 years old, he decided he wanted to milk the cow. And so he was milking away, and he had a three-gallon bucket of milk almost full, and the old cow decided to kick him. And she kicked him over backwards, and the entire bucket of milk run right down his chest and over his head. And I just was lying on the ground laughing.

188

He id   think it was so funny, but that's the most hilarious thing that I
ren ml   .

nd then, I remember the first rattlesnake Mom killed. Glenn was
in (ıp(. And she had him out on the lawn here, Tim and Jerry were out
the , ; l maybe Larry, too. I had hauled in, unbeknownst, a little
ratt sn e about ten inches long. The rattlesnake was there close to Glenn.
So ıey   ll ran in the house to tell Mom and left Glenn out there with the
ratt sn e. Well, she went out there to kill it, and she closed her eyes and
strı k ; he thing and missed it completely.

orothy spoke.

lon't know what it was, but Jerry ended up in the Marine Corp--
wa dr   ed and went to the Marine Corps. And he wrote us a letter and
tolt ıs, You have absolutely everything anybody could want." When he
livt h   , he didn't think so. But he said, "You've got a nice house, got
flaı ın you are close to the mountains." We just loved that letter, and we
stil ıaʌ it. He kind of grew up and then came back. He and his wife,
Ro , lı   down on the unit that was originally owned by Jim Caviness.

yle joked, "Maybe when I am seventy, I will give him the letter,
but ny   ıy, now he thinks it is a wonderful place."

ow Tim, he never left home. He was never gone. He stayed right
her an   worked for me and then got married and moved next door. Tim
we t   Jorthwest for two years, and when he got married, he left this
hoı ɔ a l went a fourth of a mile away.

Dorothy talked about Glenn.

lenn was seventeen when he graduated, and he worked in the oil
fiel ; fı ı while but then came back to farming. When he was just a young
boy wı   vould send him to check the water over on the hill or set it when
he as   ɪger. And he wouldn't come home. He was 1314 years old, and
he ou   be over in that place by himself. He wouldn't come home, and
it v ul   ret close to dark, almost pitch black, you know, and finally we'd
go ok   ɔr him, and he'd be sitting on the hill, daydreaming. And "Oh,
Mc ı, l e seen so many deer, and I saw a fox, and I saw this, and I saw

189

that." And that went on for I don't know how many years. "I always wanted to live here," he would say.

So finally, we quit worrying about him. We knew what he was doing.

We had a little Cushman scooter when Judy was growing up. And they just were running the wheels off that Cushman scooter, and then we traded that in, and they wanted something a little more modern. So we got a little Honda 90. And that was usually what he had when he was out sitting on the hillside.

Dorothy talked about the 4-H program. "All of our kids were active in 4-H.

Of course, 4-H was a real important thing on Heart Mountain in those years. All of our kids were ambitious. They all enjoyed 4-H." Lyle commented.

In the winter, when things eased up a bit, the neighbors would get together and talk farming. "I was younger, so I felt like I was just a kid. I remember coming over to your folks' place, Patty. Lloyd and Wallace and McHose would be talking about their mistakes and what they could do different the next year.

Dorothy said, "The good outweighed the bad those first few years. Well, we all make mistakes. Some you just learn to do better the next time and not make the same mistake again." Lyle reflected.

Oh yeah, we had a lot of wonderful crops, and we also had a lot of disasters. And we also made some stupid, dumb mistakes. I always had a saying when my wife would get after me about making a dumb mistake. I would say, well, if I wasn't out working and doing something, I wouldn't make a mistake. If I was sitting in the house, I would make a mistake.

We all laughed together at that comment.

So, on and on the storytelling would go. I loved this couple, late in years, and yet so young. They would walk me to my car, and then Lyle must have had a sense of how much I missed my own father. The tape would be turned off, but I would listen ever so intently, wanting to hear every word. And I do think every time I drove home to Shell, after being

190

wit D ithy and Lyle, I wept, because the time with them was such a
ch(sh thing for me.

FRENCH FAMILY INTERVIEW

ooking back on that time of interviewing the homesteaders, I
ren ml · well how supportive Lyle and Dorothy French were in
enc ura ng me. On a cold, June afternoon, they managed to round up the
ent e f iily for an interview. I will only be able to share a small portion
of 1 it 1 eting, but it is safely filed away for future use. The grandparents,
rig] d(n to the youngest of the grandchildren, had many stories. I was
an>)u:) go back and read Glenn's portion of the interview, but on that
Su1 ay fternoon, he was a man of few words. As I entered into the
res rc project, I knew from the onset that many of the original
hoı :st lers had already passed away but never thought that Glenn would
be 1 ke rom our community in such a short while. Later, as I read through
the 1eı ries of the three generations of families, it reinforced my energy
in 1 in on the task of preserving a piece of American history.
h: grown up with Judy French. We attended 4-H meetings and
pla ·d gether, went to 4H camp, state fair, and a host of other things, with
alv ys e happy, rambunctious joy of youth. Since Judy was the first
boı , w isked her to recite dates of each birthday, and she did quite well.
)k: I am the oldest, and my name is Judy Ann French Braten. I was
boı N ember 10, 1946, in Greeley, Colorado. Number two is Larry Joe
Fre ch, id he was born February 5, 1950, in Greeley, Colorado. Next is
Jer L French, born November 25, 1951, in Cody, Wyoming? Next is
Tir Al 1 French, born April 16, 1954, in Cody, Wyoming? And the
yoı ge is Glenn Richard French born July 8, 1955, in Cody, Wyoming.
think probably the main thing that has been with me through my
life ; tl work ethic, you know. You have to work hard and be self-reliant,
anc /ea that is probably it, work. I remember the kids.
Th(e v re a lot of kids in the community, and we had a lot of fun.

191

I took everything in 4-H. I took cooking, mostly cooking. I only took sewing a couple of years, and I didn't like that. Edna Mae McClaflin was the sewing leader. And it was fairly traumatic for me, because you had to make that silly, gathered skirt and an apron. I learned to sew later as an adult. I actually learned to sew with my children when they started 4-H. I took all the good cooking things, and gardening, and home improvement, and soil conservation.

I'm the oldest in the family, so I probably have the most vivid memories of what it was like to live in the barracks. I was three when we moved here, and we lived in the barracks until 1953, so I would have been about six. What impressed me, and what I remember the most, is how cold it was to live in that barracks. The water bucket would freeze near where we slept. Larry and I slept in one bed, his head on one end and my head on the other. We would get in bed, and then Dad would warm pillows on the stove and run them in to us. You know, to help you get to sleep. And I remember one cold night. It was so cold, and once you got your spot warmed, you just didn't roll over. Larry moved and squirmed and made me get over, and I had to warm a new spot. I was so mad at him.

I'm Gene Braten, Judy's husband. I was born and raised in Clark and could see Heart Mountain probably most of my life, except when we moved to the big city and lived there for eight years. I hated it so much, that we decided to move back. I didn't farm until I was probably 30 years old. I found out it was harder than it looked to set tubes, because I can get drenched real good. But now, I can laugh at all my grandkids and the kids that come out and want to set water. I have learned that people on Heart Mountain are hard workers, and they know what they are doing. They love doing what they do, and most everybody knows me, and I know most everybody.

Larry was the next to speak.

Probably the thing I remember most about growing up is how close our community was. We'd go down there to the Mountain View Community Club. We had Christmas parties where, gosh, some of the kids played their trombones or their flutes or whatever and had skits and Bible

sto ?s.   1 the summer, we had Bible School there. There must have been
fift of   ; that went to Bible School there. 4-H was a big deal. But the
thii tl   has always stuck in my memory here is that everybody worked
har

Se\ ral   ut when somebody was hurt, the whole community was there.
bee .   ?ars ago, Rolly Otto had throat cancer and couldn't dig his sugar
anc)ut   ey literally had to have a traffic cop stand and direct the trucks in
am   in   )ecause they had five diggers and thirty trucks, and it was just
of] s g   Kurt Lamb hurt his arm. We came, and in two days thrashed all
too on   in for him. A young guy was renting your mom's place here not
wo   d   igo. He was working in the oil fields and couldn't get his fall
all [` h ?, and five guys showed up in one day, did all of his plowing and
tha ilv   fall work for him in one afternoon. So that is one of the things
wa   a b   /s stuck with me about the community. And, of course, then 4-H
the [ea   deal. And there were ten kids that graduated in my class from
     Ve   Mountain area, just on the Powell side. So that is pretty cool.
Pai   ;ed to go fishing with J.D. Carter and his family up to Yellowstone

we   rc   h, it was so cool! We'd rent a boat at "fishing bridge." There
the at   )oats, so you could throw the anchor out and kind of float down
of : in   it a mile or so and keep all the fish you wanted. We have pictures
fry sh   rs of fish with probably fifty fish on them! J.D. always liked to
           nd it was just an absolute blast.

any iin   , 4-H, I was probably more into field crops and conservation than
anc)cc   The summer 4-H camps up on North Fork, Junior Leader Camp,
Sh(v i   Camp were always just a blast. I won a trip to the Denver Stock
nat na   horticulture and won a trip to Chicago in field crops. I was a
yea I   /inner, so I got a $500 scholarship I used at Northwest. The next
wa   se(   )n a trip to Washington, D.C. in 4-H. The highlight of that trip
wa   in   g J.C. Penney, who was 94 at the time. His first Penney's store
to : ?w   :mmerer, Wyoming. He always invited the Wyoming delegation
lun i a   ork City for four days. We were guests in his big complex for
           attended the Radio City Music Hall. I still have the Golden Rule

ruler he gave us. Probably the thing that the youth activities and achievements did most for me was that I learned how to speak in front of crowds and not be shy, so that has helped me in my sales career.

I think this community taught us to play hard. Play just as hard as you work. Everybody that grew up here definitely knows how to work. So that is what I remember. I had a blast living here.

There is one story I've got to tell you. My dad decided that he would raise a field of beans without chemicals. So here came the weeds; I mean, they were massive. So we went out and started in the middle of the field hoeing weeds. The weeds kept getting bigger, so we went at that for three weeks. My mom would just be going, "Come on, let's go, come on." Pretty soon, I looked back. I heard this thud! My mom passed out and hit the ground, and the dust just flew. I said to my brother, "Well, shouldn't we do something?" My brother Glenn said, "Just leave her lying there." By now, everyone in the room was laughing. "She'll put you all back to pulling weeds again." What really got me is we took this big field and hoed eight acres right out in the middle. We had to pull the weeds, but the bean plants came up with them. And so, my dad came up and saw all the uprooted beans and said, "Oh quit, oh quit." And that fall, I said, "Boy, I'll bet where we pulled those weeds it did better, huh?" He said, "No, I shouldn't have had you do it. It just plugged up my cutter." When I heard that, my heart just sunk; that was three weeks' worth of work. But the worst of it was that Mom had a heat stroke, so that was the last of having her help us weeding the beans.

I turned to the next son sitting near me.

Okay, I am Jerry French. I remember working on the farm, especially trying to thin 100 acres of sugar beets. My brothers and I never made it. But we always definitely put a dent in it but always had to call in reinforcements. We gave it our best shot.

4-H was big for me, because it got me off the farm. Had I not had 4-H, I would just have been buried in farm work, and I didn't want to work all of the time. So 4-H was huge to me, because I went to Chicago. I went to Junior Leader Camp three times, Soil Conservation Camp, and 4-H

194

Ca). l never forget meeting our International Youth Exchange student
fro A ralia. I met him at 4-H camp, and then he came and stayed with
us. Ie as a breath of fresh air. He was funny, and he was just joking all
the m We really enjoyed him, and we cried when he left.
went on the 4-H campout to Crandall. I never caught any fish,
but e1 yed the mountains. I always wondered where the stream came
fro . vo years ago, my son, Casey, and I walked to the end of North
Cr; da which is 18 miles one way, and we saw the snow bank that starts
the or Crandall. So I finally got to the end; I always wanted to see the
en( )f you know.
don't have to work as hard now as when I was on the farm, and
I'n la 'm not. I'm enjoying life and hiking. This homestead community
tau it how to work and how to be a survivor.

hose many years at state fair, our county always stayed with the
Pa1 C(nty delegation in the old dorm. It was the best-kept secret. The
do1 w old, but by far the coolest, and with August weather, the state
fai1 ro1 ds in Douglas, Wyoming, were stifling with heat. That is where
I b(an acquainted with Jerry's wife, Rose. I soon learned to have a great
ad1 ra n for this talented lady and an appreciation for her husband, Jerry.
Sh vo d tell me how he encouraged her talent of quilting and even built
a f1 ne r her quilts. Rose and I would always make a trek over to the big
de1)n ition building where the quilts were displayed. I remember well
the ea 1e won the Grand Champion ribbon for her quilt. I really thought
the ui vas a masterpiece of art. Here is a portion of her interview.

he big fact is that children are the most special creation on this
ear . ink that through 4-H and working with the children, you learn so
ve1 m 1 about what is important. I have been a vegetable judging coach
for in ears. I've worked with all of my nieces and nephews. One of the
fir: thi s I remember when I came here was Judy's kids, Tammy and
Ci1 y. ad just come out on the farm, and here was Tammy, getting ready

195

for county fair. She had to do a demonstration. And there was Judy, "Now come on, come on, you can do this."

I enjoyed the times I was able to be a chaperone at state fair. Seeing what the Wyoming youth accomplished was amazing. Late at night in the dorms, Teddy and Patty and the others who had grown up together would share their memories of growing up in 4-H, and I was happy to be a part of that time.

I turned to Glenn French sitting quietly, listening to all the family stories, but I would soon discover he was a man of few words.

He began.

Well, I was in 4-H. That was good, and I can't remember how many years I was in 4-H but had a good time, learned a lot, and went to 4-H camp.

Yeah, I farm up here. It is a good life. We have a good time living up here. I have made a living, worked hard, played hard, and I've had an opportunity to farm on my own. So it has been good.

I'm Tim French. The rest of them have touched on it a lot of how we worked hard, and I remember we always got to play. When we had a break, we left a trail of dust getting out of the yard. If Dad said, "You've got the afternoon," or You've got two hours," I mean, we were on our bikes and then the Honda or the Cushman, or the Honda 90 and gone. I just dearly loved San Cooley or Heart Mountain. We went to Beslonovich's and Asher's a lot. Whenever we were down there playing and we heard Dad's whistle, that meant, "Come home." I could hear it at Asher's a half a mile away. When you heard that, it wasn't, "Oh, we'll dink around for fifteen minutes." No, you got on your bike right then and headed home, or he was coming after you. But yeah, I had a great time growing up out here. I really did.

4-H was huge. I won a trip to Chicago, and then a trip to New York City and Washington, D.C. I got to go to the White House and meet President Nixon. And then we had lunch in the Rose Garden with the First Lady, Pat

196

was just amazed. New York City was so big, and you know, I
wa ore y young. I think I was 17 when I went back there. We stayed on
Tir s uare. Our chaperone said, "Now, stay in the hotel, and don't go
out / soon as he turned his back, I was out on Times Square on my
ow 1 :n I stayed out there until two in the morning, going all through
Tir s uare, and it was just unbelievable. 4-H allowed me to get off the
far lil the others said. 4-H camp was always fun, because we had hard
wo , a then, what a treat. You could go up there on the rifle range at 4-
H c nr nd you would always get in trouble, because you were given five
she s t hoot at your target. Well, there was always somebody you really
did t c e for, and they were always trying really hard. So you couldn't
hel bu ut one extra in theirs.

really liked leather craft, and I made a lot of different things. I
hac sl :p project at one time, until they got out. Gosh, I don't remember.
Th w e Columbia maybe. They were pure white. They got out on the
roa a a dune buggy hit them. That kind of wiped out my sheep project.

'e spent a lot of time in the summer hoeing sugar beets. All of
the oy had files we kept at the end of the rows. We all knew how to
sha)er hoe. We all got really good at that.

ad taught us how to hunt. We ate a lot of wild game. I still hunt,
anc bc :ve that started from when Dad used to take us up to Eagle Creek.
Th w so much fun to hike up there. We'd have our lunch before we
we ot)n the hunt, and that was always a great time.
I re ier :r getting awful cold up there, too.

remember Mom and her garden. We used to have huge gardens
like l of the neighbors did. She would can and freeze 1,500 quarts of
foc a ır.

[y name is Carrie French, and I'm almost 22 years old. I was born
Jur 25 980. And my parents are Tim and Becky French. I have a lot of
for m ories from Heart Mountain, and growing up here has been great.
I ju g luated from college. A lot of people have always told me how
the wa to move to a big city and that sort of thing, and I've never wanted
to a where but come back here. I have been raising livestock since I

197

was little, and I really love horses, so the field I would like to be in is agriculture.

It is really a neat community. My fondest memories are riding my horses around out here where it is so beautiful, and Heart Mountain is just gorgeous. I'm grateful for all the friends that I've made. I'm glad that all of our parents out here let us grow up together, and climb around on horses, and eat dirt, and throw rocks at each other. One of the things that I remember most about being out here was the old Heart Mountain Clubhouse and our parents always letting us get together for Christmas parties and Halloween. It was old, but it was just a neat place to be.

Becky added a few stories from her memories of coming to the homestead community.

It was a lot different than I expected when I married Tim and moved out here. I always thought when I was little that the farmers planted the crops, and that was all they had to do. The crops just grew on their own, and that was all that was needed--to put them in the ground, and there they were. I had no idea what all was involved in farming. But I jumped right in and learned how to drive a truck and a tractor and offered to weed some.

Music was my thing, and I wanted a piano in the worst way. I needed to make $50 to buy a piano. So Tim's mom and dad said, "Yeah, you can come thin some beets, and we'll pay you." Well, an acre would have made me the $50. I couldn't even make it through the acre. I mean, that was the biggest wake-up that I had. You know, coming out here, they work so hard, and they were so used to jumping in and doing that, and I had no idea what I was doing, absolutely none. And so, I'm ashamed to say, I never even finished an entire acre, but they gave me $50 anyway, and I went and bought the piano.

Another little mistake I made was, I was going to be like these ladies out here and make my own homemade chili. My grandmother was coming out for dinner and my family. I was going to take those beans and soak them and do everything I was supposed to do, and so I did, and it smelled so good. I followed the recipe and put in all the chili powder and

198

spi␣ ␣s ␣ l stuff I was supposed to, and the hamburger. Well, everybody
too␣ ␣th␣ spoons and took a big bite. There was this crunching sound, and
the␣ ␣oo␣ on their faces was priceless. I forgot to wash the beans before I
put␣ ␣ie␣ n the chili. Well, they were just full of dirt and sand! Tim never
did␣ ␣et␣ forget about that one. But the best thing about moving out here
anc␣ ␣na␣ ing Tim was the family has always been so good to me, accepted
me␣ ␣gh␣ way, all the people in the community. I felt like I had found my
pla␣ ␣.␣ hen we drive home from somewhere, we always look to see Heart
Mc␣ ␣nta␣ . And then we know we are almost home. Yeah, it is a great
fee␣ ␣ig␣ be home.

m Cindy Miller. My maiden name is Braten, Judy's middle child.

Ye␣ ␣,␣ wing up on the farm, you know you are an important part of the
fan␣ ␣.y. nean, it takes the whole family to do work. If your mom's driving
tru␣ ␣o␣ hatever, then you have to take care of the house, and cook, and
thi␣ ␣inc␣ hat. It's just everybody all together that helps do it. You might
not␣ ␣e␣ orking out in the field all the time, but you've got household
res␣ ␣ns␣ ilities, too. We used to raise a huge garden. You know, that was
anc␣ ␣ei␣ sponsibility that you had to do.
We␣ ␣se␣ o can for days and days and days. But it was a good thing.

hen I was in Junior High and High School, I helped out on the
fan␣ ␣.T␣ t is just part of life, and so I would help cut the hay and stuff, and,
of␣ ␣ur␣ , I wasn't very good at keeping it straight. Dad would have to
cor␣ ␣a␣ straighten it out for me periodically, because I got quite crooked
in␣ ␣y␣ drowing hay. Once, I think he had me do barley a little bit, but
wit␣ ␣ba␣ y, you've got to be a little careful, because you can shell the ends
or␣ ␣lat␣ er, but hay I could do. When Dad was baling hay, or this and that,
the␣ ␣I␣ s responsible for setting the water on the other crops, and things
lik␣ ␣ha␣ And sometimes, just like in the olden days, you had to stay home
fro␣ ␣sc␣ ol and help get things done on the farm.

eddy Jones was the 4-H Extension Agent when I was growing up.
I r␣ ␣ie␣ er going with her to livestock judging competitions and stuff.
We␣ ␣l␣ up North Fork to somebody's ranch, or something like that, and

199

do the livestock judging. I wasn't very good at livestock judging, but it was still fun to go and a good learning experience.

I think that anybody like the 4-H leaders and agents who give like they do, and I mean work with children and stuff like that, well, they help influence your life and help make you who you are. Teddy Jones, well now, she made you feel like a person, because she knew you. She knew who you were and congratulated you, or was there to console you when you didn't do good, or whatever. She was there. Yeah, and that was nice. And that was really something that people would be so willing to give to the youth.

I spent a lot of time with Grandma. She was the big, you know, the biggest influence on my life, and the big thing was working hard. That was a really big thing that she taught me.

In 4-H, I took home improvement and stuff. And my sister and I would just work all year long. We did canning, and cooking, and sewing, and stuff. When we were in

4-H, sewing was such a big thing. I mean, we made 10 or 11 outfits that we styled, and stuff. Style review took two days. Grandma and Grandpa always took their Airstream trailer into town, and we just stayed there at the fair, because Mom and Grandma worked at the fair. We would load up their trailer with all of our 4-H stuff and haul it into town, and we would spend all day long having all of our stuff judged.

I'm Todd Braten. I'm Judy's youngest. I'm a farmer with my dad and my mom. We farm about 500 acres altogether. We grow anything from corn, hay, barley, and beans. It's a farm. It has its days. What I like the most is probably baling hay all night long. Farming teaches you how to work and teaches you responsibility.

In my 4-H years, I can remember Grandma Dorothy teaching me how to judge vegetables.

I was in Boy Scouts when I was younger. I think I started in the sixth grade, because Mom started working that summer. The scout leader was her boss, and she talked her, or he talked her into getting me into Boy Scouts. I think the Boy Scouts were really what developed me and turned

me ıto ho I am today. It keeps you out of trouble. I guarantee that. And
I th ık ery young man should go through Boy Scouts. It teaches you
hoᴠ to truthful and honest, and it teaches you morals, teaches you how
to l ve ın. We went on quite a few backpack trips, fifty-mile backpack
trip in ɛ mountains. We went to the Beartooth Pass one year. We started
at l an _ake, and we came out at Crazy Creek Campground.

went to college in Dickinson, North Dakota. When I would come
hoı ɔa get between Bridger and Belfry, and I would see Heart Mountain,
yoı ɔnᴄ you're home. It just gives you goose bumps. I can tell where
I'n ıt ᴠ enever I can see Heart Mountain. It is there. It is beautiful. I've
bee oı ɔp of it two or three times, and you can just see everything. It is
jus ɔea iful.

w only able to include portions of interviews, and some have not
bee in ıded in this writing. I am hoping the next homesteader generation
wil piᴄ up from here and go on with the younger set of homestead
chi reı

DODE FULTON

ode and I sat at the kitchen table drinking coffee and watched the
hea y s ᴠw falling. The large evergreen branches were lying heavy with
the ᴠet ow, as she began talking about her childhood.

grew up in Kansas. My folks moved here when I was in the
eig h ıde. My dad came up in the summertime and worked with
far ers nd eventually, he just moved the family up here. He finally found
a p ᴄe r us and began his own farming.

ɔot married early, and my husband and I lived on a homestead on
the lat where my grandfather had homesteaded earlier. We built a house
the , a then just a little over a year later, on Halloween, Jeff was born.
oc was in the service about three years. He went in as a Navy
CB Hᴇ ᴠorked on a ship, and when he came back to California, I went

201

out to be with him and stayed until he was out of the service. After his service time, he came back and began to farm again.

Doc grew up around Powell. He always liked horses growing up, so he got into breaking horses. He spent a lot of time in those early years breaking horses, along with doing some farming, before we received our own homestead. Doc liked the homestead, and so did I. Before the homestead, Doc was renting some ground, but it wasn't very good. We have done much better here on our own homestead.

Doc was harvesting on the day the homestead allotments were drawn. The barracks was an undertaking, as I am sure we have all told you. It was good that we had them in those first few years.

We had some milk cows, but we couldn't bring them to the homestead until we got a well dug, so that was the first thing we did. After we had the cows, we would sell the cream, so that was really a big help in the beginning.

That first year of homesteading, my mom and dad lived nearby. They came and brought their tractor. My dad was farming as well, so he helped when he could. Doc's mother had moved to Billings, but she came down as often as she could. Tom, Doc's brother, was farming the original place down the road. He brought a tractor up, and they doubled up to plow. We didn't have a lot of sagebrush on our place. One of them was ahead of the other, and that was how they plowed the ground and turned it over. We had this home-place which was 116 acres, and eventually, we got an amendment. There was 27 acres of farm ground, and the rest was pasture, and we had cattle up there.

When we started homesteading, we raised dried peas, and then we eventually got green peas—"canner peas" I guess is what they called them. And then, we had a lot of hay. Then we got into beans and grain. We raised beets. I think we quit raising beets about two years before Doc passed away. He has been gone three years.

Jake was born in 1942, so he was with us when we came. I remember Swede Olson drove the children to school in his car. Gary was born May 20th, 1945. He married Dorothy Petersen in 1970, and they have

202

on(sor   Gary grew up to be a farmer. He lives about a mile-and-a-half
do\ 1 tl   road. Linda was born September 29, 1946, and had two children,
Ca 1, a   l Marti Kay. She and her husband, Dennis, live on the Powell flat
an(1a\   a farm.

/hen Charles was born, Linda could only pronounce Tuck, so his
nic 1a1   just stayed with him, and we have called him that ever since. He
wa m;   ied to Barbara Bovee on October 14, 1973, and they have four
gir]

[ike was born September 11, 1949, and he married Kim Watts.
He ot   to trucking and eventually moved to Billings. They have two
da\ ht(, Ginger and Pat.

nd then there is Carroll, who we call Pidge, and he was born June
11, 95   They had two boys, Nick and Beau. Then the youngest one,
Jan , \   ; born October 14, 1952, and she didn't get a nickname. We just
cal d 1   "Shorty." She married Tim Large. They have three children,
Jan э, (ris, and Jodie. The children were close in age. They all live close
by xc(t for Mike who lives in Billings. We try to all get together
sor tir   s. This last Christmas, there were fifty-six here, so it was quite a
hoi эft

ooking back at those early years, I don't know how we did it. I
sev d s   ne, but mostly my mom sewed for the kids. In those first years,
we 1ill   l cows and raised dried peas and did very well with the crop.

don't remember so much about the barracks. We built this house
tha ve   ised the children in. The kids laugh about how they would come
ov(h(before the house was finished. After we got the bathroom
wo in   the kids would run over here from the barracks to take a bath.

/hen we finally got the inside bathroom, it was a good thing.
Or(1a\   /, it seemed like they got to get a bath on Saturday night or
Su1 ay   nd that had to do them until the next week. When we built the
hoi э, \   re were two bedrooms upstairs and two downstairs. Now they're
full)f j   k."

ode began to laugh.

"We kept the milk cows while the children were growing up. We kept about four milk cows. We sold the milk and cream, and that was what we lived on. Those first few years, the men were able to go to school and received a monthly payment for that. It helped those first years with groceries. I was still milking cows after the kids were gone.

Jake belonged to Scouts, and I think your brother, Mike, was in that group too. Mrs. Acott was the Scout leader at the time.

Gary got into 4-H. I remember Dorothy French was one of the project leaders. Linda took sewing from Edna Mae.

In the wintertime, a bunch of the kids would all get together and go ice skating and have wiener roasts. When the kids got into sports, all of the neighbors took turns driving them to their activities. We were all busy with the farm and livestock, so that was a great help to pool the time for driving the kids. Those first few years, I don't think any of us did much in town; we stayed out here on the bench most of the time.

We always had a big garden. I still do. Of course, all the kids help me. They got me a tiller a few years ago, so that helps a lot. Yeah, Cindy comes over and helps, and she cans. I can and the rest of the kids. Janet has a garden. Linda doesn't have a garden, but about all she cares for are green beans, so I have plenty of them for her. Dorothy and Gary raise a garden, so we've got them all working anyhow, and with this, Dode laughed. Yeah, all our kids were raised on the farm, and they all worked hard on the farm.

Our community was really special. Gene Dunleavy homesteaded just about a half mile from us, and he was single. His ground was right across the road from us, so he was a ballplayer. He'd come down and play ball with our boys. He was a really good neighbor. The neighbor above us sold his unit to the Ottos, and then we had them as neighbors, and they were so special.

In our neighborhood, we always had something going on. At the clubhouse, we had square dances. The 4-H meetings were there. And I remember the Bible School. Everyone enjoyed the clubhouse, and that is where we would see our neighbors.

he boys used to like to ride their horses up on Heart Mountain.
We ac ne horse that got away from them and came home, so they had to
wa d n off the mountain. I remember we would go to Heart Mountain
at C ri las time and get a tree. There were several of the neighbors that
we w us. We would take a picnic; we did a lot of things like that.

oc liked to fish. I never did fish very much, but we went to
Su igh md fished in the summertime. We would get going on the beets.
We hir d our own beets. Doc would say, "Well, now, if you get through
wit th : beets, we'll go to Sunlight and we'll go fishing."
So he would work extra hard." Both
ode and I laughed at this.

When Doc was just a kid, he worked up in Sunlight in the
wii ert e. They cut trees down up on North Fork and snaked them out to
the ba or the electric poles that went down into Sunlight.

is harder for me now, and Doc has passed away, so I don't get
arc id much as I used to. I know the clubhouse is still used a lot. My
gir sti help with some of the dinners. They have me bake pies for the
act iti I think the irrigation meetings are held there.
Pic : v ; up here this morning talking about the elections coming up at
the lul juse. I think the grown kids are still good friends up here. He
wa say g they're going to get Wayne, too. She laughed. Yes, they are
all joc riends.

here was one year we didn't have water for the pasture, so we had
to s llt cattle. So now we have horses. Doc always enjoyed the horses.
I tl ik)w there are about sixteen horses. Doc broke horses after we
mo :d here for other people. They'd bring them in and he'd break them.
Th w n Nick got old enough, he and his grandpa broke horses.

his community was a special place and still is. When something
hap en out here on the bench, everybody was there to help you. They
all re hat things would go right for you. For instance, if you were sick,
the all e tractors would come in, and the harvesting would be done. And
the sti lo that out here on Heart Mountain. They really do give you help.

205

It is sad to see that so many of us don't farm anymore; we are just getting too old.

We were fortunate, Patty. We had a good life and good neighbors, and now, of course, the younger ones are taking over, and they are still good friends. I still like living out here. I don't want to go to town, not until I have to, anyway.

I still have a garden and do my lawn work, so I know that helps me stay strong. I have a little riding mower but still mow some of the lawn by hand. I do get lonely sometimes.

There are so many memories here of Doc and raising the family on the homestead. I remember when we planted the trees right along here. They were only five or six inches high, and it seemed like it took them forever to grow. Well, eventually Doc built the shop, and we wanted to put a windbreak back on the drain there, so we got some more trees. They were little, blue spruce trees and we just dug a real deep ditch and put it right down in that so the wind wouldn't cut them off. Carroll came home from school one day and said, 'What are you doing?' We said, 'Well, we're putting in the windbreak.' 'Well,
putting it down that deep, you are never going to live to see it.'

"Some of the trees didn't do well, but now these trees along here have done alright. But now, we didn't leave enough room between the house and the trees, so when they bring this big machinery in, they get pretty close to things. So we had one, two, maybe three trees and a big, blue spruce in the lawn, and we lost it on the corner.
We kept the lilacs as a hedge, and now it is getting big.

Of course, it is different now without Doc. He died February 11, 1998. Of course, Pidge was farming the ground before Doc passed away. Doc had wanted to quit farming. He was in good health, pretty much. He had a heart attack, and we came through that one; and he came home, and then he had another one. We brought him home. He was starting to walk, got up one morning to fix the coffee, and then he was gone.

Doc had a good life. He had never been sick very much. Heart Mountain is very sentimental to me. It is always the first thing I look for

wh I n coming home. When Doc was in the service, he always said,
'W en vas coming home, I always looked for Heart Mountain, and then
I k w vas home.'

I d ve /e stopped talking for a few minutes. "I still do that myself when
ho .") out of Ralston and see Heart Mountain. I know I am almost

FLOYD AND PAT GEORGE

had done a number of interviews by the time this interview took
pla , s I was feeling some confidence in the procedures and familiarity
of se omesteaders. The list was getting smaller with the families living
aro id)well, but I wanted to reach as many of the original homesteaders
as ss e living in other states. In the middle of July, I managed to plan
a t tl would take in several western states. It was hard to find people
at l m)r exactly where they were living, so I was very happy to be able
to f id : Georges, now living in Rupert, Idaho. They gave me directions
to eir rm. I started out early that hot, July day, thinking I had time to
spa . ien I got to Rupert, I tried to follow the instructions I had written
do 1. topped in several places to ask for directions. I drove around the
co nu :y for about two hours at midday, when the temperature had risen
to ou 100 degrees.

was so frustrated after a while, I wondered if I should just drive
on, ut knew that the Georges were expecting me. I finally pulled into
the dr :way, exhausted and embarrassed at the late hour.

hey both met me at the door and were so gracious, I was glad I
wa pe stent in finding them. We had a delightful interview, but after I
ha ur d off the tape recorder, they shared with me what they were
de ng ith personally. As I drove away from that home, I had to say a
pra :r thanksgiving that their voices were recorded.

s was the usual custom, we sat down together at the dining room
tab , a they began to tell me about their lives on the homestead. The
fan y .tory began with Pat.

207

"I was born and raised in Big Timber, Montana. I went to school there for twelve years and then went to Billings to beauty school. I later went to Seattle, Washington, and worked at Boeing Aircraft. That is where I met Floyd. I was "Rosie the Riveter," and he was a mechanic. He went into the service, and I went back to Montana where my mother was living." Floyd spoke up.

"I worked at Boeing at first, then joined the Navy. I was in aircraft work.

I was an experimental mechanic at Boeing Aircraft, and I worked on the B-29 that dropped the bomb. I went from Seattle to San Diego. There were just a few that were picked that went to the headquarters squadron in San Juan, Puerto Rico, and I was one of them.

I was raised in Bountiful, Utah. I went to high school in Davis High School and then went to Weaver College. I took a straight course of aviation and mechanic work. From there, I went to Seattle and worked for Boeing. During that time, I attended the University of Washington and studied vocational work. Because of my training, I was able to become involved in the experimental work while in the service.

Pat and I were married in 1943, and I was in the military until 1946. Our son, Dick, was born in Seattle in 1944. Diane was also born in Seattle in 1945.

Our son, Dick, was born in Seattle in 1944. Diane was also born in Seattle in 1945. Wendy was born in Montana in 1948. Wayne was born in the hospital in Powell, Wyoming, in 1951. Connie was born in 1956, and that was after we had moved to Idaho.

Pat heard about the homesteads from my brother, Harley George. He had started a dairy, and his sons are still running it. I always liked farming, and I had taken FFA [Future Farmers of America] in school. While I lived in Montana, I worked on a farm. I had a combine and a tractor of my own.

The homestead unit we got on Heart Mountain had some ground that didn't grow good crops. There weren't enough acres to support a family. I decided to make an exchange for a homestead in Idaho. At the time, I was working three farms, but I could see I was not making much money with rented ground. I will explain the exchange. In order to do this, we had to turn back the farm and our house and all the improvements to the government. Our homestead was divided up for other homesteaders in order for them to be able to have more acres, to help insure they could support a family. One year, we were hailed out. That certainly made an impact.

When we decided to make an exchange, we had an opportunity to go to Idaho, Arizona, and another place I can't seem to recall. I grew up near Idaho, and I knew there was good farming ground there. It is a lava ash, a loam; it is more of a sandy ground. I felt the markets were more established near Rupert, and that proved to be true." The conversation came back to Pat.

"The barracks we got for the Heart Mountain homestead had been the shower house at the relocation camp. The walls were filled with soap, but we had been living in the oil fields in Montana, so this was a good move for us. We were doing well money-wise at the time in Montana. Coming to the homestead was very different, but living conditions improved as far as meeting new friends and working in a community with wonderful people. Although we had absolutely nothing, I think those years in Wyoming were the happiest years of my life.

We never considered ourselves to be poor. I had a sister that was very wealthy, and she would come to visit us on the homestead with no electricity, no modern conveniences. She said, "I would trade everything I have for the happiness that you have in your home and family."

I think because our community put heart and soul into our homes, and we all worked together for the same cause is why we were happy. We loved what we were doing. At least we did. I wasn't a farm girl, but I loved it."

Floyd talked about the way the families worked together.

"Everyone was the same. We helped each other, especially when someone got into trouble. It was a wonderful way of life for anyone starting out. We weren't starting out alone; you were starting with everyone else.

209

Our children talk about those early days all the time. They had a horse and colt. Sometimes, there would be four or five children riding on the mare.

We would send them out to herd the cows. One day, they came back to the house and said, 'There are some cows out in the field, and we can't get them to get up.' I jumped up from the table and went running out there, but it was too late. The cows had already died. There is just no way could our children have all the experiences they had growing up in any other place. The rattlesnakes were something they had to be careful of in those first years. Our children were very young, but they would go out and help me feed the calves and the pigs."

Pat told about clearing the sagebrush

"One of the best things about that time was when we had to clear the sagebrush from the land. Floyd would be out working on the tractor, and the kids and I would play. Three of the children were old enough to go out and gather the sagebrush, and we would put it into tall piles. We would re-enact the story of the 'Three Little Pigs.' I would be the big bad wolf, and we gathered up the sagebrush and pretended it was the house and burned it down.

We enjoyed the family togetherness. Living the way we did, we all learned to make our own fun. Our grown children still have that ability. We did everything together.

They grew up with a strong work ethic. Some of the homesteaders would drive you crazy; they were such workaholics." Floyd added, "That is something that our kids have always mentioned, that growing up the way they did, they knew how to work hard." Pat spoke up.

"I remember we always felt safe in our community with our children. We all looked out for each other and kept an eye out for the neighbor children as well. The children were expected to behave. We were not afraid to keep the children in line. One time, when I was pregnant, I needed to have some of my teeth pulled. I didn't want Floyd to see me, so I planned the appointment when he was to be away with the troop of Boy Scouts. That was not smart on my part, as I became very sick. I don't know how Frances Roderick found out about me, but she came over to our home. She loaded up all of my wash and got the children rounded up, put me to bed, and went home and cared for them until Floyd came home.

When one of our neighbors got sick or there was a farming accident, we all rallied together to help with the work; and if it was harvest time, we got their crops in first. If we ever needed anything, our neighbors would be there in a flash. Homesteading was something that was very precious. It taught us that we had to earn our own living; no matter what, we had to earn our own living."

Floyd mentioned he couldn't think of a time any of his neighbors took anything from him or lied to him. He felt honesty was something very important in the homestead community.

Floyd talked about the service.

"I thought maybe I would stay in the service, but then I decided I would get out, and I am so glad that I went into farming. I think it is the cleanest way of life and one of the best places anybody can raise their family. It is much better than the city. The children loved it.
They all talk about growing up on the farm."

Floyd began to laugh as he thought of the toilet out in the barn.

"We had small children and the winters were so cold." Pat said, 'If you don't build me a toilet, I am going to build it myself.' Well, spring work had started, and I was trying to build the house as well. I was so busy, but I did manage to get it started and soaked the ground so it would thaw. I dug part of it, but Pat finished the digging and built the whole outhouse herself. Those homestead women were just something!"

Pat spoke.

"Our children were involved in 4-H. They learned sewing. They had one steer they raised that was just a pet, and it had great big horns. One of our girls came home from school one day and was riding Junior Horning--that was our name for the steer. Our youngest daughter walked up behind him and hit him with a stick. Junior jumped and threw the oldest girl into the canal. They've never forgotten that."

Floyd and Pat talked about each of their grown children and what they were doing in their lives. It was obvious that each of the children has grown up to be a productive citizen. Fortunately for them, all of their family live fairly close. I just wasn't prepared for Pat's next comment.

Both Floyd and Pat had been so willing to share about their life and stories of their children. I knew I needed to bring the interview to a close, as evening was coming on by now.

Pat began to speak, and I couldn't help but notice the peace that settled over her.

"Connie has just been here; she left this morning. All of our children have been taking turns coming. Diane is on a sabbatical in order to have time with us. I have cancer and have just a few weeks left. Its okay, you know. I'm so spoiled, and I look forward to death. I think it is exciting, really, to think of my Heavenly Father who loves me enough to give me the strength to have the peace that I have with the sickness. I am just grateful for all of that. I've had such a good life, such a good family, and this was certainly part of it."

What could anyone say that could be more profound than those words? I suddenly came to the realization that this lovely woman had been in a great deal of pain throughout the entire interview, and I am sure Floyd was anxious for her. No one would have guessed by the countenance of either of them. They graciously walked me to the door, and as I turned to wave good-bye to the farm couple, sadness swept over me, but also an appreciation for the privilege of spending a brief time with people who truly are the salt of the earth.

BARBARA AND DICK HANSEN

I sat with Dick and Barbara at their dining room table on that afternoon, drinking a cup of coffee, not quite prepared for such a detailed and salty interview. Later on, as I read over the transcripts of this interview, it became clear that both Dick and Barbara had played key roles of

212

leadership in many facets of the development of this productive community.

Dick began with his childhood.

"We grew up during the Depression. It was a hard time in our country, but growing up on the farm, we had livestock, gardens, milk, so I think we probably had it better than many others.

My military service was spent in the Marines. I enlisted in March of 1942 in Pueblo, Colorado. Boot camp was in San Diego, and to get my training, I went to Miramar. At Santa Monica, I attended the Boeing EC5 School. I came very close to being a rifle range instructor. After going out to the rifle range, I was the only one that made the extras. That night when we went to the range, a sergeant approached me. He explained that it had been decided that I needed to be a rifle instructor. I was surprised at this and asked if I could have a night to think it over.

I decided that was not what I wanted to do, and instead attended the Aviation Institute in Denver before the war broke out. I learned a great deal of information about planes. I went to Hawaii and became a crew chief with the Marine Aircraft Group 15 (MAG 15). I had forty-five Marine crew members I was in charge of. We repaired planes that were shot up. After the crew was finished, it was my responsibility to get into the plane and make sure it was safe for flying.

When my service term was over in March of 1946, I told my commanding officer I never wanted to go back to the farm; I would stay in aviation. I was living in Chicago after my term of service about six months, when I got a call from a friend. He had found a ranch near Granada, Colorado, and wanted me to come and work with him. The farm was owned by American Crystal Sugar Company. He had read about a homestead project in Wyoming. We both sent in an application. His name was not drawn, but my application was drawn in Riverton and Powell projects. My father came with me to check out the Wyoming homestead projects. As we drove across the barren stretches of Wyoming, everything seemed to be dried from the drought that year. My dad turned to me and said, 'Are you sure you don't want to just turn around and go back home?' By that time,

I had already made up my mind, so I kept driving. As we drove closer to the mountain ranges, there were productive farmlands, so both of us felt more encouraged. When we went to Riverton, I told the committee my application had also been drawn in Powell. They advised me to consider the Powell project first, as the land was much better.

The soil on the Riverton homesteads had a problem with seepage. The homesteaders could not make a living on the farms. The old-timers around the area wanted the land, so it was finally decided to give the homestead land to them, so it worked out for the better for them.

The unit my dad and I picked was small, and the wind tends to blow more here, but it had more Class 2 soil than most of the other units around here.

We went into Powell and bought a hammer and saw. We bought a barracks at the relocation center for $1. Dad helped me saw it in two. We found a house mover before we left and then headed back home to Colorado.

Those first three years, I didn't do much for entertainment, I just mostly worked. I put most of the farmland into seed crops to begin with. I didn't have too many problems, since I had farmed before. The ground soil was loose, so irrigating was the hardest thing in those first years.

Margaret Olson introduced Barbara and me on the steps of the Methodist church in Powell. We got married in 1953." Barbara added to the conversation.

"I grew up in Greeley, Colorado, on a farm with five sisters. My father inherited the farm from his grandfather. The 100-year-old farm is still there. Dad gave the house and surrounding three acres to the city for agricultural usage.

My sister, Frances, a fifth grade teacher, came to Powell with me. Three other sisters were teachers as well. I found a position at First National Bank in Powell as a secretary and then became a teller. I met Dick at church, but I saw him again when he came to the bank.

When my mother came to visit, we wondered if she would approve of the barracks. They were, needless to say, rustic, and when the wind

214

blew, the walls went in and out. I told Dick one of the reasons I married him was because of the view of Heart Mountain. It is beautiful up here. I grew up on a farm, so I was accustomed to farm life. We built a home in 1956. We made sure we had a view of the mountain.

Ann was born while we still lived in the barracks. She was born on July 27, 1954. Ann was named after her father's mother. Joan was born in 1956 but only lived for two weeks. And then we had Jane Isabella in 1957. She is named after my mother, Isabel. Sharon was born in February of 1960. Gary Richard was born in August of 1965.

I think our children enjoyed growing up on the homestead. They didn't appreciate all the weeding they had to do. I told them, 'If you can do this, you can do anything,' and they are. It was a lot of work irrigating. We didn't have the irrigation systems they have now.

And all the weeding of the radishes and beans was work.

We always went to Sunday school. They had Bible School at the community club. I don't think any of the families up here on the flat ever locked their doors and took keys out of cars. We just didn't have vandalism up here. I think we brought our kids up like we had been raised, and that isn't just taking them and sitting them in a corner. I think we used our hand a time or two, and I don't think it hurt them any. But anyway, I think our children have the same family values that we did in raising them.

At one time, there were five school buses that came to Heart Mountain. Nowadays, quite a few drive their own cars, but our children went clear through high school on the school bus. All of our children went to Northwest College for two years.

I hadn't been in the community very long before we lost our baby, so I still had not developed a total community feeling yet, but I certainly felt we were supported. At that time, the ladies attended the Mountain View Circle which was interdenominational, so I had become acquainted with many other wives, and they were very supportive during that time.

I think the first time I went to the community club was with Eldora Acott and Eleanor Compton who had invited me to a Circle meeting. I went in there, and I thought I have never seen so many little children or so

215

many pregnant women at the same place. Ann's graduating class was the largest that Powell ever had, and I think it was because of the number of children in this community.

Our children were all involved with 4-H. I think the community 4-H Club was one thing that helped make our families very close. Ann was the one who really enjoyed sewing. We also had horses and sheep. The children had sheep projects. Dick went to South Dakota and got some Montadale sheep. They are the prettiest sheep you ever saw."

Dick spoke.

"We took Gary with us when he was still a baby to South Dakota. The place we bought some of the sheep was a Danish settlement where Danes from Denmark had come. My original mother came to South Dakota, and my father came there. A big bunch of my relatives landed in that part. So this is where I bought the sheep, from a family named Jorgensen. My mother's maiden name was Jorgensen.

I really had not planned to go back into farming after the war, but I think it has been a good place to raise a family. They all learned to drive a tractor. Each one of our children played an important role in the farm work.

I broke horses, and all of our children enjoyed riding. The 4Horse Project was important for them.

I began raising sugar beets in 1953. In this upper part, there were only three of us in the beginning. We all shared the machinery and worked together, so it helped all of us keep the cost down for the beet crop. I quit raising sugar beets when I was approached by Northrup King to raise sugar beets. Apparently, radish seed did very well in Washington, Idaho, and Wyoming. I asked for 60 acres, and the field man allotted them to me, so that is why I quit raising sugar beets.

Many of the homesteaders began to raise malt barley for Budweiser, Schlitz, and Coors. I raised pinto and great northern beans."

Dick was helpful in explaining about the eleven amendments that were awarded later in the homestead project.

"Well, the Bureau of Reclamation had come to the conclusion that the homesteaders would need more acreage in order to make a living feasible. All of the units were awarded amendments in 1951. There was not enough land for this, so eleven of the farmers had been left out of the allotments.

We began raising sheep in 1960. Those who raised sheep worked together. We formed the Wool Board and the Lamb Board. We needed to find pasture in the summer to feed our sheep, so the Lamb Board was formed. We found land in the Beartooth Mountain Range. The Tollmans had a grazing lease up there. We had to form a band of sheep in order to use this land. I think most of us had around 100 ewes that needed pasture. Tollman hired a sheepherder for us, and they hauled our band of sheep up to the mountain range. That left us free to do our farming in the summer months. In the fall, the sheep would feed on the sugar beet tops after the harvest was done. So that worked out well.

The Lamb Board played a major role when it came time to sell the fat lambs. The telephone company would supply us with a phone with speakers. We would call the buyers and negotiate the selling of the lambs. Some of the board members got real good at weighing and grading the lambs. We loaded the lambs onto Dick Jones' trucks, and then they would be hauled to the packing plants.

The Wool Board found markets for the wool. I think most of us sheared in December and loaded the wool into railroad cars in January and February. The buyer would be there at the railroad car inspecting the wool before it was loaded into the train. It was a big job for the Wool Board. We built a big, metal ring and attached a sack about eight to ten feet long. The wool would be put into the sack and be pressed down.

Sheep production was good in those years. We sold the wool, and then we would sell the fat lambs, so it worked well for most of us. I enjoyed serving on those boards with the other guys. It was a lot of work, but we all helped each other.

217

I raised Columbia for the wool and Suffolk sheep that were rugged and sturdy. But we bought the Montadale for the 4-H projects, because they looked so nice for showing.

We lambed out in January, and it was a lot of work. There were a lot of nights I didn't get much sleep. The first winter we had sheep, we didn't have the barn enclosed in the front. We had such cold weather that year, and we lost a lot of sheep. So the next year, the barn was enclosed.

We needed to be in the barn when the lambs were born, because the ewes usually had twins. The first lamb would be okay, but when the ewe dropped the second lamb, she often would walk off and not claim it. I built lambing stalls in the sheds. When the ewes lambed, she and her lambs would be put into the stall until she had claimed her lambs, and then she could be released to be with the rest of the herd.

Sometimes, the ewe would not claim her lamb, or if there were triplets, she wouldn't have enough milk, and we would feed the lambs by bottle. The lambs fed on the bottle were called bum lambs. Sometimes we had a lot of bum lambs to feed.

There were eleven of the homesteaders who had never received an amendment, so let me tell you about how this last portion of allotments came about. A gentleman by the name of Mr. High had a school section. We were told if they didn't farm the land, it would be impossible for us to receive land because of the expense of putting in another canal. A canal was going to be dug that would feed water to the amendments up on Heart Mountain. But when Mr. High turned down this option, the land was taken away.

I was on the Irrigation Board at the time. I realized that the eleven homesteaders that had not received an amendment were getting older. I talked with Bob Fagerberg in 1970 about the possibility of putting sprinklers in for irrigation. I reminded him of the eleven homesteaders that had never received an amendment.

He and I went to Billings to attend a Bureau of Reclamation meeting. When we walked into the meeting, there sat the board members wearing black suits and neckties, and we farmers were dressed in blue jeans and work clothes.

As we sat around the table, they explained that the water rights had been taken away from the land we were wanting for amendments. It was too late; we would just have to give up the idea of getting the land. The chairman looked like a sensible guy, so I stood up and said, 'Just look at me. How old do you think I am?' He laughed and said, 'Well, you're getting up there.' I continued, "Do you think I'd ever get an amendment if I couldn't get this? Don't you think we deserve it? Eleven of us homesteaders were left out in 1951, and here it is 1974." After a few moments, the chairman replied, "I agree with you. You know what I am going to do? I am going to apply for that water right again and see that you eleven get your amendment." And so he did. The other ten did not even know that I had attended the meeting, so I went back home and told them, and they were surprised.

The names of the homesteaders that drew the last amendments on Heart Mountain were Herb Beslanowitch, Gene Dunleavy, Lyle French, Dick Hansen, Wallace McClaflin, Harold McHose, Dale Metzer, Glenn Montgomery, Tak Ogawa, Lloyd Snider, and Elmon Toler.

Your dad enjoyed the amendment. I would see him up there two or three times a day. Yes, he took good care of it.

It was good soil up on the amendments. A lot of Class 2, some Class 1 which is better than the farms below. I believe the Agriculture Department from the University of Wyoming tested the soil.

I have memories of us doing a lot of swimming. We had placed screens to protect the pumps in the canal from clogging up. We built fences with screens, but weeds would still get into the pumps. We laid logs across the canal. We would have to get down into the canal and clean the screens. I know Wallace fell in. The canal was deep. We would have to step on our toes to keep our heads above water. When the pump got clogged, it would shut off, and the sprinklers would be down, so we all spent a lot of time turning each other's sprinklers on. We all got to be great friends. I'd say

219

you couldn't have found a better group of guys than we had up there. I decided to retire from farming when I was sixty-five. When I was a kid, I had an accident while working in the hay. I broke my tail-bone and ruptured a disk, and in those days, we didn't go to the doctor. During the service, I didn't realize I had back problems, but when I got back into farming, it became a problem. I had surgery at 65 and needed to be done with farming.

VAUDINE JIRSA

As I began looking over the transcripts of my interview with Vaudine, I am so grateful for the time I shared with her. She slipped away so quickly from us, not leaving many clues that she was sick. How many times have I felt this gnawing down inside of me, wondering why the seeds of realization to write this historical account didn't come to me many years ago?

Vaudine had been interviewed in 1986 for the book, *Modern Pioneers*, but Bob was still alive then. I felt she was gracious to invite me to visit with her, as it was apparent during the interview that the gripping finger of grief still lingered with her over the death of her husband.

Several years before, her family had moved Vaudine into a comfortable condominium in the north part of Powell. As I walked up to the door that morning, I swallowed hard, put a smile on my face, and greeted her.

She was, as I remembered her so many years ago, showing age a bit around the eyes. She had the same cheerful smile, light blond hair, and soft "peaches and cream" complexion that never seemed to grow old. Even as I sat across from her, sharing a cup of coffee, it was hard to imagine that this petite and refined lady with a quiet elegance had shared in the hardships of those early years on the northern plains.

My eyes glanced around the room, focusing on a picture near the dining room. I recognized Bob from my childhood collection of faces.

"That is my favorite picture, Patty. It was taken when Bob was plowing virgin soil. And then, of course, my Heart Mountain. I think all of us felt like Heart Mountain belonged to us. The Christmas after Bob died, I saw this picture and loved it. A friend encouraged me to buy myself a gift, and I have certainly enjoyed looking at it on my wall.
Bob died November 13, 1994."

Vaudine stopped, the tears beginning to fill her eyes. We both sat quietly for a few moments, sharing this sorrowful moment. I looked away, giving her the privacy she needed, but realizing I was about to interview a

221

lady who had loved deeply, still felt a keen sense of loss, but had lived a rich life full of much joy, family, and friends.

"I moved the following year at Easter. My daughter, son-inlaw, and their children came. He had time off at Easter, but he had to be back to work in Salt Lake City on Monday morning. Several friends helped us that Saturday. It was a fast move, but we managed to get everything moved in that day. I was just sharing with my daughter, Joanne, recently of my feelings that Easter morning. We had gone to a brunch, and then they had to head back home. When I came back to my home, I don't think I had ever in my life felt so alone. But I am happy here, and this is where I ought to be now.

The homestead community was where so many young families were able to rebuild their lives after WWII. Bob was in the Signal Corps, and toward the end of the war, he was in the Air Force. He was getting ready to go to cadet training, but the war in Europe ended. He always felt they were getting ready to send him to the South Pacific, but before that happened, the atomic bomb was dropped.

His father kept him out of the service for quite a while, but he wanted to go so badly. It was important to the young people in those days to serve their country. I have said WWII kind of got people mixed up. You married people from different parts of the country, and because of the war, this is how I met Bob.

While he was stationed at Camp Crowder, he and his friend came to Pittsburgh, Kansas, for a visit. My girlfriend and I met the fellows, and then they met my mother. My mother invited the two young servicemen to live in her basement for a short while. My folks liked Bob right off. So that is how I got acquainted with Bob. The other fellow was from Texas. After a brief time, he and my girlfriend were married. We have gone to see them several times in Texas. When we first came to Wyoming, they came to see us. We have often laughed about the overalls he wore when he came to visit. He wanted to help Bob pour cement but didn't want to get his clothes dirty. So he had brought some overalls about four sizes too big for him.

We married before Bob went overseas. When he came back, it was like being married to a stranger, because we hadn't lived together long enough to have any memories or anything to base our lives on. When he came home, I was teaching at a little school close by, so while I was finishing up the year, he found a job distributing newspapers and magazines. That summer we moved to Lincoln, Nebraska. I think he read about the homesteading in one of the magazines he was selling.

Bob was a Nebraska native. I taught school there for two years, and he worked at Western Electric. He filled out an application for the Heart Mountain homestead and then just dismissed it from his mind. When we first got word that we had received a homestead, a telegram came from the Ford Tractor Company, but later on, a registered letter came in the mail.

Bob bought an old truck from the University of Nebraska and fixed it up. All of our friends helped us get ready to move. They had several going-away parties for us, and, of course, about a year later, they all came to see us in Wyoming.

We received an official notice that our name had been drawn, so in November 1949, we moved to Wyoming. We had an apartment at the relocation camp. It was a holiday...I can't seem to remember...and well, it must have been Thanksgiving. I had made a stew in the pressure cooker and drove out to where Bob was working on our unit. We ate together out at the homestead. The pressure cooker had kept the meal hot. It was just so cold in the barracks, but I wasn't about to let my parents know that everything wasn't just wonderful.

Where we had come from in Nebraska had a lot of trees. My first impression, as I looked out over the homesteads, was that it had to be the most desolate place I had ever seen. Not a tree in sight. But in those days, you did things with your husband, and that is just how it was. Of course, I thought it would get better, and it did. When a person goes to the homestead today and sees all the trees, it seems unbelievable. Right before I left the home-place, I was planting little trees everywhere.

I had never lived on a farm, so this was really a great adjustment for me. We drilled a well as soon as we could, as hauling water on those

223

dirt roads was very difficult. We eventually got electricity and everything else. I grew to love the farm. I felt it was such a good place to raise a family.

We had so much company, and, of course, my parents loved to come to see us on the homestead. When they came, Mom helped me can, and my dad would help Bob in so many ways. My parents were from Pittsburgh, Kansas. I got a flavor for farming from my grandparents who lived on a farm. I remember my brother and me spending several weeks each summer on the farm with my grandparents.

I think right away our community developed a very close loyalty to one another. We looked out for each other. The community club was our hub. The Bible School, community meetings, and I remember well the Christmas parties were our entertainment. I always played the piano for the Christmas program. Santa Claus would come, and all the children would get a sack of candy. That was always a highlight for us, you know. I think Bob was the second community club president. I know Lloyd Snider was the first but can't remember after that. Although I have moved to town, I still pay my dues for the club, as I think Bob would want me to do that. I still have land out on the bench. I rarely go out anymore. Oh, I go to weddings and baby showers, but that's about all.

In those early years, if we couldn't go to our parents' for Christmas, we would celebrate the holidays with the Cobbs and the Ashers. After our families got larger, we would have to separate the meetings, but when we had big dinners, one family would fix the turkey, and everyone else would bring other dishes. Our neighbors became our family. We did try to be with grandparents on the holidays, if possible.

We only made long-distance calls when someone died or a baby was born. It was so much different than the way it is today. I remember when Bob's mother died on May 1.

We were having one of those terrible spring snowstorms. Bud Steck came out in that bad weather and gave us the news. All of our neighbors came to help us get ready to go to the funeral. We wanted to stay with our family longer than we did, but of course, it was spring, and we couldn't stay as long as we would have liked to. At times like that, homesteaders really realized neighbors in the community made up their family away from home.

Like many of the other homesteaders, we added on to our barracks rather than tear it down and just start over. Looking back, I think it might have been better to just start all over. The kitchen, dining room, and one bedroom are the barracks. We built on a living room, another bedroom, and bath.

We had a garage attached, and when the girls were born, we made that a bedroom and built another garage. When the girls got older, they wanted their own rooms, so we built another garage and converted the present garage into another bedroom.

It is hard to give in and realize the farm is too much. I sold the house and barns, but I still own the land. It seems strange to drive by the house. My daughters tell me that it is still their farm, their home. They feel strongly about it. I think the hardest thing about being a widow is not having Bob here to help me make decisions. But I do have the girls, and they help me when we have to plan things to be done.

My daughters' families are taking me with them to Washington, D.C. in March. I went to the store and bought a Wyoming T-shirt. I want to wear it while I am in the capital. People in the east seem to be interested in the Wyoming license plate with the bronco on it.

Getting back to those early years, I remember we grew seed peas. It was a beautiful crop to look at. We had one variety that had a purple blossom, and they were beautiful. We grew potatoes and the usual alfalfa and barley. There were some of the farmers who planted flowers for seed, and that was always so nice to look at from the road.

In those years of raising seed peas, I tied so many sacks, I think I could still do it in my sleep. Of course, Bob taught me to do that, as he was a farm boy. I didn't do any plowing, but I racked a lot of beans. I used to jokingly say that was a safe job for me, as I couldn't do much harm, but I actually thought it was kind of fun racking those beans in the fall.

Both of the girls were very active in 4-H. They took sewing and cooking and did a lot of demonstrations. Jan had horse and dog projects. One year, she got the "Hard Luck Award," as her show dog died. Joanne entered the sheep lead contest. Of course, the garden project was important. I remember digging up half of the garden to get something to take to the fair. As the girls got older, it seemed like the fair came earlier each year, so it was hard to find enough produce for the garden exhibits.

I have so many good memories of our family and raising the girls on the farm. I miss the homestead, but without Bob here now, it is much better for me to be in town. I feel grateful we had the life we did here in Wyoming. So many of the homesteaders have passed away now, but those of us left are still such good friends."

GROUP INTERVIEW WITH VAUDINE JIRSA, ANN NELSON, AND RUTH OTTO

Several times, people have asked me which interview was my favorite. I have always been able to respond immediately. "All of them!" I have not seen many of the first-generation homesteaders since I married and left home in 1964. Naturally, I was more acquainted with some neighbors than others, but with each interviewee, I found the same camaraderie. After reading the transcripts and rereading them, I would have to give Ann Nelson and Ruth Otto purple ribbons for being natural historians. But each person gave insight and stories about their individual situation. Many of the comments were very similar, but that only reinforces the determination and commitment these dear families had to one another in that common goal of making a community.

I truly hope that, after the stages that families go through with losing a parent or grandparent, they will listen to the audio-tapes and read the written transcripts that are all documented and stored for future research.

I had already interviewed Vaudine, Ruth, and Ann, so I was so delighted they agreed to meet with me again. Ruth was in the last stages

226

of cancer on the morning of this interview, but none of us at that time realized Vaudine would pass away so suddenly. As I am reading over this transcript this afternoon, getting ready to put into words the delightful conversation, I can't help but take joy in the refreshing remembrance of such a wonderful morning with three homestead wives, all widows now, but each so full of the love of life.

The Jirsas, Nelsons, and Ottos had all lived in the Japanese Relocation Camp after arriving in Wyoming. Very few of the other homesteaders had this experience to recount. Obviously, there was a bond of close friendship that began with the three families in those first few weeks in a very brutally cold, Wyoming winter.

The goal of this group interview was to try to establish particular details and dates of many of the stories that had been recounted by individual homesteaders.

The first thing we talked about was the square dances of which so many others had fond memories. None of them were certain exactly when the dances started and if the evening fee was $.50 or a $1.00 a couple. Walt Scott from Powell was the caller. He owned Scott Plumbing in Powell. He and his wife went around to the local communities in the evening doing the square dances as a community service.

Ruth, of course, was so frail, but she was in good spirits, and I think the rest of us were so happy she had enough energy that morning to participate. Speaking in her soft voice with a lilt of laugher, I have such fond memories of her as she described the dances.

"It was very inexpensive entertainment, and it was good exercise. We would go to see our friends, and we had refreshments at the end of the evening. Sometimes we had sandwiches, but mostly we had dessert and coffee. And, of course, we had juice."

Vaudine and Ann laughingly chimed in. "Some of us didn't drink coffee, and some of us did. We all looked forward to it."

Each one tried to remember the year the square dances started. Vaudine spoke.

"It was early on, because my daughters are adopted, and I took one of them to the doctor when she was brand new, and they asked me if I had been square dancing last week. I kind of laughed and said, "Yes, you know my baby is adopted," as they probably wondered how I could have been dancing around last week if I had been carrying a baby.

They each described the kinds of dancing that they did in the classes.

"We did all kinds of dancing; we waltzed. But mainly, we learned to square dance. They had what they called round dancing."

Ann chuckled.

"The thing I remember is Walt Scott's dad was about 85 or 90 years old. Yeah, and he would square dance with everybody. He came out with Walt and Edna. He would come and have the best time; I think he would dance with every woman that was there.

Ruth commented.

"We did have such a good time. But I couldn't learn the little foot one, so Edna and Leonard Schafer came over, and we pushed the table aside in the kitchen and practiced so we could learn the little foot step right. Loran and I both had trouble. I guess we both just had left feet.

Ann joined in.

"We squared danced over a period of several years. When we first started, it was just the Heart Mountain group. But then, there was Pete and Ethel Wood that came to help us. There were couples from Belfry that came every time. At the peak of the dances, there were about thirty or more squares in the clubhouse, and that was a lot. Some of us would go to other places to square dance. But as the years went by, the group got smaller, and finally, they went into Powell for square dancing."

Ann and Ruth began to talk about the soap they made in the yearly years.

"Patty, one of the things I thought about after you left was how Ruth and I used to make homemade soap. We did it every summer for several years. It was Ruth's recipe. I think we went to your house to make it, didn't we Ruth?"

"I think so?"

228

Ann continued.

"I had an old, water bath canner that had a leak in it finally, and that is what we used to stir the soap. I think the canner is still sitting over in the shop or somewhere on the farm. Remember how our neighbors would save their used grease for us? They would save it, and then we would have to clean it. Ruth could probably tell you more about that."

"Well, you took the lard and heated it on the stove, and then you poured water in it, and the parts you didn't want to keep would rise to the top; you would skim off the debris and all that. Then you would have a handful of salt and begin to stir, and the salt would purify it. Then you would let it cool, and it would be so pretty and white. We continued to scoop the debris off the top. The recipe called for so many cups of lard, and a can of lye, and so much water. We would add this all together and then just stir, and stir, and stir it, like a cake. You couldn't stir it too fast, and you had to stir it just one way. If you stirred it too fast or didn't go in one direction, it would curdle. We used a wash stick or big spoon to stir."

Ann joined in.

"Yes, we would stir until it got pretty thick. Yes, it got pretty thick, and then we lined a beer box or something with freezer paper and poured it in. But before it got too hard, we would cut it. We used it for laundry soap. It just made your clothes so white."

Ruth spoke.

"One thing, if your water was hard, it didn't work very good. But our water was really nice and soft, so we could use it. The lye pretty well took out the bacteria."

Ruth and Ann both began to laugh.

Laughingly, Ruth continued.

"Yeah, I would hang the clothes on the line, and they had such a good, fresh smell from being outdoors. The soap did have a kind of lye smell. I would use a potato grater and just grate the soap into the hot water in the machine. Most of us had old Maytag washers. Usually, if I got to the overalls, the water was so dirty that I had to dump it and then put fresh water in the tub. But you had to heat the water. After we moved to the Stone place, we had a hot water heater, and it certainly helped."

"Most of us went to town sometimes to do our laundry. Mrs. Garvin, a widow lady, had some conventional washers and dryers situated in her garage. We would meet people there, and that is one way we made friends in this new community. She was certainly a nice lady. We all had so many questions, and she would always take the time to talk with us and help us. Usually, we would take our laundry home and hang it up, but once in a while, we would have them dry it.
She had a huge dryer. Do you remember that?"

Ruth, Vaudine, and Ann tried to remember the laundry in the garage.

"How many machines were there?" "I'm not sure, but I think there were three on each side." "Oh yeah, she knew these homesteaders were coming to town with their baskets full of clothes, and that was kind of a chore. Especially mothers with children and small babies."

Ann reflected.

"I remember that I would go to Garvin's at night when Earl and Ted Smith went to night school together. When it was Earl's turn to drive, I would take the laundry. Bruce and Byron would go to the laundromat while the men were at school. The twins would go into the house and play with Rodney.

In reading my letters, I came across the part where I told our parents about the bathtub situation. After Bob and Vaudine got their house plumbed and had running water, they also had a bathroom." Ann began to laugh.

"It was wonderful; I would go up to their place and take a bath."
All three friends began to laugh together as they remembered the bath.

Vaudine chimed in.

"We had two or three people who came to take a bath. It was a real treat, you know. We would have coffee and visit, and they would take a bath. Before we had electricity, we had a motor on the well that pumped our water, and early on, we had it in the house. It really became a social affair in our neighborhood."

"I was going to say the Jirsas were just a bit ahead of the average person up there with their improvements. We would go there and take baths, and then they had television long before we did, and so we would go up there and watch Liberace the night he was on." Ruth laughed again.

Vaudine added details about the Scouting program.

"My daughter always wanted me to tell about when I was a Cub Scout leader. There must have been eight or nine boys in the neighborhood that came. I left the television off during the meeting, but when they were waiting for their parents, it was a good baby-sitter. I would let them watch a program. Eldora Acott talked me into being a leader, and I used to say I did the best I could. I don't think I did any harm. I don't know if I did any good or not, but it was fun and interesting to be around young people before I had any kids. Now, my daughter is a Scout leader. When I watch her get ready to go to a meeting, she has her uniform and her hat, and she's just all business. I remember if I had a clean pair of jeans and clean shirt, I would put those on before the kids came. This is how organized we were."

The conversation shifted at this point to how the individual families heated their homes. They each commented on the morning stoves that were given to each homesteader with the barracks. Ruth said that they used coal. "We went to a coal mine over in Belfry, Montana; I believe it was the Smith mine."

"I remember one winter, Loran had to have a hernia surgery, so he went to the Veterans Hospital in Cheyenne for two weeks. While he was away, it was twenty below every day. I had to do the milking, and I wasn't giving the cow enough water, so she bloated, and it was just a mess. I ran up the hill to get Mr. Winn. He knew what to do for a cow that was bloated, so he stuck the cow, and, of course, the fumes just flew. Oh dear! He told me I wasn't giving the cow enough water, so I had to give her more water."

All three friends laughed at this comment.

"The cow healed up okay, and I learned from that experience."

Although I had already interviewed each of the homestead wives, as we concluded our interview, I asked if they could briefly summarize life in the homestead community once again.

231

Ruth spoke first.

"Well, as far as we were concerned, we didn't have that much to leave when we came up here from Kansas. We were optimistic that this was going to get better, you know, that things were going to work out. And everyone that we knew was in the same situation. Having to do without electricity was maybe a little inconvenient. But we never did think that it was all that bad, and probably carrying water was the worst thing about it, but this is the way you had to do it, so you just accepted it.

Another thing we talked about was living in the barracks.

We were just so thankful to have them to live in those first few years, because we couldn't have stayed here if we hadn't had them. I feel like most of the other families that came up here had decided that we all were going to make this our home. So you didn't spend much time thinking about how awful things were, that is just the way things were, and you just accepted it."

Ann joined in.

"I gave a lot of thought to this life for our children. I have always said that living on a farm is the best way in the world to raise boys, especially, since that is what I specialized in." Ann paused and laughed.

"I still feel that the farm, even in this more modern, faster life, is a lot better place to raise children. I don't think you sit and analyze how your life is going to affect your children and your future and all that. But you just take it day by day and make the best of what you have."

Ruth began to laugh.

"Oh, I have to tell this story. That first summer, when we began to irrigate, there were so many rattlesnakes. Remember? "Yeah, we sure remember," chimed in Ann and Vaudine. "Well, Loran would come in so exhausted that first summer after working such long hours. I think he was probably still half asleep, but Loran was always thinking there were snakes in our room when he was in bed in the middle of the night. And with no electricity! I slept on the outside of the bed, and I had a flashlight on the floor. He would wake me up, and he would say,

232

"There is a snake in bed." All of
us laughed.

"Yes, he would say, 'Get the flashlight.' And I would have to reach down on the floor and get the flashlight to turn the light on and find out there were no snakes in there. But one time, when I turned on the flashlight, I looked over, and up in the corner of the room where the Celotex didn't fit real tight, there was a mouse sitting up there looking at us. So whether he had run across the bed, I never figured it out, but anyway, that was kind of scary."

"When we came, of course, there were no roads. You just took off across country, or you took a cow path and hoped you hit the right road to go across the Alkali Creek and get over to your place. I remember one time, Loran's folks and sister and brother-in-law were coming. I told them to turn at the second bridge, and they had miscounted the bridges, so they were on the canal and couldn't get the car turned around. They could see the homestead but couldn't find a way to get over the creek. They were on the west of the canal, and finally, they inched and inched until they got turned around, and then they decided that they had to come down one road, and they finally got to our place. They were a pretty scared bunch. None of them had seen mountains much, and so, of course, we had to take them to Yellowstone. And, oh! They were scared to death. Well, I was kind of scared, too, the first time we went up Buffalo Bill Highway to the reservoir on the old road.

Loran and I had nothing in Nebraska. He had been in the service for three years and had just done some work on farms, so we certainly weren't getting anywhere there, so when we drew the homestead, we were happy. My mother said, 'You are not taking that, are you?' But then, my parents got to thinking that it really was an opportunity. I just considered it a challenge and wanted to see if we could really do it or not. I never figured it was so bad. It was lots of hard work. You worked day and night, but what do you get if you don't work?"

Vaudine began.

233

"Well, we considered it to be a wonderful opportunity, and Bob's dad and his two brothers were farmers, and, of course, there was no place for Bob. This was an opportunity to own a farm, and so we looked forward to that and thought it was something we really wanted to try and to do. I always tell the story about the old plow on the corner that was a landmark for me, when I came from the camp to take a meal to Bob up on the homestead. On Thanksgiving Day, I had made a meal in the pressure cooker to take to Bob, as he was plowing up on the farm. Someone had moved the plow, so I just drove around and around until I finally found my way."

I knew I needed to bring the interview to a close, as I observed Ruth's voice getting weaker and weaker. We had been talking together for about an hour and a half. As we all stood to go and were saying our good-byes, Ruth paused and said, "Oh, hurry and get the book done, so I can read it before I am gone."

I was already beginning to realize the magnitude of the project I had undertaken and knew the chances of completion before we said our good-byes to Ruth were nearly impossible. But as I left Vaudine's home that morning, driving away with the tears streaming down my face, I had a great sense of peace in knowing I had just sat with three heroes of my childhood--those who have loved our homestead community and had such a part in making it all happen. They have stories that will be penned to the page. Their voices will be preserved on tape. I have the awesome responsibility of putting down on paper their stories of courage, wit, and perseverance that helped shape future generations.

PAT JONES

The interview with Pat was in her home in town. Since I had seen Don and Pat, they had moved from the homestead into a nice apartment in town. How well I remember this attractive lady from the childhood years in 4-H.

"Okay, Pat, tell me about you and Don--how you found out about the homestead, where you were before it ever started."

"We were living in Powell. Both of us graduated from Powell, and we were raising our family in Powell. We heard about the Ralston Bench Project from the Bureau of Reclamation. Don put his name in the hat, so to speak, and he was one of the lucky ones, so he thought. But when they drew his name out, I was very sad. I had three babies, practically. The oldest one was three. Don was so excited, he came home from work at Case Implement and threw his cap in the door and said, 'We're moving to Heart Mountain.' I started crying immediately and said, 'I'm not going.' He said, 'Well, I'll go without you.' Well, that was just the beginning. He knew I'd go with him. I mean, he was sure of that. So, naturally, we packed up the kids and moved. We were buying our home on Avenue C here in Powell. That was in 1949. On April 2, 1950, we loaded a couple of farm trucks in the biggest blizzard we had on Heart Mountain. There were no landmarks whatsoever, there were no poles, and there were no electricity poles. There was nothing!

Don's brothers ran the ditches on both sides of the trucks and helped us get into our place. We used the barracks for a home. You could throw a cat through the wall anywhere, but it was home. And that was the beginning of our homesteading days.

Don's service was in the Army Air Corps in the Air Force branch of the military. He was with the Air Transport Command, and we were stationed all in the south. I went with him to Texas, Mississippi, and New Mexico. Our oldest son was born in Mississippi, and the other two children were born in Powell. Let's see, he flew with the B17, and he was a very thin man, and they loved the mechanic work that he did, because he could crawl in small spaces. His rank went up quite highly because of that. Both coming from Powell, we couldn't wait to get back home after he was discharged. He was in the service three years almost to the day.

Our home started on the homestead with no water, no electricity, no telephone, and just the barracks.

Don continued working for Case Implement for a couple of years. We only worked up about half of our land at first.

We built a basement home. The day we moved into our home was in 1951-52. People won't believe this, but it was 44 below zero the day we moved from our barracks into our basement home. Albert Farwell and Johnny Eichler and a bunch of the neighbor men came and helped us, and it was just heavenly. We had propane, we didn't have it plumbed or anything, and we had a well with a gas motor.

Don's father, who lived in New Mexico, gave us a heifer cow, and that was the beginning of our cow herd. It was a Guernsey cow; naturally, it had to be a Guernsey if it was a Jones. We sold cream from the Guernsey cow. After Don got home from work, he and I would go out and clear the sagebrush and burn it. All three kids were in the pickup.

One night, when we were out changing the water or something, we got lost in the field. There were no lights; no one had electricity. I thought we were going west instead of east to get back to the house. We finally turned around and made it back to the house.

We bought sheep. We started out with 200-head of sheep, and, of course, the kids were a little older by that time, so they got in on a lot of sheep herding, as we had no fences yet. Of course, they didn't like that job at all, along with many other things. I liked the sheep. When we did move to town, I missed the lambing. That was my job.

We raised cattle, and we had hogs, and chickens, and a couple of goats that ran with the sheep herd, intending to keep the dogs out of them.

We attended church every Sunday, and I still do, and I guess our children do, too. So they must have learned something from us.

We did build a new home on the basement foundation in 1954. We moved into it in January of 1955. We did all the work ourselves. It cost us $11,000, and it was about 1,400 square feet, so that was a nice job to do.

Many times, I thought if we just lived in town? My biggest wish was, if I could do like those city girls and stand out in the lawn and hold the hose while it sprinkled. That would just be the joy of my life. We finally did get a lawn, but I never did have time to stand out there and sprinkle that lawn.

Our children all graduated from Powell High School, and all but one graduated from college. Kirk was our oldest. He was born in October 1945 in Greenwood, Mississippi. Kenny was next on March 7, 1947, in Powell, and Kayleen was born in Powell in 1949.

In 1954, we were blessed with a little girl. At that time, she was the largest baby born in Powell. She weighed 10 lbs., 15½ ozs. and was 23 inches long. Since then, they have probably had bigger babies, but I know, at that time, they said it was the biggest baby born in Powell. Now she is a nice and tall, slender girl.

I think the kids were real happy at home on the farm. They had their own chores, and they did their own things. We lived on a hillside, and they had many parties on the hill with the snow sleds and inner tubes and that type of thing. We would build bonfires on the hillside for the Sunday school picnic in the wintertime at our house.

We did fun things like that. We didn't get to do a lot when we were farming, and the kids have never been able to understand that to this day. They always said everybody else went to the rodeo on the 4th of July in Cody, but none of the Jones kids did. They were always stacking hay. They were always in the field, weeding beans and stacking hay. The boys would stack, and Kayleen would drive the truck. And then, when Kara got big enough, why they taught her to just steer, and they would jump down off the truck and turn it around, and she would steer back. She likes to remember those kinds of things with her brothers.

I don't know? Seems like we had a happy time out there. I wouldn't want to go back to it, but when I think about it, it wasn't really that bad.

I think our community is one in a million. I think it's the most wonderful thing that has happened to the Powell community, has been our homesteaders. I know there are some people who are jealous of the way that we still stick together, and we ladies still have our Tuesday morning meetings. That started way back, I don't even know, in the '60s or '70s, and some of us are still doing that Tuesday morning get together. Heart Mountain people have a wonderful community, and we stick together through thick or thin.

I'm sure other communities started out the same, but it seems that all of us started with the same thing, nothing. And our children were all the same age. The men were all the same age, because they were all military. I think that had a lot to do with it, because that age similarity kept them all thinking the same and doing the same. Our kids grew up and rode the bus together and stuck together in school, and they still stick together.

Our grown kids love to talk about the homestead; they think it was wonderful. Once in a while, they will say, jokingly, 'Why didn't you move to town when we were kids?' And Don will say, 'That's why we didn't move to town--you were kids!' I think they realize now that was a wonderful place to raise them, and their morals are based on what they did and learned as children on the homestead.

I think the number one thing our children got from this way of life was they learned respect. Closeness--I think as a family, we are close. Even though our children live away now, they still feel that closeness to those neighbors they grew up with. I think the high standards and morals came from this homestead way of life. Lying to a neighbor was unheard of in our community. I don't know what we would have to lie about, because we were all equal. That was the nice part about it.

We didn't consider ourselves poor. We had so much, really. We didn't have much money, but we had a lot of other things. The children learned a work ethic. The boys didn't like milking the cows, they didn't mind the sheep, and, of course, they loved the horses and things like that, but I guess no one likes to milk cows, do they?" Pat laughed at this point.

"I think the couples loved each other. The hard work encouraged that. They didn't get to go a lot of places and do a lot of things, but love was important then.

Of course, the kids were in 4-H. The boys took dairy, woodwork, and leather. Edna Mae taught the girls how to sew. They are beautiful seamstresses today. They took cooking, and I think they also took lambs. I did a lot of driving to youth activities for the children.

The kids still talk about the Bible School down at the clubhouse. That was really important. I always handled the music part of it. I remember Bertie helping me. Kayleen and Sandy were the same age, and I remember that Sandy was so darn cute. Our children would go to the youth fellowship on Wednesday nights at church, and they would get to be with their friends. I think they sort of enjoyed going to church; they got away from home a little bit.

In the wintertime, we played a lot of games. Our kids all knew how to play cribbage. We had teams, you know, and we played cribbage. Kirk was a backgammon guy, and he played chess. He loved both of those. I didn't ever learn chess, but his dad played with him.

We had a fireplace in our house. That old fireplace would be going, and we would popcorn. They always loved it when the bus couldn't get up the hill, and that was pretty often. We would kind of lay back and have the whole day to do what we wanted to do, except the chores. The chores were there day and night, whether they were in school or home. But we haven't had storms for a long time like we had back in those years.

The storm in the spring of 1952, I think it was, we were snowed in for four days. The winds had drifted the snow over the opening of the sheep shed. It was bad, but we survived that along with many other things.

We enjoyed ourselves at the clubhouse. That was the place we all had entertainment, more than any other place. We would have potluck suppers and then a dance, perhaps. The kids would be entertained with bingo or games, or if they were too small, we had a little glassed-in nursery. They eventually installed a telephone in the clubhouse, which was good, because of the older kids leaving home with the younger ones, and then that made it a little more secure for us. I think it held our community together. I guess all of us belonged to it. I don't know of anyone that didn't belong. It was a nice old barracks meeting place.

I was a member of the Extension Club. I loved Edith Anderson. She and her husband would come to our church sometimes and sing.

239

She did a lot of work in our community.

The kids got along with each other in our community. They stuck close together, and I don't think they even thought of hurting each other, language, or lies or anything. I just think they were close and probably would stick up for each other, if necessary. We would watch out for each other's children. I wouldn't have thought anything of going up to any one of the children if they were misbehaving. You don't do that nowadays.

Coming out of the war like we all did made us appreciate what we did have. Even the little things were important to us.

When I was growing up during WWII, the Japanese Relocation Camp was here in our community. Our family liked the Japanese. I went to school with them. I was on their basketball team, and their teams would come in and play basketball. Don's parents hired them to help on the farm. My brother and I worked for a man with a hog business at the time. We hauled garbage from the Japanese Relocation Center to his hog operation, and we got to be friends with them. I was living in Ralston with my parents. My father had rented a grocery store, so we dealt with the Japanese families a good deal. My father rode a horse and did the night guarding of the fences around the relocation center at that time.

There is a lot of history in our Heart Mountain community. It has been a wonderful place to live and raise our families."

241

PART II: HOMESTEADER INTERVIEWS
SECTION 3

BOB AND IDABELLE LAWSON

Homesteading was a family affair. Everyone had a job. There were some young bachelors who received a homestead. Life was difficult for them, as they had all the responsibilities of farming as well as taking care of a home. It was not so easy in those early days to drive ten miles to town.

The community, as a whole, celebrated with those young veterans when they found a bride. One of those bachelors was a close neighbor, Bob Lawson. Memories I have of Idabelle were her energy and happy face that always seemed to have a smile.

Bob and Idabelle have moved to town. I went to visit them last winter, and as I entered their home, I was met with that same smile. It was a delightful evening visiting with them, as they were so gracious. As Idabelle would speak, I had to keep reminding myself that at least forty years had transpired since the last time I saw this couple. That same energy and fun personality permeated the evening.

Bob began the discussions.

"Well, I grew up in Concrete, North Dakota, about eighty miles north of Grand Forks. It's about fifteen miles from the Canadian border.

I heard about the Heart Mountain homesteads from a Texaco field man. I was so glad my application was accepted. We had to have $3,500, either in money or tractors and equipment. My dad gave me an old tractor and disk and stuff.

Gosh, we were lucky that first year with the seed peas we planted; we made food money on them. We had about 35 or 40 acres. That first year, there weren't many weeds, so it turned out real good that first year. Jim Brown helped us out. He was the field man.

My brother Abe and I started farming that first homestead unit together. Then he bought me out, and I bought the unit up on the hill.

243

Neither one of us had hardly any money, so we threw what we had together in order to get approved financially. That was a lot of money after the war to come up with. I think we bought our farm in 1964 and lived there until a few years ago.

Idabelle was working in a café when I met her. We went horseback riding one day, and I guess we just started going together. I guess I just charmed her. The next time I took her out riding, we rode horseback up on North Fork, and after that, we started to see each other a lot."

I turned to Idabelle. "What's your version of this story, Idabelle?"

She started to laugh.

"It must have been those big, blue eyes, cause I never ever lived on a farm before, and I didn't realize it was that much work. I thought it might be a piece of cake, but I don't know, we went together five or six months and then got married.

Bob's younger brothers, Dick and Abe, lived with us, and it was pretty nice. There was electricity but no running water. We had two bedrooms and a path. I felt like I had gone back to the sticks when I moved to the farm.

I grew up around here. My dad was a tool pusher in the oil fields, but I basically lived in Park County. In them days, the oil field workers didn't travel or drive so far. You moved when the rig moved, so we lived in Powell and then Meeteetse and then back in Powell, and back to Meeteetse. I was born on the Willwood and started school in Powell. I left and came back, and left and came back, but graduated from Powell.

I knew about the homesteads and heard people talk about it, but it isn't the same as getting out there and doing it. But I wouldn't trade it for anything. We got married September 10, 1955. So that was about five years after the rest of the families had come to homestead. I was living in town working at the Powell Café, so when you come from living in town where everything is modern, it was really different.

We had no running water or a well. We hauled water in big cream cans; it seemed like forever.

We went back to North Dakota in 1957 with our baby, Matt, to farm Bob's dad's place for a year. We stayed for just a year and moved from there to Montana, and Terry was born in Red Lodge. We lived there until '60 or '61 and then moved back to Powell.

In 1964, we bought the Lawrence Allshouse homestead. That was just about like homesteading all over again, because nothing had been done to work the fields or anything. Oh, it was a mess. The kids and I picked up rocks from the fields in five-gallon pails, and Bob would come along and dump the pails in the back of the pickup. And that was your exercise. You didn't have to worry about getting on a treadmill or riding an exercise bike. You went out and picked up a few tons of rocks. But we worked hard, and the farm began to look pretty good. We lived on the farm from 1964 to 1993. It was a long ways from town, but it was a good place to raise kids.

Our first child, Matt, was born February 21, 1957, here. We were on Bob's original homestead when he was born, with the warm morning stove. I knew he was going to freeze to death. He was born in the middle of the famous Heart Mountain blizzard, of course. Terry was born October 17, 1958, in Red Lodge. I seem to be prone to storms, because we were over between Belfry and Bear Creek getting to Red Lodge to have the baby, and I couldn't get home. Then we lived south of town when Todd was born on April 18, 1963. He was just a year old when we moved back out on Heart Mountain, and it has been home to him ever since. He can't imagine living anywhere else.

When the children were growing up, we went to the Mountain View Club, and I went to the Extension Club. We had a sewing club, which really was just more or less a gossip club. Everybody would bring their knitting or embroidery or whatever to the clubhouse and just have a good old time. It was too far to go to town. We had dances there, and the kids eventually had Halloween parties in preference to trick-or-treating. Everybody would take their candy, even if they didn't have children. In my opinion, it was a lot safer and a lot better for them to have it there where it was warm, and it saved on gas.

245

I wasn't here when the community first began, but even a few years later, we were close. Everyone was the same; nobody had anything to amount to yet. We lived in barracks with no running water. In order to survive, we helped each other. It has always been that way up here on the bench, and it still is today. We sure had a lot of good neighbors. I don't know of any bad ones. If someone was sick, all the neighbors would go combine his fields first and then go home and do their own work.

It is amazing, even the second- and third-generation kids are all doing the same things. They are out helping the older folks that are still living on their own. They don't have to be asked, they just do it. That is just the way they started out, and that is the way the kids were raised. Everybody helped each other. I personally think the world would be a better place if everyone lived that way."

Bob added comments about the coffee sessions.

"We would get together during the winter months at someone's house and discuss farming. It was a great bunch of people. At first, we had to share machinery, and even later, we would trade with each other."

Idabelle talked about her garden and chores.

"We had a big garden. We raised a good crop of weeds; they always did better than anything else. We had chickens and cows. I'd milk cows and feed bum calves on a bucket or skim the milk and feed it to the pigs. We basically had our own beef, and elk, and eggs. I had two pressure cookers I used for canning. I liked to use the glass jars. There was a cannery in town, but I preferred to stay at home, so I could keep a better eye on the children and take lunch to the field when it was necessary, which seemed quite frequently. Most of the women out here worked in the field too. It wasn't all hard work; we had a lot of fun out here."

Bob proudly added this.

"Well, Idabelle, she just drove a tractor and ran the combine and hauled grain and, by golly, she just was like one of us, you know. Idabelle, she was right in there doing all of it. She had never driven a truck, tractor, or nothing. She got good at it. No, them guys wouldn't have been here very long. We couldn't do it alone. Most bachelors didn't stay very long.

I think the thing that meant the most to me was the irrigation. When you came from dry land where your crops burned up all the time, it was nice to have that water. You could be pretty sure of a crop. Back in Dakota, most of the years it would just burn up, and there was nothing you could do about it. That first year, we didn't know anything about irrigation, and it was pretty bad, you know. We did a lot of stupid things, but it was good land, and gosh, it was just real good country up here. No alkali like there is in some other places. We did have some bog holes until drains were put in to run off the water. Tile drains were put in, and that made a big difference.

Our main crops were alfalfa, and peas, and barley, and later we had beans. We raised canner peas, so it was disappointing when the cannery shut down. It was a good cash crop; I missed the heck out it.

We had a few cows for a while. Most of the people didn't keep cattle much. There isn't much for cattle up here. It is better to raise crops and forget about 'em.

As Bob and Idabelle talked about raising their children on their homestead, they both chuckled. Bob talked about it.

We were glad we raised our kids on the homestead. I don't think the kids get in as much trouble out on the farm. Yeah, they learned to drive the pickup real little. You can't do that in town. Well, they could drive. They'd get started early--couldn't see over the steering wheel. That was kind of neat. That was what I liked about it. When we used to work in the oil field in the wintertime, the boss said he liked to hire farm kids, because they were better workers. Yeah, he always liked to hire farm boys, and that sure is the truth, isn't it, Patty?" And so, the conversation went on with this wonderful, homestead couple. What a delight it was to reminisce about those first years with a couple older but still so full of life.

CAROL LAWSON

It was a warm, summer afternoon when I drove into Carol's yard. There was a heavy windbreak of trees around the house, and it was apparent that a lot of work was still going into the lawn and flowers.

Abe had already passed away. This was a real shame, as I often heard that he was a wonderful storyteller. Carol had the look of a seasoned, homestead wife. She was warm and friendly, and I would say she was the quieter one of the two.

We began the interview with my asking when Abe and Carol were married.

"We met at a country dance there in Ralston and were married November 17, 1956. I was born in Powell. My dad had a ranch in Red Lodge. It was west of Red Lodge on the creek. His health failed, so he had to sell the ranch, and we moved back to Powell.

By the time Abe and I married, the homestead community was well on its way. Things were established. Abe's brother, Bob, had received the homestead in the 1949 drawing. Abe was in the service in Korea from 1952 to 1954. When he got out of the service, he came and helped Bob farm the homestead.

The brothers had grown up on a wheat farm in North Dakota up near the Canadian border. They came out to look at Heart Mountain homesteads in 1949. They rode the bus, and when they got to Deaver, they looked at each other and said, "What are we getting ourselves into here?"

Abe used to tell me it was a tough job, especially the irrigation those first few years. Now we have cement ditches, so it is so much better. When they came out to Wyoming, all there was to see was the sagebrush.

Abe's service time was in Korea from 1952 until 1954. I think he might have been in Japan during some of that time. Bob had received the

248

drawing for the homestead, and then Abe came and helped him farm until he went to the service.

Those first years when we were married, there was a lot of work to do, and a lot of adjustments. Ranching in Montana wasn't that much different. I helped Abe a lot. I drove the tractor doing more simple jobs like disking. The men did the plowing. I also helped out with the irrigating. We had a big garden when the kids were growing up. We canned a lot for many years.

We had three boys and a girl. Gail was born in 1958, Keith was born in 1959, Daryl was born in 1961, and Lynn was born in 1966. Gail is married and lives in Kalispell, Montana, and works as a bookkeeper for a gas company. Keith is a teacher in Salt Lake City. He teaches math in junior high and high school and is also a counselor. He was our child that always loved music. Daryl lives in Cody and works at UBC, and his wife works at WyoTech. We lost Lynn in an accident about the time he graduated. Neighbors brought in so much food, we didn't know where to put it. Yes, we felt like we had so much support during that time.

I think it was a good community where we could raise our children. I am still here, so I guess it is a good place. I probably wasn't the most social person; we always had so much work to do. We didn't get out that much. Abe was the storyteller. I wish he was here to visit with you. I am not much of a talker.

Both Bob and Abe farmed this homestead. Then Bob and Idabelle moved to North Dakota but then moved back and bought the Lawrence Allshouse homestead. So we have lived out here on Heart Mountain all these years. They sold their farm a few years ago and moved to town. But I still live out here; I like the country.

The brothers planted the windbreak in the first few years. The stand of trees has done very well. They sure had to water them a lot.

We had a lot of the activities at our community club. Abe and I used to go to the dances. By the time we were married, I think the Vacation Bible School that everyone talks so much about had disbanded, and everyone drove to town to the churches.

249

The kids still talk about the homestead. They always loved Heart Mountain. They have all climbed to the top. I never did. I guess I always thought I had too much work to do. I just think it is quite a landmark; you can see it out of Greybull. When the kids were growing up, we kind of thought our community owned the mountain. Abe had done a lot of traveling when he was younger, and he used to say he liked it better here than any place he had ever been.

We used to raise cattle. We had a feed lot with about fifty head, but then the market really dropped. I think a lot of the farmers lost money on their cattle. We raised pinto beans, alfalfa hay, and malt barley.

I don't have livestock now. Daryl comes out just about every night. He is not a town person. He likes to come out and split wood. I decided to sell the farm. When I sold the land, he had a fit. I just have about four acres now. He helps me keep it up. We used to have a big garden. Now I just have such stiff knees; the kids come and help.

We still had an outdoor John when I came. In 1959, we put water in the house and added a bathroom. We had a Stoke-a-Matic coal stove until we got natural gas. I think that was in the early sixties.

This house is the original barracks. The fellows put the barracks on wooden blocks, and it is still the same. We did put a new metal roof on, and it has really worked well. I think the house is hotter now with the new roof. I took the swamp cooler out but think I might need to have it put back in.

We were really happy when the phone lines came in. I know your family was on our line. We all managed well, I thought, sharing the phone lines.

When we could get away, we would go on picnics with our neighbors. The kids were all the same age, so they enjoyed that. None of the rest of my family were fishermen. I am the fisherman. I like to go down and fish on Alkali Creek nowadays. Over the summer, I have a friend who comes out and goes fishing with me. I go up behind Metzer and then down past the bridge. The fishing seems to run in spells. It is getting so I have a hard time getting down the banks any more. I know your brother

Wayne is a fisherman, but I haven't seen him down on the creek. I know he is probably just too busy.

Abe and I were glad we lived here on the homestead. I think everybody was working hard making a living trying to stay here. It is a nice community. Our neighbors are friendly, and we care for each other. I want to stay right here on the farm."

EDNA MAE MCCLAFLIN

"I don't think I will ever forget the day I heard the knock on the front door. Wallace had already gone to work. He got a job with Edison Electric and worked the night shift. Mike and Patty were small children then. I didn't even know Wallace had sent in an application for a homestead. I think he saw an advertisement in a paper one night at work, filled it out, and didn't think much more about it. So now the men are standing at our front door that afternoon, telling me that Wallace McClaflin's name had been the first name drawn for a homestead in Wyoming. I gathered up the kids and went to tell Wallace. I often said, 'We just felt like God had blessed us, and we were happy, as this was our opportunity for the future and our family.'

Wallace had grown up on a dry land farm out in the Panhandle of Oklahoma near the small town of Forgan. My parents lived in Gage, Oklahoma, where my stepfather was a mailman. My own father had died when I was only five, but Pop Brown really was like my own dad, and I always loved him a great deal.

Wallace and I were married before he went into service, and in a short time, he joined the Air Force. I moved to southern California during the war with the children. When Wallace came home, we bought a small, ten-acre farm on Archibald, outside of Ontario. I remember we raised sweet corn. I had been ill, and I think that working on the farm with Wallace helped me get my strength back. He missed out on most of the time the children were babies. I think that made a great impact on the families that came to Heart Mountain. We were so glad to have our

251

husbands home from the war, and we all worked together to make this community. I think that is why, from the very beginning, we all felt so close to each other. Oh, that first year or so, I got so homesick. I didn't get to see my mother for three years, and that was hard. But there was so much work to do.

Everyone worked; even the young children had jobs.

Wallace and I came in October of 1949 to meet with the Board and picked out our homestead unit. We drove through Yellowstone Park and came into a snowstorm that was really very scary for us. We were the first group to come, and I think we bonded with each other from the very first meeting. We had to come back to California and sell the farm and get things ready to move. Wallace came out earlier to get things started for farming and get the barracks moved. He did some work on the barracks before I came with the children in March. It seemed like a very long time that we were separated. Mike and Patty can still remember that trip on the Greyhound bus and the first time they saw snow very late at night.

Wallace put a partition between the living room and kitchen part of the barracks. The large bedroom was in the back part. There was a large porch on the east end of the barracks. It was several years before we got electricity. We had an old ice chest we used to keep the food cold. Growing up in Gage wasn't very modern, but this was step back, for sure. I think I missed my vacuum cleaner more than anything, as the dust just blew into that barracks. Of course, we had an outdoor toilet. The kids used to think it was funny when it blew over. I never wanted to be inside when that happened.

There was a big snowstorm not long after we arrived. I don't think any of the homesteaders were really prepared for how cold it was and all the snow. The storm began in the night, and the next morning, there was snow on the bedspread. We all got very creative in plugging up the cracks in the walls. There was no insulation, so coming from southern California, one had to learn to adapt very quickly. Before we remodeled the barracks, we had a morning stove sitting in the living room. It created a lot of heat, but I had to warn the kids to be careful, as it got really hot.

I think what we all noticed when we first saw Heart Mountain was the sagebrush and not a tree in sight. That first spring, we all began to understand about the wind. Even as busy as we all were, we began to plant windbreaks to get some relief. I don't know how many trees Wallace and I planted. It was a lot, and we also planted some fruit trees. The combination of wind, bitter cold in winter, and then later the sheep eating the bark off of the trees made for a hard time establishing the kind of windbreak that was needed.

We hauled water for a while; then we were able to have the well dug. Wallace built a well house that sits about thirty feet behind the house. He put a small heater in the small building so the water pipes wouldn't freeze. That is where I have always kept all the canning and also the big freezer later when we got electricity.

Many of the wives remember when we used to load up our children and the laundry and make a day of it in town at Garvin's laundry. She had set up a laundry in her garage. She was always so nice to us. She would help us with the laundry and have coffee for us. Her son, Rodney, was always so good to entertain our children. It was those kinds of times that we became such good friends with our neighbors.

The men got together in planning what machinery they would have to have those first few years and pooled their resources. They traded and shared equipment to get the crops planted and harvested. Of course, there were some problems, and we were all learning about this new farming life.

One of those first years, we planted viner peas. When it came time to harvest, we shared the combine and trucks. I think there were Alice and Harley Bright, Laura and Leon Banks, and Wallace and I that harvested the crop. The wives drove the trucks, unless it was your turn to furnish the luncheon meal for the working crew. We managed to get through that harvest, with the wives going to town for parts that had broken and a few other minor adjustments. Wallace and Harley figured out real fast it worked out best if I drove the truck for Harley, and Alice drove the truck for Wallace. We can laugh about it now, but this new farming life came with its stresses.

We were just too busy farming those first few years to take the time to plant a lawn. The irrigation and just dirt around the house made it hard to keep the floors clean. And then, when we got sheep, Wallace got a sheep dog. Rusty was a wonderful pet and good with the sheep, but he was a one-man dog. He went everywhere with Wallace. He was his shadow. There was such a bond between man and his dog, that there was no point trying to keep him outside. He sat right next to Wallace on the floor next to his chair, where a dirt spot was left when he left. Rusty used to go along with the men irrigating and loved to run up and down the ditch as the water came in and, of course, he was very muddy when he came home. But that was part of farm life.

Patty always had some kittens she had trained to ride in her baby buggy. Sewing for her kittens was the first indication she would be a seamstress. She would get into my stash of fabric in the closet to make all kinds of little outfits for the cats.

We named the club house Mountain View, because we all loved the mountain setting just to the west of our homesteads. I think we all felt it was our mountain. Although everyone had enough to do on the homestead, we all pitched in and turned the barracks that had been a portion of the hospital into our clubhouse.

One of the first things we did as a community was for our children. We had a two-week Vacation Bible School. Looking back, I don't know how we accomplished it, but we came from all of our faiths and bonded together. I think all of the mothers and children really enjoyed that time together. I think the faith we possessed was a very important thing to us. We taught our children to have good character, a strong work ethic, and it was very important how we treated our neighbors. In some ways, we were like a big family.

I don't think any of the families had much money. They were just young families, and the fathers had all been away fighting a war. I think we all felt in many ways we were rich; we just didn't have much money to spend. I think all of the homesteaders planted big gardens, and then the men hunted in the fall. We didn't have livestock those first few years, just some chickens, so our family ate a lot of venison. The men had so much work to do getting the farms started, so I think for the most part, the wives took care of the gardens.

The Cooperative Extension Service was a great help to the farmers, giving them educational training, and the wives as well. We were given a lot of good educational training with canning, sewing, and many other homemaking skills. I think all of us wives learned to can. My aunt taught me how to can vegetables while I lived in California, but I learned a great deal more after coming to Wyoming.

When Wallace and I first came to Wyoming in October of 1949, we rented a room from Mrs. Bosley in Powell. She was so warm and welcoming to us, that we became good friends right away. She and her husband had been in the area for a long time. They had been ranchers up on Paint Creek which is in the Clark's Fork area. Her husband had passed away, and her daughter, Bessie, and husband, Felix Hoff, had bought the ranch. Mrs. Bosley introduced us to Bessie and Felix, and they became life-long friends to us. When we moved the family to Wyoming the next March, we were leaving family in southern California. Of course, we could not afford to go back to our family in California for the holidays for a number of years. The Hoffs became our family. We had holidays together out on the ranch on Paint Creek and spent many other times together. Bessie had a beauty shop in Powell. That first summer, she needed some help, so I agreed to work with her in the shop. I would take Patty with me during the day, and Mike would work with Wallace on the farm. There was just so much work to be done on the farm that I didn't work in the shop after that summer, except at special other times through the years.

Their daughter, Phyllis, was six years older than Mike and Patty, but they became fast friends. I think she adopted both of our children as her little brother and sister from the very beginning. Even now, after so many years, they can stay up all night just sharing all the things they did as children.

A few years later, when our community became involved with 4-H, we used the clubhouse for the Homestead Hustlers meetings. Most of

255

the project meetings were held in the homes. I think most of the families participated in 4-H. And then, some of the parents became Scout leaders as well. At one time our community club, the Homestead Hustlers, was the largest 4-H Club in the state. All of the children helped with farm work and household chores. None of us could afford hired help at first, so everyone in the family worked. But 4-H, in many ways, was the icing on the cake for the kids. They all worked so hard on their projects. The young people had so much fun at 4-H camp, and then later, most of them went to state fair. There were a lot of the Heart Mountain 4-H kids that won national trips like Denver Round-Up, National 4-H Club Congress in Chicago, and even trips to Washington, D.C. This was a big deal for these kids, as many of them had never been in a big city. After many of the young people had grown up, the leaders began to take the 4-H national trips as well. We would attend the Western 4-H Leaders' Training that would be held in different locations. I remember when Patty was working with UW Extension, she and I got to go to training in Los Angeles. Those are just good memories now.

Wayne was much younger than Mike and Patty. He came with the next group of homestead children. Even as a very young boy, it was obvious he was gifted with mechanical skills. He liked to work out there on the tractor with his dad. Wallace would find some of his tools lying near the machinery and knew Wayne had been at work. This would prove to be a great asset for us, as early on, he was such a help with the machinery.

Looking back on some of the things we did with the kids, I would shake my head now. On summer evenings, the neighborhood friends liked to go rabbit hunting. They would all congregate at our house. I don't seem to remember this, but my grown children tell me I used to tell them to call their friends, and when they would arrive, I would haul bushels of beans or peas out of the bedroom and say, 'As soon as these are done, I'll take you all rabbit hunting.' That seems to be quite a stretch of the truth, but when I think about how much work we all had to do, it probably wasn't a bad idea. Anyway, we would go out near the badlands. The kids would sit on the bumpers. I only let them have one gun. I would drive real slowly, and they would watch for the rabbits. Actually, if there was a full moon, it was quite beautiful, as the light would be cast down over the formations of rock and hills. Sometimes we would get home late, but it was fun for the kids, so that was good.

In those early years, there wasn't a lot of money. The prices for crops were still very low. Back then, we didn't have the farm equipment they use today. So everybody had to do something. I believe those were good, formative years, because the kids on Heart Mountain learned the value of working and the commitment to following through. All the kids worked hard. We didn't have the chemicals back then that are used today for crops. We raised beans, and they had to be weeded. The kids would go out early in the morning and work all day in the hot sun. One thing they loved to do after weeding, coming in dirty and hot, was to head out front and get into the irrigation ditch. That was their swimming hole. Wallace dug out a place for a pond on the back of the place. That became the swimming hole for a while. Mike built a make-shift raft out of old boards and some inner tubes. Some of the neighborhood kids would come over and swim. After we put sheep and cows to pasture, the water wasn't clean, so that was the end of that swimming hole. It concerned Wallace and me, because the pond was at the back of the place, and we worried about children getting into the pond and hurting themselves, so we finally let it go dry.

Alkali Creek was at the back of our homestead. It was a large canal that was used for the irrigation run-off. The Fish and Game Department stocked it with trout, so through the years, it became a good fishing spot. One summer, Mike and his friend, Vetchel Olson, decided to take his old raft down Alkali drain. I think they had a lot of fun, but I don't really know how successful it was. We used to go over on the creek some evenings and have a wiener roast.

The irrigation ditches were always a worry to the parents. There would be a span of ditch and then a concrete drop that could be swift and dangerous for young children. One day, when Wayne was a preschooler, he was playing out on the front lawn with Rusty. I looked out and didn't see them so went to check on him. I looked all around the barns, and, of course, the irrigation ditch was always in the back of my mind. Our hired man, Dale Watts, and I started getting very concerned, as we called and called and couldn't find him anywhere. It was getting late in the afternoon, and it was getting cold. Dale said, "Edna, I see Rusty way over there by Alkali Creek, and he is running back and forth barking. I'm going to go over there." When Dale got over there, Rusty would run up to him and then run back to the creek, barking and barking. When Dale looked down over the edge, there was little Wayne. He had crawled down near the water and got caught in the fence and couldn't get loose. He was wet, cold, and just so scared. Dale came back with a happy dog and a sad and scared little boy in his arms. That was just an experience that scared all of us so badly, but we were so grateful for Rusty, as I don't know how we would have found Wayne. That day, I said a prayer of thankfulness that we had Rusty to protect Wayne.

The things we did back in those early days were really quite simple. Since Wallace and I loved to fish, if we had any time free during the summer, that is what we would do. Before we got livestock, we could take a few hours in the evening, if he had his water set. We had a Dodge pickup. We took the kids everywhere with us. I would quickly pack a picnic lunch. We would all pile into the cab and would be off to North Fork for the evening.

We met a wonderful family, the Billy Woodruffs. He had a large band of sheep up near Heart Mountain on summer range. He would stop by our house sometimes in the spring with bum lambs. That was our first introduction to sheep. During the day, I would feed the lambs with a Coke bottle, and when the kids came home from school, that was their job.

Billy invited us many times to go with him up into Sunlight to the mountain ranges up high where his sheep were. Finally, one summer Wallace said, "Okay, we're going to take three days and go." I remember the kids were so excited.

We needed to build barns before we could get into having livestock. Billy Woodruff got us started with bum lambs, and then we got into sheep. I think Patty really enjoyed her sheep projects in 4-H. Mike got involved with hogs and did very well with them.

We used siphon tubes for irrigating. It was a lot of work moving the tubes around the fields. Patty and I helped with the moving, but Mike was the one that could set the siphon tubes the best. Those first few years, the men worked so hard working with the ditches and irrigating. It is so different today with the sprinklers. Wayne was the one that helped Wallace so much with the mechanical part of the irrigating.

Hunting was something Wallace and I liked to do. In those first years of farming, we depended on the wild game for the main meat that we ate. I didn't have a gun when I went to Wyoming. One of the first things Wallace did for me was to buy me a gun. He bought me a 300 Savage with the bore and armrest sawed off, so it was just right for me. I have hunted all these years with that same gun. And then, about a year after that, he brought me home some hunting boots. I was so proud of those leather boots. I don't know if my feet would fit in them now, but for years, I wore those boots hunting and fishing. When we got something like that, in those early years, we would just cherish it, so the boots always were very special to me.

So many of the elk hunts that Wallace and I would go on would be in November, so the kids would miss out on them, as they were in school. Some of our good friends were Alvin and Garnet Cary. They owned Hunter's Peak Lodge up in the Sunlight Mountain Range. We would stay in the lodge and go with Alvin and would ride his horses back into the hunting range. Sometimes, Wallace would go up to the lodge and help Alvin with his hunters by being the camp cook and helping to get the elk packed out. At the end of the season, Alvin would take Wallace and me out with him. They had a home in Powell they lived in during the school term, so if we were hunting for several days, our children would stay with Garnet in town.

259

Garnet had a music store in town. She gave accordion lessons to quite a few children. Mike and Patty saved some money from their sheep projects and bought an accordion. Garnet loaned them another small accordion with only twelve buttons. There used to be quite a few hassles over who got to play the bigger accordion with 120 buttons. I remember they would take turns practicing in the bathroom, as the bedrooms were not heated, and it was just too cold back in that part of the house.

Garnet formed an accordion band, which I thought was a wonderful idea. They were invited to play for a small TV station in Thermopolis one time. Patty says she is still embarrassed, as she thought the group sounded so terrible, but as a mother, I was excited about the opportunity for the bunch of kids. We always had a lot of company in the summer, and usually at some time in the visit, I would have Mike and Patty play everyone a few tunes. If I waited until they were leaving, the exit was always quite rapid. For some reason, no one else seemed to get as much of a thrill as I did at watching my children play.

One evening in church, we had a music night. All the kids knew how to play was "The Blue Bird Waltz," so that is what they were going to play. Unfortunately, they got the giggles and just stood up there laughing. I was thoroughly disgusted with the both of them. Another time, I was going to sing a solo, and Patty agreed to play for me. I was going to sing "Whispering Hope," and I honestly don't know how I ever got through the song, because I would sing a phrase and wait on Patty to catch up with me, and then sing another phrase, until the song was finally over.

The Christmas at Paint Creek Ranch was always such great fun. Felix was a Swede, so Bessie had learned to make all those wonderful recipes like Swedish pudding and pancakes. One of the Hoff traditions was to serve lutefisk on New Year's Eve. It is a fish that is soaked in lye and served for the holidays. Wallace acquired a taste for it, but I never could manage the smell. The next morning, we had the pleasure of biscuits and lutefisk gravy.

One New Year's Eve, we were up at the Paint Creek Ranch with the Hoffs. They had been invited over to their neighbors', the Davidsons.

When we drove over to the ranch, it was twenty below zero. It was a wonderful party, and our family met some very nice people. About midnight, someone asked, "Do I hear water dripping off the roof?" Sure enough, a Chinook wind had come up, and in a matter of a few minutes, the temperature had gone up so fast, the snow was melting off the roof.

The wintertime was especially fun, because the Hoffs had an old sled out in the barn which Felix would sometimes hitch up to the horses, and we would take rides. The kids would go out on the hill and ride inner tubes. In the summer, we would fish the Paint Creek, and the three kids would ride horses all over the badlands up on top of the ravine.

In the summer, I would take Mike and Patty up in the hills near the ranch house. It was a great place to play, with the rock formations arranged all over the hillside. There were even some caves we used to find. We spent a lot of time looking for fossils. We found some old shells and petrified bones.

One Easter Sunday, we went to Paint Creek Ranch. At the time, we had a bum lamb, so we packed him up in the pickup with us and headed for the ranch. I had baked a cake and bought both the kids a big, chocolate Easter bunny, which they thought was really special. They weren't supposed to eat the candy until after the picnic lunch. We were just about to the ranch, coming around a sharp corner on the dirt road, when one of the wheels fell off. We sat there in the hot sun, not really able to do much. The chocolate melted all over, so that the bunny just turned into a globe, and the kids were upset. It was getting late in the afternoon. We all were hungry, but finally, someone came along and gave us a ride down to the ranch.

In later years, the Hoffs sold the ranch and moved to Idaho. We remained great friends, missed them terribly, and always had great memories of that wonderful old ranch.

My Uncle Ralph and Aunt Mamie had retired. Our neighbor across the road, Sid Blair, decided to sell, so they bought the homestead. We farmed for them and then later bought that farm. Later, we would get to have the amendment up near Heart Mountain. I think Wallace always

261

loved going to the amendment. The eleven men that had farms up on the hill became very great pals. We had sprinklers up on the amendments. The men always watched out for each other, keeping watch over the sprinklers.

In later years, Wallace was having some health issues, so he started cutting back on the size of his sheep flock. Mike Forman began to rent some of our farming ground. Wallace had always wanted to buy a boat. I had always had the desire to have a camper. So one fall, we did buy a fishing boat, and Wallace let me buy a camper. We had worked so hard for so many years, so we were very excited about our new toys. We got to go fishing with the boat some that fall. I know that was the year we went back to Michigan to see Patty graduate with her M.S. degree. Wallace took her to a boat shop to show her the kind of boat he had gotten. He was just so excited about the boat. Just two months later, we found out Wallace had cancer, and he was gone by the end of July. He had always loved the fair and had been on the fair Board for a number of years. They dedicated the Park County Fair in memory of him that year, as he died on Wednesday, the day before county fair. Wallace and I never got to go camping with the camper.
He was so young when he passed away.

Patty married and moved away from the farm. Mike came home from Vietnam after his term of duty in the service and farmed a year for his dad after his heart attack. He married a hometown girl, Linda Hart. They became missionaries in Africa. Wayne married Pam, and they are the ones who have remained farming. They built a home on the homestead across the road. Later, they built a shop out behind their house. Wayne has been a wonderful resource in the community, as he is a help to the farmers taking care of machinery. He now has become involved with a company selling liquid fertilizer, which has been a great improvement in crop production and safety. Farming has come a long way from those beginning years of homesteading. Mike and Linda will retire and come back to the homestead. Patty will stay near her grandchildren in Michigan but will make frequent treks back to Wyoming, as she feels it is a part of her.

I think Wallace and I were always so grateful to have our homestead on Heart Mountain. Of course, we worked hard. We had some heartaches and tough times, but more than that, we had a wonderful life together. We both had so much fun with the kids-fishing and hunting, and with the 4-H experiences. Our neighbors were like the salt of the earth people who we have cherished all those years. I hope my health is good enough that I can live out my life on the homestead. The farm has been a wonderful home. I can't imagine living anyplace else."

ANN NELSON

"When Earl and I heard about the homesteads in northwest Wyoming, we were living in Bridgeport, Kansas. We were raised in Kansas, fairly near each other but not in the same community.

Earl was doing some custom combining for a relative of mine, a second or third cousin. Bob and Earl met when they were in high school. Bob knew about the homesteads, and he would tell Earl about the great opportunities that could be had. He had gone north to see about the homesteads and thought he and Earl could work together and share machinery. Earl really wasn't all that interested, but Bob got him an application anyway.

Earl had traveled into southern Kansas combining without me and the twins, so when he went out to Goodwin, I thought I would go with him. When we got there, it was raining, so we wondered what we could do. I realized it was the last day we could send in the application, so we sat there in the car with the rain drizzling outside, filled out the papers, and mailed them. Earl found combining work up in South Dakota. While there, we discovered that our name had been drawn for a homestead.

We never had any doubts about coming to Wyoming. We lived in a little house in Earl's hometown of Bridgeport. We had 12 acres of ground, and I think he was working for the county. Anything we would do had to look better than what we had.

263

We came up for an interview in November of 1949. The banker back home had given me a pencil and tablet to keep notes of the trip. I remember writing as we drove from Casper to Shoshoni, noting that we never saw a living thing, only lots of bones and skeletons. But when we got this side of Cody and looked at the barracks that were on the homesteads, I said, "If they can make it, I know we can." There was never any hesitation for us in deciding to come to Wyoming.

It was a difficult task picking out a homestead unit. We were given a map, and the homesteads were marked on the corners. There were steel posts with numbers on them. Sometimes, it was hard to know where the lines were. The ground was classified as one, two, six, and so forth. Class 1 was supposed to be the best. Most of the Class 1 ground had already been picked. We decided on a smaller unit, because it did have some Class 1 soil. I believe there were about 104 acres.

For a while, we lived at the relocation camp. We lived in an apartment in the same barracks as Bob and Vaudine Jirsa. Charles and Edna Cobb moved into another barracks apartment soon after we did. We had to be out of the barracks by March 10. We worked on the homestead barracks, making it livable, and were able to move by March 1. We were only at the camp for about six weeks.

The earlier homesteaders got one barracks, but they could buy a second barracks for $1. Anyway, that's the way I heard it. By the time we came, we could only get one barracks, but Earl was able to help tear down the old hospital building. He got lumber and fixtures, so that was supposed to make up for not getting a second barracks.

We lived in the east part of the barracks and closed in the end. A Japanese family had built a little cooler on an outside part of a cupboard. That first day, we moved in and stored the groceries in the cooler. It snowed that night, and everything was frozen the next day. That night, there was a blizzard. Snow blew in and covered the top of the boys' bed. The next morning, I took paper and began stuffing the holes around the windows and filled in the cracks. We lived in the end of the barracks 'til summer. We finished the kitchen and managed to get more living space before our folks came up that first summer.

After we had been here a couple of years, we realized we did not have enough acres to make a living. There was some wasteland on our unit and a deep gully along the north side that couldn't be farmed. So, I think in about 1952, we did receive 33 more acres of amended land. We were also able to get some of the land leveled in order for more acres to be in production.

Our parents really didn't say anything about us moving to Wyoming. I am sure they did have a lot of reservations about letting us go. When we went back and told Earl's mother how long we would have to stay on the homestead, she had some misgivings. Homesteaders would have to farm the land for three years and could not be away from the farm for more than six months. She was worried that she would not be able to see the twins for three years. Of course, that did not happen, because that first summer the relatives all came, wanting to see about this new life in Wyoming.

The twins, Bruce and Byron, were born shortly after Earl got out of the service. They were born in Texas in the back seat of a car on the way to the hospital. I was horrified the first time Earl told someone up here about it, as I was just so ashamed that we did not make it to the hospital.

I didn't know enough about it at the time to even be scared. I guess "God looks after idiots and kids." Bradley was born in Wyoming in 1953.

Dr. Kattenhorn was my doctor, and I told him I didn't want to have this baby in the car. He assured me that wouldn't happen. He put me in the hospital early, and nothing happened, so I said, 'Well, just forget this, and I'll go home,' but the next morning, our third son was born. Brent was born in 1954. Dr. Kattenhorn was out of town, so Dr. Allison delivered him. After the fourth child, I gave up on having a girl. We will be happy with our four boys. For a long time, we referred to them as the big boys and the little boys, but the little boys grew up to be bigger than the big boys.

After we got the farm into production, Earl's dad kept encouraging him to sell and use the assets in another venture. One morning, I was listening to him talk with Earl in the kitchen. He said we could sell the homestead and live on the interest. I finally said, 'That's alright, but whenever he sells, he has got to sell it to a man that wants a wife and four kids.' Grandpa looked over at me and replied, 'Well, if you won't sign the papers, then there is no use talking about it,' and that was the end of that.

Bruce and Byron had to do a lot of work when they were little, picking up sagebrush. They did chores, because we had sheep. When they were in the second grade, Mary Johnson, Byron's teacher, said to me one day when I was in for conference, that it seemed to her that those boys had to do a lot of work. And I said, 'Yes, they do,' because Earl expected them to help with taking care of the livestock. They were hard workers then and have been all their lives.

In those early years, everyone in the family had to work hard, there was just so much to be done. Almost everyone had livestock, as this was an added income. We couldn't depend on just crops to make it in farming.

We had cows. I remember from the letters I wrote home, churning butter was a horrible experience for me. I don't know if I didn't have the cream the right temperature, but I would churn and churn. I would finally get butter, and it was sure a lot better eating than buying from the store. We had milk, cream, butter, chickens, eggs, and a big garden. We would split a beef with neighbors once in a while, and we ate lamb. We learned to butcher our own meat. I have always said,
'People who live on a farm eat better than people in town.'

Earl would go hunting for elk. He hunted with Harvey Adams and Bill White. There was a bunch of the guys that would go hunting together, but sometimes it was just the three guys that went together. They would go up into Sunlight to hunt for elk. One time, Earl shot an elk down in a ravine. The other fellows gave him a bad time wanting to know why he couldn't have landed one up on top of the hill. He went big game hunting for a number of years.

When Bruce and Byron were old enough, they went with their dad over by Devil's Tower several years to hunt for wild turkey.

One year, Dude Adams and I were going with Harvey Adams and Earl hunting over in the Big Horns. We got east of Lovell on the old road over the mountain. Harvey and Dude were in their truck, and we were in our car. Harvey was going too fast around a corner and turned his truck over. Dude had cooked a big pot of beans in the pressure cooker. When the cab went over, the cooker hit her in the head, so that was the end of that hunting trip.

We took pictures of the big garden we raised. I canned a lot of green beans and corn. We had our own potatoes. It was a problem in those early years canning without electricity. We had an ice chest. I had forgotten that, for a while, we delivered ice out on the flats for the polar plant. In the summer, the block of ice would thaw out quickly. We kept frozen meat at the locker plant in Cody and Powell in those first years. Neighbors helped each other out by picking up meat for each other when they would have to make a trip to town.

When we lived in western Kansas, I worked for the Farm Security Administration Office. They insisted that all farm borrowers have a pressure cooker and do canning. I bought a pressure cooker through the office and brought it with me to Wyoming. I canned a lot of garden produce with the canner.

I remember when the two younger boys came along, the older boys were already in charge of doing so many things, we didn't expect as much from them. Of course, by then we had more money and got the boys a motor scooter. Bruce and Byron let us know they never got anything like that when they were younger, but then, there just wasn't money for any luxuries. The twins were nine years older than Brad and Brent, so life was not so difficult when they went into high school.

I would never have gone back to Kansas to live. I cannot think of any reason that would have taken me back; this was home. I hated to be so far away from both sets of parents, especially after they got older. My mother lived to be 96 years old. She was in a nursing home for two years. Earl had passed away before she went into the nursing home. I knew she

267

would not have wanted to move from Kansas, but I just couldn't see myself moving back either. That was just a very difficult situation.

Earl passed away in 1990, and sometimes it seems like it has been forever. You just do what you have to do to make it through these times. I have people ask me, especially my friends down south, 'Why are you still on the farm?' I say, 'Because it is home, this is where I want to be, and as long as I can drive, I want to stay here.' As far as taking care of the place, I want to do it as long as I can. I can always hire someone to do those things I can no longer do.

Last year, my left shoulder was hurting. I couldn't use my arm and didn't know what was wrong with it. I did have the yard work done, because the clippings needed to be picked up, and I couldn't empty the bags. I was able to do the rest of the yard, though, with my riding mower. I have already done the yard twice this year, and I will just keep it up unless something else happens. It is good for me and helps keep me healthy.

The summer I was pregnant with Brad, we were shingling the house. We had friends from Kansas who helped us with that. Earl was so busy in the fields, it was impossible for him to take time off.

We built our home in 1959. By that time, we had the four boys, and we only had two bedrooms in the barracks. The younger boys were still in their baby beds, because it was not possible to fit any more beds into their room. Brad must have been getting close to six by then. It was so nice to be in our new home, but we have many good memories of years in the barracks. I think what helped all of us in our community is that we were all living in the barracks, so we learned to adjust ourselves to the situations that came up.

In our community, the neighbors visited a lot. Usually, we would get together, have a dinner, and then play cards. We all played a lot of cards in those early days. When the television came along in the mid-fifties, the card playing stopped. And, by then, we were all getting very busy with taking our children to their activities. Looking back on those times of visiting, I wish we would have continued more in the fashion of those first, early years together. We had dinners and card games throughout the winter and into the spring. We felt we needed to visit, because when summer started, there was no time for much but work.

In about 1954, we started square dancing at the clubhouse. The Deckers lived across the road, so we would have Scarlet baby-sit the children, and that was our night out. Of course, we just did that in the winter, and most of the community participated in it. It was a great deal of fun for all of us. We would all take sandwiches and cake, and after the dance, we would eat before coming home. We would have enormous crowds at the club. Couples would come from Belfry and Powell that would join us. Walt and Edna Scott would come to help us with the music, and he would call for the dances. I think we all appreciated them so much for helping us with the dances. I think we only paid about a $1 per couple to help pay for their services. Cleo Kendler and her husband came with the Scotts. She is the one that took all of the pictures and sent them to me. When we look at the pictures now, we all looked so young and skinny. After several years, Earl decided he wanted to get on a bowling team, so Harvey and Dude joined us. Unfortunately, it was on the same night as the dances. I think by that time, the dances were being held in town, but they were good memories.

The Vacation Bible School was another very important thing for our community. I believe the idea for this began at a Circle meeting held at Margaret Olson's home. That was a large group of the homestead wives. I have a book about the Bible School that Radine Ashby had, and I seem to have acquired it. There were over 100 of our children that came. Most of the mothers helped out in some way. It lasted for two weeks and was held in the community club. There was a program on the last night, and all the families would come. That was a special time for us, as we all worked together from many different churches to put it together.

We had Christmas programs, and all of the children did something. After many of them began to play musical instruments, they would play and sing during these programs. The community club met every month. Sometimes, there was a program, and then meetings, but I remember very often we had potluck dinners.

Many of us had small children when we came to Wyoming. Many of the wives were pregnant at the same time, after we lived here for a while. This group of people were the type that got things done. We were a close community that worked together. Our children were important to us. The children grew up working hard, but we tried as best we could to create opportunities for them.

4-H was a very important part of the community. You got your children enrolled as soon as they were old enough. I was the community leader for several years. It was hard to get someone to play that role, but I had two children involved, so I felt I needed to take part. I drove for a lot of the judging trips. I always had to drive for the judging on North Fork, as some of the mothers were afraid of that drive. It wasn't fun in those early years on the old road before they put the tunnel in. I had to take Brad and Brent along which wasn't easy getting them corralled and getting them to take naps.

Bruce and Brent had sheep projects and then later became interested in leather craft. I remember Larry Solberg, one of the junior leaders, would come to our meetings and help with teaching leather craft. He was very skillful in leather craft and was a lot of help. I took leather craft lessons from Mrs. Hardy, and then I was able to help the 4-Hers. When the fair was on, everybody was involved. The whole family went, and that was a big part of your life.

All four sons still live in Wyoming. Bruce is an FFA [Future Farmers of America] and VoAg [Vocational Agriculture] teacher and lives in Pine Bluffs. Byron is living in Sheridan and works on the university seed farm. Brad has a waste management company in Cheyenne. Brent is in Sheridan now, and he works in an insurance company. I don't think you could get Bruce and Byron out of Wyoming. If it was necessary, the other two would leave, but I think Bruce and Byron would be yelling and kicking every step of the way, if you tried to take them out of the state.

The grandchildren feel closeness to the homestead. For years, the kids all came home for Christmas. Not too long before Earl died, he wanted to go to Texas for Christmas, and, of course, Grandma would always drag her feet to be here for Christmas, because all the kids would come home. Then after he died, I think they all came home that first Christmas. That was the last time they have all been home for Christmas. They used to try to get here all together sometime during the summer, too, but as their families are growing up, it is getting harder to do that. But this is the hub for the family, and this is home, and that is all there is to it. They all want this place kept like it was when they were here. I will keep it as long as I can. I don't even like to think about when I can't do it anymore. Earl loved to have the kids all here, and when they came, there would be great water fights.

Earl and I started going to Texas in the winter in 1974. He was in the service in Fort Hood, so one year we were just going to take a trip, and he wanted to see what things looked like where he had been. We wandered around and got to Harlingen and spent some time looking around, and I think then the next year, we went again. We didn't stay very long that first year and were back in Wyoming by March 1st. Our parents were still alive then, so we would visit going down and then coming back. After Earl died, I felt like I couldn't go back by myself and wasn't sure I even wanted to. I stayed up here for two years, then decided, if I don't try it, I'll never know whether I can do it or not, so I went back to Texas. I hadn't been there two weeks, until I decided this is where I need to be in the winter. It makes so much more sense, because out here on the farm, it gets pretty darn quiet. I go down south and enjoy playing all winter, and I am ready to come back and go to work when spring comes. But then, by the time I work awhile, I decide it's time to go back and play.

Before Earl passed away, we had gotten out of raising sheep. We had a dog and some cats. Our dog was getting old by the time Earl passed away. She got arthritis and could hardly get up in the mornings, couldn't hear, or see, so we put her down. Oh my, did I miss her when she was gone! She was an outdoor dog, you know, and I said I didn't want another dog when I was going to be gone that much. If I was here all the time, I certainly would have a dog. I have one old faithful mother cat, and I worry about her every winter, but she comes back every year. She came back the day I got home and was sitting on the porch. She is a good hunter, so I guess that's how she survives. I enjoy having her, because she is always out here on the porch when I get up in the morning, and I have somebody to talk to.

Well, I could talk about many things, but they don't come to mind now. This was and is our family place. All of us together built our community, and it was good."

TAK AND EMMY OGAWA

I had looked forward to this visit with Tak and Emmy Ogawa. My parents, along with all the other homesteaders, have great respect for this outstanding farmer. He still farms his land, and his work ethic is nothing short of amazing.

One of the questions I asked in every interview was what the homesteaders remembered of their first impression of this community. Most of the time, especially with the wives, the comment would be made that there were no trees in sight, only sagebrush. In those first few years, most of the families planted trees for a windbreak. The wind can be unrelenting up on the flat, so not only did we want trees, but they were almost a necessity because of the harsh winds. It was hard to establish the growth of trees, so our community felt the trees that survived were of great value. After fifty years of perseverance, some of the homesteads have established a strong windbreak and some beautiful trees.

As one drives across the prairie today, it is refreshing to see those homes that are sheltered with blue spruce, elms, and a variety of other trees. As I have driven around the homesteads doing interviews for this project, I have had the pleasure, several times, of driving by the Ogawa farm and looking at the thick rows of trees surrounding their home.

There is such a thick forest of trees, that it is impossible to see the entire house from the road. This afternoon, as I drove into the driveway, my first reaction to seeing the house in full view is how very attractive it is. There is an extensive, manicured lawn with beautiful flowers in bloom.

272

This farm is obviously a well-ordered business, as all the machinery and equipment are neatly set in order. All of the barns are in excellent condition. All my recollections of the Ogawas, as I have always heard from my father and other homesteaders, are evident in this setting, nestled and protected from the harsh winds of Wyoming by many well-ordered rows of huge, blue spruce.

The eleven amendments up near the base of Heart Mountain had been awarded after I had left home. I think in the later years of farming, the amendment was, in some ways, my father's favorite pastime. The Ogawa's amendment sits just south of my parent's. Whenever we came home for a visit, we were always taken up on the hill to see the crops. Even if it was winter, we still went to the amendment. I remember so many times my father commenting about Tak. It was obvious my dad had a great deal of respect for this man and considered him a very close friend.

As a child, I had always wondered about the Ogawas. They were a Japanese family. With the remains of the Japanese camp so close, one couldn't help but wonder how it would affect our community in their reaction to this family. Although the Ogawas were considered to be outstanding farmers and excellent neighbors, I had always hoped in my heart that our community had respected them as one of their own.

As I sat there that afternoon, knowing that I was probably taking Tak and Emmy away from work, I understood why my father had always thought so much of them. They both were so warm and gracious to me. Some of the conversation that afternoon was not taped, but the openness with which they shared with me answered some of the long-ago questions I had pondered. I began the interview with the standard question, "Tak and Emmy, why did you decide to apply for a homestead and come to Wyoming? What was it that motivated you?" Tak began first.

"Well, what motivated me to get the homestead was I had a friend that drew a homestead in Riverton, and he kind of advised me. 'If you want to keep farming, why don't you apply for one of the homesteads on Heart Mountain?'

About that time, I was about twenty-three, so I was ready to start doing something on my own, because I had been working with my folks all the time.

I was a veteran. I never left the state of Texas. I was eighteen when I was drafted, but when I finished basic training, the war in Germany had ended, and then I think for a while, they didn't know what to do with me, you know, because I was Japanese. I took my basic in Camp Hood, and then from there, I went to El Paso. I was there in the honor patrol for about eighteen months. And then, when the war was over in Japan, they had no use for me, so they let me out of the service, because I wanted to farm. So after the war ended in Japan, I got discharged in April, I think, of 1946.

So, from then on, I came home and helped my folks a couple of years. They live in Idaho Falls, Idaho. On their farm, they raised sugar beets, potatoes, barley, and alfalfa. The crops were very much the same as here, except they didn't raise dry beans.

My friend, Archie Reed, sent me a telegram in August saying that my application had been drawn. I didn't hear from the Bureau until later. The potato harvest wasn't going to start in Idaho until September, so a friend and I came up to investigate and see what the soil was like on the Heart Mountain homestead project. The ground looked real good to me. I came over the Badger Basin Highway where the Reeds farmed. I had heard that the landscape had rolling hills, but when I got here, I discovered the ground was flat. Jack Black was one of the first guys I visited. He told us about the water situation on the homestead project. He suggested to go over and talk with a fellow that was thrashing beans, so that is what I did.

After I moved here, they kind of adopted me, because I was a bachelor. I didn't get married until 1954.

I had no problem with the barracks, you know, being single and everything. It was just about like camping out. I couldn't imagine the families with little kids; it was tough on them. I went over to Baker's to get my water, because I didn't have a well. In the mornings, the water would be frozen solid.

My first few years were kind of uneventful, because I didn't have a wife to nag me and support me. I just had to support myself.

I knew how to irrigate, so the first few crops I planted were peas and grain. One of the first things I did on the homestead was to put in head gates and everything. I had irrigated all my life, and I knew you had to control your water. So when I ordered water, I would order six feet of water, because that was all the water I could get through my head gate. I would irrigate about 100 acres in three days. So then I would go fishing with Cole all the other times. We'd go fishing all the time, so I did a lot of fishing in those first few years.

A few of my neighbors came over when we first got water and asked some questions about how I was irrigating. At that time, we didn't have siphon tubes. You just had to spread your water out, but we were lucky, because the roots from the sagebrush helped to slow the water down.

I wanted to rent some ground those first few years, but everyone was wanting to farm, so there just wasn't any ground, so after the water would be set, I had a lot of free time.

All of the other homestead units received an amendment of additional acres of land except eleven units. In about 1975, the Bureau designated eleven amendments, so that all of the original homesteads would now have an amendment. A pumping station and sprinklers would be required to farm these amendments.

There was a special camaraderie amongst the men in this amendment project, because we had to do everything together. We all put the gas line in, and we all had to pay for the lift pump, even though there were just four of us that would benefit from it, but then it was a big project. The lift pump was over $100,000 just by itself. So there was no way just the four of us could afford to do that, so all eleven of us that got amendments pitched in, and that is one reason we were so together on the project.

We didn't have to carry a shovel around too much in irrigating. That was one of the good things about the pivots. All you had to do was push them up and down the field. Your dad and I just pushed a button and watched the sprinklers go around.

Wallace planted some wild rose bushes up on the hill of his amendment, but I think the deer chewed on them, and they kind of got run over sometimes. They are still there, but they aren't very big. He planted two apple trees right there by the pump house, and he said, 'In about three or four years, we are going to have some apples.' But it never happened.

We planted a lot of trees on our homestead. They are mostly blue spruce and a few pine trees. I have some smaller blue spruce I am letting get a little bigger and then want to plant them up on the amendment.

We bought Hutchinson's original homestead, and that is where our home is now. He had built some buildings on this unit. Emmy and I were married in 1954. I had grown up with Emmy in Idaho. Mostly, I lived like a bachelor and had never fixed up the barracks on my original homestead and really didn't want Emmy to have to live there, as this was a nicer house. We rented Hutchinson's original homestead in 1954, and then the next year, we bought it. This homestead is the original Hutchinson unit. Hutchinson had fixed up his place, so we moved into that house. We have moved the house since then. Looking back, I think we should have built our house on the original homestead, but there were barns already built here. I wanted a shop, and some trees were already planted here. My original homestead sits right down by the corner."

Emmy told about the children.

'Well, Kim was born in 1955. I remember it was Tak's folks that came to help. We didn't have a playpen, but we had great big cardboard boxes, so that is what Kim played in. She used to spend a lot of time there on the kitchen floor. That is the way we kept track of her. I don't remember too much about those early years. I guess we were so busy. We had chickens, and pigs, and cows. We didn't think about anything else during that time. I had Kim in 1955 and Kathy eighteen months later. Then Craig was born in 1957 and Jenny in 1959. We had three girls and a boy.

In 4-H, Kim took sewing. I think Edna Mae was her leader for a long time. The two younger girls took a lot of gardening projects. Craig tried his hand at raising a steer. You know, at the last minute, you hook the steer onto a tractor so you can teach them how to lead. Just enough so Craig could hang onto the steer during the show judging contest at the fair. We had sheep. We had baby sheep and bum lambs, but I don't remember if the children ever had a 4-H lamb project.

The only thing wrong with the kids raising livestock was every time we butchered or something, you know, they had them all named. The children always asked us if the animal we butchered was their pet. We would tell them it was another, or we had bought it in town."

Emmy continued.

I know we all helped with 4-H. It was such an enjoyable time. We had such good teachers and leaders. I mean, everybody was so talented around here. We had a lot of teachers that were married up here. We looked forward to 4-H. You probably did too, didn't you Patty?

The Vacation Bible School was important. I think it was a community effort. All the kids enjoyed it, and, of course, all the parents participated, so everyone looked forward to it. We really missed it when they disbanded, and parents started driving their children to town. I don't remember the last year we had Vacation Bible School?"

Tak added this.

"There was such a sense of community here. We felt a sense of togetherness. You never heard anybody talking about someone. We had to be together, worked together--we didn't think anything of it.

The kids had a good time together, and, of course, they took pictures of each other all the time. We were so busy raising them. There were four of them close in age, so they played together an awful lot. Of course, they had their squabbles and everything, but I think they got along pretty good. One nice thing about living up here is you could yell real loud, and the neighbors couldn't hear you. They all pretty much worked, or at least they thought they did. They worked hard until they got old enough and got busy in school."

Emmy spoke up.

"The kids wanted a horse, but Tak had gotten hurt on a horse, so he never got them a horse. Same way with the bike."

I asked Emmy, if she could do it all over, would she do it again?

"Yeah, I would, if I was younger. I don't think I could have enjoyed it more. I think it is a good life. I worked in town before I married and came up here. Tak and I liked the country life a lot better. It is a good life for the kids. I think it helps them when they grow up and go out in the business world--the farm background." Tak spoke of the amendment.

"Patty, your dad and I were right next to each other. All of us with amendments checked on each other. If a sprinkler was off, we would go and turn it on automatically for each other. I remember one time when your dad first had electricity, and he was up there on the amendment all by himself taking the gas motor off. I happened to come by and saw he was having difficulty, so we worked on it together and got it fixed. That is just the way it was with us fellows. We always had trouble with the moss and stuff plugging up, and we were down every day, and sometimes twice a day, taking the moss off the screen and stuff. The screen was down there at the lift pump on the canal. We kind of took the caring of the lift pump on our own. We all checked it all the time. We had so much trouble with the moss, so later we found this rotary screen that has worked real good, and so that kind of solved that problem.

Once we got the sprinklers to going, we had a lot of time to visit, unless something happened, and then like I say, we helped each other. So I miss your dad quite a bit, you know. Well, it's quiet up there too, you know. You go up there early in the morning, and it is so quiet, and all you hear is the hum of the motors and stuff, and it is really nice up there.

My unit is right up at the base of Heart Mountain. I really like it up here. I think the mountain is a good landmark. One thing about it is it looks different from every angle. It has different figures on it whichever way you look at it. I never was to the top, only to the base.

I used to hunt, but we didn't like the wild game taste of the meat. I don't think I have hunted for about twenty years now. I did like to go hunt on the top of the mountain, but after I turned fifty, I think I quit hunting. Last time we got an elk, we had to tote it quite a ways, and it is a lot of work for not enjoying the meat. I'm not quite a fisherman, but I like to fish--mostly off the North Fork. When I first came up here, I would go fishing real often--three or four times a week. Now I just go down to Alkali Creek. That is just down below my house. I put all my gear on, which are cutoffs, tennis shoes, and my straw hat, and I just walk up the creek. I don't catch very many fish, but you know, it is so relaxing."

Tak spoke of those first years.

'Oh, yeah, sometimes with the cold, it was miserable, but you know, when you are young and like me, I never had anything and you see you have 100 acres of land, and it makes you feel good. I mean, that is what kept most of us going. We had a farm we could call our own. I think most of us felt real pride in what we owned. When I got my homestead unit, I was number 65 in line. There were about ten applicants who dropped out ahead of me. Like I say, I came up here, and everything looked so flat and looked good. Emmy and I have had a good life together in this community."

Emmy had to excuse herself, as she had a doctor's appointment. All I can say is, "Oh my gracious, what a lady she is." I knew I needed to be done, but it was so enjoyable speaking with both of them. I turned off the tape and made my way to the door. As we stood there, I ventured out of my comfort zone and asked Tak how it really was. What a kind and insightful person he is. I would have to say he is an excellent farmer, but more than that, a gentleman. As I walked away that afternoon, I could certainly understand why my father had thought so much of this neighbor and colleague he had worked with day by day for so many years.

MARGARET OLSON

I don't have a better word to describe those feelings I would have as I would once again go back and edit and put together the manuscript of this book that truly is a beloved story to me. We were the war babies, so when we arrived in Wyoming we were just entering school. Our parents were involved in all of us children.

I recall the interview with Margaret Olson. Swede had passed away on December 6, 1990 and she now was living in Cheyenne in a lovely high rise assisted living complex. I had not seen her for many years so this was an exciting day for me. She was waiting for me in the foyer when I arrived. We went up to her apartment and I could tell she was proud of her dwelling and yes it was very nice. I saw in the next room, piles of folders she had been organizing. My thoughts were, "Yes that is the room of a seasoned teacher." I always understood Margaret to be a very intelligent woman and this was evident that afternoon as she shared many intricate pieces of the stories of those early years.

She wanted me to have a meal with her in the dining room. I felt like a celebrity that day as she introduced me to so many of the residents. One would have thought I was her own daughter.

She had prepared for this visit with me as she had many research files she had saved. She took me to the office and we spent a good deal of time copying articles, documents and newspaper clips. The information she gave me would later be valuable as I put the stories of the history together for "Beloved Homeland." Of course I have saved all those documents for future research for the younger set of homesteaders.

When I left Margaret that afternoon I once again would choke back the tears that seemed to come so often from those times with the homestead wives and husbands who so lovingly shared their stories.

I was able to go back and visit with Margaret one year later, but it was obvious that her memory had declined a great deal and so I knew that It would not be possible to learn any more information and that is the way it was as the years had slipped away much too quickly.

In the research files were some stories written in booklets entitled, "I Remember When." Margaret had shared of her childhood. I thought as I read them it could be described as a precursor for preparation for her homestead life as a young bride.

She had come from generations of homestead families. Her parents moved from Nebraska and settled in Kit Carson County, Colorado about twenty miles south of Vona where they built a sod house. Margaret was their oldest child and she was born with the help of a midwife in the sod house on October 21, 1915.

I am grateful for the well written article by Sheryl Bishop Lain about Margaret. I was not surprised to learn Margaret had been the valedictorian of her high school class in Brush, Colorado in May, 1933. While teaching in Haxtun High School she met Swede Olson. He was the brother of one of her students. Sheryl writes about how Margaret described Swede, "He was the Love of her Life." He had won a scholarship to Drake. Just after one semester he returned to Colorado to farm for his mother. Swede and Margaret were married in Chappell, Nebraska on December 27, 1941.

During the war, Swede was first sent to Fort Knox, Kentucky. While stationed there Margaret was able to have a civil service job as a clerk/typist for the Post Quartermaster. Their oldest son, Vechel was born in Louisville on April 2, 1943. She told of Swede being stationed in the European theater. She recalled that day at the train station in Sterling, Colorado with the other war brides saying, "Good-bye." I can just see Margaret saying this. "Swede's brother said he'd drive me home to Haxtun but I said, 'no' I knew if I drove myself, I'd have to straighten up so I could see." They were separated for a year and a half. Swede returned home on January 26, 1947. The next great event was that their second child, Ronald was born.

Swede filed for a homestead in the Heart Mountain drawing being a WWII war veteran. Their priority number was drawn in January of 1948. They chose unit 103, fifteen miles west of Powell close to Heart Mountain. At that time their oldest son, Vechel Jr. was five and Ronald was one and a half. They moved to the Relocation center in August of 1948 from Julesburg, Colorado.

In the Heart Mountain community each family was beginning a whole new way of life farming on virgin soil, living in a barracks that needed a great deal of work and just learning so many new skills. But in spite of the heavy work load everyone took part in establishing our community club, school bus routes, telephones and so many aspects of a new community. Swede and Margaret Olson each took leadership roles in so many areas of our developing community.

That first year there was not a school bus for those of us old enough to go to school, so it was Swede Olson who drove the children in his new Chrysler. I just hope it survived the mud and snow and young ones. He had the first contract for the bus route in 1949 and then in January Swede invested in a yellow school bus, as the new homestead families were beginning to arrive.

Most of the homestead families struggled those first few years from being homesick as most of them had left family behind in other states. I always thought it was nice for the Olsons and Frenchs to have both won homestead units and to live next to each other as Margaret and Lyle were brother and sister. She told of the light plant they had which provided electricity. Most of the other neighbors did not have electricity for several years so that was almost a novelty for the rest of us. The added bonus for neighbors invited to the Olson home is that Swede would play the piano for them.

This new community of homesteaders were entering a place of virgin soil where the rattle snakes had been dwelling forever it seems. Those first years as the irrigation began to run down the ditches, this proved to be a great danger to the farmers and their families.

One story recounted by Margaret can be found in chapter 5 entitled, "Rattlesnakes."

The Olsons lived for a brief time at the Heart Mountain Relocation Camp and then moved a barracks to their homestead. They built a new veneer brick home in 1951.

I find it interesting those things that seem to stick with us from when we were young. I remember the birthday parties at the Olson home. They were always great fun for the neighborhood children. There was a wooden window that slid open from the kitchen to the dining room and I thought that was just the cleverest idea, as we could pass the cake and plates through.

My brother Mike and their oldest son Vechel were best of friends, so I have many happy memories of birthday parties and getting to come along with the guys on many of the expeditions; rabbit hunting, horseback rides and just the fun of youth.

The Olsons had a manicured lawn and an abundance of gladiolas in the garden. I always thought it was a beautiful home.

Those first few years the wives and young children were all so involved in just getting life going on the homestead but then a few years later Margaret began teaching again. I remember taking her typing class in high school. I don't think I was very speedy, but remember how much I admired her knowing she was one of our Mom's.

The crops that were grown on the Olson farm were Alfalfa, barley, spring wheat, sugar beets, potatoes and seeds, red clover and peas, green and seed. She told of the fields of multi-colored zinnias and marigolds that were grown for seed. Margaret said it was a beautiful crop but they were only paid $46 from the Utah seed company in 1954 so that was not a good investment.

It was a wonderful experience to finally have a telephone. I tell of many of the details and difficulties that went into this process in "Ma Bell Comes to Heart Mountain," in chapter 2. Each piece of settling this community would take a great deal of effort and I want to mention once again that Vechel Olson was the chairman of the committee that worked tireless for their neighbors and we are so grateful to them. The other committee members were Robert Jirsa, Herbert Wojahn, Jack Hirst and Floyd Gay.

I don't recall Margaret telling of Swede being struck by lightning for it would have a lasting effect on him. The western homesteads were right up at the foothills of Heart Mountain so the lightening could come so fast sometimes before the storm clouds. Several of the homesteaders spoke of the danger to them as they would be out in the field on farm equipment. Lyle French gave an account of that thunder storm on June 5, 1951. Swede

283

knew the storm was coming so he threw the last pea seed in the drill and shut it down. There were two tractors, a drill and a spring tooth in the ground. Jim Brown, the pea field man, was driving up to the men standing near the machinery when the lightning bolt stuck. He said it looked like a blue ball of fire. Lyle said he looked at Swede and described that his baseball cap was floating on top of his hair and from his nose to the top of his head was white. Swede finally began to bat his eyes. Swede later would suffer from a brain tumor and the family wondered if the lighting incident was related as he became ill after that. When Swede passed away the entire community grieved his death.

Swede's health declined to the point in 1957 that the farm was rented but the family continued to live on the homestead until 1961. In 1973 they sold the farm to Larry and Janet French.

I took my tape recorder with me that afternoon at the 50th homestead reunion. Margaret Olson had a story she wanted to share with me of the very early summers of harvesting.

"I wanted to share this story Patty. Swede wanted to buy a new and larger combine. He needed someone to irrigate for him while he would be away combining for other farmers. Of course all the neighbors were too busy with their own harvesting. He could not find anyone to hire for the work. I told Swede, 'if a person cannot find a job in the summer here, I don't want them around.' I finally got up enough nerve and told Swede I would irrigate the crops. I used his irrigating boots that were too large for me. I don't know, I suppose because I couldn't afford to buy my own. It was so hot that summer. One noon I stopped by a neighbor's house and told her, 'Well Annabelle found a teaching job and I think I will try and go back to teaching. Swede did pay me for irrigating that summer and he got to do his combining job so we all were happy.

In our new home we had four big picture windows. I decided I could make the drapes. I tried but it was not successful. I found a seamstress in Cody to make the drapes. When Swede came home from his combine jobs he even paid for the drapes being made so it all seemed to work out fine.

I did not even have to apply as the Deaver High School called me. I had taken off seven years from teaching in those first years of homesteading and raising our sons. I drove 32 miles to work every morning for four years and in all that time only missed five days of work from snowing roads. I then transferred to Powell High School and then later to Northwest Community College."

The Olson family gave so much to the Heart Mountain community in so many ways. And I would say that each family added to the rich story of this wonderful place called home. Swede left us way too soon and our community was sorrowful of that. Margaret continued on as she always had, that brave and beautiful person she was to us. In her own right she made contributions and received many honors and awards in education for many years after the homestead period. Margaret passed away passed on October 17, 2007 in Cheyenne.

MEMORIES OF RUTH OTTO

Very often during the time I was interviewing the homesteaders, the question was asked, "Which interview has been the best?" My quick response would be, "Each one is special, and everyone has something to add, so I can't really say that one is better than all the rest. Thus, in saying this, I want to explain why I have felt compelled to entitle one of the chapters, "Memories of Ruth Otto."

It has been some time now since Ruth's family and so many kindred friends gave their last respects to her. I canceled all previous engagements in order to attend her funeral. As I watched each of the homesteaders file into the Methodist church that morning, I could hear my breath, as I would hold it each time, studying the features of well worn, August suntans etched on wind-worn skin, with lines and wrinkles on both men and women.

I am now a Grandmother, and when I look in the mirror, I keep thinking that the homesteaders should look like me, should be just about my age. But no, they are mostly in their late eighties and nineties, and each year, the number gets fewer. With the passing of each one, my heart is very sad, as if the world has lost a great rock of stability of goodness with Ruth's passing and others like her.

I heard that Ruth had cancer. I knew it was very serious, as I asked of her state. I wanted to interview her but was hesitant, as I did not know if I would be intruding on the family. I didn't know if she was up to it; I just didn't know what to do. One morning, I was able to get some time away from the office in order to have an interview with Vaudine Jirsa. What a nice lady. I knew she and Ruth were close friends, so in asking about her, Vaudine told me Ruth had wondered why I hadn't come to interview her. I was delighted, and then upon knowing what I had always known of this woman, I was not surprised. In just a few days, I was making the trek across the Emblem Flats, which became a well-worn path in those many days of interviews. I felt anxious, not knowing if I could handle my emotions, telling myself to keep my mind clear and ask the right questions.

It was cool and overcast that morning in March. I had checked the address before I left home, so I drove up and parked at the curb. I fumbled around getting the tape recorder and tapes, paused a moment to say a quick prayer and hoped that would calm the ache in my chest.

The knock on the door brought a woman who had always had a small frame but now was so tiny and thin. Ruth smiled at me, with the smile that always seemed to be on her face. She was sick at her stomach. I knew she didn't feel like an interview. I felt like I was intruding and didn't want to be any more of a burden to her than with what she already was dealing.

"Ruth, I can come back another day when you're feeling better." No, she didn't feel well, but she wanted to have an interview anyway. I looked at her, so frail, skin as transparent as a fine, porcelain china cup. I knew it must be hard to sit on a wooden chair the way her bones protruded. "Would you like to lie on the couch while we have our interview, Ruth?" "No, let's sit at the kitchen table, but first let me show you some of the things in my living room." Pictures of her family, children, grandchildren, and her paintings were in every nook, displayed with the pride of a loving mother.

Before we began the interview, the delivery man came with the bags of liquid food, the only nourishment she could now digest. She was so matter of fact, explaining how this all worked, and how the family had a routine to help with the feedings. I was trying so hard to concentrate on what she was telling me, while at the same time, desperately pushing down the swelling tears I didn't dare let surface.

It was obvious from the beginning of this interview that Ruth had planned what she would say. I was amazed at how articulate she was. Her quick wit and memory for details were fascinating to me.

With a look of determination, speaking very softly with an erupting laugh and smile of endearment, Ruth began to speak.

"Loran and I grew up in Nebraska. I grew up about 25 miles south of Lincoln, Nebraska, on a farm. I taught school. I was only getting $45-$47 a month in a rural school. So I applied in a district north of Lincoln where I would make $80 a month. I taught in the district for four years. Loran was working in the CC camp the first year I taught there. We had organized all the young children to have a Christmas party and go caroling to the neighbors. That is when I met Loran. We hit it off and were married in 1941. Our first child, Ardell, was born. She was three months old when he was drafted. Then he didn't see her until she was 19 months old, and then again when she was three-and-a-half. Loran just happened to be home on furlough when Orin was born. He went right overseas after he went back to Fort Dix in New Jersey, and then he was gone until Orin was 23 months old. He was first stationed in England and then France. He was hit by a grenade, and the shrapnel hit his foot. When it went into his foot, it was white hot, so they just left it. They never did take the shrapnel out of his foot.

Loran had gotten out of the service in October 1945. We worked for the University of Nebraska on a farm for a while, and then we went back to where my parents lived at Adams, Nebraska. Loran was working for a cattle feeder when we heard about the homesteads. It was through a couple that had come to visit us, and they had brought a Legion magazine. They asked if we had heard about the homesteads near Cody, Wyoming.

I immediately sent a letter inquiring about the homestead project. Sure enough, in a week or so, we got information back. We had to show that we had $1,500 in the bank, which we didn't. Loran's dad put that much in the bank for us. I don't know if he ever got paid back or not. I thought about that later; I hope he did, but I don't know. Anyway, we had a cow, and some chickens, and an old, '35 Ford. In January, we received a notice that we had been chosen in the drawing for the second project on Heart Mountain.

I remember the night your folks' name was chosen. Wallace and Edna's name was the first name drawn for the third homestead project up on Ralston Bench in 1949. The drawing was done in the old theater. They used a big, bingo-type roller with the names in it. I assume the drawing for the 1948 drawing was done at the theater also.

Probably the most important thing I remember was there were no trees on the flat. We came here in April. We left home on April 5, 1948, and it took us three days to get here. We had a trailer-load pulled behind an old '35 Ford. The weather was really quite good, except when we got outside of Casper, we hit a squall, and the tarp blew off of the trailer. Loran had to go borrow some wire from a fence and anchor the tarp back down on the trailer. We got in on that day about 5:30 p.m. to Heart Mountain.

Loran asked, "Should we go to Powell or Cody for a motel?" I said, "We don't have that kind of money. We are staying right here at the relocation camp." There was still a guard at the gate then, and you had to be let in. You had to have the proper papers, so they would know you weren't an intruder. We had to have proof that we had rented an apartment there. So we unloaded, I scrubbed the floors in the barracks, and Loran unloaded our bedding. My parents and my sisters had sent enough food along, and, of course, it was cool enough that we had it in a cooler, so we had enough to eat that night.

There were construction people there, and they were hauling out stuff that belonged to the Bureau of Reclamation. There was a little café

288

and a post-office down at the bottom of the hill when we came. We had to find our barracks. They were 120-foot barracks, and our apartment was forty feet. We had the south edge of one and had to go to the laundry room to go to the bathroom and to get hot water, as there was no toilet or hot water in the apartments.

While we lived at the relocation camp, my sister got married, and I couldn't go home. She got married the 17th of June. We had been in the camp since April, and I spent most of the day of her wedding in tears. I wanted to go home so badly, but I was pregnant, and I knew that we didn't have the money. There was no way I could have gone home. I was really homesick that week, but things do pass. You have to go on, so it really wasn't such a big tragedy, but at the time I thought it was.

We knew nothing about the Japanese Relocation Camp before we came to Wyoming. We didn't know they had been placed here during the war. I was totally ignorant about how those people were living here, or why they were put here in the first place, until we got here. While they lived here during the war, they built a lot of the ditches for the homestead projects. They had their own vegetable gardens around camp. They had their own slaughterhouse for beef and pork, which I didn't know until years later.

The relocation camp was not in the Powell or Cody school district. Anything from Badger Basin Road east was in the Powell district. Anything from Badger Basin west was in the Paint Creek district up over the mountain.

Ardell was school age by then, and she would have had to ride the bus clear over to Paint Creek. If we could get her to Ralston, the bus would take her to Powell, but at the time there weren't any roads out on the flat.

I still had my teaching certificate at the time. We got together with our neighbors, the Acotts, Winns, Olsons, and Van Dykes and went over to the school district at Paint Creek and had a meeting with the school board. They gave us a petition to try and get into the Powell school district. We went to the school district in Powell, but it was too late to get Ardell into school. I taught her from September to December, and then we went back to Nebraska until March. We lived with Loran's folks those few months. My sister was teaching in a rural school nearby, so she picked up Ardell every morning. Then, when we came back in March, I taught her from March until the end of school that spring.

By the fall term, the roads were graded, so we took turns with the Olsons driving our children to Powell. That first year there were five of the kids that were in school. As more of the third drawing families moved in that year of 1949, Swede began to drive a school bus.

Ardell had to take a test before the school district would accept her into the second grade at Parkside. I really felt sorry for her though, because all the rest of the students had already been together for a year, and she came in not knowing anyone. It was hard for her the first few weeks, and then she seemed to get adjusted to the new school.

I was pregnant with Rolly when we came up here. He was born in the middle of July, and, of course, money was so scarce, so Loran applied for a job to work on the ditches. We couldn't farm that first year, because the ditches were not completed, and we couldn't get water. He got to work on the ditches up by our homestead. He helped with the upper part of the Heart Mountain units building cement turnouts. He had to quit that job in July in order to get the barracks moved to the homestead. We didn't have enough money to hire someone to do it, so Loran and Mr. Van Dyke, who was later our neighbor, helped us. They had come from Oregon. I don't know how he knew so much about everything, but he was really good at fixing stuff.

The men worked on an old '35 Chevy flatbed truck. They put big, long poles on it with dolly wheels in the back and then cut the barracks in sections, twenty-foot and forty-foot sections. They had the sections placed on railroad ties that were jacked up. They backed the truck up under the sections, and then it was let down on the truck bed.

We took the forty-foot section out of camp first. We went out the north gate, and there was a real steep hill as you turned the corner, and the truck choked about three-fourths of the way up the hill. They were supposed to throw some boards underneath the wheels to stop it, if the brakes didn't hold. Well, the brakes didn't hold, and it went right over the boards, so finally Loran backed into a bank. There was about a 35-foot drop on the opposite side. I could just see the truck and the barracks and the whole works going over there, but he got it stopped. So, then we had to go back to camp and get a tractor to pull the barracks up the hill thereafter. The old truck just didn't have enough power to pull it. We had to take the barracks through Eagle's Nest, which was quite a deep ravine. Yes, we had to go through Eagle's Nest--what a scare! When you got to the top of the hill looking out across the plain, there were no roads. So we just took out across country trying to find the one bridge across Alkali Creek to make it to our homestead.

The second drawing of homesteaders got two barracks. They would have to be cut in two, so it took quite a few trips to get them all delivered. What a relief it was to all of us when we finally got the barracks transported to the units.

My parents were living on a farm in Nebraska. It was a dry land farm, so when they had all the corn cultivated and everything, there wasn't much else they could do, so they came up to help us. They got there on July 9. I went to the hospital for Rolly that night. I was sure glad Grandma was there to take care of Ardell and Orin, and Loran was glad too. Rolly was born the next night. We brought him home from the hospital three days later. My mother was so worried, that she had been scrubbing everything with Purex. It was impossible to keep dust out of the barracks, but she had cleaned and cleaned.

The first reaction from my parents when we had decided to take the homestead was, 'Oh, you can't go, that is all there is to it.' Then they got to thinking about it and said, 'If you don't like it, you can always sell it in five years.' But after Dad came, he changed his mind. He was a good carpenter. He could use a saw and hammer, and that was a great asset. Loran and I knew nothing about carpentry or anything like that.

We needed to build some foundations for the barracks. The Bureau of Reclamation told us they were pushing down the great big chimneys of the school house and the hospital. If we cleaned the brick and cleaned up

291

our mess, we could have all the brick we wanted, so we spent days there at the camp in July before Rolly was born, cleaning brick and hauling it out. All we had to haul it in was the little, old trailer behind the car, but we hauled enough brick out to do the house and the barn. Loran had never laid brick in his life, but Dad had, so he instructed us. I mixed the mortar in one of those boat-like cement things, and they laid the brick for the foundation. That is what all of our foundations were made of. We had to put a base under it of some cement, but other than that, it was brick. One day, Loran sent Dad to town, because we needed gravel to make the base underneath the bricks. He told him, 'Now, you turn at this pile of steel.' Well, in the meantime, a truck came by and moved the pile of steel, and Grandpa got about where he thought that the steel should be, but it wasn't there. He went around and around, but he couldn't find the road that he was supposed to go on to get across the Alkali Creek. Loran finally went and got him, because he became so turned around. We have laughed about that incident many times down through the years.

The roads were not in yet, so we had to drive along the canal shoot, and then we would drive along the canal bank and follow it to the homestead. There was one bridge over the Alkali Creek to the west.

We moved into the part of the barracks that would, in time, be the barn. In evening twilight, after a late supper, Grandpa and Grandma went around the end of the barracks to get into their room, because the door happened to be on the opposite side of where we were living. They took the old lantern, both dog-tired but so happy to be a part of the beginnings of our life on the homestead. I can still see them walking around the barracks together. I was thinking the other day-they weren't quite sixty years old then. Boy, did everybody work hard that summer.

Grandma's job was to bathe the baby and wash the clothes every morning and hang them on a rope we had tied from one building to the other, as there was no clothesline then. She always kept the baby washed and the clothes all washed up.

In the beginning, I went to town a lot to do the laundry, but then Loran got a little put-put gas motor and put it on the washing machine, and it all worked good as long as he was around. But just as soon as he left, that motor would stop, and I didn't have enough strength. You pushed it like you do a motorcycle. I never had enough strength to get it started again, so then the water would get cold, and I had to put it back in the boiler and heat it up again. Washing was not convenient. Believe me, the kids had to wear their clothes several days. They didn't get clean clothes every day like we do now, because laundry was just too difficult to do. My dad fixed me a clothesline, and oh, that was such a blessing before they left. And so, we had a regular clothesline and the whole works.

We went to church at the relocation camp for the first two years. The homesteaders had a little church. There was a young man from seminary, but he worked for the Bureau in the summer, and he worked out of Cody. I don't know why he stayed in Cody in the winter. He organized a little church, and we went there the first two years. I don't know where they got their hymn books and their Bibles, but they were there. The little church was already organized when we came, so we were invited to go, so that is where we went.

When we first came, we got all our mail in Ralston. Each of the families had a post office box at Bud Steck's store. Whoever went to Ralston picked up everyone's mail. Then later, we had a mail carrier who came as far as Fulton's. He put everybody's mail in that box, and we had to go get it.

Bud Steck was so good to all of the homesteaders. He would charge our groceries until the men got their school check. All the men went to school on the GI Bill in the evening. They got $90 dollars a month, and that is what most of us lived on. I just hope everyone paid him back. There was a lumberyard there in Ralston. We got a lot of our lumber and little finishing stuff that we had to have, and, of course, you salvaged absolutely everything you could. A lot of the barracks were put together with square nails which was quite unheard of at the time.

The first year we were there, Mildred Van Dyke and I got 200 chickens. We had brought a little pole brooder back from Loran's sister, so we had it in one of the barracks. She fed them at noon, and I fed them in the morning and in the evening. We shared the cost, and when they got big enough to be fryers, we each took half of them. I took the share of fryers that I had, cleaned and dressed them, and sold them to Steck's Grocery in Ralston. I made $2.75 for each dressed fryer, but boy, was that a lot of work. It was one way to make a little money that first few years.

All of the homesteaders were so busy that summer, but after the fall work was done, we began to get together in the evenings. We played a lot of cards by the light of kerosene lamps. The wives would bake cakes. We played cards and had refreshments. Homer and Margie Winn lived north of us, the Acotts, Eldora (they called him Pink then), and Ellis Acott lived to the northeast of us, and then Bob and Mildred Van Dyke. The four families would get together and play pinochle and canasta.

I have thought about our life here, and I would do it again in a minute. I really didn't think it was so terribly bad, because we had nothing. We would never have had a farm in Nebraska, because they were so expensive, and this was the only way we could possibly have gotten where we are today.

The Carters were interested in homesteading. They were visiting Charlie and Merle Nunley. I had gone to town. When I came home, they had come over to see us and had talked to Loran about buying our place. I was just not one bit sure I wanted to sell our farm. But we decided we would sell to them, so they bought the original homestead place.

Loran was thinking maybe he wanted to go back to Nebraska. During that summer, Nebraska had a real bad drought, and the crops just dried up. I just didn't want to go back to Nebraska. The Stones lived about three miles away on lane ten. They decided they wanted to go back to Texas. He came over one evening and talked with us and said, 'My place is for sale, if you guys want to buy it.' I said, 'Yes, we'll take it.'

I loved the mountains, the climate, the farming area, and this had become home to me. So in September, the Carters moved to our homestead, and we moved to the Stone homestead, and it is where we lived for 25 years. We also bought the farm across the road--Charles Roland's place, and we bought Van Dyke's homestead. So we had three places. Rolly bought three acres, and the house is on our home place.

Now that our children are all grown, they have some stories they always tell when they get together. One of the funny ones is, 'We had a charger on the fence so that the cows wouldn't get out. It was just low enough that it would hit the dog's tail. So when they would call the dog and he would run under the fence, he would howl and yip, and turn round and round, not knowing what was going on. Of course, I didn't know what was going on, or I would have put a stop to it.' Of course, the kids liked to go fishing out on Alkali Creek. Before the upper amendments were in, we would go fishing up above our place. The kids went up there often and caught "brookies." Once in a great while, when we could get away from the farm work, our family would go up to Beartooth fishing. We had a lot of company that first couple of years. They wanted to see how we were getting along. If it was possible at all, we would always try to take them to the mountains.

The farm was not very attractive those first four or five years, but it got better. When company came, it didn't really bother me. I thought, if they don't like it, well too bad. I was perfectly happy to have a family again and all of us be together.

In those homestead families, everyone had to work. There was just no getting around it, whether you were five or ten, you had to work. Everyone had to help out, and you thought nothing of it. Those kids loaded bricks when we were cleaning them for our foundations. There were no questions, you just did it. Of course, we always had prayer around the table and often read the Bible stories, and I think that family ethic should be used more today than it is. Our family always ate together. That was just normal. When the kids were in sports, we waited until everybody came home, and we had our meal.

When it came to discipline, sometimes I think I was a little harsh and hard on the kids, because we were so busy and had so much work to do. We were just so tired at night, and I don't suppose I was as patient as

I could have been all the time, but I don't think we had many problems, really.

Of course, there were very few times the children were home when either Loran or I were not there with them.

Loran always had guns on the wall, and it was just understood that nobody touched those guns without permission. The guns were a part of our everyday life, as so much of the meat the family ate was wild game. So there was just a self-discipline with the children that they knew it was out of the question to take those guns down off the wall.

I baked bread about three times a week. Every time the children would come home from school, I always had a big slice of homemade bread with hot cocoa ready for them, because they had ridden the bus so far and were so starved when they got home. The crust was the favorite for all of them. One day, I had baked bread and had gone to town. When they came in, there was the bread, and they all wanted the crust, so they took the bread knife and cut the crust off of all the loaves. So it was no big deal that is what they wanted; well, let them have it.

The 4-H Club played a big and important role in the homestead children. The first project Ardell took was cooking. I think she went to Edna Mae's house for sewing lessons. I was a cooking leader for some time. We met for project meetings every couple of weeks, and I think all the kids really enjoyed their projects. And, of course, every project had a booklet which had to be completed.

Ardell cooked an awful lot when she was young, because I had so much to do. She baked cakes when she was ten years old. At the time, we had milk cows and had cream. She would make a sour cream chocolate cake which was out of this world, and, of course, we would eat it right away, while it was still warm. We made lots of homemade ice cream. The Schaefers and our family would have birthday parties together. They had five children, and we had six, so there were eleven birthdays that we could celebrate. Some of them were the same month. We always had homemade ice cream, made gallons of it, and then had birthday cake, and that was always a highlight in the kid's day--to have a birthday cake.

Our son Dale was six when the accident happened. After his death, I just felt I needed something, and so there was a great need for foster families. So we took babies in from 1964 to 1970. We had eleven foster children during those years.

The little Schaefer boy's accident, Dale's accident, and the Gilbert boy drowned. The community was wonderful when there was a tragedy. I don't know where I could have been where there was more support. The neighbors came, and we just all grieved together. Of course, I think in those days we really didn't talk about it as much as probably we do now, but there was certainly support. The neighbors came and supported you."

She spoke briefly of Orin's death. He was my age, and all of us had been such great friends growing up, so we shared a grief that day of his death.

Ruth and I sat there at the kitchen table quietly for a few minutes. I would not have asked about Dale and Orin, but I think it was comforting for her to be able to talk about the death of her two sons and explain how she had coped with the family tragedy.

I looked across the kitchen table that day and saw a precious woman. Even though the cancer had left her weary and worn, her face had the beauty of fine china etched with lines of a life full of loving, laughter, and wisdom. I am blessed to have known .

PART II: HOMESTEADER INTERVIEWS
SECTION 4

VELMA ROBINSON

The interview with Velma Robinson was done in my Extension office, on a conference call, so it could be taped. What a delightful conversation it was. The date was September 28, 2001. The next day was to be her birthday. She is still in her seventies, so I told her she was still a very young woman, as she is younger than most of the other homesteaders I interviewed.

Velma has sent me some very encouraging letters about this research project. I have a special file where I keep the encouraging notes, which I bring out when it seems I will never complete this task.

I knew it would not be possible to drive to Valley Mills, Texas, so I was so thankful Velma agreed to a telephone interview.

Hartwell, Velma's husband, grew up in Texarkana, and Velma grew up in Nocona, Texas. They met in Wichita Falls where Hartwell was stationed, and Velma was going to school. He was sent to camp in Larkin, California, but they stayed in touch and were later married there. Velma worked in civil service and was able to be transferred with Hartwell when his location was changed.

Hartwell's mother became very ill, and since there was no else to take care of her, he received a discharge. After she passed away, he began to work in the oil fields in Stockton, Texas.

"Hartwell Robert, Jr., was born September 23, 1943, and was five when we moved to Wyoming. Roberta was born October 16, 1946. Loretta was born in Powell, May 27, 1953. Sue was born after we came back to Texas."

Velma began to describe how they found out about the homestead.

"We moved around a great deal with the oil field work. In one location, we met a couple from Powell. We had been hearing about homesteading and were interested in looking into the possibility. They told us about the homesteads in Wyoming. We wrote to the Bureau of Reclamation in Cody for an application. Ours was the 20th name to be drawn. That was in October of 1949. We had been living in a little trailer, so we just packed everything we had in it and came. We had a little boy, five, and a little girl, two, so we brought them with us.

When we got to Cody, there was snow on the ground. We went to the camp and met with the Board. We advertised our trailer for sale. We traded the trailer to a couple for household furniture. So we had just about all we needed to live in the barracks.

We were instructed to go pick out two units on Ralston Bench. Two other candidates withdrew, so then we became number 18 in line for a homestead. We were given two barracks. One had hardwood floors, and the other didn't have a floor at all. We found a house mover, and the barracks came to the farm unit on November 11, 1949. When he arrived, we were sitting there with the furniture we acquired from the trade of our small trailer. Our new neighbor, Lyle Henderson, came and helped us move into the barracks.

While we were carrying things into the barracks, some sage hens flew over. That is the first time I had ever seen sage chickens. Both of the fellows stopped what they were doing and went and shot some.

A strong wind came up, caught the door, and blew it right off of the barracks. We put a comforter over the door to keep out the cold. We stayed there that night. We were excited; it was like camping.

We stayed out on the unit all winter. Most of the other families came, picked out their units, and went back home, but we just couldn't afford to go back to Texas, so we stayed the winter. There were several families that spent the winter, so we all got together and had Christmas together.

We were so excited about the possibility of getting a homestead, that when we sent the application in, we began to save money for the move, although we didn't hear if our name had been drawn for several months.

Some of the older homesteaders began to talk to Hartwell and were very discouraging. Before he left Texas, his boss told him if he ran out of money to just call, and he would send money to come back.
They said, "You should just take the money and go back to Texas."

300

He came home and talked to me about it. Well, I just thought about it, did some praying, and came back to Hartwell, and said, "Well, I think if the good Lord helped us get this homestead, he will help us, so I think we should stay. I'm willing to stay if you are." So we decided to stay, and I think we were both glad that we made that decision.

When Hartwell worked in the oil field, he had to be gone from home most of the time. When we got to Wyoming, we all worked together. Even though the children were small, they helped. We did everything together as a family, and it was good.

We didn't know how to irrigate. Axel lived across the road from us. He was raised here, so he knew how to irrigate. He came over and helped us all learn. Our relatives came out and tried to help with the siphon tubes and couldn't figure it out, so our little girl got down on the ditch and showed them how to create suction and set the tubes.

It was a wonderful community to be a part of. We had to do most of the work as a family in those early years. Neighbors would help each other. None of us could afford all the machinery we needed, so each of us would get different pieces of equipment and then would share.

I don't think we considered ourselves poor in those days. We had everything we needed. Of course, there weren't any luxuries or anything like that, but that didn't hurt any of us.

We came in November and stayed through the winter. This was the daily schedule. We got up in the morning. I cooked breakfast, and my husband went to the field and plowed, while I stayed in the house and baked two loaves of bread and cooked a pot of beans every morning. There was just the four of us, and we would use up both loaves of bread for the noon and supper meal.

Hartwell would come in for noon and eat, and then he would take the flatbed trailer, put the kids in the pickup, and go to the camp to work on the barracks that didn't have a floor. He tore down part of the barracks and used the materials to build a barn and garage. The kids stayed in the cab of the pickup and watched him if the weather was warm enough.

In the afternoons, I would go to the field and plow. When Hartwell had loaded the trailer with lumber, he would come home and relieve me from plowing. I would go to the house with the kids and spend the rest of the afternoon straightening nails. We plowed that first year until the ground froze. Then we worked on the house until spring.

We built a three-bedroom house with a bath, dining room, and living room. The sixty-foot barracks that had a floor was sawed in two. Part of the building was moved around to make a T-shape building which was the house.

Hartwell, Jr. and Roberta talk about when they lived in Wyoming when they get together. The younger children were too young when we left Wyoming. Those were good years for our family when we lived in Wyoming. I think it really taught our children how to work hard, because we surely did that.

The most important thing I think we had on the homestead is that we worked together and enjoyed life. We would work hard all week but would take off on Sunday and take the children to church. In the spring, we tried to get all the work done, so when May 30th came, we could take a day and go to Yellowstone Park. That was always a family day.

We had a John boat (paddle boat) in those years. We would take it to the park. We would fish there at fishing bridge and take the boat out into the lake. We would fish in the morning and then bring the trout in and cook them over a fire. After lunch, the kids would lie down on blankets in the boat and take a nap, and we would keep fishing until we caught our limit.

Roberta tells of the time when we were in the park. We had stopped to eat lunch. We didn't notice the bear, but she did. She was so scared she ran to the car, locked all the doors, and covered up her head.

Hartwell liked to hunt. He got a bear, elk, and moose. During harvest, when the peas were ripe, the ducks would come in. He enjoyed hunting ducks.

We had close friends we spent a lot of time with. Hartwell, Jr.'s good friend was Jimmy Rodriguez. We met a lot of neighbors when we would go to the clubhouse. Jean and Glenn Montgomery were good friends; they have both passed away. The Hedricks, Gordon and Beverly Hutchinson, and Don and Jo Miller are some friends I still keep in contact with. And, of course, we thought a lot of Vincent and Elizabeth Schiltz. They were good neighbors.

My husband hated the winters, but I didn't. I was so glad when winter came, so we could slow down from working outside. When it was cold, he would go to town and play Rummy. The long winters wore on his nerves. We didn't have electricity for a while, and there was no TV.

I didn't mind living in the barracks. I just thought that was all part of homesteading. We had that morning stove that seemed to keep us warm. We had brought area rugs along with the furniture, but we kept them rolled up that first winter. In the spring, when we rolled out the frozen rugs, we found snow behind them.

Hartwell went to town that first winter and bought a milk cow. We didn't have a fence for her, so we had to build a fence to keep her in. We had to haul water from the relocation camp. We had a 33gallon barrel we carried water in. It was snowing when we brought it home. When we were bringing it into the house, snow got on the bottom of the barrel. Do you know, in the spring when we took the barrel out of the house, the snow on the bottom was still there! I guess those barracks floors were cold. We didn't seem to mind; it was like camping out.

Two women from Powell taught me how to make sourdough bread. They gave me some starter. I would have to keep it by the morning stove so it wouldn't freeze. If it froze, it was ruined. I baked two loaves from the starter every day. We had to eat hardy, because we were working so hard.

Those first years, we didn't have money to buy many groceries, so we ate venison, sage chickens, pheasant, and antelope.

An outfitter in town had set out some bear meat for some hunters from Texas. They never saw any bear and finally had to go home. He asked Hartwell if he wanted to hunt for the bear. He was happy to oblige, and he did get to shoot a bear. It was time to milk the cow when they went hunting, and by the time I had the cow milked, they were back with a bear.

That milk cow was good to have. We made butter and cottage cheese. We got a separator and sold the cream to the creamery in Powell. At one time, we had three or four cows.

One year, we raised certified peas. We had a group of ladies that came and went up and down the rows and picked the peas that couldn't be certified. They were still green and could be eaten. There was a free radio program, so I submitted an ad for anyone who wanted free peas. I had one lady call and ask if they were shelled. When I said no, she didn't want them.

There were two oil wells that were drilled over behind our farm in the badlands. Hartwell got a job drilling the wells, and then when they were completed, he was hired to pump them. Another man from Powell worked with him. Every morning, they would go to the site and engage the wells. One Sunday, when they arrived at the wells, there was some poison gas. The other fellow passed out. After that incident, Hartwell was concerned for their safety. He asked me after that to pay attention to how long he was gone, and if he didn't come back, I was to go check on him.

It wasn't too long after that he never did come in, so I thought I had better go check on him. I put the kids in the pickup and went to check to see if he was safe. There was snow on the ground, and when I turned off the main road over in the badlands to go to the rig, I got stuck. There were no tracks in the snow, so no one had been there that morning.

I thought, "What am I going to do way out here? We will freeze to death." There was a load of ground grain in the pickup. I got out and put grain under the wheels and would inch back and forth and kept doing that until we got out of the snowdrift. When I finally got back in the pickup, Roberta said, "Oh, I was praying Jesus would help us get out of the snowdrift." When I got back home, Hartwell said they had already been there that morning and told me never to do that again.

One year, we lost our whole crop to a hailstorm. That was very disheartening. But then, that didn't happen so much.

We did enjoy the homesteading, but the winters were getting to Hartwell. One summer, right during irrigating, his sister got very sick, and we just couldn't leave. She died, and we couldn't get away to go to the funeral, so after that, Hartwell wanted to go back to Texas. I didn't want to leave Wyoming. I tried to talk him into staying, but he wanted to go back and live by his family in Texas.

Hartwell has passed away, so I am now a widow and live by my children, so that is good. Overall, Wyoming homesteading was a wonderful experience. I am happy our stories are being written down. I hope to come to another reunion, as I have so many fond memories of our friends."

CHARLES ROLAND

It was a blustery day in late October when I drove down the coast of Oregon from Cannon Beach to Coos Bay on Highway 101. I had lived in Oregon for two years around 1989. I have always loved the ocean. The fascination that grew during those two years for the mountain beauty and power of the ocean on the northwest Pacific coast is hard to explain to others. I had looked forward to this day. I was going to get to see Barbara and Beth Simon and Charles Roland. It was disappointing that Charles' wife, Edna, had already passed away. I did not realize how long it would take me to drive along the winding, coastal highway. It took much longer than I had anticipated. After I spent the evening with Beth and Barbara and rested, I was ready again in the morning for another interview.

Barbara helped me that next morning to find Charlie's home. It was a rainy morning, and the air had a bite to it, but I could hear the sound of the ocean and smell the salt of the sea which always gave me a feeling of wonder. Charles was waiting for us with coffee brewing. As the three of us sat down at his dining room table, once again I felt relief and satisfaction that I had taken time to come and spend this morning with these two, special families.

I could tell that Charles was happy to see us but could also sense his feeling of loss that his wife was not there with us, reminiscing of those special homestead days.

I asked Charles to tell us where he and Edna grew up.

"We both grew up in western Nebraska. She was in what they called the Sand Hills. And then her family moved to Alliance when she was, oh, I don't know, ten or so. I was born and raised on a farm in western Nebraska. I lived on the dry land farm until I went to the service. After I had been home from the service two or three years was when I got a homestead.

305

I was in the Army Corps. My service time was spent in Europe. I was in Germany for the last six months of the war. I didn't see much action, as the war was mostly over where I was.

The way I found out about the homesteads on Heart Mountain was through my dad. He found a little ad in the local paper that said there were homesteads in Wyoming. The homesteads on Heart Mountain, Riverton, and Lander were all mentioned in the ad. I think my application was number 58. I'm not real sure, but I think numbers 55 and 56 had dropped out.

I was married by this time. Rossi was born in 1946 or '47. He was just two or three years old, just a little guy.

I can remember the day I found out we had gotten a homestead. Oh! I was excited, but I wasn't sure I wanted it until I found out my name had been drawn, and then I knew I wanted it. It was hard to know if I was doing the right thing, starting out in a place that you had never seen and a kind of farming I had never done. I had never seen irrigation done, just had to stop and think for a while . There was no irrigation out in western Nebraska when I was growing up. There is now. That is all there is, but not when I was little.

The barracks had not been moved to the homestead when we arrived, so we lived in a trailer court there in Powell. I don't remember the name of the court; it was there on Main Street, but I don't think it is there anymore. That little trailer was so cold. I know there were days that it was so terrible damp in that place. The back wall had ice on it. I don't think the trailer had been winterized.

I don't think Edna minded much about living in the barracks after we moved out on the homestead. Her folks never did have an awful lot. They had a real big family and a real little house. I mean, a little house, with ten kids. So I don't think she cared that much for the farm, not that she didn't like being in the country, but she couldn't get to town to visit or anything. But then we started making friends out in our community.

That first six months was terrible. You are a long ways from friends and home and everything else. It was a very unique experience. Like I say, I wouldn't trade it for anything.

My memory of that first year was trying to figure out those cement drops. It didn't seem like that first year was worth a dang! Doing something altogether different than I had ever done. I didn't get my ground plowed that first fall. I don't remember what happened. It was too cold, too wet, or too dry. So the next spring, I just tackled it.

The GI Bill helped a lot of my neighbors taking classes that would help them with farming. But I had been already taking classes in Nebraska learning about plastics. So when I came to Wyoming, there was some kind of mix-up with changing classes, so I missed out on the first six months of classes. Most of us depended on the small amount we received to buy groceries, so since I wasn't able to go to classes, Edna struggled. Her dad came out to see us and left us 100 pounds of onions.

We didn't want to spend the money we had for farming, because if we did, what were we going to do? You couldn't borrow money. No one knows us. We had no credit rating of any kind. But Steck, yeah, he ran the grocery store there in Ralston. He saved a lot of people's hides, because he was one of a kind, I'll tell you. I didn't know what we would have done without him. He let the homesteaders charge their groceries in his store. I just hope everyone paid him back.

We sold the homestead in March of 1971 to Loran Otto. Later, the house and outbuildings were sold to someone from out east. Our children were young when we came to Oregon, so they didn't have a chance to get involved in 4-H.

I know Heart Mountain was a wonderful community. Everybody helped everybody. Everybody's kids were just like your kids when they came to see you. You decided if they weren't going to do something, and you told them, and nobody's feelings were hurt. The kids did what they were told. You couldn't ask for better neighbors. Loran and Ruth Otto were just wonderful people. Now, all the neighbors were special, as far as I'm concerned. If you needed help, it was there; you didn't ask, it was just there.

Our family liked to fish. We did a lot of fishing in the summertime, when we had time. But we didn't often go very far, because we would have to get home to change water most of the time, at least twice a day. So that

was one reason that we fished at Buffalo Bill Dam, because it was so close. A few times, we fished on Crandall
Creek. We usually fished with our neighbors. I remember going with Loran Otto, Elmer Collar, and Otto Andersen. I don't think I ever went fishing by myself.

In those first years in Wyoming, we raised a lot of dry edible peas to start with. That was one of the main crops for about three years, and then alfalfa, malt barley, and beans. There wasn't much of a price for alfalfa hay then, but that was a good crop to get the ground built up and get the nitrogen in the ground without putting fertilizer on it.

I tried a dairy for three years. It was one of the worst mistakes I made in my life, trying to have a dairy out there. I didn't have a very big one, and we didn't have any market. The markets had never materialized, and it broke a bunch of us. My light bill the first six months I had the cows was more than my milk check. We just had no place to sell it.

Edna and I started square dancing down at the club. I can't remember everyone, but there were Elmer and Tiny, Dick and Lois, Otto and Katie, Charlie and Merle that I recall. I just can't remember everyone that went. We took instructions, and, oh, we had a ball.

We had community club meetings every month, but it was more of a get together than anything else. The women met there a lot for their different types of meetings.

There were times some us didn't get paid for our hay after it had been hauled. That made it really rough on the farmers out here. By the time we left, they had put a scale there at the clubhouse to weigh the trucks. I don't think there was enough room to weigh a semi. But it was just a convenience for the farmers up here. We had to drive to town to get our hay bales weighed, so having the scale at the clubhouse saved all of us time. It was a certified, state-inspected scale.

Now, as far as our neighbors, I can't ever think of a time I was lied to. As far as I'm concerned, if somebody said they would do something, they did it. Or if somebody said this is what happened, it happened.

If somebody got sick during harvest time, you went and helped them. Merle Nunley was in a car wreck in the spring, and everyone went and helped get the ground ready to plant. When I got burned, the neighbors came and did my harvesting.

I'll tell you how I got burned. I was trying to do something I knew absolutely was not smart. That is usually what happens in accidents, farm or otherwise. I had a bunch of peas that were so ripe they were popping. I was trying to get done, and I was using a track combine. It had a Wisconsin four-cylinder, air-cooled engine. It had a five-gallon gas tank. I didn't want to run out of gas out in the middle of the field, because if it ever quit, it would take an hour to get started again. It wouldn't start until it had cooled down. I could crank my arm off, and it still wouldn't start. So, I thought, I'll take a half can of gas, and when I need some gas, I'll just turn the combine off where nothing is running except the motor and pour real easy, real slow, and be real careful. I could add a couple of gallons to keep me going. Well, I must have spilled some on the manifold, because it caught fire. It burned my hands and wrist and face real bad. I was doing something I knew I shouldn't do. You never put gas in a motor when it is running.

I think what I remember the most was the good times the kids had growing up on the homestead. They sure got into stuff. Rossi and Debbie got into their heads how they could tease Greg. Greg was scared to death of bears. He would go into orbit if he saw a bear.

I don't know how old they were, but they were little. Greg wasn't in school, and Debbie must have just started. Anyhow, they took catsup and smeared it all over Debbie, and she went out on the lawn and lay down. Rossi took Greg to the window and said the bear got Debbie. Well, that did it for Greg and the bears from then on! Yeah, we were up in Yellowstone Park, and a bear was coming through. I don't know, at least fifty yards away. It was quite a ways away, and Greg saw the bear. He went into the car and locked all the doors, so we couldn't get in, and we couldn't get him out either. There was a lot of that kind of stuff.

One thing we never did was let our kids swim in the canal. We were close enough to the drop where it went under the road, and it was just too dangerous. I told them, don't you ever let me catch you in that canal! The water is cold, and there are too many things that can happen. Now, if you want to swim, we will take you to town or something.

I remember in the spring when we would start irrigating, you couldn't even keep your hand in the water very long. Coming off the mountain, that snowmelt was cold.

We sold the farm in 1971 and came out here to Brookings. The people in Brookings are real nice, but they are not farmers. Yup, it was a lot of fun, a lot of hard work, but it was a great place to be there on the farm."

PAUL AND LILLIAN SCHILTZ

After retirement, Paul and Lillian moved to a lovely home in Powell on the west side of town. I began the interview this afternoon, first asking Lillian where she grew up.

"Well, I'm originally from Bismarck, North Dakota, and I've been married fifty-four years. We are lucky to be alive today. I'll let Paul talk, while I get all the children's birthdays in mind."

"I was born in a little town in North Dakota. My parents came from Minnesota in about 1910 and homesteaded there. I was born in 1917 which makes me a WWI baby. My dad didn't go to the service, because he had three children.

I was the third son of Leonard and Theresa Stadtler Schiltz, born at my dad's North Dakota homestead on May 21, 1917. Preceding me was my oldest brother, Lowell, born Sept.18, 1911, and next was Vincent, born May 17, 1914. Following me via the same outlet was my sister, Felicitas, born on June 4, 1923.

Dad homesteaded the 160 acres in 1909 and went back by train to marry my mother in 1910. They rented an immigrant railroad car to come from Caledonia, Minnesota, to Taylor, North Dakota. Our home was located four miles northwest of Hirschville, so-named after Hirsch who had a grocery and general purpose store and also ran the post office.

I got my public education at a rural, one-room schoolhouse for all eight grades. When it was miserably cold or a blizzard, Dad would take us to school in the sleigh filled with straw and cover us up with buffalo robes.

I went to high school in Richardton, North Dakota. I attended Assumption Abbey. It was run by thirty-five Benedictine priests, and they really were good teachers. They wouldn't even let us look at the girls, as far as that went. So I had a good education. I graduated in 1934 as valedictorian from my class. I got a job right away with what was then called FSA. I worked there about a year, I guess. I made $60 a month. I had to pay $20 a month for room, board, and washing. So we had $40 left over to squander. I also went and helped my folks. Then I went to Michigan and worked in a factory for about a year. I ran a lift transporting stuff all over the factory. I didn't like the climate. I got tired of that job, so the company let me do piecework for a while.

On December 7, 1941, the Japanese had attacked Pearl Harbor. The Nazis and Fascists were already invading Poland and other neighbors, and the main force was in North Africa. Hitler and Mussolini were the dictators."

Paul talked about his service time.

"When I was drafted, they sent me to airplane mechanic school for about three months, and then I went out to California and went to another school at Burbank, and they taught me about the 820 attack bomber and how everything worked on it. About halfway through my aircraft technical course, I was recalled to have a physical for the service. I passed with red, white and blue colors.

When I got overseas, I never saw one, so all that training didn't do me much good. Seems like I was in a lot of places during my service time. I was in Liberia for a few months. From there, I went up to Tunisia, and that was the nicest climate I have ever lived in. There was always a breeze off the Mediterranean. The buildings were all bombed when we got there. We had to sleep in those buildings, and then the United States came in and rebuilt them all. I think I spent sixteen months there before I got shipped back to Bismarck, North Dakota, where I met Lillian. I was then sent to Great Falls, Montana, and stayed there until the end of the war.

One night while in Bismarck, I was canvassing the town when I ran into five girls on the street ready to leave for a class picnic. They were short of boys, I guess, because they invited me to the picnic near the river. Afterwards, before I had to leave for my basic training, we went into a

311

restaurant and had buffalo sundaes. That's about the time I singled out a cute, freckled redhead named Lillian Danielson. Little did I know she would be my future bride. I dated her a few times before being shipped out."

Lillian joined in at this point.

"I was in my last year of high school, and Paul was in the service. We both were in the town of Bismarck at that time, and we wrote back and forth for a year-and-a-half or two years. I know I was too young to get married, but we did get married, and we're still married today. I was seventeen at the time."

Paul continued.

"I got a one-week furlough and was home on V.E. Day (Victory in Europe). That's the first time I got home to see the folks since entering the service, a period of over three years. On V.E. Day, people about went nuts with celebrations in all the towns, but we still had the Japanese to contend with.

In October 1945, I got my special orders to report to the Lincoln, Nebraska, Air Base, where I was given my mustering-out pay and sent back to Bismarck, which I didn't mind, as I would meet my girlfriend again, and from there to home.

On July 9, 1946, Lillian and I were married at St. Patrick's Cathedral in Bismarck. Before the wedding, I checked all the stores for a new suit and a white shirt to get married in. All I could find at the time was a brown suit. For our honeymoon, we went to the Black Hills in South Dakota.

Looking for an apartment was something else. We finally got a basement room from a widow who used to be our neighbor at the farm. Lillian didn't like sitting around all day while I worked, so she got a job at the S & L Dept. Store. In the spring, I quit my job and went out to the farm, bought a Ford tractor and plow, and used Dad's tractor and machinery to farm on a share basis.

The year of 1948, Paula was born on May 25th. Dad would rock her a lot and later help teach her to walk and would play with her.

Cecil was born on January 31, 1951. He was crawling around and always carrying off my pencils and tape measure while we were finishing the house. I told Lill, 'That kid must be going to be a carpenter,' and I was mostly right.

We've had a good life. I can't complain. We have two children. Paula Corton, our daughter, is up in Mead, Washington, and has a nice family. She had one boy, and he got married this past summer. And then we have Tyler, and he got married a couple weeks ago."

Lillian spoke.

"When we were first married, we lived with Paul's dad. Yeah, I think we were there about two years, dry land farming with Dad. We raised flax and wheat. My mother had passed away at that time. We had a couple of years that we had real good crops, and then we were hailed out."

Paul continued.

"After that experience, Lillian and I moved to Idaho and got a homestead. The homestead was near Caldwell, Idaho. That group of homesteaders was called the Black Canyon Project. The land was nothing like Heart Mountain. The water was pumped to the farms. There were days when it was 105 degrees in that area. We had sixty-four acres of land. The soil was hard to irrigate. We would chase the water, and in the mornings, the ditches would be washed out. We started a dairy for a while. It was supposed to be a Grade A dairy farm, but we couldn't get any quotas so ended up selling the milk to Simplot to be made into powdered milk. It was the same kind of powdered milk we had overseas, that I hated so much. It would ruin the coffee. But the dairying was not so much fun, so in 1957, I decided to sell the place.

In Idaho, we had rainy weather all winter and had to stack our bales of hay about eighteen high, plus putting another two layers of straw bales on top of that so it wouldn't get rotten. We had a lot of fog and black ice, but you hardly ever saw any snow. If you did get some, it was gone in a day or two. I think the most snow we ever got was about seven inches one winter. I like the climate here much better, although it is a lot windier.

Lillian had worked at Glen Evans tying flies and then went to work at the courthouse for a while working as a clerk. That is when we bought this 120-acre farm from Jim Lanik.

My brother, Vincent, had received one of the Heart Mountain homesteads in 1949.

In the fall of 1959, Fred and Betty Rose and I took off for Powell, Wyoming, to look over farms. We went through Yellowstone Park, took the wrong turn in the junction, and hit big snowdrifts up north. We had to turn back. We stayed at Vincent's, and Fred found a farm he liked, and I made an agreement to buy the 121 irrigable acres for $32,000. The home was built new but needed some trim and doors on the inside. It was ready to stucco on the outside. About that time, there were only a few of the 49 original homesteaders in Idaho still on their farms. Most had gone broke.

When we came to Heart Mountain, we enjoyed our neighbors. They were all so friendly. They all seemed to know our names, but we had a hard time at first remembering their names. We took up square dancing, and we used to go to all the meetings at the community club. The homesteads over in Idaho were more spread out, so the community was not as close as we found here.

We grew mostly grass seed on this farm. Sometimes we had to wait a couple of years to sell the seed to get a decent price." Lillian talked about the 4-H Clubs.

"I enjoyed the 4-H program. I was a leader for seven years. I taught leather craft. I would have about eight or nine members at the meetings. Paula, our daughter, enjoyed the sewing project the most. She did very well in her 4-H years. Our granddaughter, Alisa, still enjoys 4-H. She has become a beautiful seamstress and takes many honors. I think one of the big advantages for our children were the good schools in Powell. They both got an excellent education here.

I told Paul when we first met that if I ever get married, I won't marry a farmer, but he convinced me. I have to say now that it has been a good life. On the farm, I enjoyed helping Paul with the irrigating and running the tractor. I felt like I was a hired man. I helped him milk on the farm in Idaho but not here in Wyoming.

The reason we moved to town after retirement was because of the snowstorms out on Heart Mountain. We didn't have a snowmobile, and if we got sick, we didn't want to be out on the farm, so we decided to move into town. Now we are right across the street from the nursing home. I told Lillian I'm saving my wheelbarrow, so when I get ready, she can wheel me over there."

314

Paul and Lillian both agreed that the most important thing about living on the Heart Mountain homestead was the way the neighbors stuck together. They appreciated how much the homesteaders enjoyed each other and the influence of the community club. Lillian added, 'Even now when some of us live in town, we still feel like we are a part of the community and enjoy seeing each other. It was a good place to live, and life was good to us on the homestead.'

BETH AND BARBARA SIMON

I drove down the Oregon coast to Brookings to meet with Beth and her daughter, Barbara. I had hoped in the interviews I would be able to reconnect with this family. Fortunately, when I interviewed Edna Cobb, she had helped me find them. Sharon Simon and I had been best of friends for such a short time, and then their family had moved back to Oregon. For years, I had asked around, trying to find out where she had gone after she grew up. We had been reunited after all these years on my way out to Oregon, and so this afternoon, I would again be able to see her mother and sister Barbara.

Beth has lived in Brookings for a number of years. When I went to interview Beth, her husband, Tom, had already passed away. The view of the ocean was breathtaking, and then I found myself at Beth's home which was nestled in a hillside, surrounded by evergreens. Beth Simon and her oldest daughter, Barbara, were there to visit with me.

Beth began with how they happened to come to Wyoming. "I think Sharon was in the sixth grade when we came to Wyoming. We farmed there for about two-and-a-half years. I think we farmed Glenn and Cookie Ball's farm. I think they had come from Sweet Home, Oregon. They wanted to come back to Oregon, so we wanted to see if we liked the homestead, so we farmed their place.

It was so cold when we moved to Wyoming. We went during the Christmas holidays. When we arrived, everything was frozen up, including the septic tank. I think Tom built a fire with about twentyfive tires before he got thawed out enough so that things would work.

I would try and hang clothes on the clothesline, and they would freeze before I could put the pins in them. So I would bring them in the house and lay them across a drying rack. They would lay stiff until they softened up enough to flop down on the sides. We weren't used to that kind of dry cold, being that we had come from Oregon.

We weren't in Wyoming that long, but I do remember the families that were there and the cooperation and fun we had together. The schools and the children were wonderful. That first winter was so cold, but in the spring, we finally got warmed up.

We couldn't get up the hill for the mud in the road, and the first Easter we were out there, we went to church in Powell. On the way home, we got stuck in the snow just past Montgomery's house on the way to where we were living. Tom had to walk home to our house and get the tractor to pull us the rest of the way home. The worst of it for Tom was that the kids, I, and Grandma Hansen, that is my mother's mother, were at our house with a cooked turkey. Cal and Alta, Mom, and Pappy were at their house with the desserts. We never could get together that day, as we both were snowed in. They ate the desserts, and we ate the turkey.

I thought the people in the community were all wonderful. But they were all homesteaders, and we weren't. We were a bit older than most of the rest of them. I went to work at Kopriva's Hardware in Powell. That was okay, but there were times when it was so cold going to work in town.

We were only committed to stay one year on the homestead. We thought we might be able to find something else we could do in the community. We stayed a second year, and Tom worked for Pat Fielding. Then he drove a propane truck up into Montana and down into southern Wyoming.

Cal and Alta Musser have both passed away, so let me tell you something about them. Alta lived in Crescent City, and we grew up in Brookings. About a week after Cal came home from World War II, we went to Crescent City for a dance. Tom and I, along with some friends, Jack and Joyce Miller, and Cal went together. That is where he met Alta.

I think it was pretty-near love at first sight. They were married in Fortuna, California. It is a little town south of Eureka. I can't remember the date they were married; I think it was May 12, 1947. Well, anyway, they lived here in Brookings until they went to Wyoming, and that was in 1949. Johnnie was born here, and Glen was born in Wyoming.

I think they enjoyed homesteading. I don't think they enjoyed that first winter in the barracks, the wind blowing through all the cracks and every sound the neighbors made. They were pretty thin walls. But I think they were pretty anxious to get out to the homestead itself. They lived at the relocation camp until they got the barracks divided and moved it out to the homeste. My mother and father came to the homestead and lived for a few years. Then when they came back to Oregon, Cal and Alta moved on that place. Cal was my brother, and John and Zana Musser were our parents, Mom and Pappy.

Cal loved homesteading, but Alta's folks lived over in Eureka, Oregon, and she would get pretty lonesome for them. Of course, they would come out and visit every once in a while. But I think they finally decided to move, because her parents and our parents were getting old. He used to have a poster hanging in his bathroom that said, 'If I had a million dollars, I'd keep right on farming until it was all gone.'

Barbara added a comment.

"Yeah, there was one thing he liked when he'd get back to Oregon, and that was rain. Every time it rained, he would go out and wash his car. He thought the rain felt good. He said he never got that kind of rain in Wyoming."

"Tom and I enjoyed the square dances. I don't remember much about the dances, except we used to have such a good time, good callers, and lots of good dances. We took the square dance classes down at the clubhouse. The hardest dance that they ever taught was the "Salty-Dog Rag."

We used to go to the community club quite a bit. I think those things helped the community to be close. And also, the young couples had come from all over the country. They didn't come with friends; they came by themselves and made friends here.

Our time in Wyoming was a brief time in our lives, but our three girls made friends, and t was a special time for Tom and me. "

LLOYD SNIDER

I knew when it came time to finish this interview, I would struggle. I had hoped that the book would have been published by the time that Lloyd passed away, but that was not going to happen. I have deep-seated memories of Lloyd and Bertie. They both made a huge impact on my life. Sandy was just a baby when the Sniders moved to Wyoming in 1950. I always thought she was such a cute baby. She was a few years younger than Mike and I, but we always considered her part of the group.

Bertie had passed away before this project began, so I will rely on the significant research conducted by Winifred Wasden to interject some of the flavor of Bertie's life. 1

I remember going home during the time that Bertie was so ill. My own life was going down one of those tributaries that was difficult. I had come home to spend a few days with my mother. They called and wanted us to come over that evening. I walked in, and there they both were, sitting at the kitchen table drinking coffee, the same as it had always been from the time I was a young child. Bertie was so thin, her face puffy from medication, and she was on oxygen. Not a word about how she was feeling; her whole attention was on me and my welfare. It wasn't long after that she passed away, and I grieved deeply at her passing.

Later, I wished that I had probed for details of her childhood. Bertie was born in 1914, so she would have been part of WWI. Her family was German. When I was a young girl, she used to tell me of the difficulty she had, as other children would taunt her because she was German. It is strange, in a way, how a person can hear something like that and put it way back in a memory bank, and in a split second, the realization of what has been said comes back years later. This is not the time or place to tell all the details of that time of my teaching stint in Russia. But as soon as possible after returning from a teaching stint in Saratov, Russia, I drove over and met with Lloyd.

During my time in Saratov, I noticed German architecture in the buildings throughout the city. The two teachers assigned to caring for me gave me background history of many German colonies that had made their way over into Russia and had settled in towns and cities along the Volga

River. During the horrible reign of Stalin, whole towns and people were wiped off the map. There would have been no way one could have tracked the family heritage. One afternoon, I met an English professor who could have passed for Bertie's twin. She not only looked like Bertie, but she had that same lilting laughter that I had always enjoyed hearing when visiting with Bertie.

One of the leaders of the Heart Mountain women, Bertie Snider, came here from California where she had been an executive secretary, a member of the Women's Ambulance and Transport Corps in San Francisco, and a worker for the Red Cross and USO.

On Heart Mountain, she continued her community involvement. She was a twenty-five-year Extension Club member and a volunteer for the "Reach to Recovery" program for the American Cancer Society.

She was active in her church, loved sports, played the piano, traveled, and regaled her many friends with her delightful sense of humor and keen insights into human nature. 2

Lloyd came to see me when I was living in Oregon. My children had always heard so much about Bertie and Lloyd, and after that visit, they came to realize why he was so special in my life. Because he and my father were such dear friends all those years, it was as if, in some ways, he brought a piece of my father with him whenever we saw each other. When Lloyd passed away, my brother Wayne was one of his pallbearers, and this was a comfort to me. He had always been a support to Pam and Wayne, just as he had been to Mike and me. Lloyd and Bertie both invested a great deal of themselves in the Heart Mountain community.

I always knew that Lloyd was an innovator and an achiever. Even as a young child, I often managed to sit quietly and listen to my dad and Lloyd discuss farming--what to do the next year, how not to make that mistake again, and just how much they both enjoyed working together.

When I came back to Wyoming and took a position with UW Cooperative Extension, I gained an insight into how far-reaching Lloyd's influence was in agriculture. I will just mention a few highlights of his successful career in farming to give you, the reader, a glimpse into this very special man, Lloyd Snider.

In 1983 he was named Seedsman of the Year by the Wyoming Crop Improvement Association and was selected Outstanding Agriculturist by the UW Chapter of Gamma Sigma Delta, honorary agriculture fraternity, in 1984. In 1991, the University of Wyoming presented him with an honorary Doctor of Laws degree for his contributions to agriculture in Wyoming. In 1995, he was selected as a Wyoming Agriculture Citizen of the Year by the Wyoming Livestock Roundup.

Lloyd worked closely with the UW specialist Ken Faulkner, Extension Sheep Specialist, and Ray Field, Animal Science Specialist in conducting a variety of experiments.

Lloyd and his daughter Sandy developed a flock of Hampshire sheep and were able to certify three meat sires in this breed, more than any other breeder in the U.S.

Lloyd served his community as a member of the Powell School Board for 12 years, including five years as chairman. He was a member of the Park County Planning and Zoning Commission and chairman for three years between 1975 and 1982. He was also a member of the Park County Predator Board and chairman for three years from 1981 to 1987. 3

The list of accomplishments could go on and on, but now I will step back into those first few years all those young veterans and their families came together to become a community.

Just as it always had been, I came in and sat at the Snider's kitchen table.

Lloyd poured me a cup of coffee, and he began to reminisce.

"Bertie and I were living in northern California, right up near the Oregon line on a ranch. I was working for my dad. I was intending on becoming a partner with my father. He was coming along in years, and we tried to buy land there, but it was too high. We wondered if it was a satisfactory thing to do. We had an opportunity to buy land down where Bertie was raised near Fresno, but the land needed to be leveled and pipeline and wells drilled, so we decided against it.

We had friends over in Klamath Falls, Oregon, which was near the Lake Reclamation area, so we visited them quite often, and it was beginning to look like maybe that was not too bad of an idea. So when this opportunity came, I applied for it. In those days, when you were already thirty years old, you didn't have much income and wondered what in the heck you were going to do with your life, you paid attention to notices in the post office and anything else you could discover for jobs or opportunities. This was my seventh filing for a homestead. I filed in Moses Lake, Idaho, and down in a central Arizona project a couple of times. I lucked out and had a chance for an interview in Riverton, Wyoming, at the same time my application was accepted for a homestead unit here on Ralston Bench.

Bob Fagerberg encouraged me to come here, and this helped Bertie and me to decide to come and look at the situation. We got here in early October, along with your parents and several others in the first group who were interviewed. I guess we visited with the banker and visited around town. We talked to two or three of the older homesteaders, mostly from the Willwood. We didn't see many of the Heart Mountain settlers at the time, as they were just getting started, and it seemed like they were hard to find. Well, we decided to give it a try.

Bertie was born and raised on a very small farm. She was an auditor at the time. Her folks had raised her on a 37-acre chicken ranch with a vineyard and alfalfa fields outside of Fresno. When she thought of the possibilities of 115 acres, it seemed good to her. I didn't have any doubts, and I don't think she ever said anything other than probably, 'would we rather be in Fresno?' and neither of us thought there would be a good opportunity there.

We were making a living in northern California, but it didn't seem like the long-range opportunity we were looking forward to. My dad said, "Go, I can find a hired man."

Sandy was born in April, and we came here in October and left her at home with her grandmother. I stayed with Lyle and Dorothy Baker. Bertie and Dorothy went back to California. Lyle and I stayed here until just a couple of days before Thanksgiving. We dug a basement and got our house assigned and water on 35 acres of ground.

I got hold of a tractor and plowed up some ground, 35 acres or so. We felt we were off and running with that much ground plowed." I wanted to add comments from Bertie at this point.

"You see, we had six months after we made our selection and were awarded a unit to move our family. We got our unit on October 12th. I went back to California after the drawing because Sandy was four months old and that was our baby. Lloyd stayed at the Heart Mountain Camp. He and three other guys stayed and plowed and got their buildings moved and then Lloyd came home the day before Thanksgiving. In February 1950, he bought an old truck and then they put sides on it and came with our furniture. Sandy and I didn't come until March because that gave him a chance to put linoleum on the floor and put shelves in the corner and other things to get the barracks ready and that was it for seven years. We had electricity though, after three years, so that wasn't bad. Then I could use my electric stove. I had brought a gas stove and I don't know what was the matter with it, but no matter what you put in the oven, it was done in twenty minutes. We baked our own bread and made cakes from scratch and pies and all kinds of stuff.

We had the whole cotton pickin' unit to move. You know, it's just a steel post with a number on it, and there was nothing else, so he just kind of picked out a location close to the edge of the farm and set her down. The barracks had holes in the wallboard. There was no insulation. There was just that tarpaper on the outside and wallboard on the inside, and when the wind blew, man alive, the curtains flopped out, and when the dust blew, dust just came in. I stuffed everything full of newspaper. Lloyd had his socks in all the holes. I used to wrap them up into a ball when I washed them. When I first came and saw the socks, I asked Lloyd, Why did you do that? He replied, 'Just wait till the wind starts blowing, Bertie.' And the wind did blow, and then I understood all too well.

That first winter we were here in 1950, it was forty degrees below zero, and we just nearly froze to death. We used to go up to the neighbors' cause they had a hotter morning stove than we did.

We played a lot of cards. We didn't have TV; we didn't have radios half the time. My brother gave me a little battery radio, but then the batteries would go dead, so there you were with nothing. And you couldn't spend much time reading, because your light was so bad. Kerosene lamps aren't very good for light, so you went to bed early and got up early and tried to stay warm. We didn't think it was that bad, but the average age

322

was in the twenties. We all had little kids; we all had the same kind of houses. It just depended on how you fixed them up. We used to scrub and wax those floors, and we'd clean windows
'til the panes fell out. 4

Bertie laughed as she told about the toilet.

"Our neighbors used to joke about the toilet in the back room. I think we were the only ones with an actual toilet at first. Lloyd had hooked it up to the septic tank. But we had to haul buckets of water to fill it. But that was still better than going outside at night in the winter. We planted a lawn in the back for Sandy to play in, but the front was just dirt and rocks."

I was glad that Bertie had told about setting up the community club.

Lloyd was the first president, and I am sure she played a big role in the first organization teams of work.

"We fixed up the community building together. We had lots of talent up here. There were guys that came that were carpenters. Some were electricians; some of them could do almost anything. The men laid the foundation for the building. It was a big building. It was the barracks that was a wing of the hospital. I think the men had to move it in three sections. The problem was that they had to make the concrete by hand. They had to have a hand mixer, because there wasn't electricity yet. The men were so darn busy, but they worked together in teams. They put in hardwood floors. But we women waxed and scrubbed, and we washed the windows, and put up curtains, and painted the whole thing.

We'd have from seventy-five to a hundred kids at Bible School, and we all taught. We all had different grades, and different churches sponsored it every year. If the community wanted to do anything, we would just all get together. We didn't have phones and had to go to Ralston to get the mail. Since we lived on the road to
Ralston, we had a lot of neighbors drop by."

Lloyd continued reminiscing of the early years.

"From the very beginning, of course, we had hardships, but we all just determined to have a community, and we worked together and helped each other and became very good friends. Even when we were away, we are always so happy to see neighbors from Heart Mountain.

I think it was the same for most of us up here those first few years. You had an awful lot of work to do, and you didn't know too much about what you were doing. You weren't sure what was going to work, so you just had to try.

We worked together to get things established. We shared machinery and planned together, as money was tight. We couldn't afford to hire help at first, so we helped each other a lot. A lot of us hired someone to move the barracks and to drill the wells. Bertie and I hauled water for a while. We have pictures of Sandy as a toddler out at the pump handle trying to pump water."

Lloyd told about that first year of farming.

"We had a pretty good crop of peas the first year on 35 acres. Everybody needed cash desperately to operate, you know. So then we started some other things. We planted some alfalfa, and hopefully, it would make a better crop the second year of harvest. We still didn't understand just exactly what we were supposed to do. I don't think any of us made very much money the first three years, mostly just a case of trying to stay here.

The Cooperative Extension Service played a role in helping us gain knowledge about our farming needs. I had been exposed to the Extension Service through the University of California at Davis. We had farmers' advisors from the university in our county, and I had done a couple of fertilizer plots with them. My dad and I built a chicken house according to the specifications they provided.

Jimmy Nicholas was the Park County Ag Extension Agent when we came to Wyoming. He was a real good advisor, as far as I was concerned. We talked about alfalfa seed and certified seed. I started raising red clover seed. I knew early-on the rewards of keeping the place clean. Today we can raise seed, because during the first four years or so, we didn't let the place get dirty with wild oats and that sort of thing. When you have to take wild oats out of red clover seed, you get the idea real fast.

The UW Extension Service agents took a lot of time with us. I can remember one lecture that was given about how we should have a plan to take care of our kids if we hit the bucket, you know, that sort of thing. I know Bertie and your mother would go to Extension meetings where they were given a lot of educational help on different topics. They had a lot of good ideas for opportunities to help us succeed.

I remember when I was ten years old and involved with 4-H. Then I became involved as a junior leader. We would go to the California State Fair there in Sacramento. We would pull in on the train there in Davis and live at the UC Davis campus. It was awe inspiring. Yeah! I was fourteen before I ever got to a big city or on a train even. Bertie and I were so happy that Sandy won a 4-H trip to Chicago. That was a big thing to her.

We were also enthusiastic Farm Bureau people, and I had a close friend that was a graduate at Davis. He lived a few miles from us, and we had gone to school in Sacramento together for a couple of years. At the time, everyone was trying to learn as much as they could. You know, this was right after WWII. Everything was expanding. People wanted tools, wanted to buy cars. And there was a market for everything. In those days, it didn't take long to understand the person that raised the most crops made the most money. And you had to be real careful about your expenses. A lot of us learned to be production oriented. We wish now we had been a little more market oriented.

We still believe in crop rotation that they told us about in the beginning. This gated pipe is a wonderful thing. We used to have two men go change water, and now one person can do it.

We use chemicals differently now than we used to. We are very careful with what we use. Everything costs, you know. Chemicals aren't even offered that are real dangerous anymore. But there is still a lot to think about.

This homestead community was a good place to raise a family. You can't escape some understanding of the work ethic. You live in one place for quite a while, and you have almost the same neighbors. Another thing you can't escape from is the honesty and treating people in a fair manner. Doing people the way you would want them to do you. This is the thing that you learn in the country. I think every one of our kids, including you, that rode the bus learned about that pretty fast, you know. This behavior stuff, if we don't learn it, we are in trouble. And then soon, the rest of the kids don't like us either. I guess we never thought much about trying to get someone else to do this work for us; we just did it. It was an opportunity that we were prepared for, and we wanted to do it, and I believe we raised our kids pretty much the same way. You have to get out and study and just do the best you can. Yeah.

The 4-H program was a very important part of our community. Most of the kids participated. The parents taught the projects and got the kids to their judging and the fairs. Bertie and I were just so tickled when Sandy won a trip to 4-H Club Congress in Chicago. I think a lot of the homestead kids won trips to Denver Roundup, Chicago, and Washington, D.C.

We had the homestead, and then we bought Ashby's homestead, and that is where Bertie and I built our home. We bought the Ball unit just south of the first two units. Sandy came back home after working several years away, and that is where she has built her home there on the corner, with a view of Heart Mountain.

We thought if we had three farms, it could provide a retirement, and it is working well for us."

LOIS AND JIM SPIERING

I had looked forward to the interview with Lois and Jim. In the beginning of this research project, I had scheduled a meeting with the homesteaders. I remember that Lois was there, and she had been so encouraging. The Spierings lived only about two miles from our homestead. Their property dropped down under the Eagle's Nest hill. I remember the winding road that my brother and I used to drive down when we were teenagers. As I slowly wound down around the hill, I drove at a much slower speed than in those former days.

At the bottom of the hill, set into a ravine, was a lovely home with beautifully manicured lawns and trees. Lois met me with her contagious smile, and I was escorted out onto the deck.

I had not seen Jim since childhood, but he remembered me as a teenager.

Jim began the conversation.

"I grew up on a dairy farm west of Portland, Oregon. I grew up knowing how to work. The farms were homesteads back in the 1830s and '40s. The old-timers had cleared the land, and when I was growing up, there were a lot of prairies and some scattered timber. My father was in the logging and sawmill business when my folks got married. In 1919, they moved out to western Oregon two weeks before I was born. Later, I joined the Navy to get away from the cows.

After I got out of the Navy, I met Lois. She was a young, blond, attractive lady that worked in the same office. I worked in the lab in the back, and she worked up front in the office. Anyway, she would go traipsing through every so often. We'd all whistle at her."

I turned to Lois and asked her how many times a day she would go through the lab.

Laughing, she told us, "It was often."

"Jim heard about the homesteads from his brother who had applied for a homestead in California but didn't receive one. Jim began to apply for all the homesteads from Columbia Basin on down to Yuma, Riverton, and then at Heart Mountain."

"I ended up getting a homestead here, and then later, I heard that my name had been drawn at Riverton, but I decided to stay here.

The main problem we had on this homestead was the rocks. After our sons grew up, I got a rock picker. They give me a bad time about that."

Lois joined in.

"When we came to Wyoming, we were married. We had a one-year-old boy, and we were expecting our second child. He came a month early, so we were here about three weeks when he arrived."

"I never looked back. I was ready for an adventure, and I never did regret it. We lived in the barracks, but I figured it was just temporary. We were going to move the barracks like most of the other homesteaders did. It cost money to move them, so we decided to just tear it down.

We were out there cutting the barracks in half. I was taking out the nails. We met a carpenter, and he told us he could build us a house for a certain amount of money and was encouraging us to build a house, so we did. We built our first home up on the hill, on the homestead, using the wood from the barracks.

We came to Wyoming in March 1950. Jim came out earlier bringing everything we owned, returned to Oregon, and we came back with him in the truck."

Jim talked about his dad.

"When my dad came to Wyoming, he drove through Idaho and saw some beautiful farms. When he arrived, he couldn't say anything good about this place after he came out here once. I was digging rocks out of the ground when he came. He was going to show me how to dig around the rock, so he picked up the pick, hit a few times, and got enough dirt out to get in his eyes. He said, 'This is the toughest place I've ever seen.' So he was ready to go back to Oregon. I don't think he really ever changed his mind. He would come to see us, but he never did think much of the place. It was too dry, too desolate. He was used to the green hills of Oregon.

The way we felt was, all you could see in Oregon was hills and trees, but here you can see what is underneath; that always impressed me.

We felt it was a helpful, friendly community to come to. You could buy things on credit, and they would never question you. I bought a combine one time and told the dealer, 'I'll pay for it when I get some money.' He said, 'Okay.' No notes, no nothing.

I think the people in the community welcomed us, because the Powell area had been developed by the homesteaders from the beginning.

The group of veterans in the 1949 drawing had come through WWII and had started settling down with their families. That was really a disturbing lifestyle during the war years. It disrupted a lot of people mentally and physically. When the families came here, they were ready to settle down.

There was a feeling of who did what, when, and where. This last group of homesteaders that came in had pretty well made up their mind what they were going to do. Of course, a lot of the original homesteaders are either here or their families are still here on the homesteads. I guess the heart of the community was the hard-working kids.

The community club was a hub for our community. We worked real hard getting the original building. We had to move it up in sections, and then we worked a lot on it so it was useable. That brought the people together a lot more, I do believe, because of working on projects like that.

One thing and another drew us together. We worked together finding new crops and making a go of it.

I raised any crop I thought I could make some money on. I only raised sugar beets one year on rented ground. My dad was a seed grower, so when I came out here, I started raising seed. I raised red clover to start with. And then I went to alfalfa seed, grass seed, all kinds of seed crops. Sometimes you could sell what you raised, and sometimes you couldn't. But basically, there was always an effort for seed crops. I worked a long time getting the barley in just to be able to work with Coors and Budweiser.

Those first years, the fellows took classes in town from different local teachers to learn skills in farming. The GI Bill paid us about $90 for taking the classes. For most of us, that paid our grocery bills.

They tried to tell us all about feeds and feeding for cattle. I'd seen a lot of the guys put in fencing and corrals and all that stuff to get enough money to build a house. I had already figured out if I wanted to take care of cows, I wouldn't have time to raise seed and do a good job of it."

Lois talked about the children.

"The guys were all out in the field, so somebody had to be around to take care of things around the home. We had two sons in the beginning, and then three more sons. They were all born in the spring. A friend said that is Wyoming time. Jerry was born in Oregon in 1940. Ken was born in 1950, and Gene was born in 1953, Kelly in 1956, and Tom in 1958. So we had five boys and no girls. So Jim ended up getting a lot of help. But that's okay. I just figured I'm the queen bee. We told the boys the girls would come later. But they had to help with the dishes. Dad didn't like to do dishes, but he made sure they helped Mother.

We had a big garden. I did a lot of canning. I had canned some in Oregon. I used to come home with bushels of fruit to can, and I canned everything in the garden.

The only social life we had was getting together with our neighbors. All of the children out in this community were young, so there were no baby-sitters. We would just scoop up the baby basket and go visit. We mostly stayed home, or we went to the drive-in movies. We did a lot of camping and going on picnics. I think Gene was a month old when he went up to Lion Creek. He was in a basket with mosquito netting over him. Everybody just took their kids along.

That was just about all you could do.

When we lived in the relocation camp, we met Ed and Bernice Schaefer. They moved out on their homestead before we did, so they invited us over for dinner, and we became good friends. We played a lot of pinochle. I remember one time it was 30 below. Ed got on the tractor, pulled the car and came up, and we played pinochle. I mean, you worked really hard in those years to have a social life, but that was why friendships became so special. We didn't have our families here, so maybe that is why we all became so close.

All of our sons are grown now. Jerry became an electrical engineer and lives in West Linn, Oregon. Ken is a professional artist, and he lives in Spokane.

Gene went into geology, so he has been all over the world and presently lives in Spain. Kelly is farming the homestead and is presently buying it. Tom works for the Heart Mountain Irrigation District, so he is close by.

All of our boys feel a close tie to the homestead. They can't wait to get back. It is home. When they were young, we would go back every year to Oregon to visit Grandma and Grandpa."

"My parents and Lois's parents lived out west of Portland, within five miles of each other. For Christmas, we would go out there every year and spend a month. Then the boys got in school, and the time we would spend was a little shorter, but we went out there every year. Then when they started getting married, they still wanted to make the trip. And I said, "We're going to have to get a Greyhound bus, or forget it.""

Growing up on the homestead gave our sons the ability to work and the willingness. Even though we had many discussions, some of them quite vocal about doing work, in the end, the knowledge and the capability to be able to do a day's work was what they learned. To me, that was tremendously important. They grew up on a farm, and they knew what work meant.

All of the boys knew their contribution was important, even if it was just picking up rocks. I had a hard time convincing them picking up rocks was important. I used to tell them after we picked up rocks off the field, 'Doesn't that field look a lot better since we got the rocks off it?' And they would moan!"

Lois talked about the 4-H projects.

"Oh, let's see. Tom took cooking, Ken did leather craft, Gene was interested in the fish hatchery. I remember the bench that got painted to go to the fair. I think that was Kelly's, and the paint wasn't quite dry, and we were taking it to the fair. Tom would be baking cakes like mad, trying to get one that was good enough to take to the fair. They all had their experiences. I mean, a lot of it was, the fair is coming down on us, we better get busy. We've got to get this done. I think it taught us parents patience. When kids live in the country, it is nice to have 4-H so they can get together with other kids.

Now that the boys are raised and we are not farming, we go south in the winter. A lot of the homesteaders go to Mesa and Yuma, Arizona, in the winter, and I believe they have a reunion in February. It's funny, people get away from their local surroundings, and they look up some more Wyoming people wherever they go.

I think our community was close, because our children were all about the same age. They all grew up together, and the only social life was getting together. That didn't continue after TV came along, so that is too bad."

Jim, Lois, and I continued talking for a while. It was a balmy, warm summer evening as the sun began to set. I looked out over the lawn and trees, knowing that Jim still did almost all of the yard work. It was apparent that Lois still took great care in taking care of their home. What a rich life they have had with their sons. The interviews with these homesteaders proved over and over to me the rich heritage they have passed on to our generation. Working alongside our parents day by day gave all of us something of which to be proud.

BILL WHITE

I made the call to set up an interview but found myself a bit nervous, as I had never really known Mr. White, except from a distance.

331

As a child, I certainly had many questions about him, wanting answers, but never felt I dare ask. The voice on the other end of the line was so pleasant. He seemed as if he were looking forward to our interview.

I walked up to his door that morning a bit nervous, not knowing how the interview would turn out. After leaving his home that morning, I spent a good deal of time doing some soul-searching. Not wanting to invade the privacy of another's past, I pondered what I should share in writing. After looking over the transcript of our visit and remembering the graciousness of this older gentleman, I came to the conclusion that his misfortune in war found a solace and healing in the community that so loved him and his wife. For that reason, I will record the story shared that morning, walking softly with reverence into his past.

I had not seen Bill White for at least forty years. He stood in his doorway that morning, tall and slender but a bit stooped, a handsome man, with charcoal gray hair. What struck me most was his gracious hospitality and gentle voice. I began to relax as I began to sip the cup of coffee he offered me. He was living in a comfortable apartment in Powell. Clara, his wife, had passed away, and the homestead had been sold.

I started with the standard question I asked all the homesteaders, "Bill, how did you and Clara find out about the Ralston Bench homesteads?"

"Well, it was shortly after the war. We were living in Chicago. We had gotten married a short time before. I read about the project in a publication, which I can't seem to recall. I thought I had always wanted a piece of land of my own, so this could be a great opportunity. My name was drawn, but it was 126, and there were only 114 units. I didn't think much more about it. Being so far down on the list, I really didn't think we would be called.

Eventually, we were called. We came and looked over the project. I discovered that it was irrigation land, so thought it would be a good opportunity. My wife and I talked it over and decided we would come. After I got here, I thought I had made a big mistake though. The soil on our homestead unit had a lot of seepage the first few years, after the irrigation started."

I asked Bill to explain to me what he meant by seepage.

"Well, when you start irrigating, if there is a sort of something in the ground, either clay or gravel, or a bed that has a block in it, the water comes to the surface and it brings up alkali salts, and then the sun evaporates the water away and leaves the salt in the ground. You can't raise anything, as it kills all the vegetation. On our unit, there were about forty acres with alkali.

The Reclamation District put in a drain shortly after that. It took time to leach the alkali out, but after a while it did. The land became more productive. Then I was given an amendment of another eighty acres, so the farming became more livable. The amendment was about one-half a mile northeast of my unit, and it became some of the best land I farmed. After the land began to improve, prices got better, so farming turned out fairly good.

I grew up in a farming area and had done a lot of farming work. My folks didn't own a farm, but I worked a good deal on my uncle's farm. I worked eleven hours a day for ten cents an hour. Clara was born in Chicago, but then her folks moved to Indiana and had a chicken farm. Her father added to the farm income with a huckster wagon. In those days, many of the farmers didn't have cars. He went out into the country with groceries, tobacco, eggs, and butter. We would trade groceries for eggs, or people would pay cash for supplies.

I wasn't raised in the city, but Clara was. I don't think city life was what Clara wanted either. During the war, she worked for a furniture company, but I can't seem to remember the name. Shortly before we got married, she worked for Merrill Nut House. They had all kinds of nuts that were in small stores all over the United States. She did the books for them. I think they treated her real well, but in the long run, she was glad she had come to Wyoming.

We didn't get married until after the war. I worried about her when we came. I didn't think she would like it at all, you know, but after she had been out here a short time, I was ready to go, and I think she would have stayed here anyway. Yeah, she liked it real well after she was here for a while and everything. You know, we had it fairly tough like everybody else. Of course, she worked in town for a while, because we had a lot of expenses and not much money. She worked for the Bureau of Reclamation.

It was better when she quit working, because I really needed her at home to help me. We never had children, but she still played a big part in farming our homestead.

When we first came, the Bureau of Reclamation had control over everything until we proved up on our homesteads, and then it went into a district. There was a district with a supervisor, and then we had ditch riders who helped us with the water and canals. They took care of the water business, and if anything went wrong with the canals, they took care of that.

We had a barracks 120 feet long and twenty feet wide. I cut it in two with a hand saw. I just got up on the roof and started cutting down halfway on one side, and then cut down on the other side, and then across the floor. We hauled one part over and put it up on blocks. I got a gas refrigerator. And I remember we had a potbelly stove. I was trying to fix up the barracks a little bit before Clara came out in March of 1950. I went and bought some paper drapes and stuff to go in our bedroom to make it look halfway livable.

We bought a little, bottled gas stove after she came out. We had a rollaway bed that we slept on that first night. We hadn't cooked on the stove yet, and in the middle of the night, there was an explosion. The top of the stove lifted up a little bit and slammed down, you know.

Clara was sleeping on the side next to the stove. She rolled right over the top of me; it just scared her to death. It was a slow leak somewhere, and the gas accumulated, and the pilot light set it off. It didn't really explode but enough to raise the top of the stove, but in the middle of the night, it sounded like an earthquake. We got the leak fixed the next day, but I don't think either one of us ever forgot how that scared both of us.

We didn't have a phone in the early years or TV. If we wanted to see someone, we would just get in our pickup and go see them. We did a little square dancing and played a lot of cards. On Friday, we could go to town to the VFW and American Legion, and they had slot machines. On Friday, they had a free lunch, so sometimes we did that.

We hauled our drinking water at first in milk cans. In some ways, we were better off without all the modern conveniences. But then, it is nice to have a washing machine to wash clothes and have running water.

334

Running to town did interfere with the work that had to be done. We couldn't have livestock at first without a well.

After we got a well, we bought some ewes off the range. I would get about 125 ewes, and then we would lamb them out in the spring and sell the lambs in the fall. Seems like we had Colombia and Ramboulet. The Ramboulet sheep had a better quality of wool.

I always hated to sell the sheep. You know, you get to know each one of them. They have a personality just like people. One year, I had twelve ewes with triplets. That just doesn't work. So I would have some bum lambs to feed, because most of the time, the mother just didn't have enough milk.

We had chickens and pigs. We weren't fixed up right for the pigs, so they just drove us crazy. I remember one time I was going to sell some of them. Wayne Lewis and I worked and worked to try and get the pigs loaded. He wanted a pig that hadn't been loaded, but we were so frustrated, we stopped and went into the house and drank a cup of coffee. When we came out, there was that pig in the pickup. After we had worked so hard with the others, and there she was, sitting in the pickup bed.

We lived in one end of the barracks and kept the chickens in the other end. Sometimes, we kept the lambs in the barracks to keep them from the cold. I did have one cow, but she bloated on the alfalfa. It seems like a lot of us had trouble with the alfalfa in those early years. The cows and sheep would bloat; it was a real problem.

We butchered the chickens, put them in the freezer, and kept a few for eggs. We always had a garden, and that was more work than forty acres in the field. But we did always have a garden. Clara canned a lot, and then later when we got electricity, we froze a lot of things. We had a big asparagus bed too. It was hard to start. It took years, but it was so nice. It got so there was nice, big asparagus spears and tender sprigs in the early spring. But the next owners of the farm didn't want the asparagus bed and plowed it up, after it took so long to get started."

As Bill White and I sat at his dining room table that spring morning talking about those early days of homesteading, I found myself reliving with enjoyment so many long- ago memories of the homestead gardens and livestock that unavoidably became family pets.

As we sat there quietly talking, the phone rang, bringing with it an oppressive change in the interview that would leave me a bit shaken and perplexed as to what I would be responsible for in future days and weeks in my recollection of our community history.

Bill had just asked if I wanted another cup of coffee when the phone call came. As he began to answer questions, speaking into the receiver, I couldn't help but hear the seriousness in his tone. I felt uncomfortable, not wanting to eavesdrop, but I was sitting there facing him, not knowing if I should quietly leave or remain. The conversation went on for about half-an-hour. After Bill had hung up the receiver, he came back to the table apologizing for the interruption. "Can you believe it, right in the middle of our interview, I get this call." The man who had called obviously had gone through a bit of difficulty finding Bill's name in the phone book.

Bill began to tell me how he had just returned from a reunion with a bunch of soldiers who had been in the Philippines during WWII. They had been captured and had to surrender to the Japanese.

I didn't want to invade his privacy, so I asked Bill if he was uncomfortable talking about the horrific experiences he had lived through. But the phone call had brought the memories back like an unrelenting snowplow that hurls everything aside in its path.

"Was it easy for you to talk about your experiences when you returned from the war?"

There was a pause, and then he began to speak.

"Well, it wasn't so much that I didn't want to talk about it. There were very few people that were interested in it. Even my own family never mentioned it."

"Bill, are you sure people weren't interested? I remember even as a young child seeing you for the first time, you were still very thin when you and Clara first came. I know our community was very interested in your story, but I am sure no one wanted to pry into such a bad experience."

"Absolutely, and if I said something about it, they would change the subject, you know. And it is quite a bit that way with a lot of people even today, you know. They don't want to talk about it. They aren't interested. They don't care and don't want to talk about it. And others, I think they figure that it might bring back too much, but when you go through something like that, you don't ever forget it. It is just so coincidental that, while you are interviewing me, this fellow called. There are a group of lawyers who are trying to go back and find out exactly what happened and where we were in the camps.

I became a prisoner of war in 1941. I was in the camp for 3½ years. I guess they were about as cruel as was possible to be. A lot of the men were murdered. We didn't understand the language, so we didn't know what they would be telling us to do. Some of the prisoners were very belligerent. They said, 'They're not going to do that to me!' Or, other men said they couldn't eat the rice, they felt they just couldn't live in such conditions so would just give up. Of course, a lot of the men died from deficiency diseases. I never realized what poor nutrition could do to a person.

We first got scurvy. Our legs would swell up like balloons, you know, just from the water. It made us swell up, and I think we all got that. I mean, it was just the lack of certain nutrients in our diets. If we would have had some fresh fruit, or if we could have had some protein--but all we had was rice, rice, and more rice, and not really enough of that, you know. So it was a miracle that any of us got back, really. I had malaria, and that gave me a lot of problems. We had no medicine, and we had no medical care. Whatever disease we got, we either got over it, or we died. They made us eat some kind of soup with some kind of weeds or vegetables that must have had some kinds of nutrients that helped us early on. When we were captured, we were taken to Japan in a boat. On the boat, we got steamed barley or rice. We were all crammed down in the bottom of the ship. That was one of the worst things. They talk about the death march, but I think that trip to Japan was a lot worse for me. It was hot down there, for one thing, and they just packed us all in there like sardines. We couldn't even lie down at once, and there were no sanitary facilities.

"What was it about you, Bill? You must have had a lot inside of you to survive?"

"Well, I was kind of dumb. I thought, it won't be over six months at the most, and I can take anything for a while, you know. But after six months was over, I thought, oh, it can't be much longer, you know, and I just sort of kept going. I guess you would say I must have had a little faith

337

somehow I would get out of this mess. If it hadn't been for the atomic bomb, I don't think that any of us would have gotten out, because they had orders to kill us all if the Americans landed on the island of Japan. I woke up one morning, and the guards were all gone. All of us prisoners couldn't imagine what happened. We had no idea. After they were gone, we started breaking down. We'd get a little information here, and a little information there, you know. Then the B-29s came over and dropped a lot of food and things. The Red Cross finally came in and told us to stay there. They were making arrangements to take us out. It all happened in a matter of two weeks after the bomb fell.

I was in the hospital in Letterman for probably six weeks, and then I went to Fletcher for a year and a half. I wasn't really injured. I went all through the war and never really got any shrapnel, never got any wounds of any kind. That was a blessing, because I remember the march. They call it the Bataan Death March, because it was impossible for everyone to keep up. It was hot and dry, and we didn't get any water. Some of the men would collapse, and they would just come along and bayonet them with their guns. When we saw men falling, we would try to help them, but it was just impossible. They just murdered a lot of the prisoners.

When we were captured, we had to give up our arms, and once you give up your arms, you are helpless. Anything they tell you to do, you have to do, and they are the boss. If you don't do it, you take the consequences, you know. So there was no choice! No choice! It is a terrible situation to be in. You can't imagine, but they did torture us in a lot of ways. Not only individually but the whole bunch. If somebody goofed off or just anything could set them off, they would cut off our water, or they would make us sit out in the sun for hours with no hats or anything, you know. Just to punish us; it was a mass punishment. That was how they forced us to do what they wanted us to do. They disciplined us in many ways by holding off food and water, or sometimes they would run us through a line and take bamboo sticks and whack us across the back; well, I hate to get into this."

"Bill you don't have to talk about this!" He continued to recall the war.

"I think the war was mostly about greed. The Japanese were going from one island to another, and no one was giving them any opposition. They got into Shanghai. They went along the coast of China, and all the islands, and they plundered everywhere they went. I think the only thing that kept them out of Australia was that we held them off there in the Philippines, and they got reinforcements. The unit I worked with was tracking the Japanese with radar. We knew the planes were flying over the islands months before we were captured.

We reported it, but nothing happened. They hit us the same day they hit Pearl Harbor.

It was a day's difference across the dateline, but it was the same time. We could have been a lot stronger, but they commanded all our planes to the ground. That left us almost defenseless, because we had lost so much, that if we had the planes to keep them from landing, we could have been a lot stronger. And then we got low on ammunition and food, because it was impossible to supply us. We were ordered to surrender to the Japanese. We didn't have any choice. You are on an island thousands of miles from home, what are you going to do?

I was on Luzon, the main island in the Philippines. I was in an Army unit. We were attached to the Air Corps. Radar was new at the time, and we had a radar mobile unit in the prairie. We were in the northern tip of Luzon when the Japanese came in. After we were captured, we had no outside news, so we didn't know about anything that was going on in Europe. We were completely isolated from the rest of the world. We never had recreation of any kind. It was just work, eat, sleep, work, eat, and sleep.

Our soldiers were just common people, you know. So were the Russian soldiers, and so were the German soldiers, and so were the Japanese soldiers. They were just common people. A lot of the Japanese people are real nice people. I have nothing against them, you know. They would have loved to do something for us, but they couldn't, because they would have been treated the same way we were. This was a war situation, and the soldiers were taught to hate us, because we were bad. A soldier goes to war, and he is given a rifle or a bazooka or whatever, and you use it to fight the enemy. They are shooting at you, and you shoot back or you are killed, one of the two. I mean, you have to defend yourself. So it was a terrible situation to put anyone in.

I mean, all these boys that went to war, they were just common people, and I mean, they were farm boys or city boys. They were like you

339

and me, but they had to do what they had to do. And, you know, they can work you up until you think you are right, whether you are always right or not.

But anyway, when you get in a situation like that, you don't have any choice. It is a terrible thing.

When we were on the march, the Filipino people, although they had very little themselves, would put their lives in danger to try and give us a little food. They would come out to where we were and try to give us something, like a candy they made with coconut and molasses. They had it wrapped in leaves. But the Japanese soldiers would come along and kill them.

It was a terrible time. I don't know if we have learned anything from all of this. War is a terrible thing. You know, most wars are either about religion, military, or greed. Down through history, I don't know that we learn from war, as it seems to keep repeating itself. One thing we learned in WWII was the destruction of the atomic bomb. I think it has kept us from any major wars for some time now. If we ever do get into a major war, it is going to be terrible, because there just won't be much left. Because the atomic bomb that we used on Japan is just a baby compared to the hydrogen bomb they have now. I didn't see Hiroshima, but I went through Nagasaki, and I mean, it just completely wiped out everything. Everything throughout that valley was just completely wiped out. On the hillside, you can still see a few trees where just the tips of them were damaged.

Once in a while, I still have nightmares, even now. But I guess that is just the way it is. I do have memories about all of it, and I do seem to think about it a lot. I still have friends that are scattered all over. They are about my age or maybe a couple of years younger.
Two of my friends from the war just died recently.

The body is an amazing thing. But that is the thing about deficiency disease--you can be deficient for a long while, but if you get the proper things, you recuperate and regenerate, and so your body does come back in time, you know. But we were so thin, you know, and then we put on weight so fast. But it wasn't a solid weight. It was kind of puffy-like, you know. But then, later on, we came back to somewhat normal, I guess.

340

Well, I said I thought coming to the Wyoming homestead was probably the best thing that ever happened to me, even though it was tough from the start financially.

We didn't suffer too much. We always had something to eat. We always had something to wear. We had friends and a good life. I think it was probably the best thing that ever happened to me and Clara. I'm not sorry at all. I'm just glad that I had the opportunity, and that somebody else decided not to stay, so that I got a homestead, although it wasn't one of the better units. No, I have no regrets about it at all. I am glad it happened, and I met so many nice people. You just couldn't pick any nicer people than those in this community."

CHAPTER 7: REFLECTIONS OF A HOMESTEADER'S DAUGHTER

If one were to have a searchlight in hand, looking down the passages of time, would it be possible to comprehend those images of life and destiny before us? I dare say life itself, with the experiences that come alongside, is the teacher that weaves a pattern of life. The sunrise and sunset are only reminders that we live one day at a time.

I have taken the journey back into the memories of early childhood and those first few years of smelling sagebrush on spring mornings. This experience has caused me to stretch, and at times, my soul seems to be parched from the longing for those days of childhood.

And yet, this morning as I pen those thoughts on the page once again, I have a sense that those experiences of new beginnings for our little community are with me yet. Those moment-by-moment happenings, along with this incredible sense of destiny, have been infused into my spirit, not only by my parents, but also by those many neighbors who went before the children of this generation.

THE GREATEST GENERATION

As children growing up, we always know that, one day, our parents will not be with us any longer. Those in my generation who lost fathers in the war never had a chance to know them. They can only go back and rehearse the stories over and over in their minds of the details, if they are available, of how their fathers gave their lives for this country.

I remember well in the late sixties, when my son was just a toddler. All across our country, riots were breaking out on college campuses. Haight Ashbury was flooded with hippies. Great educational edifices were being burned to the ground, along with the American flag. As a post-war

343

child growing up on a homestead, this was a horrific sight to see on the evening news. As one thinks of time and place, it was a very short time since the end of the Great War.

Even today, when I drive by a cemetery and see row upon row of white crosses, I am gripped with gratitude for the great sacrifices made in order for our children to live in freedom.

Since the beginning of this research project, so many of those interviewed have passed away. I felt challenged in putting down the words spoken by these very special neighbors. Some of the interviews were very short. Others, such as Ann Nelson and Ruth Otto, were historians from the onset of those first years of homesteading. The day I went to visit with Bill White will always be fresh in my mind. I never would have approached the topic of his experience in a concentration camp. But in such a gracious and kind manner, he spoke without being asked. How I managed to sit there without weeping because of what he survived is a relief to me.

A few days ago, as I was working on this manuscript, I went to my treasure trove of books and pulled out a very special book, *The Greatest Generation Speaks*, written by Tom Brokaw. As if that weren't enough, I finished the evening watching videos with Tom Brokaw done by NBC News about "The Greatest Generation."

The next morning, as I came into my office for a day of writing, I saw a picture of my father on my desk. It was as if he were saying, "You are so close to the home run for this story...come on, you can make it." It didn't help my emotions to look over and see that picture, in a steel-gray frame, given to me by my brother Mike and his wife, Linda, for Christmas. As I studied the faces of those handsome young men, I saw hope and courage as they stood in front of the bomber plane that would take them deep into Germany. In just a short while, those men would be in the freezing, cold waters of the English Channel. Only my father and another pilot would come back to American soil.

In the pre-dawn hours this morning, it seems as if I were dreaming about my father. I was speaking with him of his life experiences, only to wake and know he has been gone for so many years now. It seems like today, I too have added "wind in my sails" as I reminisce about stories of life out on the windy plains of Wyoming. I have had the privilege of hearing stories that very well could have been lost with time, if I had not persevered to bring them to the forefront.

A SENSE OF TIME AND PLACE

As the thoughts and frames of mind developed from day to day in writing this story, the phrase, "A Sense of Time and Place," seemed to capture the essence of what I was portraying. The other day, I began to wonder about those words, so simple and yet so profound. Plagiarism is something of which I never want to be guilty, so I looked up the word combination, and sure enough, there was a long list of very similar phrases using these words. I will make mention of one title, *A Sense of Place, a Sense of Time*, by John Brinckerhoff. As I glanced through the list of books with very similar titles to mine, I found it very interesting that the topic for each book was about growing up in a particular place.

There is something within each of us that longs for that sense of time and place--that needs to be part of something and someone. Even that one who possesses an orphan's heart has a longing to know his/her parent. There is a sense of belonging within family, and if that family has the privilege of being part of a close-knit community, there is an added component of resiliency.

Life sometimes has a way of coming full circle. That is how it felt for me when I returned to Wyoming after living away for so many years. I was privileged to take a position with the University of Wyoming Cooperative Extension as a Family Consumer Extension Educator. Early on, I discovered an extensive research project done by the University of Idaho Cooperative Extension entitled, "All Families Have Strengths." This would prove to have a great impact on me in the path I would take.

The documented research reinforced what I had already experienced as a child growing up in a close-knit community. Significant work by Dolores Curran affirms those characteristics of the Heart Mountain community.

The family who owns a rich sense of kinship is able to withstand stresses and disappointments that destroy other families. It's able

345

to do so because its members have the support that comes from knowing that they are not alone, either in the neighborhood or in history. It is in this kind of family that individuals are loved not for what they have or do but for who they are; members of the family.[1]

One of the qualities that stands out in my mind of creating that sense of time and place on those cold, wind-swept farmlands of Heart Mountain was the work ethic in which everyone in the family and community played a role. Even the small children had tasks. To the person looking on, the jobs might have seemed insignificant, but it gave that family member a sense of belonging. Time after time, I would hear husbands speak of the vital role played by the wife. Those homestead women were amazing, and I am proud to say my mother was one of them.

FEED THE CHICKENS

In those early years on the homestead, every family member had a job. After coming home on the school bus, one of my chores was to feed the chickens. I didn't have a horse yet, so I had to get by with a long stick with a rope tied at the top to substitute for reins. I made trails out through the weeds and could entertain myself for a good deal of time in my fantasy world of being a cowgirl. One night, it was almost dark when my dad asked me if I had fed the chickens. Of course, that was the last thing on my mind. I don't remember so much that he scolded me, but he did sit me down and explain to me that the family was depending on me to do my part on this homestead; those chickens were depending on me. I never cared a great deal for those chickens, because they would peck my hand when I gathered the eggs, but that night I began to have empathy for those chickens out in the barn. Later in life, when something would arise when determination and loyalty were needed in a situation, I would hear myself say, "Just get up and go feed the chickens."[2]

WORK ETHIC: A GIFT PASSED ON

"Lazy" was not even part of a homestead family's vocabulary. The common goal of building a life on virgin soil and facing the elements of nature required backbone and a work ethic that was indelibly impressed into one's character. In many of the interviews, the parents would describe the chores of the small children. To some, this might seem a harsh way to raise children, but actually, it created a sense of belonging and community.

As one takes the curtain of time and pulls it back, it is interesting to see how those day-by-day conversations with young children take hold and have a glue-like ability to stick for a lifetime.

I remember one day when I was about ten. It was a hot summer day out in the sweltering hog house. My day's assignment had been to shovel out the manure from four of the pens. As I would heave each shovelful out the door, I would grumble and complain to myself, not realizing my dad was standing there at the double door listening to me. He walked in and stood there, didn't scold me, but just began to speak in those few words of the dignity one finds in those hard-working farm men. "Pat, no matter what work you are doing, always take pride and do the best you can." I am sure he went on out to the field that day, not even thinking how profoundly those words would follow me throughout my life.

It was many years later in late June of 1986. Our father had only a short time to live, as cancer had moved throughout his body. I had not come to the realization he would be leaving us so quickly, but he knew. All of the family had come home to the homestead. My son, Craig, was sitting near his grandfather, and I could hear the conversation. "Craig, when you go out into the workplace, about every week, stop and ask yourself a question. "Am I doing the best at my job for my employer and for myself?"

I have always felt that the group of young people living in the homestead community had been given a special gift by knowing how to work hard. There is just something satisfying at the end of a day, when one has worked hard and done the best they could in a situation.

Last summer, my daughter's three sons decided they wanted to start a business mowing neighbors' lawns. They spent all day planning. Kameron even made up a little flyer and sent his younger brothers door to door. They didn't get any takers, but I thought it was a grand idea. A few days later, I was out in my back yard talking with my neighbor. He had just had heart surgery and couldn't mow his lawn. I told him about my grandson. Don't you know, the best promoters are always the grandmas? Well, he wanted to give this young man a chance. It was a very hot day when my daughter came with Kameron. I wanted to encourage him in his new business. I pulled out my weed eater and touched things up just a bit. As we worked together, I spoke of the importance of doing a job well-- taking pride in everything we do. Oh, my goodness, where did I hear those same words when I was a young girl? I would say it was that hot day in summer when I was cleaning out hog pens and my father happened to come by.

THE INVESTMENT IN YOUTH

If it were possible to roll back time, one of the first things that I would do is thank those significant people who made such an impact on my life. After so many years, having the privilege to visit those neighbors and friends from my childhood was priceless. The parents took part in making our community a place where children could thrive and grow. Taking time out of a heavy farming load to make room in children's' lives for Vacation Bible School, Scouts, and 4-H are some of the rich memories.

When I was a youth, I worked long and hard in 4-H just as all the other young people. I never realized, at the time, the sacrifice that was made for us. I have often wished I could thank Edith Anderson, my Extension Home Economist, who gave so much of herself. She always walked with a cane. I never asked her why, but it must have been difficult, as she traveled a great deal.

Long after we had grown up, our parents played a major role in the 4-H program. It would be impossible to count the number of children who learned many skills on the farms out in our community.

My mother would have about twenty 4-H youth in her sewing club. Of course, as a teen-ager, I spent many hours at the kitchen table helping young children learn how to sew. At times, I would grumble under my

348

breath, but later as a teacher, I realized what a gift I had been given in learning teaching skills at such an early age.

One day, after I was grown and had children of my own, I was visiting with my dad. He made the comment, "Patty, always invest in young people." I followed in my parents' footsteps, because not only do I love my own children, I just love all children and want to be involved with them in some way.

It was a hot day in August at the Big Horn County Fair. After the Monday judging, I spent the rest of the week packing 4-H projects for state fair. It was a huge job, and the sweltering heat in that cement block building with a tin roof seemed to leach out all energy. Each year, I had a goal. I wanted to have all the items labeled and ready to pack on Thursday. Sheep judging day was on Thursday, and I had a special place in my heart for the sheep. This was a big day at the county fair. The judging would begin early and go into late evening. Since I was a judge myself, I had great respect for those judges out there all day in the August sun. It was late afternoon by the time I finally managed to pull a folding chair out under the tree to watch the classes of sheep being judged. As I sat there, memories of my dad came back. I thought of those times as a child, when he was there encouraging me as I showed my sheep at the Park County Fair. I have a faded, purple ribbon tucked away that I won for my Columbia ewe. It has a story and memory so tender to me now.

Each year, I tried to talk myself out of the melancholy that seemed to seep right down into my weary bones. The fair manager, John Haley, came over and sat down beside me. I knew I was tired, but the weariness I saw in him was far greater. He began to tell me about the many years Lloyd Snider and my dad would come over to judge the sheep. "You know, Pat, I had so much respect for your dad. It would be long after the sun had gone down, and I would see him over there in the barns after such a long day of judging, encouraging a 4-Her about what they could do the next year with their sheep." I think that would paint a picture of Mom as well, as she continued for many years to teach sewing. That could be a description of the Heart Mountain community, as all the parents invested in the youth.

DEATH OF A FATHER

Long ago, I came to peace with the great Shepherd of Heaven with the death of my father. Harboring grief each year on the day he died, July 26, 1986, is not what he would have wanted. But now, as I sit quietly with gentle classics playing in the background, I am reminded of that time. It would be easier to pass lightly over this passage in the McClaflin family, but for you, the reader, who is facing that time with a parent, or maybe your own home going, I will for a brief reprieve go back and relive that sorrow.

Christmas was almost here, and my parents were coming from Wyoming to spend the holidays and attend my graduation celebrations. I was going to walk down an aisle to receive my diploma for a Master's Degree. It seemed like a dream, but it was now a reality.

Growing up on that northern Wyoming homestead taught me many life lessons that I still practice today. From an early age, it was understood that my father's greatest desire was to see his children have college degrees. On many occasions, as I rose at 4:00 a.m. or studied way into the midnight hours, the look of pride that I knew I would see on my father's face as I reached out to clutch that diploma gave me a relentless drive.

It had been a blessed Christmas time with the folks, and now they were sitting in the family room as we were about to take them to catch their plane home. My father suddenly had an excruciating pain in his back. He became so uncomfortable that, upon arriving home, he went for a checkup. When the test results came back, it was discovered that he had lung cancer, and it had moved on to his liver. He was given two weeks, and the maximum time for him would be five months.

Just as I had done years before when my father had suffered a severe heart attack, I asked God to give me a gift of faith. So many friends came alongside our family during that time and prayed. I remember times in the night when I would slip into the living room, moonlight creating shadows on the walls, and I would lie across the carpet weeping for a miraculous healing for this daddy of mine.

One Sunday morning, a lady came up to me after service. She apologized as she handed me a note written on yellow tablet paper. "I am sorry this is all the paper I had one day as I was at work. This message came to me as I thought about you praying for your father." I thanked her and went off to be alone as I read the words. "Your Daddy has something he wants accomplished and he needs someone to agree with him in prayer." I opened my Bible to the passage she had written down. It read:

"Now May the God of hope fill you with all joy and peace in believing, that you may abound in hope by the power of the Holy Spirit. Romans 15:13 NKJV

How I needed to hold onto hope; I wasn't feeling much joy, so these words became imprinted on my soul.

That night, the prayers changed. I wasn't sure what that message on that scribbled notepad meant, but I prayed fervent prayers that my father's desire would be granted. All the family came to Wyoming in June, and on the last night, a long table was stretched out in the living room so that every member, including the smallest child, could be seated. Daddy wanted to stand and bless the meal and the family. I still had not come to the realization that our father would be with us for just a brief time. It is so good to know this Great Shepherd of humanity, but in the valley of death, He has to be the most precious to those who love him. I am reminded of the scripture in Psalm 116:15, "Precious in the sight of the Lord is the death of His saints."

A few weeks later, our family was at church camp near London, Ontario. It was during the song service, and it was already hot and humid. The minister led the congregation in the old hymn, "I Surrender All." To one who is not attuned to hearing God's voice, it is hard to describe how clearly He does speak to us. As I sang the words of that beloved hymn on that old campground, the reality came to me. That afternoon, I went off alone with an old chair and sat, looking out on the lake. For hours, I stared at the water. A few days later, the call came, and my husband booked a flight for me to Wyoming for that afternoon. My heart hurts for families, as I now understand the heartache that accompanies watching the ravages of cancer in those we love so dearly.

My brother, Mike, and his wife, Linda, were missionaries in Africa, so it was a concern that they would make it home in time to see Daddy.

351

Later, we would reflect on how God had taken care of the smallest details during the time of our father's illness.

One afternoon, I slipped into Daddy's bedroom. He lay there so still, hardly able to speak. The few words I spoke were in such desperation. He looked at me with eyes deep-set in his gray face. With a croaking voice barely above a whisper, his words burned into my soul: "I'll never give up hope; I'll never give up hope!" How could I possibly know that in just a short while, my faith would be tested as it went through fiery trials? And years later, when I sat in a crushed car out in the middle of nowhere, in sub-zero weather with my life on a precipice, those words would flood back as if my father were sitting right next to me. At those times in my life, there was always that underlying remembrance, "I'll never give up hope," and it would cause me to hold onto the Lord's hand with all my might.

The hours before the ambulance came for my dad are a fog at this time, but I remember that Daddy didn't have on the pajamas I had gotten him for Father's Day. I spent hours looking for his gift, finally decided on a pair--cobalt blue, cotton satin, with piping around the collar.

Now they were lifting him onto the gurney, his suffering was unbearable, and the faded brown pajamas were frayed around the collar. Of course, I mentioned this to no one. Why would I be so frantic about a pair of pajamas when everything was winding down, and no one could stop it?

In the morning hours, the death rattle came. I would slip out into the hall with the kindly nurse who was wearing a soft-pink sweater, and she would explain to me what was happening. All of our family were there that July morning with Daddy. I stood for hours there next to his bedside, trying to put into my memory every crease and line of his face.

When death came, he just dissolved down into the pillow like an ancient gray tent being folded up; then hemorrhaging came, and he was with God. 3

The homestead out on the northern prairies of Wyoming will always have a special place in my heart. The memory of coming around the corner of the kitchen and seeing the smile break out on my father's face for the joy of seeing me will always be burned on my memory. After his death, whenever I returned to the homestead, I wanted to drive up to the amendment and look for the wild rose he had so fondly planted years before. One of my coping skills when walking through grief or facing a great challenge is to put my thoughts into a poem format. Thus, sadness at the sense of loss in missing my father turned into a poem.

WILD ROSE BUSH ON THE HILLSIDE

Brambling, falling, winding down a path of rocks and sagebrush,
Your delicate color of crimson painted on the tiny petals,
Wild rose bush, oh dear and wonderful little wild rose bush.

Your journey down this hillside has survived many a year of toil
and perseverance.
The heavy truck wheels, not realizing the treasure of memories you
hold have crushed and bruised many of your branches. Yet you
remain there on the hillside for those of us who come to look for
you once again.
Somehow thinking you can roll back time,
But then you are only a little wild rose bush Planted so
long ago.
Lovingly nourished by buckets of water carried from a long distance
By a man with sunbaked skin,
A gentle spirit,
One possessing a quiet wisdom.
He loved the beauty of this farmland protected by
the mountain's shadow.
It is not only I who come searching for you on windswept mornings in
the early spring
But others who were his special friends.
Those who carried his coffin on that stifling summer day in July.
Even after all these years, I remember them
standing over on the side.
Glistening moisture in the eyes revealed their sense of loss.

As I watched his friends huddled there, it seemed the heat of the sun
pressed my spirit down into the earth.
But now as I look about for you, little flower
My heart takes on a joy of knowing a war veteran who was able to come
home to family.
Those early mornings at the break of dawn, those tillers of the soil
shared a bond as they stood together after water sprinklers had been
turned on to irrigate the crops.
The water shooting in the air caressing the sky with circular motion
playing its own symphony in life's patterns.
They drank coffee together out of mugs, made plans, shared the
load of work, and talked of life.
The two apple trees planted by the shed were not as fortunate as you,
little wild rose bush.
Chemical sprays and truck wheels crushed them long ago now.
But the memory of my father planting the trees, feeling even now the
great anticipation he had at sharing the golden fruit with his friends
somehow soothes this heart within me.

Brambling, falling, winding down the hillside.
Wild rose bush, oh dear and wonderful little wild rose bush.
You hold memories for us,
Somehow your delicate presence on the hillside brings a calm,
not tangible in human words, but a hushed silence. Brambling,
falling, winding down the hillside, Wild rose bush, or dear and
wonderful little wild rose bush.

Patricia McClaflin Booher, April 9, 2002

Life has a way of going on. Those times of the loss of a loved one or
other struggles that seem to be part of the human frame can bring a measure
of depth or bitterness, and each person chooses the outcome.

Many of the 4-H leader trainings were held in Laramie, Wyoming, at
the university. Through the years, my parents made many trips there,

354

sometimes in winter. I often heard my mother say, "You never want to get caught in a storm in Shirley Basin." Oh, how true that statement was.

In the very beginning, when seeds were being planted in my thoughts for this research project, I would never have dreamed how it would all play out. It was as if it took on a life of its own. Receiving a sabbatical in order for me to do the research was a joy beyond words. Through this whole process of completing this book, I have relied heavily on faith and also those roots of bravery in taking the risk. Those qualities were born into my character in that "sense of time and place" in the Heart Mountain community. I have borrowed this story of the car wreck from my Shepherd book. I am so grateful that I have come through that time out there on that cold winter day in early February.

CAR WRECK IN SHIRLEY BASIN

I drove away from home that morning with relief as I saw the sun filtering down through the clouds. I was hoping the rays of amber, layered with a mist of pink, cotton candy softness were a promise of a warmer day than it had been in this northern Wyoming country in early February. I was in for a brutal surprise that would forever change my destiny, and with this, a passion for life that would ever drive me on.

I was an Extension Educator with the University of Wyoming. My office was housed in the county courthouse in Big Horn County, right at the base of the massive and rugged Rocky Mountains. I lived in the small hamlet of Shell, and from the picture windows in my living room, I could see right into the canyon, a wonderful place to live for someone like me who loved the beauty of nature.

The university is in Laramie, which was approximately a seven-hour drive from my home. Traveling was an ongoing part of my job, as many times I found myself doing programs all over the state. Because I was so used to long trips, I had pondered for days why I had such an unsettled feeling. I had called my mother several days before, asking her to pray for me, as I couldn't shake this uneasiness. I had a habit of rising early to watch the sunrise coming up over the mountains, because I didn't want to miss the splendor of such beauty.

355

The Sunday morning I was to leave, I was up at five, long before I wou 1 see the first gray glimpse of dawn. As I sat in my chair, with my gaze fixed on the eastern skies, sadness came over me. Although it wasn't an o tion, I just wished that I could stay home. Finally, around seven, I finis ed loading my bags in the car and returned to lock the front door. This wasn't a usual custom, but on that morning, I opened the door, looked arou d at my familiar things, and said, "Good-bye, little home." I started my oyota Camry, headed down the hill, and began my long trek to Lara nie. On my many journeys, there was a familiar awareness that angels wou 1 accompany me. I would pray that the Lord would send angels to trav along with me, and this morning was no different.

As I drove through Basin, I realized I had to get hold of this mel icholy mood, or it was going to be a very long day. I reached into my stasl of recordings and pulled out a tape of sermons from my daughter Shar 1, who lived in Seattle. On a regular basis, she would send me tapes of h Pastor, Reverend Steve Schell of Northwest Foursquare Church. The topic was on praying many kinds of prayers. I popped it into the cassette play r. The words he spoke were like healing salve to my emotions as I drov down the highway. By the time the tape had finished, my mood had beer elevated into a tranquil stage, and it relieved me as I calculated I had clipr ed off an hour of my journey as I drove down into Thermopolis. Driv ng through Wind River Canyon, regardless of season, is a scenic plea ure. It was always a relief to see Shoshone laying out there on the hori: on, as it was a halfway point. For as long as I could remember, this stop off place was like the very end of somewhere.

I cruised through the small town and headed to Casper. For the next wo hours, I sang old hymns. There have been times in my life that it seen ed as if Christ were sitting in the seat right next to me, and this was one of those days. The melancholy mood had melted into a feeling of strer gth and peace, as the songs brought so many memories of a lifetime of e perience.

Just a week before, I had received word that I had been awarded a year s sabbatical to complete a Qualitative Research Project. I was still so exci ed about the news, and it was going to be wonderful to have time to

356

share my gratitude with friends who had been such a support to me through all the hard work of accomplishing the task of writing.

Much planning had gone into this week, as close friends with which I had grown up, who also worked in Extension, would be attending the week-long training. We had arranged to have adjoining rooms at the motel. Each of us had stashed junk food into coolers. This had been the arrangement on previous trips, which had proved to be disastrous to anyone staying in the rooms adjacent to ours. We were the greatest of friends, and as the week would become tiresome, the evenings would grow in warmth and much laughter, as old stories were rehashed. I had always been blessed with an overactive sense of humor, so my retelling would take on new and colorful dimensions. And, of course, being the true-blue friends that they were, they would laugh at my antics.

By the time I had left Casper, it was the middle of the afternoon. The constant wind that customarily engulfs this area was unusually strong. Since the sun was still shining, I did not realize, as I drove along, that the temperature had plummeted. As I looked back at the Medicine Bow Mountain Range to the northeast, I saw dark volumes of seething, angry clouds coming down upon Shirley Basin. This was an area surrounded by a mountain that created its own climate. I had remembered my mother commenting in the past, "You don't want to get caught in Shirley Basin when a storm comes up. "

Now, my mother was one of those homestead pioneers who took on a form of bravery not common to the modern-day woman. Her words had resonated in my storehouse of memory, and for that reason, if I had to drive through Shirley Basin in the winter; I was always relieved to see the sign, "Medicine Bow, 22 miles."

My Toyota Camry began to pull to the side of the road because, as I quickly realized, the wind had risen to gale proportions. I slowed down and gripped the steering wheel, trying to hold the car in my lane of traffic. Loneliness seemed to engulf my thoughts now, along with those feelings of foreboding that had left home with me. I began to quote the 23rd Psalm over and over. I had just finished the last verse, "And I will live with you forever and forever and forever." Suddenly, I cried, "Dear God, send me more angels!"

As I came down a hill, my car must have hit a patch of black ice, combined with wind gusts which caused the vehicle to begin a spin that went around and around in huge circles into the oncoming lane. Of course, there were no cars in sight, but as I spun around the second time, screaming the name of Jesus over and over, terror struck my heart as I saw, out of the snow flurries, a huge snowplow coming directly toward me.

I was amazed, as I realized I was going to see God at that very moment. Thoughts passed so quickly, and there was an awareness of how close I felt to His presence all through that day. It felt like a dark force had pushed me from behind, right into the side of the huge plow.
Then the darkness came.

Someone was banging on my window. I was gasping for air, as the blasts of wind were brutal on my face. I opened my eyes to see a look of panic on the face of a man I did not know. The winter elements of wind and cold had given him deep, wind-burned wrinkles in his face, but he had a look of kindness. I would later feel badly for the driver of the snowplow, as he thought I was dead. My car was on the side of the road, with a lone hubcap from the front wheel lying in the middle of the pavement. The snowplow was parked across the highway, the side of the bed smashed, and the snow blade bent up into the air. I felt disoriented, and all I could think was for him to call my brother, Wayne, who lived on a farm near Powell.

The highway patrolman quickly arrived. He brought me a small quilt to wrap around my legs. It would take an hour for the ambulance to arrive. As I sat there, with most of the windows shattered, I realized the car was crunched in all around me. My car seat was broken; glass was everywhere. I looked down and noticed that my stomach had begun to swell. I lifted my shirt, and the entire front of me was purple. Panic seized me for a moment, as I knew I was hurt. Would I freeze or bleed to death out here so far away from my family? Instantly, as the thought came, I saw my son's face with such a depth of sorrow in his eyes. My father's memory came to me so clearly as if he were right there in the car. I took great strength from the last words my father spoke to me before his death from the ravages of cancer, "I'll never give up hope, I'll never give up hope."

I quickly assessed my situation and came to the conclusion, "I am not dying today, I'm not cold, and I'm not going to cry. I am going to be

358

thankful for that kind man over there sitting in the cab of the snowplow and the poor fellow out there having to wave the traffic around the debris my car left in the road."

I later was told the temperature had plummeted to more than twenty below. I just wanted to go home, but that was not going to happen, as the roads were closed behind me.

When the ambulance arrived, five volunteers had come to help. By this time, the sun had gone down, and the cold and wind currents had dropped again. The front passenger door had been shoved almost to the middle, so I was relieved they got the door open. A man got in and lifted me up out of my seat, as the others managed to get me out from the passenger side. When the full impact of the wind blast hit me, I cried out but then became immediately sick. The gurney felt like stone, and it was hard to lie back. The last thing I wanted was to throw up, knowing I probably had some broken ribs. I kept requesting blankets, as I couldn't ever remember a time in my life when I had been so cold. I was so grateful for the many people who helped me that night, but I had an ache in my heart, as I wanted my family.

How many times throughout my life have I discovered, through some of life's small details, how much God really cares for us? My director, Glenn Whipple, came to the emergency room; this meant so much to me. To my amazement, the local pastor of the Assembly of God, who just happened to be my childhood Sunday school teacher,
Dave Garrett and his wife, Jean, came and stood by my bed until I had stabilized. I noticed that Dave's arm was in a sling. He had just come through a horrific car accident himself. I knew he was in a great deal of pain, but it was such a relief to me that they had come.

That cold February day seems but a memory to me now. There is one thing everyone who comes so close to death can agree on--you are forever changed as you realize you have been given more time on this earth.
4
In those next few months, recovery was slow. I never remember a day feeling sad or even scared, just grateful I would see leaves coming on the trees for another season. This time of reprieve could appear to be a halt to progress on the research and writing of chapters for the homestead book.

But now, as I look back on that time, a deeper level of character and grit were forming. I had time to think about family and those close-knit friends who had been such a source of courage, so one day I penned a poem, and I will share it with you.

FOREVER FRIEND

Seasons come and go, spring, summer, fall, and winter, A time for crying and time for laughing, A time to be silent, a time to speak.
In all of these seasons there is glue that runs down into the crevices of the soul,
And upon the open wounded places of the heart.
This adhesive is what brings courage in the most trying of times,
Brings a smile upon a face masked in tears,
Hope is renewed because of this glue,
An ointment so valuable no price tag can be placed on it's worth.
What is the glue, you ask?
Let me tell you in a hushed tone of reverence.
This is my forever friend.
That one who believes in me when I am discouraged,
Who sees beyond today and helps me remember my dreams,
Forgives me when I don't deserve it,
Will cheer me on when I pursue the destiny and visions for my life, will grow old with me,
And we will remember the seasons fondly,
The tears, the laughter, the disappointments, and the triumphs.
The spring, the summer, the fall, and winter.
My forever friend, and that is you.

Patricia McClaflin Booher

After the cold, winter day out in Shirley Basin, I was warm again, and life went on, but it was never the same. I slowly recovered, worked hard during my sabbatical year, and spent another year with the University of Wyoming. My eldest is a son by the name of Craig. For many years, he had wanted me to come back to Michigan, not just for visits, but to live. Finally, one day in the early morning as I was watching the sunrise, I knew I needed to be near those grandchildren, telling them "lamby" stories and investing in them on a regular basis. The decision was not easily made, but much soul-searching went into this process.

Teddy and Ronnie Jones came alongside me in the moving process, which always seems to be more difficult than we want to acknowledge. We drove across Interstate 80 with an auto transport in tow. I sat in the front with Ronnie and my little Yorky dog, Timmy. Teddy sat in the back seat holding onto their sheep dog with a heavy hand. He was a very smart dog, but he made me nervous, as the look in his eye suggested he had thoughts of the tasty morsel with shaggy ears sitting in the front seat.

Craig, Sandy his wife, and my daughter Rachel, her husband Mitch, and all the grandchildren met us with open arms that cool and crisp day in late October. I was so hoping there would still be some golden, vibrant red leaves holding on for my friends from Wyoming to see. So it was with great delight, as we came around the south edge of Lake Michigan, that my Wyoming friends would be greeted with smashing, bright crimson leaves. Life is a trade-off. Wyoming has the rugged mountains that will always be a part of me. And then we have Michigan, with its lush foliage and so many types of trees and lakes. I will never acquire all their proper names.

CHAPTER 8: PASSING THE BATON

I feel a sense of relief as the final chapter is coming to a close. Growing up in the Heart Mountain Homestead Community has been a gift that has followed me throughout my life. I don't know that I ever again will be so emotionally torn in writing down a piece of history. But, alas, as I look about at those unfinished manuscripts on my desk just waiting for this book to be in print, I am very cognizant that without this passion and soulful ache, words written down are just another book sitting on the shelf.

When I look back to that morning that I walked into the office of Karen Williams, Professor of Early Childhood Development at the University of Wyoming, I had no idea what seeds would be planted in my life. I would say now of this incredible journey back to a "Sense of Time and Place," that it is probably a good thing that I did not know at the time the obstacles I would face and mountains I would have to climb as the research would unfold into layers and layers of rich history and stories of another time. Works such as this and others to come will certainly not come to pass in future generations without that same component of resiliency that compels those sojourners to live out their own dreams in such a way that all obstacles will be overshadowed with a sense of purpose and destiny.

My first introduction to Qualitative Research came from Professor Williams as she showed me her collection of the Foxfire Series by Eliot Wigginton. I have acquired some of his work, and hopefully, I, too, will have a complete series in the future. I have to thank Ben Silliman, UW Cooperative Extension Family Life Specialist, as he was instrumental in introducing me to research in Family Resiliency that would greatly impact my own research project. And, of course, without the green light from my Director of Extension, Edna McBreen, none of this work would have been possible.

It wasn't long before I discovered the research project had taken on a life of its own. The next Extension Director, Glenn Whipple, encouraged me to apply for a research sabbatical. At the time, it seemed but a dream that I would have such good fortune. Glenn wanted to be the first to congratulate me when the news came to him on campus. When he called my office in Big Horn County, I screamed so loud into the phone, I am sure he was deaf for the rest of the day? I was so full of joy at the news, I could hardly contain myself.

The research would prove to be a costly endeavor. I wrote for one grant after another. This was not a lost cause, as I would discover that I was refining the research by the grueling task of writing those lengthy grant applications. My secretary, Dori Noyes, became one of my cheerleaders as I worked with passion applying for one grant after another. A young lady came into my office one day and gave me a grant proposal. Dori came into my office and said, "Come on, just try one more time." Well, wouldn't you know? I did receive the grant from the "John Anson Foundation." The gentleman who contacted me by letter was on the foundation board who reviewed the grant proposals. He was a professor from Harvard.

I interviewed as many of the original 1949 homesteaders as possible. By the time I was conducting research, many of the neighbors had passed away or lived so far away I could not reach them. Sometimes I was able to conduct the interview by telephone. The most enjoyable interviews were done sitting around the kitchen table with the neighbors from childhood. I remember traveling to Cheyenne to conduct an interview with Margaret Olson. It was wonderful to see her in the beautiful, assisted living apartments to which she had retired. She had many files of documents and pictures we copied that day. She filled me in on so much of the early history. I was very impressed with how intelligent Margaret was, and how she remembered so many details. Just a year later, I visited her once more, but it was apparent her memory had slipped away; that was the last time I was able to see her.

THE MIGHTY COLUMBIA RIVER AND HER TRIBUTARIES

I find myself thinking back to those very first months while beginning the research project. I had taken a few weeks of reprieve to concentrate on writing and planning the project. The northern Pacific coastline tends to be my muse. I rented a small cottage in Cannon Beach, Oregon, where I wrote day after day. One morning, I drove over to Astoria and, to my great delight, found a bakery/coffee shop in an old Victorian house perched up on the side of a mountain looking down on the great Columbia River.

As I sat quietly writing and looking out on this immense body of water moving silently and powerfully along, I felt overwhelmed. I was beginning to grasp the realization that the first seeds planted would need a much greater expanse of time, energy, finance, and courage. As the research progressed, I became aware that my contribution of bringing back the history of my childhood community would need to be limited, for the most part, to the beginning stages of those first few years. My brother, Wayne, was born in the next set of children on the homestead. Hopefully, there will be a writer in that group who will take this story to the next layer of history, family, and community. All of the research and documentation I have acquired will be safely housed at McCracken Research Center in Cody, Wyoming, and at the American Heritage Center at the University of Wyoming.

As I look at the journal that was written on that morning in Astoria, gazing at the mighty Columbia River, I detect some fear and intimidation, wondering how I will ever bring this project and book to completion. In the next few days, I pulled out maps and studied history pertaining to this river in the northwest regions of the country. As I followed the tributaries flowing into the mighty Columbia River, I thought about my own life experience. I will describe just a few of those tributaries that have come from a great distance of time in my own life.

A summer afternoon when I was a young girl comes to mind. I stood with my father, looking out the picture window of the living room at heavy, black clouds. Darkness settled over the homeland, as large hailstones began pelting the lawn. In just a few moments, the summer crop had been destroyed. I looked over at the deep furrows of disappointment on my father's face. "Daddy, why don't you do something different than farming? You have worked so hard, and now the crop is gone." He looked at me and said, "What could our family do that could be a better life then this?"

Many times during the arduous task of writing the homestead manuscript, I have looked over at my father's picture sitting on my desk and whispered, "Thank You!" Those small tributaries of life that began on the homestead have flowed into a stream, ever moving forward with a taste of courage and richness for the love of life itself.

Not only did the homesteaders have a "Sense of Time and Place," but that same essence was passed on to the children growing up. Later, when I had grown and was raising my family in the Detroit area, I began to have an understanding of how unique our homestead community was. For many years, I taught high school and adult education. Regardless of the topic taught, stories would emerge of the lambing sheds, planting, harvesting, and the sense of belonging that came from my "growing up" community. I will have to say I was always amazed at the response of the audience. At times I would see grown men moved to tears. I became aware that most of those dear city dwellers had never experienced what I had commonly taken for granted in those day-by-day childhood happenings.

Years later, I returned to Wyoming and took a position with the University of Wyoming Cooperative Extension as a Family Life Educator. Early on, I discovered "All Families Have Strengths," a research project compiled by Cooperative Extension Educators with the University of Idaho. During those years with the university, I did a great deal of educational programming in the area of Family Resiliency. I often referred to research conducted by the Idaho Extension Educators. One of the contributing authors is Dolores Curran who has written, *Traits of a Healthy Family*. She lists "Six Signs of a Healthy Family." One of those signs correlates with what I discovered in the research I conducted.

The family has a person and/or place that serves as a focal point:

> Sometimes this person is referred to as the "family switchboard operator." This person knows which family member is doing what, where, when, and how at all times. It is to this person's house that the family usually gathers for special occasions. It is to this house that people go for a feeling of belonging. 1

> In the past, we were able to gather at "the old homestead' for nurturing, love, and assurance, but there are few old homesteads for today's families. Curran says that "our increasingly mobile

culture is doing away with such homes, and healthy families cite this as a great loss." 2

During those years I worked at UW Extension, I had the pleasure of teaching many different groups in varied settings. I often taught resource-based programming in the area of "Family Strengths." I referred to research from *Traits of a Healthy Family*. "Families who treasure their traditions and rituals seem automatically to have a sense of family. Traditions are the underpinning in such families, regarded as necessities not frills." 3

To enhance the presentations, I would always follow up with an evaluation from the audience. Hands down, if the segment, "Family Traditions and Rituals" was part of the workshops, it would be listed as a favorite. I learned very quickly, if I was addressing a group of youths and asked the audience for their own examples of "Family Traditions and Rituals," to make it a voluntary response. For I found if a young person came from a troubled family without any traditions or rituals, the body language of that child, slumped in the seat with head cast down, spoke volumes.

This did furnish me with an opportunity to encourage individuals that they could become the source within the family to create meaningful traditions that could be passed on. To create a tradition or ritual does not require spending a great deal of money. It just takes that quality of planning and a family member willing to be the baton carrier. I will give just a few of those simple but meaningful examples from our family's stash of traditions.

Mother had an old, gray crock she used for years to make her sweet pickles. When I grew up, I had her teach me how she made potato salad, as it was always something special. My own children grew up feeling the same way about my potato salad. I learned very quickly that in order for the potato salad to taste like an Edna Mae's salad, it had to have her sweet pickles. For many years, every time I went back home to the homestead, I would always go out to the well house before leaving and take several jars of pickles. Sometimes, I would even pack them in my suitcase when flying home. At times this proved to be a disaster, if the jar broke in flight.

I often thought I should learn to make my own pickles, but then they wouldn't be from Mom's stash. It just wouldn't be the same. Last summer,

I ran out of pickles, so I knew I had to carry on this tradition of making sweet pickles. I needed to pick up that particular baton for the family.

A very dear gardening friend, Carol Johnson, gave me a package of Amish pickling cucumber seeds. I have a small yard, so every portion that is free has flowers. I went out with my special seeds and planted them in the yard around the flowers. I watched over them every day. Finally, I had gathered enough cucumbers to fill a metal tub. I so wished I could have had Mom's crock. Pam, my sister-inlaw, said she would mail it to me, as she knew how much I treasured it, but we decided it was just too risky. It was so old, and the thoughts of it getting broken squelched the idea.

I followed Mom's recipe to the letter but still felt I needed to call for more instructions. It was a two-week process, so every day I would go down into the basement where it was cooler and check on my new-forming pickles. It was such a satisfying feeling the day I canned the pickles. I don't know that they are as good as my mom's pickles, but they are close, so I will keep trying. I would say this pickle story could classify as a family tradition.

In my own family, every holiday menu will have as a main staple my cherry pie and croissant rolls. I began making the rolls before Craig was born. Many years ago, I gave the recipes to my children. When I still lived in Wyoming, if it wasn't possible for me to fly to Michigan for the holidays, I could almost count on a call from Craig, wanting me to tell him how to make the rolls. He had the recipe before him, but it wasn't like having Mom there.

Now I am in Michigan, so the family tradition of cherry pie and croissant rolls is still carried out. Now I try to have one of those grandchildren coming alongside me, learning Grandma's love of baking, so that one day this experience will flow on down those tributaries of family tradition.

One might ask why is it important to build on those everyday happenings that go into making the foundation of healthy families. As families collectively come together with a sense of belonging, it brings the cohesiveness and glue that forms a strong community, just as we have observed in the Heart Mountain homesteaders.

As has been described in this work, the completion of the homestead projects in the early fifties would bring to an end the era of opening new communities for homesteading. The number of families growing up on farms has decreased in our nation, but that does not mean we cannot still have that sense of community. There are many reasons for the isolation and exclusion one can find in today's society. Building a sense of community, whether it is in a farming setting or in the inner city of a large metropolis, takes a great deal of trust and just plain hard work and commitment.

During those many interviews with my neighbors, I always asked the question, "Can you ever remember a time when a neighbor lied to you?" I always received the same response, "Absolutely not!" I always thought so much of Lloyd Snider. He and my dad, almost on a daily basis, would connect and talk farming or just enjoy each other's friendship. I liked his answer to this question. "Well, Patty, in our community we were going to be neighbors for a long time. We wanted to respect each other and for sure tell each other the truth. You know, in farming you spend a lot of time alone out on the tractor, so it gives you a lot of time to think about those things that really matter the most." Within that homestead community, the parents created many of the tributaries that flowed into the lives of the young people. We were taught the principles of strong character, respect for others, and the importance of being a good neighbor and a faithful friend.

RUSSIAN CONNECTION

I will relate briefly my experience in 1997 teaching at Saratov University in Russia. The story of how this all came about will be told another time. What I do want to convey is what I discovered when I arrived at the beautiful, old university that morning. It was apparent at one time that that the edifice was a spectacular building, but now it was in need of much repair. As I ascended the stairs with the English Administrator, I saw old women bent over, sweeping with brooms made out of twigs. After several hours, I needed to go to the restroom. The teacher who was in charge of my duties was hesitant. I finally realized that she was embarrassed, so I went back into my bag of life experiences and began to tell her about the out- door John or (better called outhouse) our family used. I didn't bother to tell her it had been many years since the old outhouse had

369

been torn down. We went down the hall to the restroom. What I found were several stalls with only a hole in the floor. I didn't find the luxury of soap, drying towel, or toilet paper, so I quickly learned to be prepared for the next day's encounter. I felt so badly for my newfound friend, as she was so ashamed of the conditions in the university.

I had received a UW International Grant in order to teach at the University of Saratov. The topics I taught were "Creative Thinking," and "Leadership." The topics might seem commonplace in our society, but there in Russia, conditions were far different. Two teachers were assigned to escort me to the various schools in order for me to conduct lectures. I am not free to give their names, but I will say that in just a short time, a bond of friendship developed between the three of us. Several times, they took me to view the monument of cranes in flight.

It was situated on a hill overlooking the city of Saratov and the mighty Volga River. They explained to me why there were so many beautiful buildings in the city that were of German architectural design. Many colonies of people from Germany had settled all along the Volga River. Unfortunately, many of those people, cities, and towns had been completely annihilated under the dictatorship of Stalin. My friends told how it was estimated that more than twenty-thousand citizens were murdered under the brutal reign of Stalin. It has been more than a half century since the end of WWII, and the country is still shrouded with sadness and grief. When we walked down the street together, they were both eager to share with me what had happened to their country but spoke in whispers, looking around as if someone were watching us. By the time I had been invited to Russia, the Communist government had fallen, but even after almost a decade, there was still a sense of fear in the citizens.

I will never forget the experience of standing in front of college students in the packed university rooms. It was difficult for the older professors to grasp what I was saying, but the young students had a spark in their eyes. It was not until the last day of lectures that students would come to the front and seemed almost to mob me. Several students came near and whispered to me that they were also poets and would slip me poems they had written.

When one understands that, during the reign of terror under Stalin, all the creative thinkers, leaders, and poets were killed, it helps to put into perspective the fear that still seems to hover like a gray cloud over that nation. In the evenings, while working at Saratov University, I wrote "Russian Connection." The news column consisted of what I had observed each week, my feelings, and the outcomes of topics I was teaching. I was always very careful to omit names and places that would put my Russian colleagues in jeopardy. The news article was sent out to the Wyoming newspapers each week. After returning home, I was delightfully surprised that so many across the state had followed my comings and goings each week while in Russia.

When I was a young girl, our special neighbor, Bertie Snider, used to tell of when she was a young girl. Her family had come from Germany. Because of her heritage, some of the other children at school would taunt her; this brought her much sorrow. I had forgotten those stories told by Bertie until one afternoon, just before I left the city of Saratov. At the end of my teaching term in Saratov, I was addressing a group of English professors. So much had gone into being able to fulfill the dream of going on this journey to Russia. My own experience of coming to love these people from so far away, and to see how desperately they wanted to grasp onto the freedom of what I was teaching, moved me deeply. As I stood before those dedicated professors who worked in such meager conditions, emotions beyond my control came over me. It didn't help to realize, as I was looking over that group of professors, that I saw a face I recognized. The lovely woman looking back at me could have been Bertie's twin. I tried to go on with the lecture, but instead of words, a sob came up out of me. I desperately tried to compose myself but to no avail. When I finally was able to speak in just a whisper, I described to them why I had been so compelled to come to Russia, and how, for many years, I had prayed for the Russian people.

They were astonished to see before them an American who was so moved with compassion for them in their conditions. In just a few moments, they were all up out of their seats coming around me and hugging me with a beautiful sense of comradeship. As I look back on that day, I can't help but know that the same brave and raw courage I saw in my parents and neighbors as a young child had developed within me a brave heart that propelled me to another place. I would say that, on that afternoon, a homesteader's daughter from the windy plains of Wyoming went to a faraway place and connected with Russian professors. And with those bonds of friendship, a "Sense of Time and Place and Community" were formed.

DEAR HEARTS AND GENTLE PEOPLE

I find it interesting how a thread of a song from long ago in childhood can evoke such deep emotions. As I bring this portion of the Heart Mountain Community story to its completion, I remember a song I have not thought about in years. In the last few days, the words of each line run through my mind.

The Mountain View Community Club was a hub for the neighbors to gather together. When I was still very young, I remember a talent show that had been planned.

My mother took me to town one afternoon to look for sheet music at the Bonner's Five and Dime store. I had never sung a solo before, so I wasn't very sure of myself. I just knew I loved to sing. Mom worked and worked with me, and in few days it was time for this shy, little girl to get up in front of all those big adults. My knees were shaking as I began to sing, but as I looked out at all those loving neighbors, my small, lyric soprano voice began to swell with confidence. I loved the words of the song, as I thought everyone in the world had the same of kind of kindred spirit as our little homestead community.

The melody that keeps coming to mind was made popular by Bing Crosby. I am sure many of my readers have not heard the verses, but I think the words just might warm your heart also.

I love those dear hearts and gentle people Who
live in my home town.
Because those dear hearts and gentle people Will
never ever let you down.
They read the Good Book from Fri till Monday
That's how the weekend goes
I've got a dream house I'll build there one day With
picket fence and rambling rose.
I feel so welcome each time that I return

372

That my happy heart keeps laughing like a clown I
love those dear hearts and gentle people Who live
and love in my home town.

Endeavors such as this of going back into the past and creating a place of memories for the family and the inheritance of growing up on a Wyoming homestead are of great value. The impact it will have for younger generations is how we, in our golden years, take part among the living. I often say, "Believe it or not, it's not all about me."

A few years ago, my son Craig and his wife Sandy invited me to go with them to the high school state wrestling finals. I was so happy to be invited. For two very long days we sat in the stands at the Palace of Auburn Hills. We sat on the front row where there was no way to get out, so when I needed a break, I was graciously helped up by the men around our seats. That was an accomplishment, since I am not as thin as I used to be. When we came that first morning, we didn't know anyone's name around us. In just a short amount of time, we became like a family. There were twelve mats down in that big arena with continual matches taking place. All of us sitting in that corner became very keen on the family of the wrestler who was coming up next. We screamed and yelled for the young people down there giving everything they had to win. When a wrestler won, we all cheered, but when he/she lost, we all felt the loss together. We were community.

"DON'T DIE BEFORE YOU'RE DEAD"

Throughout this story of the Heart Mountain Community that I fondly remember, I have often mentioned those childhood friends I connected with after many years. I refer to them as my "Forever Friends." Two of those special friends are Teddy and Ronnie Jones who keep resurfacing in my life, as I write about life on the homestead.

A few years ago, Teddy called and invited me to attend a conference with her, "Women of Faith," in Billings, Montana. I decided to go and was pleasantly greeted by many old friends from the Powell area. I have fond memories of those few days with Teddy. A phrase that was repeated over

373

and over by Sheila Walsh, an inspirational speaker at the conference, still resonates in my mind.

"Don't die before you're dead."

This phrase brings me back to a time in those early years. In the late fall, crops needed to be harvested. The short growing season on the Ralston Bench posed a problem for farmers. Everyone in the family was required, as time was of the essence. It would be getting cold in October by the time we got home on the school bus. We would change our clothes and be out in the bean field with our parents, carefully racking the dry bean shells into rows so Dad could come along with the combine. After some time, Mike and I would start complaining. "Is the job done? We're hungry and cold. Can we go in the house now?" Mom's reply would always be the same. "The job's done when the job's done."

That sense that each of us played a role in bringing in the harvest can be a metaphor such as a small trickle of water coming off of the great Rockies from the spring run-off. Such a small amount of water, but later it finds its way into the Snake River which flows into the mighty Columbia.

I can think of another time that those small tributaries of water became like a mighty river of life for me. It was a time I would have to rest heavily on the courage I was taught as a child and the faith in God that had been planted deep in my soul. The winds of adversity were blowing like a howling gale against my little crumpled car out in the middle of nowhere in Shirley Basin. I had taken on the role of historian, putting down in print those stories of life on the homestead. I had picked up the baton, and I couldn't lay it down now. I just decided I had to live through the experience, so I told myself I wouldn't die that day, and I didn't!

This morning I went out into the sunroom for that quiet time I spend reading the Bible. As I opened up the cover, I happened to notice my handwriting. The caption read: "Presented to Wallace McClaflin on March 14, 1986." We had all come home when it was discovered our father had a very short time to live. In those last months of his life, he would read this small leather-bound Bible day after day. It had just been a few months since my parents had attended my college graduation in December. It had been a wonderful holiday season with the family as they celebrated my great joy in the completion of those years of study. Who would have dreamed that, in just a few months, the news would come that our father was in the final stages of cancer.

As soon as we received the news, I came home to the homestead. I tried to think of something that would give my dad courage, just as he had done for me so many times throughout my life. I suppose I could say that the parchment paper that had my name imprinted with an M.S. Degree was one of my most treasured personal possessions. I put it in a wooden frame and placed it in my luggage. When I arrived at the homestead that evening, I came into my parents' bedroom where my father was. I placed the college certificate on the wall where it could be easily viewed from the bed.

How I managed to complete my college education just took raw grit on my part, but what always propelled me on was knowing my parents wouldn't miss my graduation for anything. Just to see the smiles on their faces kept me going. Just knowing in those midnight hours of study, that simple sentence, "The job's done when the job's done." It was in late July when the call came, and in just a few hours I would be getting on a plane for Wyoming. When I saw our dad, I just couldn't believe it. When everyone else was in the other part of the house, I slipped in by his bed, knelt down, and leaned up close to his face. With a croak just barely above a whisper, he looked at me with that look I had loved so well. "Pat, I'll never give up hope, I'll never give up hope!"

I have often referred to the work done by Erik Erikson in relation to the eight stages of life. In the eighth and final stage of life, "Integrity versus Despair," I have penned a quote that parallels what we are relating in reference to living with purpose: "Only in him who in some way has taken care of things and people and has adapted himself to the triumphs and disappointment adherent to being, the originator of others or the generator of products and ideas—only in him may gradually ripen the fruit of these eight stages." 4

I have known individuals who have lived their last days on this earth in great despair. At times, I have been asked to attend a person's funeral, so that there would be someone sitting in the audience. And then I have attended funerals where there was great sadness, as the individual had given such an investment to others that their passing on to be in Heaven would leave a great vacancy. They had completed this journey of life with the

375

utmost integrity. In other words, they had left a rich inheritance to those they loved.

In that summer of 1986, my own three children were growing up. I was still a high school teacher in the Detroit area. It had never occurred to me that, one day, I would return to Wyoming and become an author. But, alas, those tributaries of life always moving downward into that ocean of life with such wide expanse have a way of propelling each of us into that destiny of purpose that can either bring Integrity or Despair. It is a personal choice.

Every season of life is important. It is possible in that last season, when strength seems gone and many times health is a challenge, that one can settle into despair and forget the purpose and destiny they had in life. The longer I live, the more I am convinced that the final thrust of the race into finishing life can impact our family and friends and the entire community more than we could ever know. "The relation of adult integrity and infantile trust influences the potential that healthy children will not fear life if their elders have integrity enough not to fear death."5

How could my father have imagined that one day, out in a brutal storm, his daughter would be at such a precipice between life and death, and those words spoken at his bedside would come back? "I'll never give up hope."

CLOSING THOUGHTS

These are trying times in our nation. Many families are out of work. There are many discussions and points of view on just how to govern this great land of America. I don't know of any family in this community who does not have electricity. In fact, we have so many modes of communication, I can't even begin to keep up. And yet, as I look about me and observe young families today, I don't know that they are that much different than the homestead community in which I grew up. Parents love their children. They want the very best for them.

The nightly news concentrates on the sensational, but I am thinking about those day-to- day kindnesses that are all around us--that person who runs into a burning building to rescue persons he has never met--that neighbor who so kindly shovels out my driveway when the heavy snows

376

come, knowing my respiratory system is not what it used to be. How does one have the words to thank such kindness?

I have often wished that the age span between Mike, Wayne, and I had not been so far apart. Wayne came along in the next group of young people on Heart Mountain. It seems as if Wayne and his wife Pam have been the "watchmen on the wall."

Mike and his wife Linda went off early as missionaries to Africa. They returned to the states when he became the Regional Area Director for Africa for the Assemblies of God. When they retired they moved back to Wyoming and built a beautiful home on the homestead. Although Mike has retired he still is the Special Assistant to the President of Convoy of Hope.

Wyoming will always be a part of me, and I will want to come back often, but the draw of children and grandchildren in Michigan has taken me there.

When I do visit the homestead community, I am delighted to see Wayne and Pam taking that same interest in their neighbors, as they often congregate out in his shop where he works on the farming machinery for the community. If there is a snowstorm, as homesteader Tiny Collar knows, before long, Wayne will be coming into her yard to shovel her out and make sure she is safe.

A few years ago, Pam and Wayne told me of Glenn French and his terminal illness. His parents, Lyle and Dorothy, had been such a wonderful support to me during the interviewing process. They told of Glenn as a young boy and how he loved to take time to sit out on the hillside and just absorb the beauty of the mountains. On the afternoon the family gathered to share in the interview, I discovered Glenn was a man of few words. I checked with Pam and Wayne throughout the summer, as I was so concerned for Glenn and his family. When his illness was discovered, it was in its last stages, so he would not see another harvest.

In the last few days, as I have been editing the homestead interviews, I pulled up the Powell Tribune on the internet and read the beautiful obituary for Glenn written by Tessa Schweigert. She captured that spirit of the Heart Mountain Community that still remains after all these years in those she interviewed.

Weeks after Glenn French's death, farmers in the Powell

377

Valley gathered together to harvest the fields he planted last spring. "It's a community effort of people who saw a need and filled it. And it's a tribute to my brother," said Larry French. "He was one of the kindest people I ever knew."

After planting his barley and hay crops last spring, Glenn French was diagnosed with cancer. He remained a faithful, dedicated farmer throughout the spring and summer. "He knew he was terminal once his crop was in the ground," said Kelly Spiering, a fellow Heart Mountain farmer. "When one farmer hurts, we all hurt."

On a hot August weekend day, a group of Powell-area farmers left their own fields to harvest Glenn's barley fields in the shadow of Heart Mountain. Around 50 people showed up to help; operating three combines, more than a dozen trucks, making lunch, and pitching in however they could to ensure Glenn's fields were harvested successfully.

"Other farmers in the Powell area have stepped up to help harvest Glenn's remaining acreage," Mike Forman said. "It's the nature of the Powell community as well, but even more, the Heart Mountain community," Forman said. "A lot of people have offered to help. It's neat to be a part of a community that steps up to the plate."

"Family and friends remember Glenn as a committed farmer, hard worker and good steward of the soil he farmed. Glenn would sleep in his pickup during the harvest time, checking moisture levels to make sure it was perfect and then begin harvesting," Spiering said. "Even in his final days, Glenn's commitment and love for farming remained unwavering. He irrigated Thursday morning and died Monday. I truly hoped he would be here to see this and run the combine," Spiering added. "It just didn't work out that way." 6

Many times, I have been concerned for Pam and Wayne, because I knew that at harvest time, or in the haying season, they would both work around the clock getting in the crops. Those early homestead wives worked right alongside their husbands, and in many ways I see those same qualities in Pam and other farm wives out on Heart Mountain. Farming has gone through a metamorphosis of change through the years. Wayne takes me up to see the huge sprinklers and tries to explain all the workings of them, but I am not sure I fully understand. In the last few years, more and more of those circling silhouettes of water can be seen throughout the homestead community. Water conservation and efficiency in irrigation have come a long way from those early years in the fifties.

Several winters past, our mother was very ill. My daughter Rachel, her husband Mitch, their four-year-old son Luke, and baby Max flew back home in the February cold to see her. Luke always wore his rubber boots everywhere. He had several pairs. He liked to mix up the colors, so on that blustery, Wyoming day, he had put on his blue dinosaur and green frog boots. He liked to go for walks with his parents in the north field. I think he was fascinated by the huge sprinkler sitting out there in the plowed field. He had found the deep ruts made by the heavy, metal wheels that made a circular motion throughout the field in the summer irrigation season. Luke wanted to take one last hike on his path in the field before we left. We all felt sadness at leaving Mother. I think the family was beginning to realize that our mother's wish of living on the homestead throughout her lifetime might not be possible.

I decided to walk with Luke on his trek along the sprinkler path and was glad I had bundled up, as the wind had a brutal bite to it that afternoon. Mitch captured the picture of Luke heading into the wind that day. When I saw the picture, it seemed to capture the thoughts and feelings of passing on the baton of rich inheritance to the next generations of families.

We had always hoped our mother could live out her days on the homestead, in that house that had started out as a barracks but later was a lovely brick home surrounded by lawn and a variety of trees.
Her remaining years would be in a nursing home.

This last June I flew back to Wyoming to see my Mom. I had given her a copy of the Homestead manuscript, but had always hoped to be able to place the finished book in her hands. The morning I left I had a deep sense I would not see her again until I greeted her in Heaven.

In the last stage of finishing all the parts and pieces of publishing, I have many times been weary but in those moments I would reflect on the prayer my mother said over me when saying goodbye that morning. It would seem she was a young pioneer woman all over again, as the words were full of hope and courage. I truly believe that morning with my dear mother, so tiny now, she was passing the baton of destiny to her daughter.

During that visit we made plans for our mother's 100 year birthday on January 3, 2020. She almost made it. Heaven became the home of Edna Mae McClalfin on November 27, 2019.

One generation passes the baton of living on to the next generation, but the basic need of a sense of belonging to a community still remains. I hope that I am an encouraging voice that gives "wind to the sails" of young parents raising their children today. I do believe that life as we have known it in the last few years might be changing, and maybe that is a good thing. We just might be spending more time at home. We might be digging into the soil and planting nutritious gardens. Maybe we will take the time to get together with our neighbors and bring a potluck picnic to our block party. I must bring this story to a close. But really, it is just the beginning chapter. And with the second chapter, the next generation of young people from those farmlands of Wyoming will tell their own stories. It is time to pass the baton to the next generation of brave young people who will have their own challenges that will take courage and perseverance.

WIND IN OUR SAILS

Some folks want to settle into the retirement years With slippers,
easy chair and life that is easy.
And then there are those of us who just have to head into the wind.

There is a sense of destiny
Regardless of the personal cost or sacrifice.
We march to a different drummer. This dear
soul just never gives up.
The God of Creation is always searching out
Those brave souls who love life to the fullest,
Yet take time to feel the most tender moments and have
compassion for another passerby.

Not an easy thing to choose; this life full of courage to face any
challenge.
These dear souls have a single focus as they look Ahead coming
into harbor.
Adjusting to the winds of adversity they have come
To understand a deeper meaning
to the preciousness of life.

What makes this journey of courage and persistence
Full of joy are those kindred spirits that come along our path; Sometimes
in the most trying of times.
To have such a friend could only be that special blessing The Shepherd
of Heaven brings to pass.
And so today my dear friend, I bless your life with prayers that
Will give wind to your sails as you have been So
faithful to walk with me In my own path of
destiny.

Patricia McClaflin Booher

For I know the thoughts that I think toward you, says the Lord, thoughts of

peace and not of evil, to give you a future and a hope.

Jeremiah 29:11 NKJV

PHOTO ALBUM

Our homestead community felt like Heart Mountain was our own. This view was taken from the location of the Heart Mountain Relocation Camp setting. The mountain is north of the highway between Powell and Cody, Wyoming.

PEL – PHOTOGRAPH

(Courtesy of Paul Lewis)

Wallace and Edna Mae McClaflin were married December 14, 1941.
(Courtesy of McClaflin family album)

1st Lieutenant Wallace McClaflin in London while serving
as a B17 pilot with the U.S. Army 8th Air Force
(Courtesy of McClaflin family album)

The first group of Heart Mountain veterans with
their wives in front of the REA building in 1949

(Courtesy of the Shoshone Irrigation District
and Jo Miller)

Fifty year reunion of the 1949
Heart Mountain homesteaders

(TJ's Portrait Studio, Powell, Wyoming)

Mike and Patty McClaflin in front of the barrack home
(Courtesy of McClaflin family album)

Paint Creek ranch: Edna Mae, Patty, and Mike McClalfin riding their favorite horse Lady

(Courtesy of Phyllis Hoff Sammons)

Patty McClalfin, age six, the first spring in Wyoming, as   she rode through the sage brush trails with her stick horse.   (Courtesy of McClaflin family album)

The homesteaders spoke of the outhouse which was
common place for me. Paul Lewis took a picture of the
McClaflin outhouse that has not been in use for many
years.
I speak of the outhouse in the "Russian Connection," in
chapter 8.

PEL – PHOTOGRAPHY

(Courtesy of Paul Lewis)

Paint creek Hunters: Jim Caviness, Wallace McClaflin and
Felix Hoff

In those early years on the homestead the wives grew
Gardens and the husbands were the hunters. Venison was
the main course for most families

(Courtesy of Phyllis Hoff Sammons)

Second generation:

Mike McClalfin, Patricia McClaflin Booher and
Wayne McClaflin

(Courtesy of Mitch Ross)

Four Generations

Frist Row: Edna Mae McClalfin, Pam McClalfin, Rachel Ross,
Max Ross, Patricia McClalfin
Second Row: Mitch Ross, Luke Ross, Wayne McClalfin, and Mike
McClalfin

(Courtesy of Mitch Ross)

REFERENCES

Book Cover

Luke Ross walking on the north pasture on the McClaflin
  Homestead. Picture donated by Mitch Ross

Chapter 2

1 Churchill, Beryl Gail. *Dams, Ditches and Water, History of the
   Shoshone Reclamation Project.* Cody, Wyoming:
   Rustler Printing and Publishing, 1979, p. 84

2 Ibid., p. 80

3 Bonner, Robert, and Beryl Churchill. *Land, Water and People,
   The Shoshone Project.*

4 Reclamation documents, 1949. (These documents are located at the
   Shoshone Irrigation District Office, 337 East 1st Street, Powell, WY
   82435.)

5 Land and Survey Office, Cheyenne, Wyoming,
   March 8, 1957

6 "He Gets First Choice." Powell, Wyoming: *Powell Tribune,*
   Tuesday, October 11, 1949

7. "Lucky McClaflin." Powell, Wyoming:
   Powell Tribune, Thursday, October 13, 1949

8 "Applicant for Homestead Interviewed Tuesday." Powell, Wyoming:
   Powell Tribune, November 10, 1949

9 U.S. Department of the Interior. Homesteader Application

10 Bonner, op. cit., p. 20

11 Bonner, op. cit., p. 17

12 Churchill, *The Dam Book.* Cody, Wyoming: Rustler Printing
   and Publishing, p. 17

13 "Water Tunnel Disaster." Powell, Wyoming: *Powell Tribune,*
   May 8, 1986, Issue 30

Chapter 3

1 Stanley, Jerry. *I Am an American.* New York:
   Crown Publishing, 1994.

2 Kidston, Martin, "New interpretive center opens at former

Heart Mountain internment camp in Wyoming." *Billings Gazette*, Sunday, August 21, 2011, p. A8

3   Mackey, Mike. *Heart Mountain, Life in Wyoming's Concentration Camp.* Casper, Wyoming: Mountain   States Lithographing, 2000, p.16.

4   Inada, Lawson Fusao. *Only What We Could Carry.* Berkeley, CA: Heydey Books, 2000.

5   Mackey, op. cit., p. 16.

6   Churchill, *Dams, Ditches and Water, op. cit.,* p. 86

7   Larson, T. A. *History of Wyoming.* Lincoln, Nebraska:

University of Nebraska Press, 1965, revised, 1978, p. 479

8   Hagel, Scott. "Bond of Camp Life Endured."
Powell Wyoming: *Powell Tribune*, Homesteader Edition, July 19, 1988, p. 8

9   Excerpts taken from Mary Blackburn interview
(located at American Heritage Center, University of Wyoming)

10 Kessel, Velma Berryman. *Behind Barbed Wire, Heart Mountain Relocation Camp.*
Billings, Montana:
Topel Printing, 1991, p. 1

11 Ibid., p. 123

12 Ibid., p. 43

13 Ishigo, Estelle *Lone Heart Mountain.* Los Angeles, California.

14 Anderson, Ritchie & Simon, 1972, p. iv 14 Inouye, Mamoru.
The Heart Mountain Story.
San Francisco, California: Mamoru Inouye, 1997, p. 3
Ibid., p. 9

15 Mackey, Mike. *Remembering Heart Mountain,*
Essays on Japanese-American Internment in Wyoming.
Casper, Wyoming: Mountain States Lithographing, 1998, p. 65.

16 Ibid., p. 73

17 Larson, op. cit., p. 480

18 Inouye, op. cit., p. 67

19 Mackey, *Remembering Heart Mountain*, op. cit., p. 95; excerpt from Douglas M. Todd,
Cover Report, 1945, Operations Division, RG210/WRANA
20 Mackey, *Remembering Heart Mountain, op. cit.,* p. 20

Chapter 4

1 Churchill, Beryl Gail. *Challenging the Canyon. A Family Man Builds a Dam.* Cody, Wyoming

2 Bonner, op. cit., p. 4

3 Bonner, op. cit., p. 3

4 Churchill, *Challenging the Canyon*, op. cit., p. 10

5 Churchill, *Challenging the Canyon*, op. cit., p. x

6 Bonner, op. cit., p. 21

7 Churchill, *Dams, Ditches, and Water,* op. cit., p. 1

8 Churchill, *Dams, Ditches, and Water,* op. cit., p. 8

9 Churchill, *Dams, Ditches, and Water,* op. cit., p. 10

10 Churchill, *Dams, Ditches, and Water,* op. cit., p. 14

11 Churchill, *Dams, Ditches, and Water,* op. cit., p. 14

12 Bonner, op. cit., p. 7

13 Bonner, op. cit., p. 8

14 Churchill, Beryl Gail. *The Dam Book.* Cody, Wyoming: Rustler Printing and Publishing, 1986, p. 4

15 Ibid., p. 9

16 Ibid., p. 12

17 Bonner, op. cit., p. 8

18 Bonner, op. cit., p. 11

19 Churchill. *Dams, Ditches, and Water*, op. cit., p. 78

20 Churchill. *Dams, Ditches, and Water*, op. cit., p. 86

21 Churchill. *Dams, Ditches, and Water*, op. cit., p. 88

Chapter 5
1   Powell, Wyoming: *Powell Tribune*, July 1950
2   McClaflin, Booher, Patricia. *Reflections of a Wyoming Shepherd on the 23rd Psalm.* Bloomington, IN: Authorhouse, 2009, p. 19
3   Ibid., p. 112
4   Ibid., pp. 62-64

Part II – Interviews
1   Wasden, Winifred. *Modern Pioneers*. Powell, Wyoming: Northwest College Production Printing, 1998, p. 229
2   Obituaries, Lloyd Snider. Powell, Wyoming: *Powell Tribune,* May 3, 2007, p. 2.
    3   Wasden, op. cit., p. 231

    4   Wasden, op. cit., p. 235

Chapter 7
1   Curran, Dolores. Traits of a Healthy Family. Minneapolis, Minnesota: Winston Press, 1983.
2   McClaflin, op. cit, p. 53
3   McClaflin, op. cit, pp. 80-83
4   McClaflin, op. cit, pp. 11-15

Chapter 8

1   Curran, op. cit., p. 204
2   Curran, op. cit., p. 205
3   Curran, op. cit., p. 210
4   Erikson, Erik. *Childhood and Society.* New York, New York:
       Norton and Company, 1963, p. 269
5   Ibid., p. 269
6   Schweigert, Tessa. *Glenn French Obit.* Powell, Wyoming:
       Powell Tribune, Wednesday, September 14, 2011.

Appendix A

Churchill, Beryl Gail. *The Dam Book.* Cody, Wyoming, Rustler Printing
       and Publishing, 1986, p. 95.

Appendix B

Shoshone Irrigation District Office, Powell, Wyoming

APPENDIX A

GLOSSARY OF DAM BUILDING TERMS FOR LAYMEN*

Acre-foot: An acre-foot of water covers one acre of land one foot deep.

Adit: Man and equipment access shaft, coming from the side into a tunnel.

Apron: Protective pad, usually concrete, below a dam.

Axis: Horizontal center of a dam.

Barrel of cement: Equal to four cubic feet, or four sacks. Each sack is one cubic foot and weighs 94 pounds. Cubic-foot-per-second (cfs): Often called a "second-foot", 450 gallons of water per minute.

Concrete arch dam: A thin concrete arch which transmits the pressure to the sides (abutments).

Concrete gravity dam: Proportioned so its own weight provides the major resistance to the forces exerted upon it. Willwood and Corbett dams are concrete gravity dams.

Curtain wall: In most cases, is a series of grout holes, grout barriers in the foundation below a dam which increases the   length of the percolation path. At Buffalo Bill Dam the curtain   wall was similar to a retaining wall.

Face: Downstream side of a dam.

Head works: Controlling gates and valves of a dam.

Heel: Upstream base of a dam.

Left, right abutment: Left and right abutments are determined by looking downstream. Abutments are the point of contact between a cliff and dam. Toe: Downstream base of a dam.

Churchill, Beryl Gail. *The Dam Book.*   Cody, Wyoming, Rustler Printing and Publishing, 1986, p. 95.

APPENDIX B

FIRST HEART MOUNTAIN HOMESTEAD
DRAWING IN 1947

UNIT	HOMESTEADER NAME
01	Herbert Grund
02	Alexander Brug
03	Jim Walters
04	Robert Roggli
05	Kenneth Stapp
06	Wayne and Earline Smith
07	Elmer and Mrs. Thomas
08	Lambert and Anna Kitchin
09	Chris L. Younglove
10	George Satterfield
11	William and Joan Ross
12	Allan and Sharon Long
13	Herschel Mason
14	Not taken
15	Wilbur Williams
16	Wilbur and Frankie Amend
17	Howard and Hester Talbot

18	David and Florence Tuff
19	Raymond Hensley
20	Lynn Torrance
21	Robert and Roberta Skaggs
22	Denver O. Mayes
23	Edward and Avis Zenonianni
24	Karl and Marjorie Kaufman
25	James F. Minnehan
26	Philip and Roma Bare
27	Dale and Jeanne Good
28	John McCabe
29	Dean and Rosamond Baker
30	Daniel and Edith LeBlanc
31	Ray and Blanche King
32	William Shellhase
33	John and Merle Perkins
34	Leonard J. Erie
35	Ray Bjornestad
36	Mark Stevens
37	Harry and Pauline Reinstma
38	Russell D. Tolland
39	Rudy and Doris Jolovich
40	Albert Johnson
41	Donald and Rose Ann Dye

66   Lyman Hopkins

67   Charles and Jean Robinson

68   Leonard and Francis Brand

69   Jim and Helen White

70   Pete Milohov

71   I.J. and Lola Frank

72   Harvey and Helen Latham

73   Deforest Neville

74   Kenneth and Alla Calver

75   Roy Meyers

76   Arthur and Alvina Oster

77   Wallace and Mae Thompson

78   Glenn and Jean Mangus

79   Calvin Weymiller

80   Donald B. Stewart

81   Fred and Mary Giles

82   Charles and Fern Patrick

83   Lewis A. Gates

SECOND DRAWING, 1948

89   Forrest and Carole Allen

90   Herman and Jackie Rauchfuss

91   Leo and Wilma O'Gorman

92   John and Ruth Long

THIRD HOMESTEAD DRAWING, 1949

UNIT	NAME OF HOMESTEADER
114	Not Taken
115	Marion and Pearl Aimone
116	Doc and Dode Fulton
117	Gene and Frances Dunleavy
118	Charles and Merle Nunley
119	Charles and Edna Cobb
120	Dick and Barbra Hansen
121	Herb and Lois Beslanowitch
122	Elwyn Thawley
123	Chester and Adele Denton
124	Ira Martin
125	Don Riley
126	Ben Knouse
127	Jay and Norma Kirby
128	Winfred Chalk
129	Lawrence Allshouse
130	Albert Gay
131	John S. Donnelly
132	Glen and Jean Montgomery

133	Kenneth Cunningham
134	Charles and Edna Roland
135	Earle and Lucille Wilson
136	Cal and Alta Musser
137	William Stone
138	Otto and Katie Andersen
139	Lyle and Dorothy Baker
140	Gordon and BeverlHutchinson
141	John and Frankie Hildreth
142	Roland and Dorothy Hogg
143	Francis Meins
144	Harry and Margaret Miller
145	Orville and Pat Bjornestad
146	Elmon and Zelma Toler
147	Orlin and Vada Tirrell
148	Tak and Emmy Ogawa
149	Floyd and Pat George
150	Dale and Millie Metzer
151	Billy and Vivian Imboden
152	Bob and Vaudine Jirsa
153	Elmer and Tiny Collar
154	Harold McHose
155	Jim and Edith Lanik
156	Leon and Laura Banks

157	Harley and Alice Bright
158	Not Taken
159	Paul Eileen Etheridge
160	Jesse Stark
161	William Cook
162	Vince and Lois Spiering
163	Joseph and Susan Storm
164	Bill and Alberta Jackson
165	Cyrus Rogers
166	William and Pat Brown
167	Jack and Carmen Hirst
168	Phillip Ell
169	Wayne and Nevabelle Lewis
170	Lawrence Powers
171	Not Taken
172	Not Taken
173	Robert Gibbons
174	Marvin and Hannah Bodle
175	Roldo and Leora Duston
176	Arthur Howard
177	Robert and Iva Darling
178	Bill and Katherine Larkin
179	Herb and Farell Wojohn
180	Don and Pat Jones

181	Norman Neilson
182	Glenn and Cookie Ball
183	Albert and Georgia Farwell
184	Joseph Kock
185	Theodore Crawford
186	Bill and Claire White
187	Not taken
188	Bob and Vivian Bishopp
189	John and Betty Eichler
190	Ardan Hortin
191	John and Loyal Krauter
192	Al and Ann Kamm
193	Eldon and Radine Ashby
194	Ed and Berniece Schaefer
195	Bob and Idabelle Lawson
196	Lloyd and Bertie Snider
197	Harvey and Dude Adams
198	Clarence and Gail Randolph
199	Sid Blair
200	Wallace and Edna Mae McClaflin
201	James and Laura Caviness
202	Jamie and Rena Hash
203	Don and Frances Roderick
204	McKay and Ruth Avery

205	Vince and Elizabeth Schilitz
206	Don and Jo Miller
207	Hartwell and Velma Robinson
208	Carl and Waneta Hill
209	Lyle Henderson
210	Pat and Faye Fielding
211	Daro and Donna Larson
212	Delbert and Maurine Hollcroft
213	Earle and Anne Nelson
214	Harry and Pearl Cullen
215	Larry Trudeau
216	Not Taken
217	Not Taken
218	Leo and Claire Hollcroft
219	Leroy and Annabelle Holmes
220	Loran and Margaret Henderson
221	William and Adelaid Wibel
222	Don Millie Case
224	Clarence Schoonover
225	Frank and Carol Jolovi

BOOK ORDER INFORMATION

Photo by "A Pair of Photographers" www.apairphoto.com

Patricia McClaflin Booher weaves a tapestry of life experience,   mingled with aspects of creativity, family resiliency and faith in her   stories. The outcome brings a sense of time and place across   generational lines. She received an M.S. degree in Human Recourses, Family and Child Development from Eastern Michigan University.

"Beloved Homeland" Book Cover Design

PEL-PHOTOGRAPHY

To find more information on books and ordering go to:

patriciamac.com and Amazon.com

"Beloved Homeland, Growing up on a Wyoming Homestead"
Soft Cover
"Reflections of a Wyoming Shepherd on the 23rd Psalm"
Soft Cover   E-Book   Hardcover

Books to be released in the near future:
"Timmy the Timid, Timmy the Tender, Tools for Coping with Grief"
"Lessons of Life I learned in my Garden Patch"

Rock Pavilion Press LLC

Made in the USA
Las Vegas, NV
18 October 2022